TANKS

AND ARMORED FIGHTING VEHICLES

TANKS

AND ARMORED FIGHTING VEHICLES

OVER 240 OF THE WORLD'S GREATEST VEHICLES

Robert Jackson

Bath · New York · Singapore · Hong Kong · Cologne · Delhi · Melbourne

This is a Parragon Publishing book
First published in 2007

Parragon Publishing
Queen Street House
4 Queen Street
Bath BA1 1HE, UK

Copyright © Parragon Books Ltd 2007

Editorial and design by
Amber Books Ltd
Bradley's Close
74–77 White Lion Street
London N1 9PF
www.amberbooks.co.uk

Project Editor: Sarah Uttridge
Design: Graham Curd
Picture Research: Kate Green and Terry Forshaw

Printed in China

ISBN 978-1-4054-8664-4

Picture Credits:

All © Art-Tech/Aerospace except the following:

Alcaniz Freson's S.A: 18(t); 41; 49(b); 56; 59(t); 60(b); 62(b); 63(b); 64(b); 73(b); 74; 80; 83(b); 88; 89(r); 135; 165(b); 179(r); 195(b); 249. **Amber Books:** 8(b); 10(b); 19(b); 42(b); 50(b); 51; 53(b); 59(b); 65(t); 66(t); 69; 92(b); 102; 103(b); 104(t); 106 (both); 108(b); 110; 114; 119(t); 120 (both); 121(b); 123(b); 126; 138/9(b); 142(b); 144 (both); 149-50 (both); 152; 157(t); 159(t); 160(b); 172(b); 182(t); 189(t); 193(l); 198; 200(t); 210; 215(b); 217(b); 218(t); 219(t); 221(t); 228(b); 233(b); 234/5(b); 236; 242(t); 259(t); 262; 272(b); 273; 278(b); 283; 284(b). **Art-Tech/MARS:** 97(b); 138(t); 196 (both); 207-8 (all); 216; 220; 222; 231 (both); 232; 239; 242(b); 243(b). **BAE Systems:** 7(t); 11; 253 (both); 292-3 (both); 314 (both). **Bovington Tank Museum:** 24-6 (all); 30(t); 31; 33-4 (both); 37; 46-7 (both); 55; 57; 70-1 (both); 82(t); 101; 111-3 (all); 133; 148; 151(t); 161; 174(t); 180(b). **Corbis:** 163 (t). **Daimler-Chrysler:** 248 (both). **De Agostini:** 226/7(b). **Christopher Foss:** 136; 197; 206; 246; 266-7 (both); 275; 279(t); 282; 285; 288; 295; 299; 301-2 (both); 304; 308-9 (both); 311. **Terry J. Gander:** 27(b); 28-9 (both); 145. **Rheinmetall Landsysteme GmbH:** 291(b); 313 (both); 315 (both). **Richard Stickland:** 13(t); 38(t); 39-40 (both); 79(b); 93; 100(t); 122(t); 131; 143; 166; 190; 252; 269; 276; 303; 307. **TRH:** 7(b); 8(t); 12; 13(b); 14; 17(b); 19(t); 20; 21(t); 23; 27(t); 30(t); 32; 35-6 (both); 42(t); 43-4 (both); 45(b); 48; 52; 54; 58; 60(t); 61(t); 62(t); 63(t); 67-8 (both); 72; 73(t); 77; 78(t); 79(t); 81(t); 83(t); 85-6 (all); 87(b); 89(l); 90; 94 (both); 98; 100(b); 105; 107; 108(tl); 108(tr); 109(b); 115(t); 116-7 (both); 119(b); 121(t); 123(t); 132(b); 137 (both); 140-1 (all); 146(b); 153(b); 154(b); 156; 160(t); 164(b); 165(t); 167(t); 168-9 (both); 170(t); 172(t); 175; 176(b); 177 (both); 179(l); 181(b); 184; 186(t); 187(b); 188; 193(r); 194(t); 199; 200(b); 202-4 (all); 211(t); 212(b); 213; 215(t); 219(b); 224(b); 225; 229(t); 230; 238; 241; 247; 250; 255(b); 256-7 (both); 261; 264; 265(b); 272(t); 284(t); 297(b); 306. **US DOD/US Army:** 9(b); 254; 263(b); 297(t).

CONTENTS

6

INTRODUCTION

Lieutenant-Colonel Ernest Swinton was a British engineer. In September 1914 he recognized that the war in Europe was likely to end up as a stalemate of trench warfare. He proposed the building of armored fighting machines capable of breaking through enemy trench systems. The French had similar ideas, although their initial proposals only envisaged armored tractors designed to break through barbed-wire entanglements.

Above: *Armed with a 2.95in (75mm) main gun, the M24 Chaffee light tank was introduced into service in 1944. In the postwar years it was used as the basis for a new family of fighting vehicles.*

Left: *A large proportion of Soviet armored strength in the 1950s and 1960s was provided by the T-54 and T-55 series of MBTs. They are the most widely produced tank in history.*

The first attack by British Mk I tanks took place on September 15, 1916, and achieved only limited success. On November 20, 1917, the British launched the first tank offensive in history, when 476 tanks forced a 12-mile (19.31km) breach in the strongest sector of the Hindenburg Line at Cambrai. The Germans never produced more than 13 tanks in any one battle and remained deficient in their armor. The British, by contrast, had a total of 1184 tanks on the Western Front by July 1918. The first-ever tank-versus-tank engagement took place on April 24, 1918, when three British Mk IVs met three German heavy A7Vs. One of the German tanks was knocked out, although not before three lightly armored Whippet tanks had been disabled.

The British tanks were designed so that their crews could react quickly to a situation and, because of this, they were often able to disrupt German infantry attacks in open country. Often, the movement of the armor was directed by army cooperation aircraft. The largest-scale tank action of World War I took place on August 8, 1918. On this day, 604 Allied tanks took an exhausted German army corps by surprise, and overran it.

Left: *Vickers light tanks advancing through the desert. They proved virtually useless during the early campaigns of World War II, and were adequate only for armored scouting.*

The lessons of World War I were not lost on Germany's military leaders under the Nazi regime. Although the British were the first to experiment with a fully mechanized fighting force in the 1920s, they tended to use their armor for direct infantry support or for reconnaissance. The Germans adopted a different tactic. Under the guidance of General Hans Seekt, they developed the tank as an instrument of mobile warfare and formulated the classic Blitzkrieg (Lightning War) tactics. These allowed their Panzer divisions (preceded by ground-attack aircraft like the Junkers Ju 87 Stuka dive-bomber) to plunge deep into enemy territory and create corridors that could then be exploited by mechanized infantry.

These tactics worked well in the Battle of France and in North Africa, although in the latter case the Germans were ultimately foiled by Allied air supremacy. Even then, however, their armor was still capable of inflicting serious losses, such as in the Battle of the Kasserine Pass in Tunisia in February 1943, where the 21st Panzer Division destroyed 103 American tanks and caused over 2500 casualties. The tactics also worked well in the early stages of the German attack on Russia. Russia's heavily armed KV-1 and T-34 tanks were a shock, however. Their 0.30in (76mm) guns could penetrate the Wehrmacht tanks' armor while remaining immune to German antitank munitions.

To meet this new challenge, the Germans launched a program to build a generation of massive, heavily armored fighting vehicles. Two of its products were the Tiger and the Panther. The 43-ton Panther tank, with frontal armor of 3.27in (83mm) thickness, a

speed of 28mph (45km/h) and a main armament of one 2.95in (75mm) gun was, without doubt, the best tank produced by any side during World War II. Elements of this design were reflected in postwar armored fighting vehicles like the British Centurion.

The 49-ton (49790kg) Centurion Mk 3 of the late 1950s was an outstanding example; it had an electronically stabilized 3.28in (83.4mm), and later a 4.13in (105mm) gun. When it began to be phased out of British service in 1960, other nations were keen to acquire it, and it continued to be used into the 1990s. Together with the American M48, it wrought havoc on Egypt's Russian-built tanks in the 1967 Arab–Israeli war.

The Panther and the Centurion were first models in a line of armored fighting vehicles that culminated in two excellent designs used in the Gulf War of 1991, and again in 2003. America's M1 Abrams and Britain's Challenger have proved themselves capable of taking on the latest Russian-designed equipment and destroying it with almost ridiculous ease. They will certainly rank alongside the Panther as the most effective tanks ever built.

Below: *The Centurion tank arrived just too late to see action in World War II, although a few took part in some minor infantry support operations. It had to wait until the Korean War to see serious combat.*

Tanks became more effective during World War II, and so it became inevitable that a tank destroyer was called for. As the war progressed, these armored fighting vehicles became an important part of any army's inventory. In some cases, they were the result of improvisation; in North Africa, for example, the early desert campaigns produced some extraordinary scenes, particularly on the Italian side. Large-calibre guns were mounted on whatever chassis was available and operated by a small crew who did not have the benefit of armor protection.

It was the Germans who took the lead in the development of effective tank destroyers when they were confronted with excellent Russian tanks like the T-34. Some of their earlier designs (such as the Elefant) were slow and cumbersome and had a disastrous combat career. Later in the war, however, they produced some superlative tank destroyers, in particular the Jagdpanzer IV and the little Hetzer, while the Americans developed the excellent M18 Hellcat. In the years following World War II, however, the tank destroyer virtually disappeared as a separate category of fighting vehicle.

Today, the armies of the world have a huge

range of armored fighting vehicles, developed to suit every purpose. Combat engineers, for example, have a considerable array of mine-clearance systems at their disposal. One of the most basic is still the flail tank, developed by the British during World War II for the assault on the Normandy beaches. This consists of a rotating drum with chains suspended from it, attached to the front of an armored vehicle.

Above: A formidable foe when first encountered, the Panzer VI Tiger tank was too ponderous to be used in an aggressive role. It could also be knocked out by rocket-firing aircraft, as the action in the Falaise Gap in 1944 showed.

Left: One of the finest tanks in the world today, the M1 Abrams led the armored action in both wars against Iraq. It is constantly being updated to make it viable well into the 21st century

Left: *The deadly little Hetzer—the name means "baiter," in other words someone that lures something into a trap—was one of the most effective and best-designed tank destroyers of World War II.*

As the drum rotates, the chains strike the ground and detonate any mines that are activated by pressure or vibration. As the width of the flail drum exceeds the width of the armored vehicle, the latter clears a broad swathe though the minefield, opening a path for other tanks. An added advantage is that several tanks clearing paths through a minefield create a considerable amount of dust and smoke from exploding mines, obscuring the advance of friendly armor.

One variant of the flail tank is the mine roller, which works on the same principle as the flail. Attached to the front of a tank, it exerts sufficient downward pressure on the ground to detonate mines, but is too heavy and solid to be itself affected by the explosions.

The mine plow is the most effective combat-proven solution to the antimine problem, and has several significant advantages over all the other systems. It physically removes mines from the path of an armored vehicle, removing any doubt as to whether a mine has been neutralized or not. The plow can be carried by all heavy armored vehicles without significantly reducing their mobility. An additional asset is that it can be brought into use instantly, whenever a minefield threat is identified.

The full inventory of "special" armored vehicles available to the modern combat engineer was brought into play during Operation Desert Storm in 1991. These vehicles breached the defensive perimeter the Iraqis had built around occupied Kuwait from the Gulf to the Iraqi border. Before the infantry and armored divisions attacked their targets, engineers with special tanks had the task of filling ditches with plastic pipes to serve as crossing points, others laid armored bridges. Other heavy vehicles were used

Below: *Without doubt the most famous Allied tank of World War II, the Sherman is seen here in its specialist role as a flail tank, its task being to clear a path through the minefields that the Germans had laid on the Normandy beaches.*

Left: The excellent Challenger 2 entered service with the British Army in June 1998 and the last of the 386 tanks on order was delivered in April 2002. Deliveries for Oman were completed in 2001. Challenger 2 has seen operational service in Bosnia, Kosovo, and Iraq.

to flatten the sand berms and to clear paths through the enemy minefields.

Allied combat engineers brought their full arsenal into play at various points of the so-called "Saddam Line." The US 1st Infantry Division (nicknamed the "Big Red One" because of the large figure "1" that forms its insignia) carried out a classic assault on the Iraqi defenses. This allowed the British 1st Armoured Division to come through the sand and trench fortifications both unhindered and at speed.

Helicopters lifted squads of reconnaissance troops over the top of the sand berms to form a defensive screen against possible Iraqi counterattacks. Then, combat bulldozers smashed gaps in the outer sand walls for tanks taking position in support of the infantry. Throughout the operation, artillery pounded Iraqi positions to the rear. Combat engineering tractors, towing explosive hose equipment, moved through the breaches in the sand berms (made by the M9 Ace armored bulldozers) and fired their high-explosive charges across the enemy minefields, which blasted clear lanes through them. Engineers followed on foot, marking safe routes for the British tanks to follow. Bundled pipes and fascine bridges were dropped into the antitank ditches.

Once the Challenger MBTs had crossed over, the American engineers bulldozed sand over the top of the fascines to make a roadway for the US 1st Infantry Division's wheeled support vehicles. In all, the "Big Red One" cut 16 lanes through the berms and minefields over a two-mile front. It deployed its own armor and artillery to the north, protecting the flank of the British advance, while further north still, the US 1st Armored Division engaged and annihilated the Iraqi Republican Guard, whose Russian tanks were no match for the American M1 Abrams.

Infantry fighting vehicles followed, supporting the armor and keeping pace with it. These are essentially troop-carrying light tanks, exemplified by the excellent British Warrior and the American Bradley. The whole Desert Storm operation provided a classic example of how armored fighting vehicles of all types should be used, as well as (in the case of the Iraqi Army) how they should not.

This book tells the story of the tank, from its first use to break the stalemate of trench warfare in World War I, to the present day, where tanks and other armored fighting vehicles are helping to confront the "War on Terror." Much has happened in terms of technology in the first years of the 21st century, but although continual advances in firepower and fire-control systems continue to be made, the basic role of the tank, and its associated fighting vehicles, remains much the same as when it was first developed.

Chapter 1

THE QUEST FOR MOBILITY

The first tanks were used on the battlefields of the Western Front in World War I. Not only were they slow, lumbering models, they were also intensely vulnerable to artillery fire. From 1917, French designers led the field in designing infantry support tanks with an emphasis on lightness and speed. The increasing speed and mobility of these newly designed tanks created a need for armored vehicles in which infantry could be transported into battle.

Above: The Vickers medium tanks were among the fastest when they entered service in the 1920s. They were one of the first tanks to have their main armament mounted in a revolving turret.

Left: A Tank Mk I moving up into action at Thiepval in September 1916. The wire mesh screen over the hull was for protection against grenades. The clumsy steering wheel at the rear was soon discarded.

The quest for speed and maneuverability created its own problems, however, notably that with the power available at the time, armor had to be sacrificed. This spelt disaster, and was demonstrated on numerous occasions in the limited conflicts between the two World Wars: Small, lightly armored tanks may have been speedy, but they fell victim repeatedly to the arsenal of antitank weaponry that was being developed.

The conflicts of the 1930s demonstrated a need for three types of armored fighting vehicle—the heavy main battle tank (acting like a "battering-ram" to break through enemy defenses), the medium tank (exploiting the breakthrough created by heavy tanks), and the light tank (performing rapid reconnaissance and command tasks).

Experiments during the interwar years revealed a whole diversity of new uses to which tanks could be put, from laying bridges to crossing rivers under water.

LITTLE WILLIE LANDSHIP

Little Willie was a rudimentary model, but was the world's first practical armored fighting vehicle. It was designed and built on the initiative of the British Admiralty, and in particular of Winston Churchill.

Below: For security reasons, Britain's first armored vehicle was known as a tank. The name became firmly entrenched in military parlance and remains in use today.

Strangely enough, it was the British Admiralty that provided the impetus for the development of armored fighting vehicles in World War I. In February 1915 Winston Churchill, then First Lord of the Admiralty, set up a Landships Committee to investigate the feasibility of developing a basic machine. This was originally intended to transport troops; it would cross deep and wide, and would be able to suppress enemy weapons, especially machine guns.

Prototype vehicle

The idea was taken one step further by Colonel Ernest Swinton of the Royal Engineers, the official war correspondent at GHQ British Expeditionary Force in France.

He held discussions with a friend (Colonel Maurice Hankey, Secretary to the Committee of Imperial Defence in London) about the idea of a cross-country tracked vehicle, based on the design of prewar tractors. The result was an 18-ton prototype tracked armored vehicle. It had a rotating turret and became known as "Little Willie." It was built by Fosters of Lincoln and underwent trials early in 1916.

Little Willie was eventually abandoned because it did not have the required trench-crossing capability. However, its automotive, transmission, suspension, and track systems were adopted by later armored fighting vehicles. Its riveted boxlike shape also brought the word—tank—into military parlance.

Specifications

Armament: One 2pdr (1.57in/ 40mm); one 0.303in (7.7mm) Maxim MG and a varying number of 0.303in (7.7mm) Lewis MGs

Armor: 0.23in (6mm)

Crew: 2 plus 2 or 4 gunners

Dimensions: Length 18ft 2 in (5.45m); Width 9ft 4in (2.8m); Height 10ft 2in (3.05m)

Weight: 18 tons (18,289kg)

Powerplant: Daimler 6-cylinder gasoline developing 105bhp (78.29kW) at 1000rpm

Speed: 2mph (3.2km/h)

Range: Not available

The Quest for Mobility
1916 France

CHAR D'ASSAULT ST. CHAMOND

Despite being classed as a tank, the Char d'Assault St. Chamond was in fact the ancestor of all self-propelled guns to be used in the future. It served during most of World War I.

Specifications

Armament: One 2.95in (75mm) mle 1897 field gun; four 0.315in (8mm) Hotchkiss MGs
Armor: Maximum, 0.67in (17mm)
Crew: 9
Dimensions: Length 28ft 11.5in (8.83m); Width 8ft 9in (2.67m); Height 7ft 9in (2.36m)
Weight: 22.64 tons (23,000kg)
Powerplant: Panhard, 4-cylinder gasoline, 90hp (67.1kW), plus gasoline-electric drive
Speed: Road, 7.45mph (12km/h)
Range: Road, 37.3 miles (60km)

These tanks actually fell into the category of assault guns. They were based on the Holt chassis and track system, and had serious cross-country defects. They were of very limited tactical use because of the length of the hull, which greatly restricted the traverse of the main armament. Nevertheless, they were used with some effect from April 1915 until the end of World War I, and acted as forerunners of all types of self-propelled guns that have been created up to the present day. The AFV was designed by Colonel Rimailho and built at Homecourt, the St. Chamond factory. One of the drawbacks of this model was that it used a gasoline engine to drive an electric transmission system, and this led to a substantial weight increase. Another problem was caused by the length of the hull: This extended both fore and aft of the tracks by a considerable distance, and so the tank often became stuck in uneven terrain.

Above: *The length and bulk of the Char d'Assault St. Chamond, compared with the limited length of the track run, made the vehicle unwieldy and difficult to handle in some conditions.*

Supply carriers

As the St. Chamond tanks were gradually withdrawn from use and replaced by more effective fighting vehicles, some were converted to supply carriers and were used in this role in the last days of World War I.

The Quest for Mobility
⚒ 1916 France

SCHNEIDER CHAR D'ASSAULT

France's first true tank was distinct from a self-propelled gun. However, the Schneider Char d'Assault had many defects and suffered serious losses in combat, mainly in artillery battles.

Above: *A Schneider tank moving up to the front line near L'Eglantiers on the river Oise.*

Right: *The designers of the Schneider Char d'Assault also made the mistake of superimposing a large and bulky hull on a short track run, making the vehicle unstable when crossing obstacles.*

The Schneider Char d'Assault was the brainchild of Colonel J.E. Estienne. He had made an in-depth study of the American Holt tractor's track-and-chassis system. The contract to develop the concept went to the Schneider Company, which was already producing armored tractors for the French Army. In January 1915 Schneider's chief designer, Eugene Brillié (who had already been involved in designing armored cars for Spain) went to the USA to study Holt tractors for himself. He came back with a proposal for a Tracteur Blindé et Armé (an armored and armed tractor) that was based on the Baby Holt tractor chassis. The design that emerged was a simple armored box mounted on the tractor chassis, with a short 2.95in (75mm) gun mounted on the right-hand side, and with provision for two machine guns on ball mountings. In practice, the Schneider Char d'Assault suffered from many of the same problems as the St. Chamond, caused by its long hull extending fore and aft of the tracks.

Defects

The defects of the Schneider Char d'Assault were dramatically revealed at the battle at Chemin des Dames in April 1917. A total of 132 tanks of this type were deployed here, and as many as 76 were lost, mostly to artillery fire.

Specifications

Armament: One 2.95in (75mm) gun; two 0.315in (8mm) Hotchkiss MGs

Armor: 0.43in (11mm) or 0.315in (8mm)

Crew: 7

Dimensions: Length 20ft 6in (6.32m); Width 6ft 8in (2.05m); Height 7ft 6in (2.3m)

Weight: approx 11.8 tons (12,500kg)

Powerplant: Schneider, 4-cylinder, gasoline, 55hp (41kW)

Speed: 5mph (8.1km/h)

Range: Road, 49.7 miles (80km)

The Quest for Mobility
✖ 1916 UK

MARK I MEDIUM TANK

It was Britain's tanks that finally broke the stalemate on the Western Front in World War I, overcoming the enemy's trench systems. The first of these was the Mk I—noisy, smelly, and prone to breaking down.

Above: The Mk I was fitted with an antigrenade mesh on top of the hull, as seen in this photograph.

Specifications

Armament: Two 6pdr (2.25in/57mm) guns; one Hotchkiss 0.303in (7.7mm) MG

Armor: 0.23–0.47in (6–12mm)

Crew: 8

Dimensions: Length 32ft 6in (9.7m); Width 13ft 9in (4.12m); Height 7ft 11in (2.41m)

Weight: 28 tons (28,450kg)

Powerplant: Daimler 6-cylinder gasoline developing 150bhp (111.8kW) at 1000rpm

Speed: 3.7mph (5.95km/h)

Range: 22 miles (37.8km)

The British Mk I tank of 1916, known first as Centipede, then as Big Willie, and finally as Mother, was born out of a need for a tracked fighting vehicle that was capable of crossing a 12ft (3.5m) trench. The design that evolved was unlike anything seen before. The rhomboidal-shaped vehicle had tracks carried right around the hull, and a sponson on each side to house 2.25in (57mm) guns or machine guns. Mother was tested for the first time on January 16, 1916, and successful trials were completed within three weeks. Orders for 100 examples of the tank, now called Mk I, were placed in February, and training of the first crews began.

Above: Originally, the Mk I tank was fitted with a wheel at the stern for steering purposes. This was found to be quite ineffective and was soon discarded, applying brakes to the tracks proving a better option.

Insight into the future

The Mk I first went into action on September 15, 1916, when 32 vehicles were employed along a five-mile front. They were successful, especially when several tanks operated together. A few days later, a single British tank moved ahead of the infantry and cooperated with a low-flying aircraft to capture an enemy trench. This was a dramatic pointer to the future.

The Quest for Mobility
⚒ **1917 France**

RENAULT FT-17 LIGHT TANK

Arguably the finest tank of its era, the Renault FT-17 Light continued in service for many years after World War I. Some countries were still using it as a frontline tank in 1939.

Specifications

Armament: One 1.46in (37mm) gun; one or two machine guns
Armor: 0.47in (12mm)
Crew: 2
Dimensions: Length (with tail) 16ft 5in (5m); Width 5 ft 7in (1.71m); Height 7ft (2.13m)
Weight: 6.485 tons (6589kg)
Powerplant: One Renault liquid-cooled four-cylinder gasoline engine developing 35hp (26kW)
Speed: 4.8mph (7.7 km/h)
Range: 22 miles (35.4km)

The French FT-17 light tank was designed in 1917 and had a huge impact on future tank design. It featured a rotating turret mounted on top of the hull, and also had a rear-mounted engine. Because of the French War Department's enthusiasm for super-heavy tanks, the FT-17 might never have been produced had it not been for the enthusiasm and continuing support of Colonel Jean-Baptiste Eugène Estienne. He persuaded key figures in the French military that a light infantry support tank would be a valuable tool. The first FT-17s were deployed in March 1917 and were first used in action in May 1918. In July of that year, enough of these tanks were available that 480 were concentrated for a successful French counterattack near Soissons. The FT-17 was also used by the American Expeditionary Force in France from the summer of 1918. The type continued to serve in substantial numbers for years after World War I. Several variants, such as command vehicles, were produced. As Renault did not have the capacity to produce the large numbers of FT-17s on order, production was allocated to various subsidiary manufacturers.

Above: The Renault FT-17 infantry support tank was one of the most successful of the early armored fighting vehicles, although it was difficult to maintain. Thousands were produced.

Below: This example of an FT-17 features a cast, rather than a riveted turret. The original FT-17 was not used in action until May 1918, but after a slow start large numbers were deployed.

The Quest for Mobility
✂ 1917 Germany

A7V STURMPANZERWAGEN

The A7V Sturmpanzerwagen was Germany's first viable tank, and was successfully used in the Ludendorff Offensive of March 1918. It fought the first-ever tank-versus-tank battle.

Above: *The A7V was armed with up to seven machine guns, which meant that it had to carry a large crew. The interior was consequently cramped and uncomfortable, with available space strictly limited.*

Specifications

Armament: One 2.24in (57mm) gun; six or seven 0.312in (7.92mm) MGs

Armor: Maximum, 1.18in (30mm)

Crew: Up to 18

Dimensions: Length, overall, 26ft 3in (8m); Width 10ft (3.05m); Height 10ft 10in (3.3m)

Weight: approx 30 tons (30,480kg)

Powerplant: Two Daimler-Benz, 4-cylinder gasoline, each delivering 100hp (74.5kW)

Speed: Road, 8mph (12.8km/h)

Range: Road, 25 miles (40.2km)

Developing armored fighting vehicles had a much lower priority for the Germans than for the British and French during World War I. By 1917 the Germans were on the defensive, and it was argued that tanks, as offensive weapons, had no place in defensive strategy. Nor did they have a part to play in the war on the Eastern Front, as the Russian armies were on the verge of collapse. The A7V Committee was formed in October 1917 to study the concept of the armored fighting vehicle. By the end of the year this committee had designed a machine based on the Holt suspension. A year passed before an order was placed for 100 examples of a 30 ton (30,480kg) fighting vehicle—the A7V Sturmpanzerwagen.

Above: *The A7V was Germany's first successful tank design, and was used to good effect during the Ludendorff Offensive of March 1918. It took part in the world's first tank-versus-tank battle.*

Ludendorff Offensive

The Germans only ever managed to produce 20 A7Vs, relying on captured German and French AFVs to bolster their armored force. Despite this, four A7Vs—together with five captured British Mk IVs—played a vital part during the Ludendorff Offensive of March 21, 1918. They advanced in the wake of a five-hour artillery barrage and punched a five-mile hole through the British defenses at St. Quentin.

The Quest for Mobility

✗ 1917 UK

1917 MARK IV TANK

Britain's Mk IV tank took part in the first-ever major tank battle at Cambrai in November 1917. The battle might have proved decisive if proper tactics to exploit the tanks' success had been formulated.

With its 105hp (83kW) Daimler engine, the British Mk IV tank was badly underpowered and relied on relatively flat and even terrain to keep its momentum. The Mk IV was very difficult to command and control in action: It had a crew of eight, and the conditions were hot, cramped, and noisy, making voice contact impossible. Its increased thickness of armor was capable of deflecting German armor-piercing bullets, but its bulk

and slow speed made it very vulnerable to artillery fire, and it burned readily when hit and penetrated.

Unsprung suspension

The Mk IV's suspension was completely unsprung, which gave a very rough ride and made it difficult to engage targets accurately while on the move. Nevertheless, the tank struck terror into the German troops, who

Above: Although heavy and slow, the Mk IV tank was a formidable opponent and struck terror into German troops. Conditions were far from comfortable for the eight-man crew, as the suspension was unsprung.

Specifications

Armament: One 2.24in (57 mm) gun (male); four 0.303in (7.7mm) machine guns (female)

Armor: 0.47in (12mm)

Crew: 8

Dimensions: Length 26ft 5in (8.05m); Width 12ft 7in (3.91m); Height 8ft 2in (2.49m)

Weight: 28 tons (28,449.31kg)

Powerplant: One 105 or 125hp (78 or 83kW) Daimler gasoline engine

Speed: 3.7mph (6km/h)

Range: 35 miles (56km)

Above: *The Mk IV was heavily armored and could withstand all types of small arms fire, but its low speed made it vulnerable to artillery. It often suffered serious losses when advancing through a barrage.*

strongest defenses of the Hindenburg Line at Cambrai. This was in conjunction with an artillery barrage and was the first time armored fighting vehicles had played a dominant role. The cost was high, however, and 179 tanks were lost. This might have been a decisive breakthrough, had the supporting British troops not stopped to reduce each strongpoint in turn instead of driving ahead in depth. The attack petered out in stalemate and the Germans sealed the breach in their line.

Tank-versus-tank battle

On April 24, 1918, the first tank-versus-tank engagement took place at Villers-Bretonneux between British Mk IVs and German A7Vs. Fifteen German tanks were involved. They attacked in three groups toward their objectives—the Bois d'Aquenne and the villages of Villers-Bretonneux and Cachy. The three tanks in the leading German group attacked British infantry at Villers-Bretonneux and were engaged by three Mk IVs. One was armed with a 2.24in (57mm) gun and the other two (so-called "female" Mk IVs) with machine guns. In a protracted engage-ment, the Mk IV armed with the 2.24in (57mm) gun, commanded by Lt. Mitchell, knocked out one of the A7Vs and hit two others, although without noticeable effect. The encounter took place when the two groups of tanks were about 400 yards (365m) apart.

overestimated its hitting power and were daunted by the seemingly inexorable progress of these armored monsters over trenches and through obstacles that had previously seemed impenetrable.

Cambrai attack

On November 20, 1917, a massed attack by 476 British tanks punched a gap 12 miles (19km) wide and 4 miles (6km) deep into the

Below: *The shape of the Mk IV meant that it was far more suited to crossing serious obstacles than its French and German contemporaries. This example is demonstrating its trench-crossing agility.*

The Quest for Mobility
1917 UK

MEDIUM MARK A (WHIPPET)

Unlike previous British tank designs, the Whippet was fitted with a revolving turret. It played a vital part in the fighting retreat of the British Army during the German offensive of 1918.

Above: *One notable feature of the Whippet was its large mud chutes, visible here under the track tops. Another recognition feature was the tank's complex turret shape.*

Right: *This Whippet medium tank shows signs of battle, the dirty marks imply that its has been across some muddy terrain during fighting.*

The British Whippet medium tank was designed for the rapid exploitation of the tactical opportunities that arose after heavy tanks had penetrated the enemy's defenses. It was a little less vulnerable than the Mk IV, and had the advantage that it could be produced quickly in large numbers. The first prototype was tested in February 1917, equipped with a revolving turret taken from an Austin armored car, and 200 production examples were ordered in March. The first Whippets became operational in December 1917 and seven of these took part in the second tank-versus-tank engagement at Villers–Bretonneux, and Cachy in April 1918. This took place a few minutes before the British Mk IVs engaged the German A7Vs. In this action, one Whippet was destroyed and another was damaged by a German A7V, but the surviving Whippets caught two German infantry battalions out in the open and inflicted 400 casualties on them. Before this, Whippets had played an important part in covering the retreat of the British divisions recoiling before the German shock troops in the spring offensive of 1918. Whippets took part in several of the British Army's postwar actions, notably in Ireland and North Russia.

Specifications

Armament: Four 0.303in (7.7mm) Hotchkiss MGs
Armor: 0.2–0.55in (5–14mm)
Crew: 3
Dimensions: Length 20ft (6.09m); Width 8ft 7in (2.61m); Height 9ft (2.74m)
Weight: 14 tons (14,225kg)
Powerplant: Twin side-valve Taylor JB4 gasoline engines developing 50bhp (37.85kW)
Speed: 8mph (12.8km/h)
Range: 40 miles (64km)

The Quest for Mobility

1918 France

FCM CHAR 2C HEAVY TANK

The Char 2C was one of the heaviest tanks ever built, and was the subject of a massive production order. This order was canceled with the Armistice, and only a few were ever built.

Below: *The massive bulk of the Char 2C is apparent in this photograph (taken in 1940), dwarfing the figure of the soldier standing beside it. The main production order was canceled following the Armistice.*

Specifications

Armament: One 2.95in (75mm) gun; four 0.315in (8mm) Hotchkiss MGs

Armor: Maximum, 1.77in (45mm)

Crew: 12

Dimensions: Length 33ft 8in (10.27m); Width 9ft 8in (2.95m); Height 13ft 1.5in (4m)

Weight: approx 67.9 tons (69,000kg)

Powerplant: 2 x Daimler or Maybach, 6-cylinder gasoline, 520hp (387.7kW) in total

Speed: Road, 7 45mph (12km/h)

Range: Road, 62.1 miles (100km)

The origins of this heavy French tank are obscure, and the vehicle appears to have been surrounded by much political maneuvering, much of it revolving around Brigadier Estienne. He recognized that the Char 2C would need a huge allocation of funds if it were to be produced in any quantity, and saw it as a threat to the future of his pet project, the FT-17 light tank. General Mouret, head of mechanized development at the French War Department, had allegedly accepted a bribe from the FCM Company to allow them to develop the heavy tank, and he insisted on three prototypes being built—of 30, 40, and 62 tons (30,500kg, 40,600kg, and 63,000kg) respectively. None of these had been built before the end of the war, but Marshal Philippe Pétain, now head of the French General Staff, asked for 300 of the heaviest variant to be ready by March 1919. This order too was canceled after the Armistice, but a prototype—the Char 2C, weighing 69 tons—was completed and 10 production examples were delivered in 1921. They were still serving at the outbreak of World War II. One example was captured by the Germans and taken to Berlin for exhibition purposes.

The Quest for Mobility
⚔ 1918 UK

MARK IX TANK

In 1917 Britain led the field in the development of what would later be called the armored personnel carrier. This was a sensible solution to the problem of infantry mobility and protection.

Below: The Mk IX was designed to carry 30 troops or 10 tons (10,160kg) of supplies.

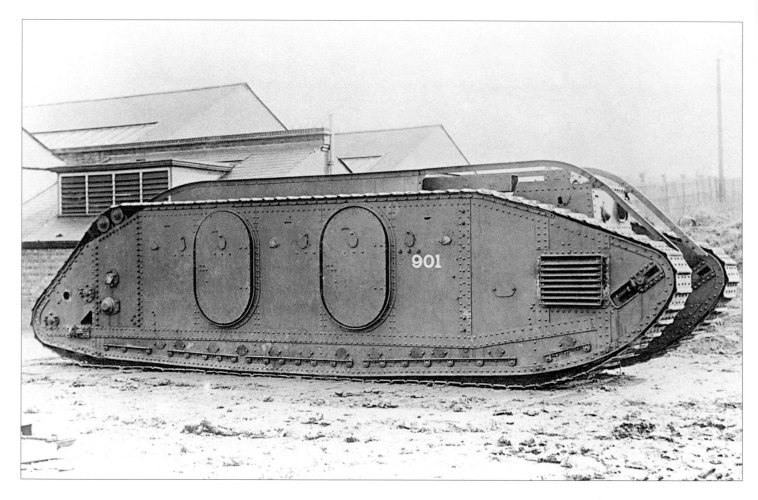

The British Mk IX armored fighting vehicle was the world's first armored personnel carrier. It was designed by Lieutenant G.R. Rackham. His task was complicated by an initial requirement for the hull to be fitted with sponsons so that the vehicle could be turned into a tank in case another AFV project (the Mk VIII tank) proved to be a failure. A production contract was awarded to Armstrong, Whitworth, & Co. of Newcastle upon Tyne, and construction of two prototypes began in September 1917. In the event, only three Mk IXs had been completed by November 1918 and only 34 were produced in total.

Armored ambulance
The Mk IX was intended to accommodate 30 fully equipped troops, and, in its supply role, could carry 10 tons (10,160kg) of cargo. Eight loopholes were incorporated in the hull, through which the troops could fire their rifles. The Mk IX continued in use after the war, and at least one was converted as an armored ambulance. The sole surviving tank is in the Museum at Bovington, in Dorset, UK.

Specifications

Armament: One 0.303in (7.7mm) Hotchkiss MG

Armor: 0.47in (12mm)

Crew: 4 plus 30 men or 10 tons (10,160kg) of stores

Dimensions: Length 31ft 10in (9.78m); Width 8ft 3in (4.11m); Height 8ft 8in (2.64m)

Weight: 26.52 tons (26,950kg) unladen

Powerplant: Ricardo 6-cylinder gasoline engine, 150bhp (111.8kW)

Speed: 3.5mph (5.63km/h)

Range: 20 miles (32km)

The Quest for Mobility
⚒ **1918   UK**

MEDIUM MARK C TANK

Below: The Medium Mk C tank was an agile fighting vehicle, but plans to produce it in quantity were abandoned with the end of the war.

Like so many other promising AFVs, the Medium Mk C tank had a short career. It was the subject of large orders, only for these to be canceled at the end of World War I.

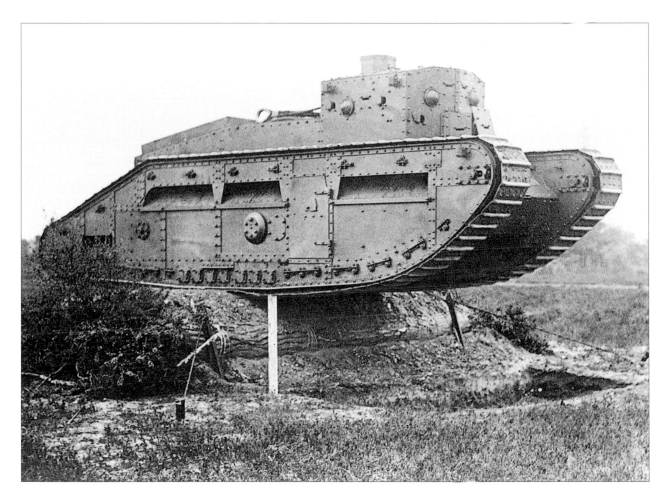

Specifications

Armament: Four 0.303in (7.7mm) Hotchkiss MGs (female)

Armor: 0.24–0.55in (6–14mm)

Crew: 4

Dimensions: Length 26ft (7.856m); Width 8ft 4in (2.71m); Height 9ft 6in (2.94m)

Weight: 20 tons (20,320kg)

Powerplant: Ricardo 6-cylinder gasoline developing 150bhp (111.8kW) at 1200rpm

Speed: 7.9mph (12.64km/h)

Range: 75 miles (120km)

Also known as the Hornet, the British Medium Mk C tank came too late to serve in World War I. It was the result of a rivalry that developed between two former colleagues, Sir William Tritton of William Foster & Co. and Major Walter Gordon Wilson. Tritton, without consulting Wilson, had designed the Mk A Whippet in 1917, and so Wilson had set about designing a rival AFV, the Mk B. Tritton's response was to order his chief designer, William Rigby, to design a still-better vehicle, the Mk C. An initial batch of 200 Mk C tanks was ordered,

and this was later increased to 600. All orders were canceled at the end of World War I, and only 36 partly completed vehicles were left on the production line. These were finished and issued to the Tank Corps, together with 14 additional vehicles that had been built from spare parts. The Medium Mk Cs were issued to the 2nd Tank Battalion and did not take part in postwar operations overseas, being regarded as too valuable. Four Mk Cs took part in the 1919 victory parade. From 1925, the type was replaced by the Vickers-designed medium Mks I and II.

The Quest for Mobility
⚒ 1918 USA

HOLT GAS-ELECTRIC TANK

The Holt Gas-Electric tank was the first true AFV to be developed in the United States. It was too complex, however. Its engineering led to excessive weight that adversely affected its performance.

Below: The ugly Holt Gas-Electric tank was based on the series of tractors designed by the Holt Manufacturing Company. Only a single prototype was built.

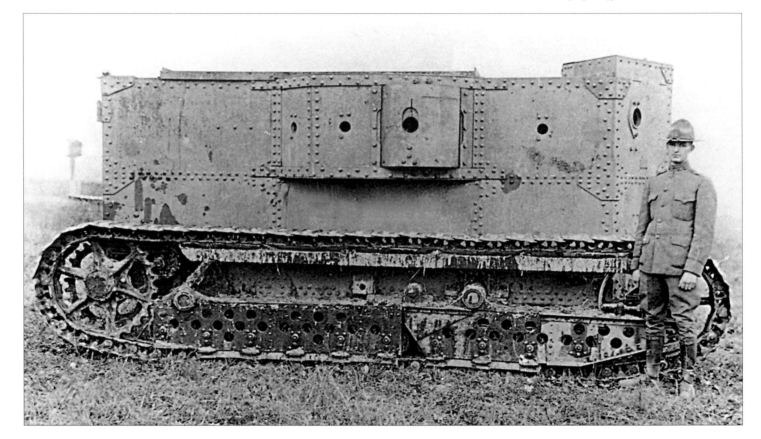

The Holt Gas-Electric was a collaborative venture between the Holt Manufacturing Company (later to become Caterpillar Inc.) and the General Electric Company, and was the first tank to be developed in the USA. A prototype was completed in 1918 and embodied the vast experience gained in the design and construction of the Holt tractor series, incorporating a lengthened and modified suspension with 10-road wheel on either side. The four-cylinder engine was fitted with a GEC generator driving an electric motor for each track, a system that had also been used in the French St. Chamond design. To prevent overheating of the transmission, a complex water-cooling system was installed. This added to the weight and bulk of the vehicle. Like the St. Chamond, the Holt vehicle featured a 1.46in (75mm) gun mounted in the nose, and sponsons on either side of the hull were designed to mount a machine gun each.

Only one Holt Gas-Electric vehicle was ever built. Trials showed that its performance was generally unsatisfactory, especially on sloping ground, and the design was abandoned.

Specifications

Armament: One 1.46in (75mm) mountain howitzer; two 0.3in (7.62mm) MGs usually carried

Armor: 0.59in (15mm)

Crew: 6

Dimensions: Length 16ft 6in (5.03m); Width 9ft 1in (3.12m); Height 7ft 9.5in (2.38m)

Weight: 25 tons (25,400kg)

Powerplant: Holt 4-cylinder gasoline, 90hp (6.7kW), used as generator for two electric track motors.

Speed: 6mph (9.65km/h)

Range: Not known

The Quest for Mobility
1919 USA

MARK VIII INTERNATIONAL TANK

Conceived in 1917, the Mk VIII International was a collaborative effort between Britain and the USA. The end of World War I meant that it was never produced in large numbers, as intended.

Below: *The Mk VIII tank was issued to the US Army immediately after the end of World War I.*

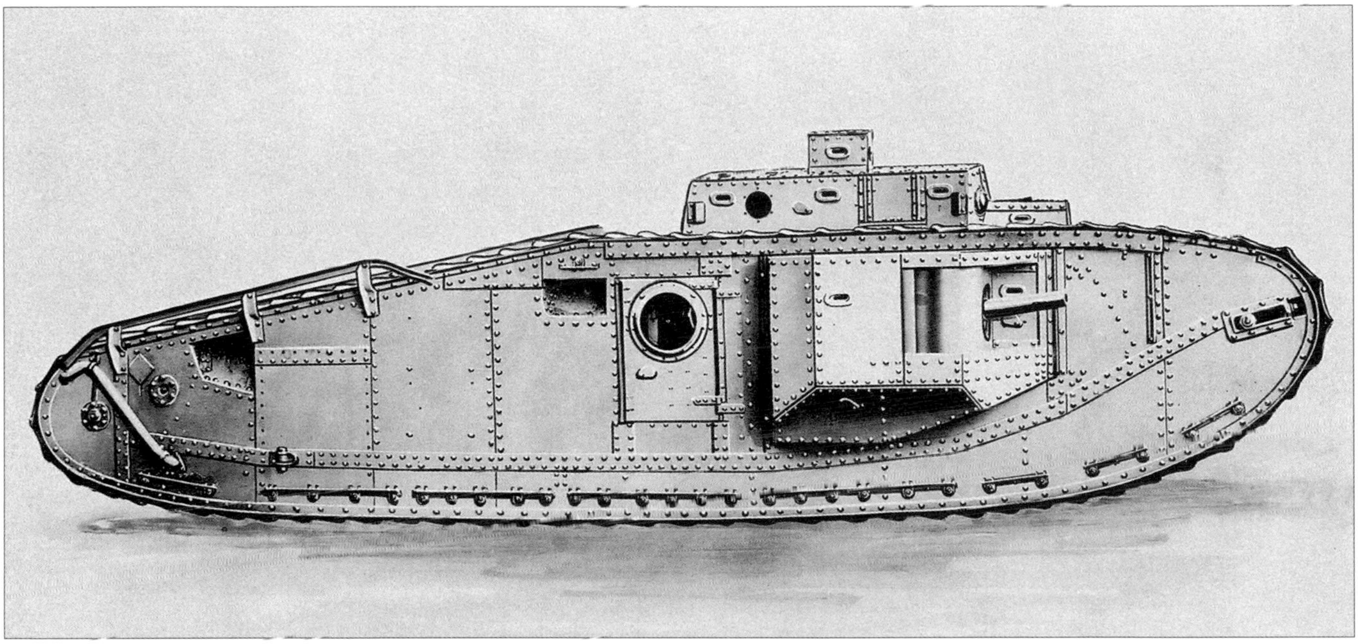

Specifications

Armament: Two 6pdr (2.244in/57mm) OQF guns; seven 0.3in (7.62mm) Browning MGs
Armor: 0.63in (16mm)
Crew: 11
Dimensions: Length 34ft 2.5in (10.4m); Width 12ft 6in (3.81m); Height 10ft 3in (3.12m)
Weight: 37 tons (37,592kg)
Powerplant: Ricardo 12-cylinder gasoline, 300hp (223.9kW)
Speed: 6.5mph (10km/h)
Range: 50 miles (80km)

The Anglo-American Mk VIII tank was the first AFV to be produced as a result of international collaboration. In June 1917, two months after the United States declared war on Germany, an approach was made by the US government to purchase British tanks for use by the US Marine Corps. The most modern British tank in production at that stage was the Mk VI, and the Americans believed that they could produce a more powerful version. A little while later, the US Army took on the project, and a rather ambitious program was agreed whereby 1500 Mk VIII tanks were to be produced by the end of 1918, with the two participating countries supplying agreed components. Trials of the prototypes were completed after the end of World War I and it was decided to build 100 Mk VIIIs in the United States. These were built in 1919 and 1920, and were issued to the 67th Infantry (Tank) Regiment. The British ordered 1500 examples from various manufacturers, but only one prototype and 24 vehicles manufactured from spare parts were produced.

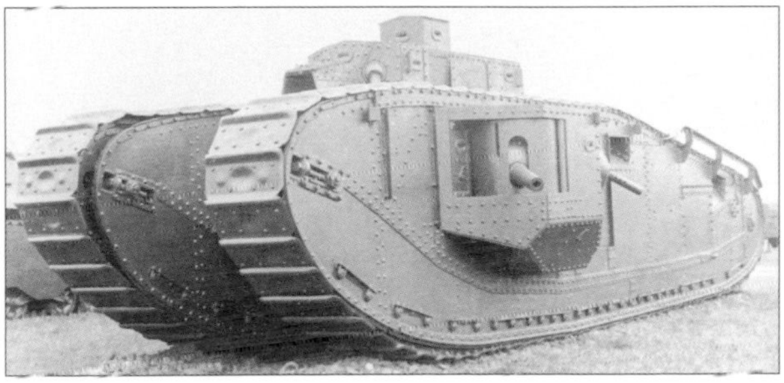

Above: *The evolution of the British-designed tank, from the lozenge-shaped design of the early AFVs into the more classical lines of the modern tank, is apparent.*

The Quest for Mobility
⚒ 1918 USA

SIX-TON MODEL 1917

In the aftermath of World War I, many nations resorted to copying British and French tank designs while taking time to develop their own AFVs. The Six-ton Model 1917 was one such example.

This six-ton fighting vehicle was an American copy of the Renault FT-17, the best-known French tank of World War I. Some 950 were built under license in the USA, in addition to the 500 or so that were delivered direct to the US Army. The FT-17 remained the principal US Army fighting vehicle for some years. Of the American-built vehicles, 374 were infantry support tanks, and 50 were fitted out as radio command vehicles. During World War II, some were delivered to Canada and the United Kingdom as training vehicles. The FT-17 and its derivatives were among the most widely used tanks of the interwar period, some of the American machines being deployed to the Philippines and Hawaii. They served in almost every limited war of the 1920s and 1930s, playing a key part in the Russo–Polish war of 1920, the Spanish Civil War, and the Chinese Civil War. In 1940 the French Army still had eight battalions of FT-17s, each with 63 tanks, and three independent companies with 10 tanks each. Many of these were seized by the Germans and used for airfield defense and internal security in the occupied countries.

Specifications

Armament: One 1.46in (37mm) cannon or one Colt 0.30in (7.62mm) MG

Armor: 0.67in (17mm)

Crew: 2

Dimensions: Length 16ft 5in (5.0m), with tailpiece (M1917A1) 17ft 4in (5.28m); Width 5ft 9in (1.9m); Height 7ft 7in (2.30m)

Weight: 6.47 tons (6580kg)

Powerplant: Buda HU modified 4-cylinder water-cooled, 42hp (31.34kW)

Speed: 5.5mph (8.9km/h) (M1917A1 10mph (16km/h))

Range: Road, 30 miles (48km)

Below: *The US Army was just one of many overseas customers to purchase the Renault FT-17. It gave the US a sound foundation in armored warfare.*

The Quest for Mobility
⚒ 1923 Italy

FIAT 3000 LIGHT TANK

Reliable and easy to produce, the Fiat 3000 was yet another offshoot of the remarkable little French FT-17 light tank, the most widely used of its type in the world in the 1920s.

Specifications

Armament: Two 0.26in (6.5mm) MGs, or one 1.46in (37mm) gun; one 0.236in (6mm) MG

Armor: 0.63in (16mm)

Crew: 2

Dimensions: Length 11ft 9in (3.58m); Width 5ft 2in (1.66m); Height 7ft (2.20m)

Weight: 5.41 tons (5500kg)

Powerplant: Fiat 4-cylinder gasoline, 65bhp (48.5kW) at 1700rpm

Speed: 15mph (24km/h)

Range: 60 miles (95km)

The Fiat 3000 was the Italian version of the Renault FT-17, and 180 of these splendid AFVs equipped five battalions of Italy's first armored regiment, formed on October 1, 1927. The Fiat 3000 had a relatively short career in Italian service. It was regarded as obsolete at the beginning of the 1930s and was replaced by a new generation of armored fighting vehicles developed by the Ansaldo Armament Company of Genoa.

The first of these was the Carro Veloce (Fast Tank) CV.33, modeled on a British design. Despite this, the Fiat 3000 continued to serve as a training vehicle for several years more, and some may have been used in the Italian campaign in Abyssinia

Above: This Fiat 3000 has been much modified from the original FT-17 design, fitted with additional side armor and a redesigned turret. Note the mud chutes in the side armor plating.

(Ethiopia) in 1935, where they would have proved very effective in counter-insurgency operations.

It is not know whether any Fiat 3000s served in World War II, although they were possibly used in the East African campaign of 1941, which ended in the defeat of the Italians by British and Dominian forces. Some Italian Fiat 3000s are known to have deployed to Spain with the Italian Expeditionary Force in 1936.

The Quest for Mobility

⚒ **1923 UK**

VICKERS MARK I AND MARK II MEDIUM TANKS

The Vickers medium tanks were among the fastest of their kind when they entered service with the British Army. They were well armed, but their armor protection was poor.

Below: The Vickers Mk I tank was considered to be the first "fast tank" to enter service with any army. The main factor that contributed to its speed was its sprung suspension.

These so-called Vickers medium tanks—the Mk I was actually designed as a light AFV in 1922—were the principal British AFVs used in ongoing mobility trials during the 1920s. The design of their fighting compartments and general layout was a long way ahead of any contemporary AFV, as was their general reliability and radius of action of 150 miles. The Vickers Mediums were speedy (an attribute helped by sprung suspension) but they had a low track life. Starting was mechanically and magneto-assisted. Their high-velocity 1.85in (47mm) gun was designed specifically to engage other tanks, leaving their machine guns to engage other targets. The biggest drawback to the Vickers Medium tanks was their pitifully inadequate frontal armor, which had a thickness of only

0.31in (8mm). The designers of these medium tanks had been instructed to create a turret layout of maximum efficiency, in which the commander could directly instruct the gunner to maintain rapid and effective application of fire. They decided on a three-man layout, which was to become standard in most later turret designs.

Specifications

Armament: One 1.85in (47mm) 3pdr gun

Armor: 0.246–0.315in (6.25–8mm)

Crew: 5

Dimensions: Length 17ft 6in (5.33m); Width 9ft 1in (2.78m); Height 8ft 9in (2.68m)

Weight: 13.2 tons (13,411.82kg)

Powerplant: One Armstrong Siddeley V-8 engine of 90hp (67.1kW)

Speed: 13mph (21km/h)

Range: 150 miles (241km)

Left: The Vickers Mk I and II were one of the first tanks to have their main armament mounted in a revolving turret.

The Quest for Mobility

1928 Soviet Union

MS (T-18) LIGHT TANK

After relying on foreign tank imports for some time, the Russians produced a tank design of their own in the form of the T-18, the first of a long line that eventually culminated in the excellent T-34.

Specifications

Armament: One 1.46in (37mm) Model 1916 gun; two 0.3in (7.62mm) Hotchkiss MGs

Armor: 0.236–0.866in (6–22mm)

Crew: 2

Dimensions: Length 11ft 6in (3.5m); Width 5ft 9in (1.76m); Height 6ft 11in (2.12m)

Weight: 5.32 tons (5410kg)

Powerplant: Fiat 6-cylinder gasoline, 40bhp (29.8kW) at 1500rpm

Speed: 9.9mph (16km/h)

Range: 37.3 miles (60km)

This tank was the first operational armored fighting vehicle of Soviet design, and although it suffered from many inadequacies, including being underpowered and undergunned, it gave the Russians experience in tank design and construction that they had previously lacked. The prototype was built in 1928 and entered service the following year. Production ended in 1931. The concept of the T-18 stemmed from a specification for a light infantry support vehicle issued in 1924 by the newly formed Tank Bureau. The first prototype was designated T-16, which emerged as the T-18 after some improvements to the engine and hull design had been incorporated. The manufacturer's MS designation stood for Maliy Soprovozdiniya (which literally means Small Escorting). The tank was produced by the Leningrad Bolshevik plant.

After its withdrawal from frontline service in 1932, the MS (T-18) was allocated to military training units. One unusual feature of this tank was the turret armament arrangement, in which the 1.46in (37mm) main armament and the machine gun were offset at 45 degrees to one another.

Below: *The odd-looking little T-18 was the forerunner of a long line of Soviet tanks leading to the technology used during World War II. It served until 1932.*

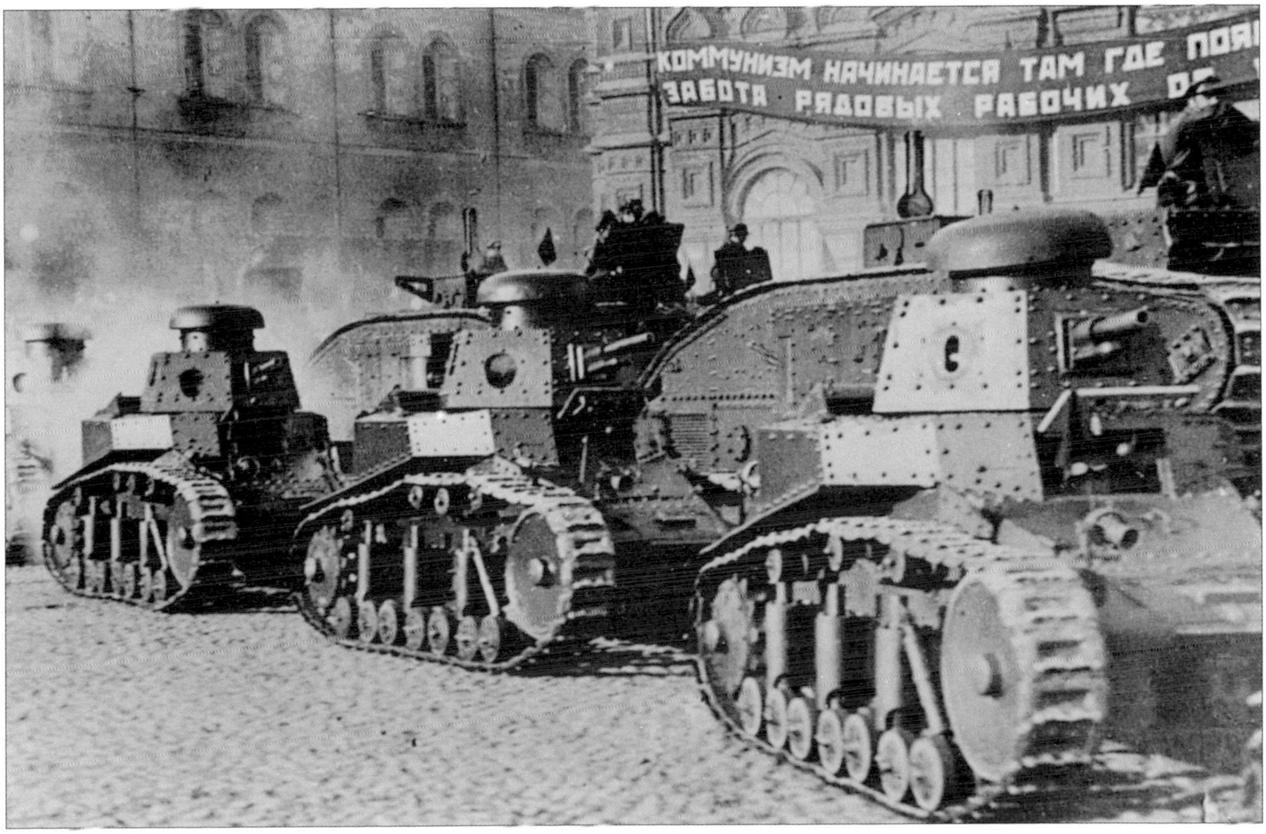

The Quest for Mobility
✖ 1928 UK

VICKERS SIX-TON TANK

The Vickers six-ton light tank was the model for many other tanks that were designed around the world in the 1920s, and in some cases, as in the Soviet Union, was copied down to the last detail.

The Vickers six-ton light tank was initiated as a private venture by Vickers, and although it was not taken up by the British Army it was acquired by many overseas armed forces and, in the case of the Soviet Union, was faithfully copied as the T-26. During the interwar years, the Vickers six-ton was the second most common tank design in the world, after France's Renault FT-17.

Mk E

Originally known as the Mk E, the prototype was built in 1928 and was produced in two versions, the Type A with two turrets (each mounting a Vickers machine gun) and the Type B, with a single two-man turret

Above: The Vickers six-ton light tank, although it was not adopted by the British Army, was an instant export success.

mounting a short-barreled 1.85in (47mm) gun and a single machine gun. This design, known as a duplex mounting, proved very effective, as both guns could be brought into action at the same time.

The British Army evaluated the Mk E, but the reliability of the suspension was considered unsatisfactory and the tank was rejected, whereupon Vickers sought export markets for the design. Although the tank was produced in the Soviet Union, it was also supplied to Bolivia, Bulgaria, China, Greece, Finland, Portugal, and Thailand.

Specifications

Armament: One 1.85in (47mm) gun; two 0.303in (7.7mm) machine guns

Armor: 0.39–0.98in (10–25mm)

Crew: 3

Dimensions: Length 15ft 9in (4.8m); Width 7ft 10in (2.39m); Height 7ft 8in (2.33m)

Weight: 10.3 tons (10,460kg)

Powerplant: One 80-98hp (60-70kW) Armstrong Siddeley Puma gasoline engine

Speed: 17.4mph (28km/h)

Range: 124 miles (200km)

The Quest for Mobility
⚔ 1929 UK

CARDEN-LOYD TANKETTE MARK VI

A cross between a light tank and a machine-gun carrier, the Carden-Loyd Tankette was a huge success on the export market, being cheap to purchase and reproduce.

Specifications

Armament: One 7.7mm (0.303in) Vickers MG

Armor: 0.2in–0.35in (5mm–9mm)

Crew: 2

Dimensions: Length 8ft 1in (2.46m); Width 5ft 9in (1.75m); Height 4ft (1.22m)

Weight: 1.5 tons (1525kg)

Powerplant: Ford Model T gasoline engine developing 40bhp (29.8kW) at 2500rpm

Speed: 25mph (40.2km/h)

Range: 90 miles (144km)

Although sometimes classed as light tanks, the Carden-Loyd series of AFVs were actually intended to be machine-gun carriers. The first, the Mk IV, started as a private venture by Major General Le Q. Martel and was subsequently manufactured by Vickers for the home and the world export markets. Production began in 1927. Exports were a success: The Tankette was purchased by Canada, Chile, Czechoslovakia, France, India, Italy, Japan, Poland, and the Soviet Union, who used it to develop their own T-27 design. The Mk VI and earlier versions were also used by the British Army,

Above: The Carden-Loyd Mk VI failed its trials with the British Army, but 270 examples were eventually purchased for use as artillery tractors.

which took delivery of 270 examples. One variant, the Mk III, was produced by the Royal Ordnance factory. The purpose of the Tankette was the rapid deployment of troops armed with machine guns, which were not intended to be fired from the vehicle itself, although a tripod mounting for a machine gun was attached to the front of the hull. The Tankettes could also be used to tow light howitzers.

The Quest for Mobility
⚔ **1931 France**

RENAULT CHAR D1 INFANTRY

In 1935, the most modern tank available to the French Army was the small 13-ton D1. This was equipped with a 1.85in (47mm) gun and two machine guns, but it was expensive and heavy.

France's preoccupation with light and cheap infantry support tanks (which had much to do with the massive success of the FT-17 and its derivatives) continued in the 1930s with the development of the Renault Char D1 Infantry, of which 160 examples were built between 1932 and 1935. Originally fitted with an FT-17 turret, later models featured an ST-1 turret armed with a 2in (47mm) SA-34 gun. The Char D1 was intended to equip autonomous tank battalions assigned to infantry divisions for armored support. In 1935 the D1 was the most modern tank available to the French Army; however, it proved to be more expensive and heavier than

its specification required, and it was soon replaced by the more effective Hotchkiss.

D2

A follow-on version, the D2, with heavier armor, entered service in 1937, but only one battalion was equipped with it. Some D1s and D2s were captured by the Germans and issued to the armed forces of some of Germany's allies, or used for training purposes.

Below: *The Char D1 was a modern design that compared favorably with other AFVs of its class in the mid-1930s, but it was replaced by the Hotchkiss.*

Specifications

Armament: One 1.85in (47mm) SA 34 gun; two 0.295in (7.5mm) mle 1931 MGs

Armor: Maximum, 1.57in (40mm)

Crew: 3

Dimensions: Length 15ft 9.3in (4.81m); Width 7ft 1in (2.16m); Height 7ft 10in (2.4m)

Weight: 13.78 tons (14,000kg)

Powerplant: Renault, 4-cylinder gasoline, 74hp (55.2kW)

Speed: Road, 11.55mph (18.6km/h)

Range: Road, 56.9 miles (90km)

The Quest for Mobility
1931   France

RENAULT UE CHENILLETTE

The little Renault UE Chenillette was a very versatile utility vehicle, and was widely used throughout the world in support of France's colonial interests. Many were used by the Germans.

Specifications

Armament: None

Armor: Maximum, 0.354in (9mm)

Crew: 2

Dimensions: Length 9ft 7.7in (2.94m); Width 5ft 9in (1.75m); Height 4ft 1in (1.24m)

Weight: 3.25 tons (3300kg)

Powerplant: Renault, 4-cylinder gasoline, 38hp (28.3kW)

Speed: Road, 18.6mph (30km/h)

Range: Road, 62.1 miles (100km)

Produced in the early 1930s, the Renault UE was in widespread service at the outbreak of World War II. It was a small, tracked armored vehicle with a two-man crew. Many of these models were captured and pressed into service by the Wehrmacht and used on all fronts. In German service the vehicle was known as the Infanterieschlepper (infantry tractor) UE 630F. It was considered by many users to be the finest vehicle of its kind in the world—a claim that was entirely justified. It was also an excellent towing vehicle, and was able to transport supplies across terrain that was unsuitable for wheeled vehicles. As an infantry support vehicle in

Above: *The Renault UE Chenillette was the approximate equivalent of Britain's Bren-gun carrier and served much the same purpose. It served in large numbers during and after World War II.*

German service, the UE could be armed with one or two MG34 machine guns. The UE was widely used by the French in Indo-China, and, in the late 1930s, represented the only effective armored vehicles available to the French colonial forces, as most of the light tanks that had been deployed there at earlier dates were no longer roadworthy. The UEs were formed into motorized detachments.

The Quest for Mobility
1931   Poland

TK-3 TANKETTE

In September 1939, the Polish Army's T-3 Tankettes were sent into action against the invading German Panzers in actions that were full of valor but ultimately hopeless.

Below: A German soldier poses in front of a captured Polish TK-3 after the conquest of Poland in September 1939. Most TK-3s were destroyed in the fighting.

The Polish Army's TK-3 Tankette series of AFVs was based on the two-man Vickers Carden-Loyd Mk VI design. Poland purchased a single Mk VI in 1929 and subsequently ordered 10 more, together with spare parts. The British design was progressively modified by Polish engineers, and manufactured as the TK-1 and TK-2. In 1930 a heavier and much-improved variant, the TK-3, was produced and entered service with the Polish Army in 1931.

Difficult targets
About 300 TK-3s were produced by the PZI (National Engineering Works) at Ursus, near Warsaw. The Tankettes formed the main body of the Polish Army's armored force at the outbreak of World War II, and although they were no match for the German armor of the time, they were ideal for reconnaissance and infantry support—their small size and low profile made them difficult targets. The TK-3s suffered heavy losses during the German invasion of Poland in September 1939. About 24 were fitted with a 0.79in (20mm) cannon just before the outbreak of hostilities, and these were much better placed to engage the lighter types of German armored vehicle than those armed with a single machine gun.

Specifications

Armament: One 0.312in (7.92mm) MG or one 0.79in (20mm) cannon

Armor: : 0.157–0.317in (4–8mm)

Crew: 2

Dimensions: Length 8ft 6in (2.65m); Width 5ft 10in (1.78m); Height 4ft 4in (1.35m)

Powerplant: Ford A 4-cylinder gasoline, 40bhp (29.8kW) at 2300rpm

Speed: 28mph (45km/h)

Range: 125 miles (200km)

The Quest for Mobility
⚒ **1931 Soviet Union**

BT-1/BT-2 LIGHT/MEDIUM TANK

The Russian BT-1 and BT-2 were the first in the line of fast tanks that saw a great deal of service in the troubled years of the 1930s, when the Soviet Union was involved in various border disputes.

The Russian BT series of light and medium tanks was based on the designs of J. Walter Christie and in particular the Christie T3 tank of 1931, although it was completely redesigned by Soviet engineers (with assistance from their American counterparts). A single T3 tank, delivered to the Soviet Union for evaluation in 1930, received the designation BT-1, while the first Soviet-produced model became the BT-2.

BT-7

The ultimate Soviet derivation of Christie's design was the BT-7, which incorporated numerous improvements and entered service with the Red Army in 1935. The BT tanks were fast and maneuverable, although these attributes were only achieved at the expense of armor, the lack of which made the tanks vulnerable. Some BT tanks were tested under operational conditions in the Spanish Civil War and were used during the "Winter War" against Finland between 1939 and 1949, when they suffered heavy losses to Finnish antitank weapons. The earlier BT tanks also saw service in the Far East, where the Soviet Union became embroiled in border incidents with Japanese forces occupying Manchuria in the late 1930s.

Below: *This Soviet BT light tank, seen during the fighting in Manchuria in the late 1930s, has had its tracks and turret removed, as well as much of its armor, probably to serve in a secondary role.*

Specifications

(BT-2)

Armament: One 1.46in (37mm) Model 1930 gun; one 0.3in (7.62mm) DT MG

Armor: 0.236–0.51in (6–13mm)

Crew: 3

Dimensions: Length 18ft (5.48m); Width 7ft 4in (2.23m); Height 6ft 4in (1.92m)

Weight: 11.02 tons (11,200kg)

Powerplant: Liberty Aero 12-cylinder gasoline, 400bhp (298.5kW) at 2000rpm

Speed: Unknown

Range: 187 miles (300km)

The Quest for Mobility
⚒ 1931   Soviet Union

T-26 LIGHT INFANTRY TANK

Russia's T-26 tank saw widespread service in the years between the wars and gave much-needed experience to the Soviet Army, leading to the development of better tactics.

Above: *Later models of the T-26 were fitted with a single turret, as pictured in this photograph. In this configuration the vehicle was designated T-26B.*

Left: *The 1931 model, seen here, was one of the many variants of the T-26. It had dual turrets, usually mounting a pair of 0.3in (7.62mm) machine guns, but sometimes carried a 1.46in (37mm) gun.*

The T-26, a mass-produced version of the British Vickers Type E six-ton tank, was an extremely important milestone in the development of the Soviet Union's armored forces. Not only did it provide a substantial nucleus of Russian tank men with practical experience of operating what was then a modern armored fighting vehicle, but it also led directly to many improvements that would be incorporated in later generations of Soviet AFVs. These improvements would place them among the finest in the world. The initial models of the T-26, the T-26A series, had twin turrets each mounting a machine gun (or later, one machine gun and one cannon), but this configuration was soon abandoned in favor of the more practical single turret, in which guise the AFV became the T-26B. This served in large numbers from 1933. Around 5500 were produced before production ended in 1936. The T-26B was followed by the T-26S of 1937, which had a turret of improved design and was of all-welded construction. Earlier models had been riveted, but in 1934, during a series of clashes

with Japanese forces on the border between Manchuria and Mongolia, it was found that when a T-26 was hit by enemy fire the rivets tended to pop out and ricochet around the tank's interior. This had deadly consequences.

Spanish Civil War

The Soviet Union supplied 362 T-26Bs to the Republican government during the Spanish Civil War, where they proved to be far superior to the German Panzer Mk Is and Italian CV33/35s, which were armed only with machine guns. With its relatively light armor, however, the T-26 was vulnerable to antitank weapons such as the German 1.46in (37mm) towed antitank gun, and this deficiency was hammered home during the conflict with Finland in the winter of 1939-40, when dozens of knocked-out T-26s were captured, repaired, and pressed into service.

During the German invasion of Russia in 1941, the T-26 could hold its own against enemy light tanks, but it was completely outclassed when it came up against the Panzer Mks III and IV.

Specifications

(T-26)

Armament: One 1.77in (45mm) Model 1938 L/46 gun; two 0.3in (7.62mm) DT MGs

Armor: 0.39–0.98in (10–25mm)

Crew: 3

Dimensions: Length 15ft 9in (4.8m); Width 7ft 10in (2.39m); Height 7ft 8in (2.33m)

Weight: 10.3 tons (10,460kg)

Powerplant: GAZ T-26 8-cylinder gasoline, 91bhp (67.9kW) at 2200rpm

Speed: 17.4mph (28km/h)

Range: 124 miles (200km)

The Quest for Mobility
1931 Soviet Union

T-27 TANKETTE

Yet another design based on the well-tried Carden-Loyd model, the T-27 Tankette proved to be a useful counter-insurgency vehicle in the hands of the Red Army. It had an advantage that it could be transported by air.

Below: The Red Army found the T-27 reliable and simple to operate, but it coped poorly with swampy and snowy terrain due to the narrowness of its tracks.

Specifications

Armament: One 0.3in (7.62mm) DT MG

Armor: 0.354in (9mm)

Crew: 2

Dimensions: Length 7ft 6in (2.29m); Width 5ft 1in (1.55m); Height 3ft 7in (1.1m)

Weight: 1.7 tons (1727kg)

Powerplant: GAZ AA 4-cylinder gasoline, 22bhp (16.4kW) at 170rpm

Speed: 28mph (45km/h)

Range: 100 miles (161km)

Based on the Carden-Loyd Mk VI, which was produced under license in the Soviet Union, the T-27 was developed during the 1930s and featured a larger hull than the original British design. It also had an improved running gear and a mounting for a Soviet 0.3in (7.62mm) DT machine gun. The T-27 entered service in February 1931 and, during its useful life with the Red Army, was used mainly as a reconnaissance vehicle. It was deployed in 65 tankette battalions, each equipped with about 50 T-27s (although this number was later reduced to 23). The T-27 was air-transportable, the concept being proven in the mid-1930s

when the AFV was airlifted over considerable distances slung under a Tupolev TB-3 bomber/transport. The T-27 was widely used in the troubled 1930s to help put down local rebellions in the central republics of the Soviet Union. Some were still in service in 1941, and it is known that a few took part in the defense of Moscow.

Experiments

Quite a number of T-27s were also used for experimental purposes, being fitted with flamethrowers and recoilless cannon. The T-27, which had a very cramped interior, was not popular with its crews.

The Quest for Mobility
✖ **1931   Sweden**

STRV M/31 TANK

Sweden's tank production got underway with a good deal of help
from the Germans, who smuggled tank parts into the country.
The first indigenous design was the m/31.

The Stridsvagn m/31 was the first tank to be produced in Sweden, and it came to fruition with German help. After World War I, the Germans hid much war material from the Allied Control Commission, and some of it found its way to Sweden. The Swedish government paid 100,000 Swedish Krona for 10 LK.II light tanks, which were taken to pieces and shipped to Sweden disguised as boiler parts and agricultural equipment. They were then reassembled and put into service as the Stridsvagen m/21. The Swedes rebuilt these tanks, making several improvements before turning to an AFV of indigenous

Above: *The Stridsvagen m/31 was Sweden's first tank, and was based on a German AFV, the LK.II. The tank was known as the L-10 in Swedish Army service.*

design with the help of German designer Josef Vollmer. Although the Strv m/31 was the first Swedish-produced tank, it came about as the result of German backing—the German government had become a major shareholder in the Landsverk Company, which manufactured the vehicle. The Strv m/31, also known as the L-10 in Swedish Army service, began to replace the m/21 from 1931.

Specifications

Armament: One 1.46in (37mm) gun; two MGs

Armor: 0.354in (9mm)

Crew: 4

Dimensions: Length 17ft (5.18m); Width 7ft (2.13m); Height 7ft 4in (2.23m)

Weight: 11.31 tons (11,500kg)

Powerplant: Bussing V6, gasoline, air-cooled, 140bhp (104.5kW) at 2500rpm

Speed: 25mph (40km/h)

Range: 125 miles (200km)

The Quest for Mobility
✖ 1932 Germany

SDKFZ 231 RECONNAISSANCE VEHICLE

Germany was forbidden to produce tanks under the terms of the Versailles Treaty, and relied heavily on armored cars. These could then be manufactured under the guise of agricultural vehicles.

Below: *Although its off-road performance left a lot to be desired, the SdKfz 231 gave the German Army an armored capability at a time when the country was not allowed to produce tanks.*

Specifications

Armament: One 0.79in (20mm) cannon; one 0.312in (7.92mm) MG

Armor: Maximum, 0.57in (14.5mm)

Crew: 4

Dimensions: Length 18ft 3.3in (5.57m); Width 5ft 11.6in (1.82m); Height 7ft 4.6in (2.25m)

Weight: 5.61 tons (5700kg)

Powerplant: Daimler-Benz M09, 6-cylinder gasoline, 65hp (48.5kW)

Speed: Road, 40.4mph (65km/h)

Range: Road, 124 miles (200km)

The first German armored car to be produced after World War I, the six-wheeled SdKfz 231, was based on a modified 6x4 truck chassis. The vehicle was equipped with two driving stations, one in the rear (so that a second driver could quickly take control and drive it in the opposite direction). The rear driver also doubled as the radio operator. The SdKfz 231 entered service with the German Army in 1932 and began to be replaced in 1937 by eight-wheeled vehicles, which were to become standard in the Wehrmacht. Their replacement did not mean immediate withdrawal from frontline service; some numbers were used in the Polish and French campaigns, but after the Battle of France they were used for internal security and training.

Limited off-road ability

One of the main problems with the SdKfz 231 armored car was that its six-wheel configuration gave it strictly limited off-road mobility, whereas the later eight-wheelers could cope with all kinds of terrain and were greatly prized in North Africa, where they were widely used for fast reconnaissance by the Afrika Korps.

The Quest for Mobility

⚒ **1932 Soviet Union**

BA-10 ARMORED CAR

Russia's BA-10 armored car was anything but an effective vehicle, but large numbers were captured by the Germans, who found them useful for second-line duties such as security patrols.

Below: Although Russia's BA-10 armored car had the appearance of a World War I-vintage fighting vehicle, it was well-suited to the terrain and distances of the USSR.

Left: *A BA-10 armored car in the snow of a Russian winter. This photograph was probably taken during the Winter War with Finland in 1939–40, in which many BA-10s saw action.*

A heavy and unattractive vehicle, the Russian BA-10 (Broneavtomobil 10) armored car was developed from the older BA-3 and BA-6 AFVs, and was not much of an improvement on them. Produced by the Gorki automobile plant, it was based on the chassis of the six-wheeled GAZ-AAA truck, incorporating some reinforcement and a modified suspension. The turret was mounted at the rear, over the twin rear axles, and could mount either a 1.46in (37mm) tank gun or a 0.5in (12.7mm) heavy machine gun.

The BA-10 was produced in several versions, the later ones seeing only limited production. The first of these was the BA-10M, which had a turret taken from the T-26 light tank and which was armed with a 1.77in (45mm) gun. Considerable numbers of BA-10s were still in service when Germany invaded the Soviet Union in 1941, but losses were heavy and many were captured by the Germans, who pressed them into service as the Panzerspähwagen BAF 203r and used them for second-line duties such as antipartisan operations. Those still in service with the Red Army had virtually disappeared by mid-1942.

Specifications

Armament: One 1.77in (45mm) gun; one 0.3in (7.62mm) DT MG

Armor: 0.63in (16mm) hull, 0.236in (6mm) turret

Crew: 4

Dimensions: Length 15ft 5in (4.7m); Width 6ft 10in (2.09m); Height 7ft 11in (2.42m)

Weight: 5 tons (5100kg)

Powerplant: GAZ-MI 4-cylinder gasoline, 50bhp (37.3kW) at 2800rpm

Speed: 54mph (87km/h)

Range: 199 miles (320km)

The Quest for Mobility
1932 Soviet Union

BT-5 LIGHT/MEDIUM TANK

Early Soviet tanks like the BT-5 relied heavily on a good turn of speed to ensure their survival. In a pitched battle, however, they were extremely vulnerable to antitank weapons.

Specifications

Armament: One 1.77in (45mm) Model 1932 gun; one 0.3in (7.62mm) DT MG

Armor: 0.236–0.51in (6–13mm)

Crew: 3

Dimensions: Length 18ft (5.48m); Width 7ft 4in (2.23m); Height 7ft 3in (2.2m)

Weight: 11.52 tons (11,700kg)

Powerplant: M-5 12-cylinder gasoline, 350bhp (261.2kW) at 2300rpm

Speed: 43mph (70km/h)

Range: 124 miles (200km)

The BT-5 (Bistrokhodny Tank, or Fast Tank) was one of a series of cavalry tanks produced in large numbers by the Russians between 1932 and 1941. They were well armed, but relied on their mobility for survival, as they were lightly armored. The BT tanks were convertible AFVs, which meant that the tracks could be removed and a chain drive engaged to the roadwheels, permitting the tank to travel at high speed on roads, the vehicle being steered by pivoting the front wheels.

Below: *The BT series led directly to the design and production of the T-34, which was to play a key part in the war on the Eastern Front.*

Battle duty

A battalion of about 50 BT-5s served on the Republican side in the Spanish Civil War, where they were successful against the lighter tanks used by the Nationalists, but in the Winter War against Finland they suffered heavily at the hands of the Finnish antitank defenses, which were well organized, well camouflaged, and expertly dug in. The ongoing development of the BT series led directly to the splendid T-34, which was just beginning to replace the older models in June 1941, at the time of the German invasion of the Soviet Union. Many BT-5s were lost in the early stages of the campaign.

Chapter 2

EXPERIMENTS IN ARMOR

The 1930s saw ongoing experimentation in the development of armored fighting vehicles. The radio control of armored formations now became routine, and in the early years, armies used the so-called "infantry tank," a lightly armored vehicle reliant on speed and agility. As the decade progressed, however, two distinct types of tank evolved, both of them in the medium category. One was designed to support an infantry attack and the other, armed with a high-velocity weapon, was designed to destroy other tanks.

Above: *A Vickers Mk V light tank pictured as a museum piece. The Mk V had an enlarged turret to take two men, raising the number of crew to three.*

Left: *The Renault R-35 light tank was typical of the fighting vehicles of this era. It was designed to replace the excellent FT-17 in service, but never quite succeeded in doing so.*

Many of the tanks produced by the leading nations in the 1930s owed their inspiration to British designs. During the previous decade Britain had led the world in tank design and manufacture, exporting tank models that were widely copied and developed by the armed forces of countries such as the Soviet Union. By the mid-1930s, however, Britain had lost its way, and it was Germany and France who emerged as innovators in the design of new armored fighting vehicles. Different categories of AFV began to emerge, too, one of the most important being the armored personnel carrier. AFVs of this kind had been used on a limited scale in the last months of World War I, but now it was the Germans who developed them and formed Panzergrenadier divisions, in which highly mobile infantry could keep pace with the rapid advance of the tank echelons. This formed a key element of the Blitzkrieg concept that was to meet with devastating success in the early years of World War II.

Experiments in Armor
⚒ **1933   Czechoslovakia**

CKD/PRAGA T-33 TANKETTE

Although it received unfavorable report during testing, the T-33 Tankette was accepted for service with the Czech Army. The Czechs never used it in action, but the Germans did.

Below: Although it was disliked by the crews who tested it, the CKD/Praga T-33 was selected for production.

In the 1920s, the government of the newly created independent state of Czechoslovakia realized that if their embryo nation was to survive, it would need to build up a thriving and modern armaments industry. This it succeeded in doing with remarkable speed, the Skoda company of Pilsen, in particular, quickly becoming world-renowned for the quality of the weapons it produced. In 1927, the CKD (Ceskomoravska Kolben Danek) Company was formed by the amalgamation of four tank-manufacturing firms, and this enterprise set about manufacturing a tankette called the T-33, which, like many others of its type, was based on the British Carden-Loyd Mk VI, some examples of which had been obtained by the Czechs.

Unsatisfactory testing

Crews who tested the T-33 reported that they did not like it, but it went into production for the Czech Army anyway. Seized by the Germans in 1939, many CKD Tankettes were used in action on the Eastern Front in 1941. About one-quarter of the armored fighting vehicles used by the Germans between 1940 and 1941 were of Czech origin.

Specifications

Armament: Two 0.312in (7.92mm) MGs

Armor: 0.47in (12mm)

Crew: 2

Dimensions: Unknown

Weight: 2.46 tons (2500kg)

Powerplant: Praga 4-cylinder gasoline, 31bhp (23kW)

Speed: 22mph (35km/h)

Range: 62 miles (100km)

Experiments in Armor

⚒ **1933 France**

AMR 33 LIGHT TANK

Below: Early trials showed that the AMR-33, although very agile, was noisy, poorly balanced, and lacked sufficient range for it to be effective.

The French AMR 33, built by Renault, was mechanically unreliable and suffered heavily in the Battle of France, as much from breakdowns as from enemy action in combat.

Specifications

Armament: One 0.295in (7.5mm) MG

Armor: Maximum, 0.51in (13mm)

Crew: 2

Dimensions: Length 11ft 5.8in (3.5m); Width 5ft 4.5in (1.64m); Height 5ft 8in (1.73m)

Weight: 5.4 tons (5500kg)

Powerplant: Renault, 8-cylinder gasoline, 84hp (62.4kW)

Speed: Road, 33.5mph (54km/h)

Range: Road, 124 miles (200km)

In January 1932, the French War Department issued a specification for a three-ton light AFV armed with a single machine gun, optimized for the rapid reconnaissance role, as its name (Automitrailleuse de Cavalerie type Reconnaissance) suggested. Against strong competition, the contract was won by Renault, who designated the vehicle AMR Renault Modèle 33, or AMR 33. Production was slow, mainly because of financial difficulties, and the first AMR was not delivered until June 1934. The last came off the production line in September.

Service history

At the outbreak of World War II, the AMR 33 was in service with the French Army's 1st and 2nd Light Mechanized Divisions, each of which had three squadrons of AMR 33s to support their motorized infantry. The lightly armored AMR 33 suffered severely in the Battle of France, as much from mechanical problems as from enemy action. The few survivors were used by the Germans for patrol duties in France itself after the occupation. Today, one AMR 33 is on display at the Musée des Blindés (Tank Museum) at Saumur.

Experiments in Armor
⚒ 1933 Italy

CARRO VELOCE CV 33 TANKETTE

The Italian Army had a fixation about cavalry tanks, leading to a series of vehicles classed as Carro Veloce—Fast Tank—developed by the Ansaldo armaments manufacturing company.

Below: *This CV 33 has been stripped of its turret and appears to be in use as a reconnaissance or command vehicle.*

From 1933, a new generation of fast, lightly armored tanks was developed by the Ansaldo Armaments and Heavy Industry Company for the Italian Army. The first of these was the Carro Veloce (Fast Tank) CV 33, which was an improved version of the Vickers Carden-Loyd Mk VI. Designated L3/33 in military service, the CV 33 and a developed version, the CV 35 (L3/35), saw operational service in Abyssinia (Ethiopia) in 1935 and in the Spanish Civil War, where an Italian armored force was virtually wiped out at Guadalajara by far superior Russian-built T-26s. After the Axis invasion of the Balkans in 1941, some numbers of CV 33s

and CV 35s were deployed to Yugoslavia for antipartisan duties, some being captured by partisans and used against their former owners.

Under-armored

The casualties suffered by the CV series of tankettes in various conflicts should have convinced the Italian military that the sacrifice of armor in order to achieve speed was not a good formula, but it did not. Right up to the end of their participation in World War II, the Italians continued to produce tanks that were under-armored and no match for those of the Allies.

Specifications

Armament: One 0.26in (6.5mm) MG or two 0.315in (8mm) MGs

Armor: 0.59in (15mm)

Crew: 2

Dimensions: Length 10ft 5in (3.17mm); Width 4ft 8in (1.42mm); Height 4ft 3in (1.30mm)

Weight: 3.15 tons (3200kg)

Powerplant: Fiat 4 cylinder gasoline, 42bhp (31kW)

Speed: 26mph (42km/h)

Range: 78 miles (125km)

Experiments in Armor

1933 Russia

T-28 MEDIUM TANK

The first operational medium tank in the world, Russia's T-28 incorporated several innovations, including radio equipment. Its inadequate armor caused problems in action.

Below: *Although assured of its place in history as the world's first operational medium tank, the T-28 was too cumbersome to be really effective.*

Right: *The bulky design of the T-28 is apparent in this photograph. It suffered appalling losses during the Winter War of 1939–40, where its inadequate armor was easily penetrated by Finnish antitank projectiles.*

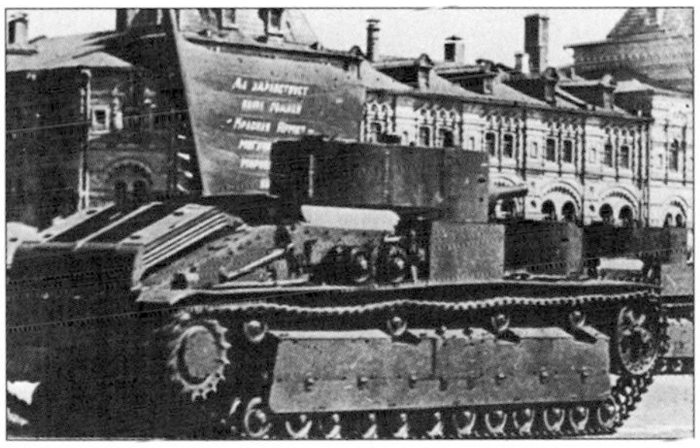

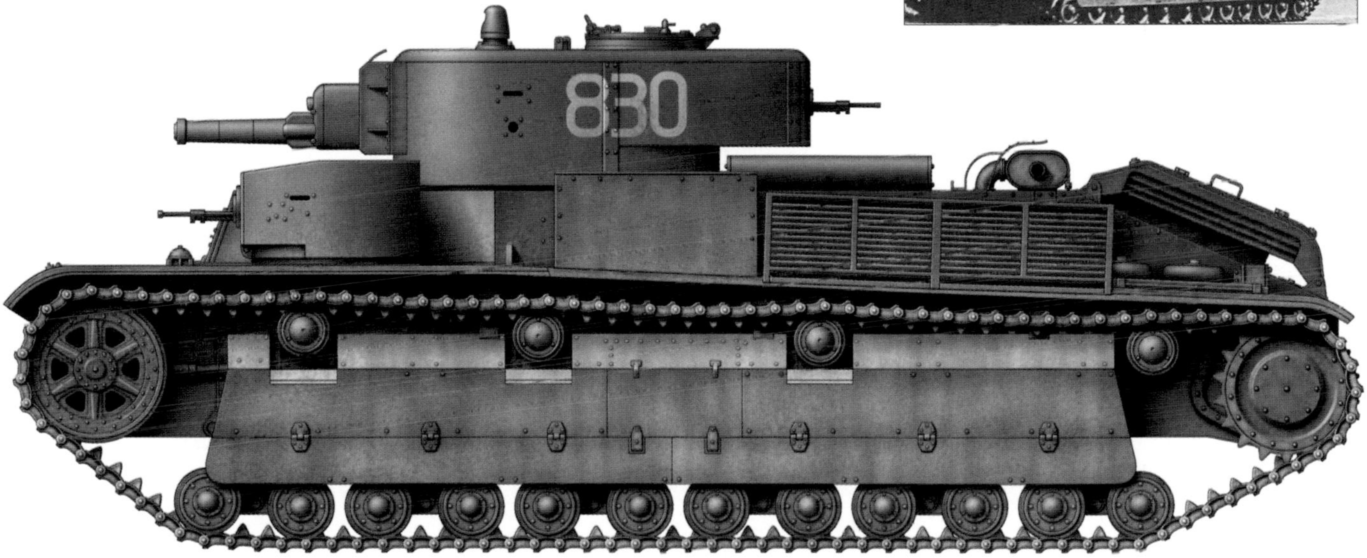

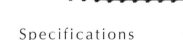

Specifications

Armament: One 3in (76.2mm) Model 1927/32 L/16.5 gun; three 0.3in (7.62mm) DT MGs

Armor: 0.39–1.18in (10–30mm)

Crew: 6

Dimensions: Length 24ft 5in (7.44m); Width 9ft 5in (2.81m); Height 9ft 3in (2.82m)

Weight: 28 tons (28,500kg)

Powerplant: M-17L 12-cylinder gasoline, 500bhp (373kW) at 1450rpm

Speed: 23mph (37km/h)

Range: 118 miles (190km)

In many respects Russia's T-28 was a prime example of how a tank should not be designed. Despite this, however, it was the first operational medium tank in the world, and therefore deserves its place in history. Even though some of its design features were influenced by earlier British experimental AFVs (notably the Vickers types), it was of indigenous design and paved the way for future Soviet medium tank developments. The prototype was completed in 1931 and was equipped with a 1.7in (45mm) gun, which was replaced by a 3in (76mm) weapon in the first production model, the T-28A, which was issued to Soviet armored units from 1933.

T-28B

The next production variant, the T-28B, appeared in 1938, and featured a new long-barreled 3in (76mm) weapon with a better performance. The main armament was housed in one large turret, which was flanked by two smaller ones housing machine guns, an arrangement that was fashionable in the early 1930s. All T-28s were equipped with radio, which was mostly lacking in the tanks of other nations at that time, and had mounts for antiaircraft machine guns. The T-28's participation in the Winter War of 1939–40, when it suffered grievous losses to Finnish antitank weaponry, revealed the inadequacy of its armor, which was upgraded later.

Experiments in Armor
⚒ **1933 Russia**

T-35 HEAVY TANK

Russia's T-35 heavy tank was a failure. It made for an impressive sight on ceremonial parades in Moscow, but was little use for anything else. Its brief combat record was very poor.

Specifications

Armament: One 3in (76.2mm) L/16 or 24 gun; two 1.77in (45mm) guns; six 0.3in (7.62mm) MGs

Armor: 0.39–1.18in (10–30mm)

Crew: 11

Dimensions: Length 31ft 11in (9.72m); Width 10ft 6in (3.2m); Height 11ft 3in (34.3m)

Weight: 44.3 tons (45,000kg)

Powerplant: M-17M 12-cylinder gasoline, 500bhp (373kW) at 2200rpm

Speed: 18.6mph (30km/h)

Range: 93 miles (150km)

Left: The T-35 might have made an impressive sight on parade, but it was less than impressive in action. Its five turrets proved difficult to control and the bulk of the vehicle made it hard to maneuver.

Below: This view gives a good idea of the bulky nature of the T-35. In action, the tank was prone to continual mechanical failure, most being abandoned by their crews.

The T-35 heavy tank was intended to complement the T-28 medium tank in action, but in the event it turned out to be a failure. Equipped with five gun turrets, the T-35 had the task of breaking through strong fortifications to create gaps that could then be exploited by the T-28. The prototype T-35 appeared in 1932 but was found to have severe defects in its transmission system. Work on it was halted in favor of a less-complex prototype, which was accepted for production in August 1933. A production line was opened at the Kharkov Locomotive Factory, which turned out two initial batches of 10 T-35s. Only 65 tanks were produced in total, mainly due to its complexity and cost. Between 1935 and 1940 the T-35s served with the 5th Independent Heavy Tank Brigade in Moscow, where they made an impressive sight on parade.

Surviving tanks

In 1941 the survivors were assigned to the 34th Armored Division in the Kiev Military District and sent into action against the invading Germans. Most of the machines broke down and were abandoned before they came into contact with the enemy, however. Today, one surviving T-35 is on display at the Kubinka Tank Museum in Moscow.

Experiments in Armor
✖ **1933 Russia**

T-37 LIGHT AMPHIBIOUS TANK

Although the Russian T-37 drew its inspiration from the Carden-Loyd Tankette, it was not a copy of this earlier model. The Russians took the best features from the British vehicle and then improved them.

Below: *The T-37 light amphibious tank was produced in several different versions from 1935 onward, and saw combat during the early phase of the German attack on Russia in 1941, where it was completely outclassed.*

Specifications

Armament: One 0.3in (7.62mm) DT MG

Armor: 0.157in (4mm) hull, 0.354in (9mm) turret

Crew: 2

Dimensions: Length 12ft 3in (3.75m); Width 6ft 11in (2.1m); Height 5ft 6in (1.82m)

Weight: 3.15 tons (3200kg)

Powerplant: GAZ AA 4-cylinder gasoline, 65bhp (48.5kW) at 2200rpm

Speed: 35mph (56.3km/h)

Range: 115 miles (185km)

The inspiration for the T-37 light amphibious reconnaissance vehicle was Britain's Carden-Loyd AE 11 amphibious tankette, several of which were purchased by the Soviet Union in 1931. However, the T-37 was not a copy of the British AFV, which the Russians only used as the basis for a developed version. This resulted in the T-33, which was subjected to numerous trials and found to be unsatisfactory.

Design changes

After substantial redesign, the vehicle emerged as the T-37, which entered production in 1933 and incorporated major improvements, such as a suspension based on that of the French AMR 33 light tank. Production continued until 1936, and the T-37 was built in several versions. One of the most important of these was the T-37TU command vehicle. This was equipped with a large radio frame aerial around the upper hull, and in due course this was replaced by a pole aerial. Despite the fact that it was becoming obsolete, the T-37 was used in combat during the early stages of Operation Barbarossa in 1941, sometimes engaging vastly superior German armor. It had largely disappeared from frontline service by the spring of 1942, as had an improved model, the T-38.

Experiments in Armor
1934 Germany

NEUBAUFAHRZEUGE V UND VI HEAVY TANK

This massive tank had little value to the German Army other than one of propaganda. When it was deployed to Norway during the German invasion of 1940, its sheer weight caused problems.

The Neubaufahrzeuge V, also called PzKpfw V, meaning "new construction vehicle," was an impressive heavy tank that had considerable propaganda value for the Germans. One model was displayed at the International Automobile Exhibition in Berlin in 1939. This machine represented an early attempt to create a heavy tank for service with the new Wehrmacht, but it was cumbersome and slow, and did not fit in with the Blitzkrieg (lightning war) tactics then being developed by the Germans. Development started in 1933, and since the German Government was still bound by the restrictions imposed by the Treaty of Versailles, forbidding the production of certain war materials, the tanks were built under the guise of large tractors. Only six of these tanks were produced, three of which were used in the invasion of Norway in April 1940 (one being lost after it became stuck in a marsh and was blown up by German engineers). The Neubaufahrzeuge V was produced by Rheinmetall-Borsig; an alternative design, the Neubaufahrzeuge VI, was built by Krupp. The surviving Mks V and VI were scrapped sometime in 1942.

Below: *It is easy to see why this tank was of such propaganda value to the recently formed Wehrmacht. It had to be built in secret, masquerading as a heavy tractor design. Only six examples were produced.*

Specifications

Armament: One 2.95in (75mm) gun or 4.13in (105mm) howitzer; one 1.46in (37mm) gun; three 0.312in (7.92mm) MGs

Armor: Mild steel, up to 2.756in (70mm)

Crew: 6

Dimensions: Length 24ft (7.315m); Width 10ft (3.05m); Height 8ft 11in (2.72m)

Weight: 35–36 tons (35,560–36,575kg)

Powerplant: 6-cylinder gasoline, 500hp (372.9kW)

Speed: Road, 22mph (35.4km/h)

Range: Road, 87 miles (140km)

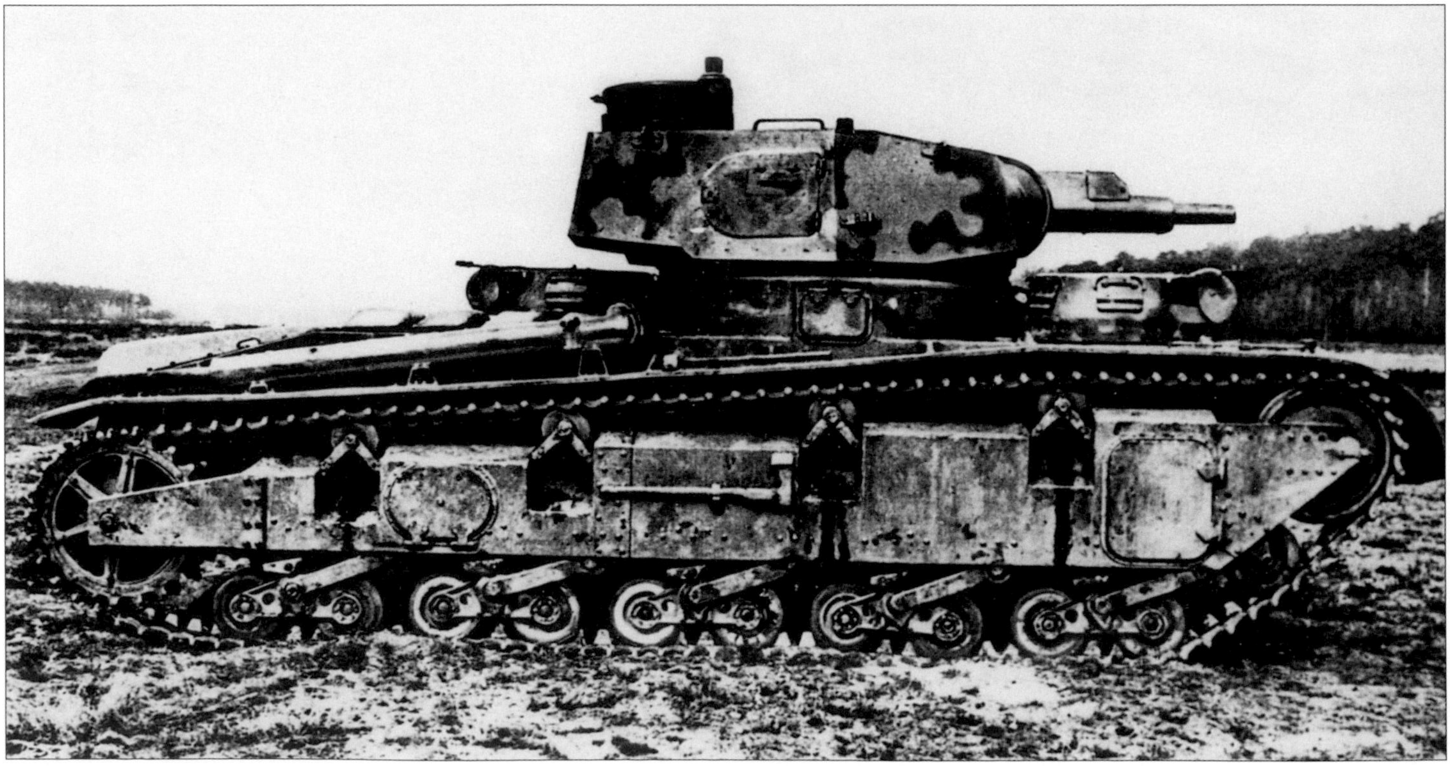

Experiments in Armor
⚒ 1934 Germany

PANZERKAMPFWAGEN I

The Treaty of Verailles forbade Germany to manufacture tanks, and

so the Germans had to produce their first post-World War I tank,

the Panzer I, in strict secrecy.

Above: *Panzerkampfwagen I tanks fording a river during the Polish campaign. Note the driver's observation slit, positioned to the left of the turret. The tank carried a crew of two.*

Below: *The Panzerkampfwagen I was a good tank for its day, but it proved to be too light and vulnerable to be really effective in action. Nevertheless, it was more than adequate in the Polish campaign. The tank is marked with white crosses on the turret for identification purposes.*

Specifications

Armament: Two 0.312in (7.92mm) MGs

Armor: Maximum, 0.51in (13mm)

Crew: 2

Dimensions: Length 14ft 6in (4.42m); Width 6ft 9in (2.06m); Height 5ft 7.7in (1.72m)

Weight: 5.8 tons (5893kg)

Powerplant: Maybach NL38TR, 6-cylinder gasoline, 100hp (74.5kW)

Speed: Road, 24.8mph (40km/h)

Range: Road, 95 miles (153km)

The Panzerkampfwagen I (PzKpfw I) was the result of a specification issued by the German Army's Waffenamt (weapons department) in 1933, calling for a light armored vehicle that could be used mainly for training purposes. Several companies submitted tenders and were awarded contracts to develop prototypes. The vehicle designed by Krupp was selected for further development. To conceal the true military nature of the vehicle, the Henschel Company received an order to produce an initial batch of 150 "industrial tractors," but by the time production started in July 1934, all pretense of secrecy had been abandoned by the Nazi regime. The tanks came off the production line under their correct military designation.

Light and vulnerable

The PzKpfw I was evaluated under operational conditions in Spain, and by the time Germany invaded Poland in September 1939, the Wehrmacht had over 1400 of these tanks on charge. The campaign in Poland showed that the PzKpfw I was too light and vulnerable to be effective in the front line, but despite this some 500 were used in the French campaign of 1940. The vehicle was phased out of frontline service in 1941.

Experiments in Armor
1934 Japan

TYPE 89B MEDIUM TANK

The Japanese were experts at examining the fighting vehicles of other nations, particularly those of Britain, and getting the best out of them to produce designs of their own. The Type 89B was a good example of this.

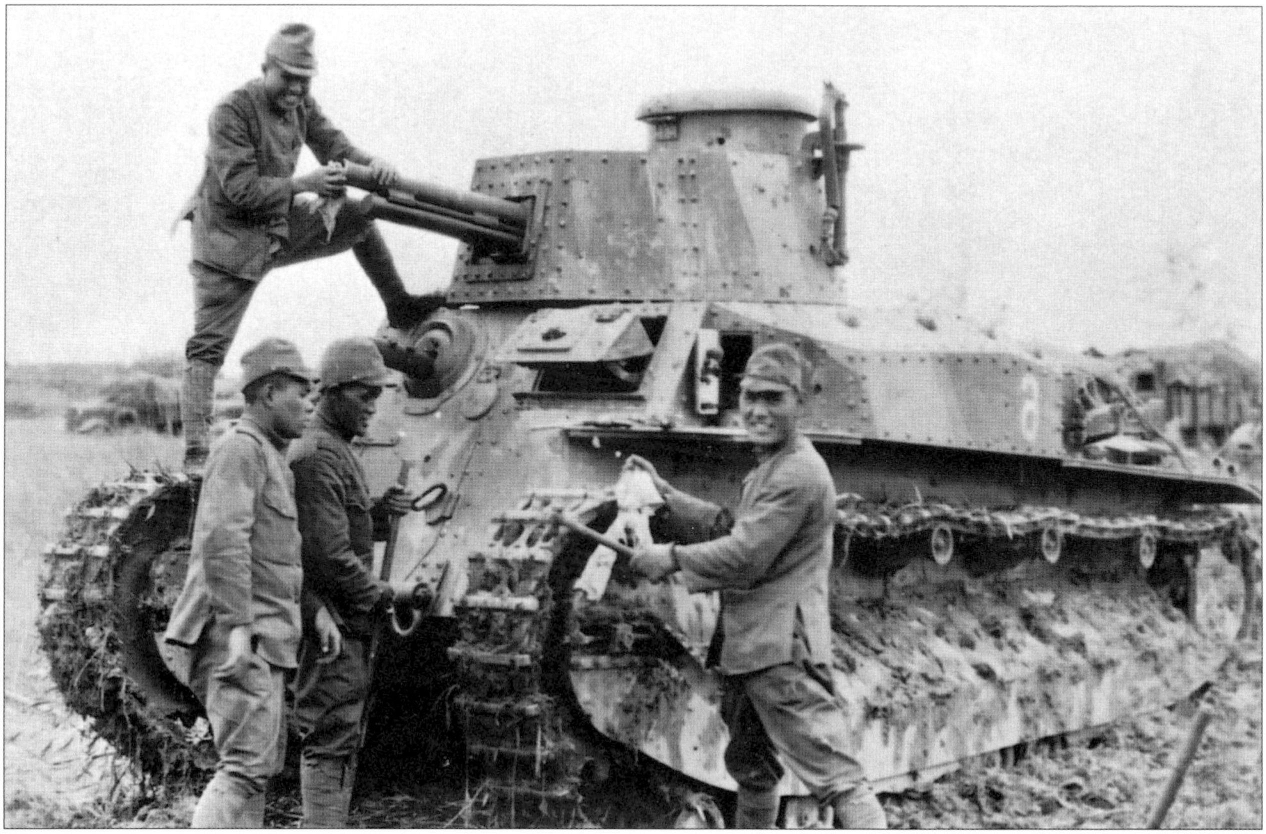

The Japanese Type 89B was a medium tank and owed some of its features to the Vickers Mk C, some of which had been purchased in 1927. The Type 89B made its appearance in 1932 and was first used in action at Shanghai in 1932, when it operated in support of Japanese Marines who were engaged in a landing operation. In December 1941 it saw operational service in Malaya and Singapore, and was used in Burma and the Philippines in 1942, although it was in the process of being replaced by more modern tanks. Most of the surviving Type 89Bs were transferred to China after these operations, where they saw further action.

Above: *The Type 89B was one of the first Japanese tanks to enter production. It was based on the Vickers Mk C, evaluated in 1927.*

Type 89A

The early model Type 89 tanks, designated Type 89A, were equipped with gasoline engines, but operations in Manchuria showed that these were prone to freezing up in conditions of extreme cold and so were replaced by diesel engines in the Type 89B. Other improvements in the Type 89B included the replacement of multiple armor plates by a single sloped front plate.

Specifications

Armament: One 6pdr (2.24in/57mm) gun; two 0.26in (6.5mm) MGs
Armor: 0.67in (17mm)
Crew: 4
Dimensions: Length 18ft 10in (5.73m); Width 7ft (2.13m); Height 8ft 3in (2.56m)
Weight: 12.79 tons (13,000kg)
Powerplant: Mitsubishi 6-cylinder diesel, 120bhp (90kW)
Speed: 16mph (26km/h)
Range: 106 miles (170km)

Specifications

Armament: One 0.26in (6.5mm) MG

Armor: 0.47in (12mm)

Crew: 2

Dimensions: Length 10ft (3.08m); Width 5ft 4in (1.62m); Height 5ft 4in (1.62m)

Weight: 3.35 tons (3400kg)

Powerplant: Mitsubishi Type 94 4-cylinder inline, 32bhp (24kW)

Speed: 24.9mph (40km/h)

Range: 124 miles (200km)

Experiments in Armor

1934 Japan

TYPE 94 TANKETTE

The Type 94 Tankette served in all Japan's campaigns from China in 1934 to the end of the Pacific War, and proved itself to be a very useful utility vehicle that could hold its own in combat.

The Japanese Type 94 Tankette was yet another small fighting vehicle based on the Carden-Loyd Mk VI. It was intended for light reconnaissance and patrol duties, and also for towing ammunition and supply trailers. As the vehicle was intended for operation in hot climates, it was provided with asbestos insulation to protect the two occupants—the driver (seated to the right of the front-mounted engine) and the commander (standing at his back inside the small turret). The small turret was unpowered, and to traverse it the commander had to push his shoulder against the machine gun. A company of Type 94s, usually consisting of six vehicles towing tracked trailers, was assigned to each Japanese infantry division.

Development

More than 800 Type 94s were manufactured and further development led directly to the Type 97 light tank. The Type 94 was used in all Japan's campaigns from 1934 onward, and surviving vehicles were still in use at the final surrender in 1945. Many are still to be found in tank museums all around the world.

Left: Type 94 Tankettes on parade. The Type 94 was a popular and effective AFV and owed its origin to the British Carden-Loyd Mk VI. It saw a great deal of service during Japan's campaigns in the Pacific and Southeast Asia, right up to the end of the war.

Experiments in Armor

1934 Poland

7TP LIGHT TANK

The 7TP light tank, derived from the British Vickers six-tonner, was a much better AFV than the German Panzer II, with which it came into conflict in September 1939 during the German invasion.

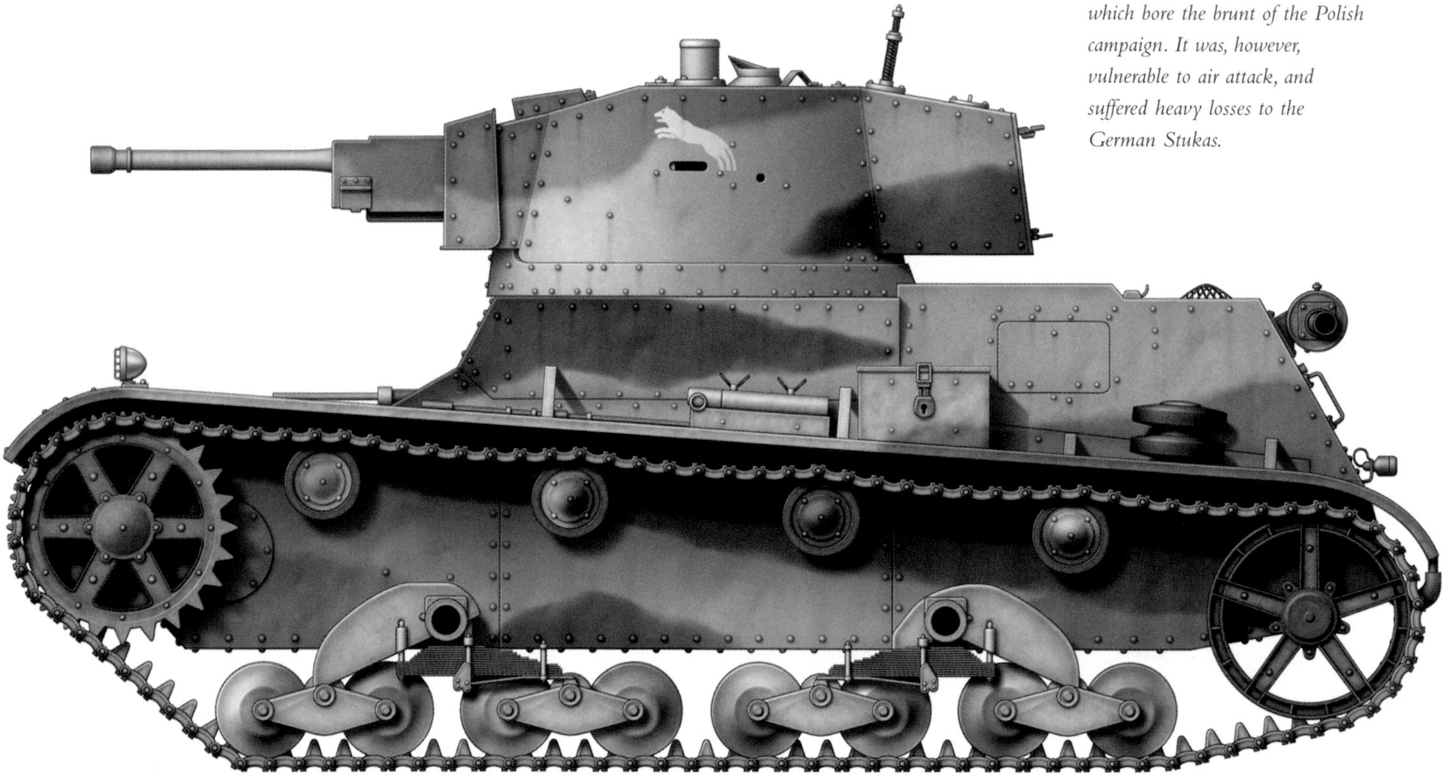

Below: *Poland's 7TP was an excellent light tank and a better AFV than the German Panzer II, which bore the brunt of the Polish campaign. It was, however, vulnerable to air attack, and suffered heavy losses to the German Stukas.*

The excellent Polish 7TP light tank, which made its first appearance in 1935, was a development of the British Vickers six-ton Mk E, and it was the standard tank in service with the Polish Army at the outbreak of World War II. It was a much better fighting vehicle than its German contemporary, the Panzer Mk II.

Design modifications

Taking the basic Vickers Type E design, Polish engineers incorporated some important improvements, the first of which was a reliable diesel engine. The vehicle was also equipped with a 1.45in (37mm) tank gun and improved frontal armor. Other modifications included the installation of a periscope, an efficient air-conditioning system, and a radio. Total production of the 7TP ran to 132, plus four prototypes. Two principal versions of the 7TP were produced, one with twin turrets and the other with a single turret. During the Polish campaign of 1939, the 7TP equipped two tank battalions. Some numbers were captured by the Germans and were used mainly as artillery tractors. Had it not been for the war, the 7TP might have enjoyed considerable export success, as several nations, including Sweden, had expressed great interest in it.

Specifications

Armament: One 1.46in (37mm) gun and one 0.312in (7.92mm) MG, or two 0.312in (7.92mm) MGs

Armor: 0.197–0.67in (5–17mm)

Crew: 3

Dimensions: Length 15ft 1in (4.6m); Width 7ft 1in (2.16m); Height 6ft 7in (2.02m)

Weight: 9.4 tons (9550kg)

Powerplant: Saurer 6-cylinder diesel, 110bhp (82kW)

Speed: 20mph (32km/h)

Range: 100 miles (160km)

Experiments in Armor
⚔ 1934 Sweden

STRV L-60 LIGHT TANK

German influence was apparent in this Swedish light tank, one of a series of vehicles designed by Joseph Vollmer, who had been responsible for German tank designs in World War I.

Below: The Swedes cut a lot of corners by using German design expertise in developing their armored forces. The L-60 light tank was a case in point.

Specifications

Armament: One 0.79in (20mm) cannon; one MG

Armor: 0.512in (13mm)

Crew: 3

Dimensions: Length 15ft 1in (4.60m); Width 6ft 7in (2m); Height 6ft 10in (2.08m)

Weight: 6.8 tons (6900kg)

Powerplant: Bussing-NAG V8 gasoline, 160bhp (119.4kW)

Speed: 28mph (45km/h)

Range: Not available

The Swedish L-60 light tank was a product of Joseph Vollmer, the German chief designer of the Landsverk Company. In Germany, Vollmer had been responsible for the A-7, K-Wagen, and LK-I/II series of AFVs. In 1921, he had designed Sweden's first indigenous tank, the Stridsvagn m/21, which was produced in several different variants and which was fitted with a Daimler engine powerful enough to provide a respectable road speed. Building on this experience, Vollmer went on to design other tracked and wheeled vehicles, including the L-10, which was purchased by the Swedish Army under

the designation m/31. This was followed by the L-30 light tank, some of which were sold to Eire and Hungary, and the L-60, which was further developed to become the Strv m/38 in Swedish Army service.

Home-produced goods

Although Sweden could readily have purchased modern armored fighting vehicles from other nations, the fear that a European war might cut her off from spares and support led to a growing reliance on home-produced material, a trend that was to continue until the present day.

Experiments in Armor
🔨 1935 Czechoslovakia

LT-35 MEDIUM TANK

Many modifications had to be made to this tank before it was fit

for service, and even then it remained unreliable. It was not one

of Czechoslovakia's better designs.

Below: *The LT-35 was not one of the best tank designs to emerge from the Skoda Armaments Factory, but it was used by the Germans during the Polish campaign and also in France.*

Produced by the Skoda Armaments Factory, the LT-35 light tank entered service with the Czech Army in 1935. Its early prototypes, designated T-11, failed to complete their acceptance trials. They revealed many design faults, and substantial modifications had to be made before the type was finally fit for operational service as the LT-35. Even then, it proved to be unreliable, and it was not until 1943 that its problems were finally overcome.

Sold

The tank was sold to Romania, which purchased 126 units under the designation R-2. In 1939, over 200 LT-35s were seized by the Germans and then incorporated into the Wehrmacht. About 80 of these machines were allocated to Slovakia. Slovakia had become a German ally and fought on the Eastern Front in World War II. In addition, 219 machines were built by Skoda for the Wehrmacht, and these formed the bulk of the 6th Panzer Division during the campaign in France in 1940. The type also equipped the 1st Light Panzer Division during the Polish campaign of 1939. The LT-35, as the Panzerkampfwagen 35(t), continued in German service until 1942, when it was replaced by tanks of German manufacture.

Specifications

Armament: One 1.46in (37mm) cannon; two 0.312in (7.92mm) MGs

Armor: 0.59–0.98in (15–25mm)

Crew: 4

Dimensions: Length 16ft 1in (4.9m); Width 7ft 1in (2.16m); Height 7ft 3in (2.21m)

Weight: 10.5 tons (10,670kg)

Powerplant: Skoda T-11 6-cylinder gasoline, 120bhp (89.5kW) at 1800rpm

Speed: 22mph (35km/h)

Range: 120 miles (190km)

Specifications

(Char B1-bis)

Armament: One 2.95in (75mm) gun; one 1.85in (47mm) gun; two 0.295in (7.5mm) MGs

Armor: Maximum, 2.36in (60mm)

Crew: 4

Dimensions: Length 20ft 10.7in (6.37m); Width 8ft 2.4in (2.5m); Height 9ft 1.8in (2m)

Weight: 31 tons (31,500kg)

Powerplant: Renault, 6-cylinder gasoline, 300hp (223.7kW)

Speed: Road, 17.4mph (28km/h)

Range: Road, 111.8 miles (180km)

Experiments in Armor

⚒ **1935 France**

CHAR B1-BIS HEAVY TANK

The French Army deployed around 400 Char B1s in May 1940. These might have made a huge difference to the outcome of the Battle of France, but they were not used properly.

Below: This view shows the position of the Char B1's main armament of a 2.95in (75mm) gun and the secondary, turret-mounted 1.85in (47mm).

France's Char B1 traces its development back as far as 1921. It was somewhat archaic in appearance, although it was in fact an excellent heavy tank, with many advanced design features that included self-sealing fuel tanks. Later described by the German Panzer General Heinz Guderian as the best tank in the field in 1940, it was fitted with one 2.95in (75mm) and one 1.85in (47mm) gun, and two heavy machine guns. During the campaign of 1940, German antitank gunners found that their shells simply bounced off it.

Too complex

Its main disadvantage was that it was technically complex, which increased the risk of breakdown and made it unsuited to

Above: The Char B1 was a good fighting vehicle, but it was over-complex and had a limited endurance. It was also expensive to produce, which reduced the French Army's order at a time of economic constraint.

mass production. It also used a large amount of fuel, which cut down its endurance to a little over five hours, and it was expensive, costing one and a half million francs per vehicle. It was not until January 1940 that the French were in a position to begin forming two heavy armored divisions (Divisions Cuirassées), followed by a third division in March. The final production model of the Char B was the B1-bis, which had a more powerful engine, thicker armor, and a revised turret design. Some were used by Germans as training vehicles.

Experiments in Armor

1935 France

HOTCHKISS H-35 LIGHT TANK

France's other light tanks might have made a better showing in the Battle of France had it not been for poor battlefield tactics and training. The Hotchkiss H35 was no exception.

In the fall of 1935, as part of a modernization program initiated by General Maxime Weygand (the French Army Commander-in-Chief), several new armored fighting vehicles were ordered into production. The first of these was the 12-ton Hotchkiss light tank, initially fitted with a 0.98in (25mm) and later a 1.46in (37mm) gun. Two hundred of these tanks were ordered, together with 300 Renault R.35 infantry support tanks. The first production vehicles were delivered in September 1936, and by the outbreak of war in 1939, some 640 had come off the production line.

H38 and H39

From 1936 onward, the basic production model was joined by two upgraded variants, the H-38 and H-39, which had more powerful engines and thicker armor. Despite this, all the Hotchkiss light tanks suffered terrible casualties during the Battle of France, but this was partly due to poor tactics: The French continued to use their armor in small infantry support groups rather than massing it in large formations to take on the Panzers. Many Hotchkiss tanks were captured by the Germans and used in various capacities for the remainder of the war, while others, abandoned by Vichy French colonial forces, were used for some time by various Middle East armies.

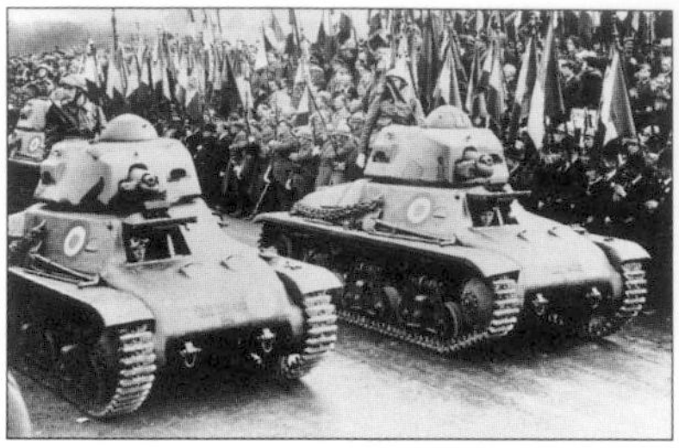

Above: *Hotchkiss H-35 light tanks on parade. After World War II, many H-35s that had served with the Vichy forces and subsequently been abandoned saw further service with some Middle East armies.*

Specifications

Armament: One 1.46in (37mm) gun; one 0.295in (7.5mm) MG

Armor: Maximum, 1.57in (40mm)

Crew: 2

Dimensions: Length 13ft 10in (4.22m); Width 6ft 4.75in (1.95m); Height 7ft 0.6in (2.15m)

Weight: 10.43 tons (10,600kg)

Powerplant: Hotchkiss 1935, 6-cylinder gasoline, 75hp (55.9kW)

Speed: Road, 17mph (27.3km/h)

Range: Road, 93.2 miles (150km)

Below: *The Hotchkiss H-35 was one of the best French light tanks, and served throughout World War II in the hands of Vichy France and the Germans, who captured many examples.*

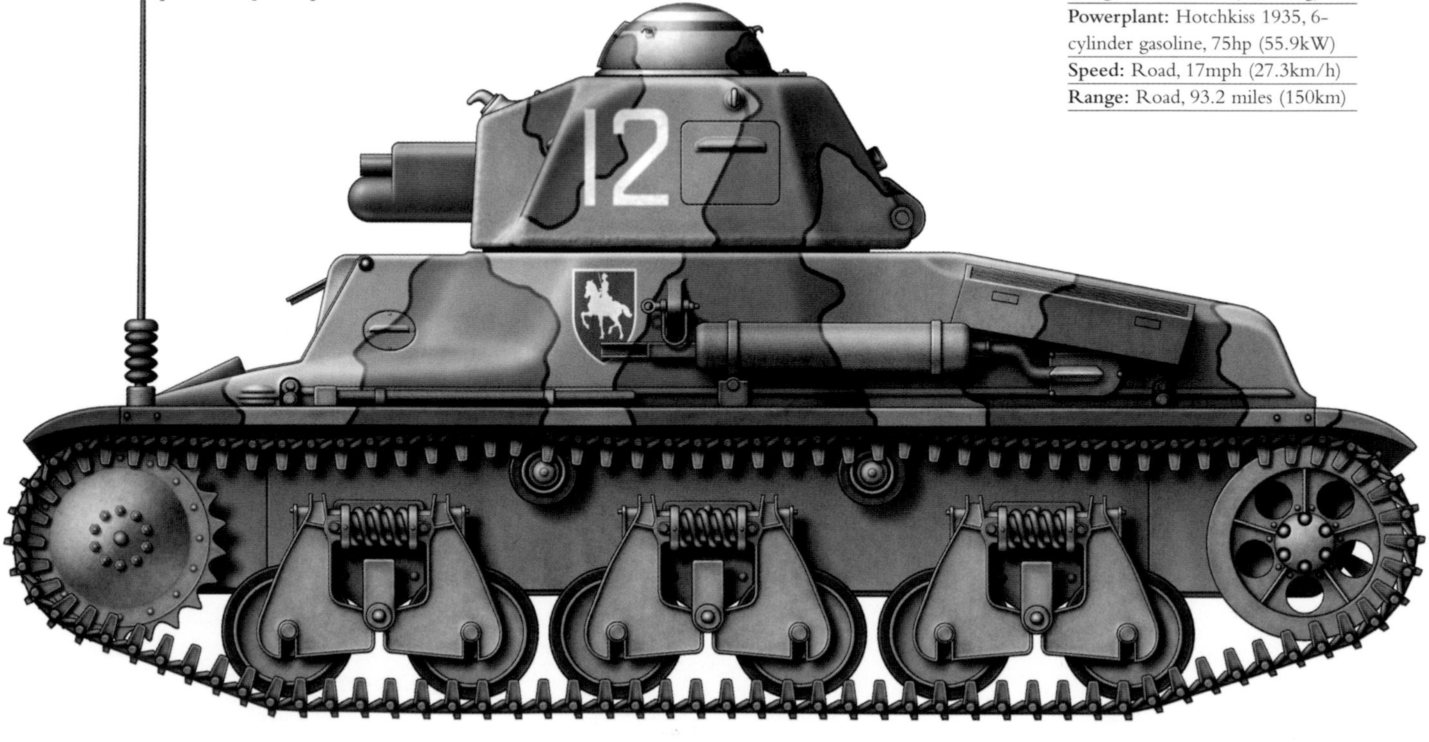

Experiments in Armor
1935 France

PANHARD AND LEVASSOR TYPE 178 ARMORED CAR

The French, like the British, had large colonial possessions overseas, and the armored car was the ideal vehicle for patrol work. The Type 178 armored car was designed for this use.

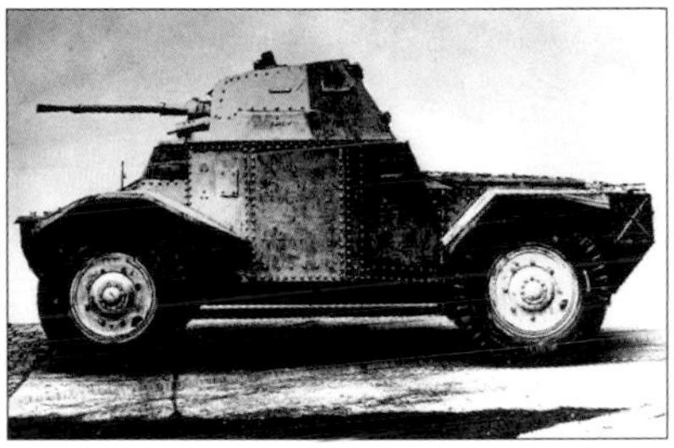

Above: *This view shows the Panhard's clean lines to good advantage. The armored car was developed in the first place to police France's North African colonies, and was designed for rapid deployment.*

Specifications

Armament: One 0.98in (25mm) cannon; one or two 0.295in (7.5mm) MGs
Armor: Maximum, 0.512in (13mm)
Crew: 4
Dimensions: Length 15ft 8.6in (4.79m); Width 6ft 7in (2.01m); Height 7ft 9.4in (2.15m)
Weight: 8.07 tons (8200kg)
Powerplant: Panhard ISK 4F II bis, 8-cylinder gasoline, 105hp (78.3kW)
Speed: Road, 44.7mph (72km/h)
Range: Road, 186 miles (300km)

The Panhard and Levassor 178 armored car, which first appeared in 1935, was intended for service in the North African colonies, where the French were experiencing continual unrest. Patrols in soft-skinned vehicles were becoming increasingly easy targets for terrorists. A light armored vehicle was needed that would be able to deploy rapidly and negotiate most types of terrain with its large-diameter tyres. Soon after the beginning of the Battle of France, the Panhard's short 1.46in (37mm) gun was deemed to be inadequate. This was replaced by a 1.85in (47mm) weapon, although there was not enough time to modify more than a few of the AFVs in this way. The Panhard 178 remained in action to the final hours of the French campaign. Some of these tanks took part in the last battles on the River Loire in June 1940, days before the Armistice. In June 1941, 140 captured vehicles of this type were issued to German units. Rail wheels were fitted to 43 of them, so they could be used for railroad-protection duties.

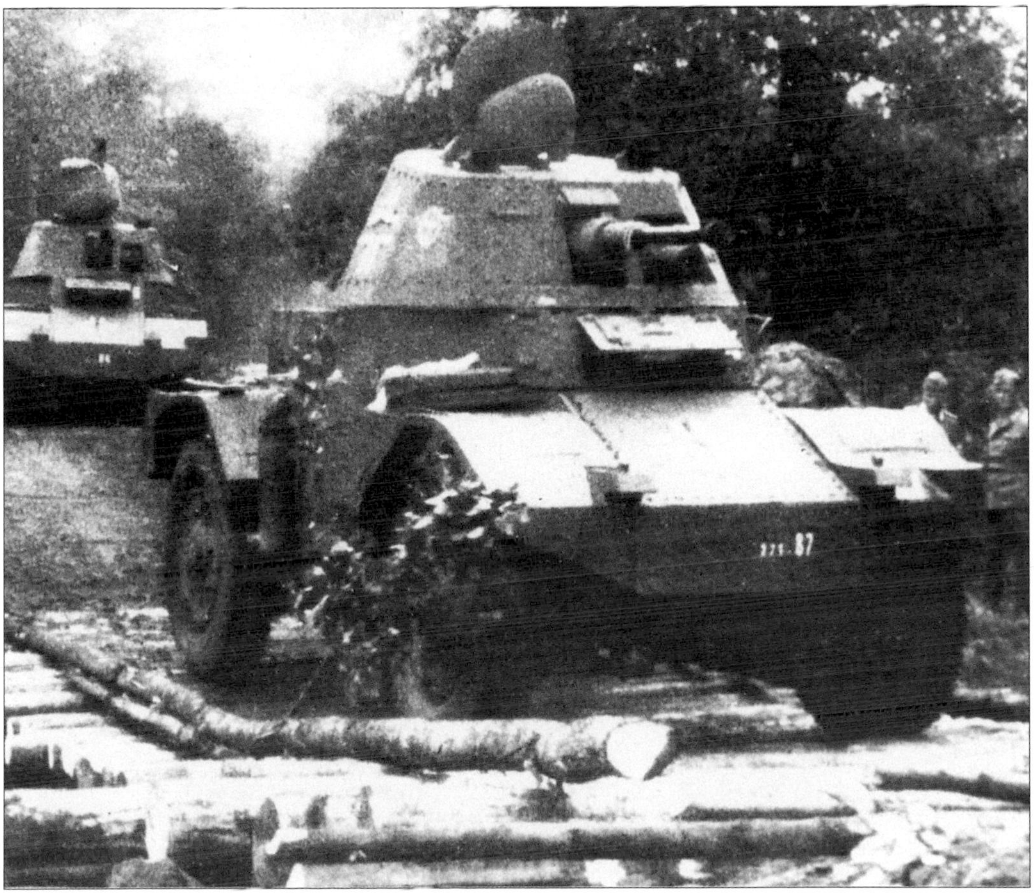

Right: *These Panhard armored cars have been pressed into German service (note the soldiers in German uniform looking on). The vehicles are negotiating swampy ground, over which tree trunks have been laid.*

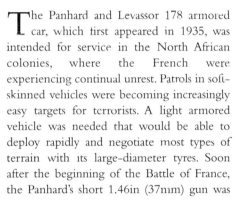

Experiments in Armor
✂ 1935 France

SOMUA S-35 MEDIUM TANK

The SOMUA S-35 was well-protected and agile, and was the finest tank in the world in 1940, incorporating many novel features that had escaped the attention of other designers.

Left: *The SOMUA medium tank was an excellent design, but its development was plagued by industrial disputes and successive changes of government. It never reached France's frontline armored units in sufficient numbers.*

Specifications

Armament: One 1.85in (47mm) gun; one 0.295in (7.5mm) MG	
Armor: Maximum, 1.57in (40mm)	
Crew: 3	
Dimensions: Length 17ft 7.8in (5.38m); Width 6ft 11in (2.12m); Height 8ft 7in (2.62m)	
Weight: 19.2 tons (19,500kg)	
Powerplant: SOMUA V-8 gasoline, 190hp (141.7kW)	
Speed: Road, 25.3mph (40.7km/h)	
Range: Road, 143 miles (230km)	

The SOMUA (Société d'Outillage Mécanique et d'Usinage d'Artillerie) was designed in response to a requirement for a new cavalry tank issued in 1934. Two prototypes were built, and an order for an initial batch of 50 tanks was placed in 1935. The official designation of the tank was the Automitrailleuse de Combat Modèle 1935S, although in practice it was commonly known as the SOMUA S-35. A fast, hard-hitting tank, with an excellent 1.85in (47mm) main armament, the SOMUA had one major drawback: Its commander was also the gunner, and was expected to direct the tank at the same time as loading, training, and firing the main gun. The turret itself was a version of the APX-1, also used in the Char B1. This tank's experience of real combat revealed a design defect: The upper and lower halves of the hull were joined by a horizontal ring of bolts, and if this joint line was hit by an antitank projectile, the vehicle split in two.

Innovations

The SOMUA's innovations included self-sealing fuel tanks on either side of the rear-mounted engine. Each tank was equipped to carry a radio transceiver, but a shortage of the required ER28 sets meant that only the commander's tank in a platoon of five vehicles was radio-equipped. Throughout the period of its production, the SOMUA was plagued by industrial disputes and other labor problems. It consequently entered service at a much slower rate than had been planned.

In action, the SOMUA could outpace and outgun the German Panzer III, but the German tank was much more reliable mechanically. The SOMUA experienced problems with its complex suspension. Despite its problems, the SOMUA acquitted itself well during the Battle of France. In battle, the SOMUA battalions suffered more from dive-bomber attacks than they did from enemy tank engagements.

Below: *If the SOMUA had a design fault, it was its high profile, which made it an easy target. The commander also had to act as the gunner, which made it difficult for him to exercise control in combat.*

Experiments in Armor
⚒ **1935 France**

RENAULT R-35 LIGHT TANK

This two-man infantry tank was designed in accordance with the concepts developed in World War I. The Renault R-35 was built in the erroneous belief that tank warfare had changed little since 1918.

Above: *The R-35, outclassed in combat, found a useful working life in other applications, such as a recovery vehicle. The example seen here is fitted with heavy chains for recovery purposes.*

Below: *The Renault R-35 was developed in a hurry by its parent company, which was eager to beat Hotchkiss in the race to secure French Army orders, and was rushed through its trials.*

Specifications

Armament: One 1.46in (37mm) gun; one 0.295in (7.5mm) MG

Armor: Maximum, 1.57in (40mm)

Crew: 2

Dimensions: Length 13ft 2.27in (4.02m); Width 5ft 11.8in (2.13m); Height 6ft 11.8in (2.13m)

Weight: 10.43 tons (10,600kg)

Powerplant: Renault, 4-cylinder gasoline, 85hp (63.4kW)

Speed: Road, 12.5mph (20km/h)

Range: Road, 80.1 miles (130km)

The Renault R-35 was designed in response to a French Army requirement for a light tank to replace the Renault FT-17 in the infantry support role. Seventeen companies responded, among them Renault, who raced to beat Hotchkiss in producing a prototype. Renault succeeded. An order for 300 units was placed in April 1935 before trials had been completed, such was the urgency that gripped France's military leaders because of German rearmament.

R-40

In 1938, the Polish Army gave two R-35s a thorough evaluation, and was not impressed by the quality of the vehicles. Nevertheless, since the Polish Army was short of tanks, they placed an order for 100 units, the first 50 of which were delivered in July 1939, only weeks before the German invasion. On May 10, 1940, at the start of the Battle of France, R-35s equipped 21 battalions, each with 45 vehicles. By this time a modified version, the R-40, with a revised suspension, was also in service. Large numbers of R-35s were seized by the Germans and proved invaluable for garrison-patrol duties in the occupied countries, and many were used as artillery tractors during the invasion of the Soviet Union.

Experiments in Armor
⚔ 1935 Germany

PANZERKAMPFWAGEN II

The Panzer II bridged the gap between the Panzer I and later, much more viable armored fighting vehicles. Crews used it to practice the tactics that could take the future Panzer divisions to early victory in World War II.

The PzKpfw II was in the nature of an interim light tank, ordered in 1934 to bridge the gap between the Panzer I and the new generation of AFVs, the PzKpfw III and PzKpfw IV. The specification called for a 10-ton armored vehicle mounting a 0.79in (20mm) gun in a fully revolving turret. Henschel, Krupp, and MAN of Augsburg all responded; Krupp's proposal was the simplest, involving the mounting of a 0.79in (20mm) cannon and machine gun in the existing PzKpfw I, but it was the vehicle developed by MAN that was selected for production.

Industrial tractor

The firm produced several prototypes under the cover-name Landwirtschäftlicher Schlepper (industrial tractor), and the vehicle was accepted for production. MAN was responsible for the chassis and Daimler-Benz for the superstructure. The first production PzKpfw Ausführung A tanks were delivered in 1935 and production continued well into 1942, despite the experience of the French campaign of 1940 showing that the vehicle was obsolete. Several variants were produced, one of the most interesting being an amphibious version intended for the invasion of England in 1940.

Above: *A Panzer II (right) in France during the German invasion of May 1940. The Panzer II played a key part in ensuring the rapid German victory. The other tank in the picture is a Panzer 38 (t).*

Specifications

(PzKpfw II Ausführung F)
Armament: One 0.79in (20mm) cannon; one 0.315in (7.92mm) MG
Armor: Maximum, 1.38in (35mm)
Crew: 3
Dimensions: Length 15ft 9.4in (4.81m); Width 7ft 5.75in (2.28m); Height 7ft 0.6in (2.15m)
Weight: Approx 9.5 tons (9650kg)
Powerplant: Maybach HL62TR, 6-cylinder gasoline, 140hp (104.4kW)
Speed: Road, 24.85mph (40km/h)
Range: Road, 124 miles (200km)

Below: *The Panzerkampfwagen II was intended as an interim design pending the introduction of more effective AFVs like the Panzer III, but it continued in production for a long time and saw much action in World War II.*

Specifications

Armament: One 1.46in (37mm)
Type 94 or Type 98 cannon; two
0.303in (7.7mm) MGs
Armor: 0.47in (12mm)
Crew: 3
Dimensions: Length 14ft 5in
(4.38m); Width 6ft 8in (2.06m);
Height 7ft 3in (2.18m)
Weight: 7.28 tons (7400kg)
Powerplant: Mitsubishi NVD
6-cylinder inline diesel, 120bhp
(89.5kW)
Speed: 28mph (45km/h)
Range: 152 miles (242km)

Experiments in Armor
⚒ **1935 Japan**

TYPE 95 HA-GO

The Type 95 Ha-Go was the first light tank of Japanese design to go into full production, and saw service in China and the Pacific, enjoying a good deal of success in the early months of service.

Below: The Type 95 was derived from the Type 89, seen here on parade. The Type 89 was one of the first Japanese tanks to enter production and was in turn derived from the Vickers Mk C.

The Type 95 Ha-Go Japanese light tank was used in China and throughout the Pacific War. It was also known as the Type 97 Ke-Go. It was the first Japanese light tank to reach production, although its design was based on an earlier experimental vehicle, the Light Tank Type 89 Experimental Tank No. 2, which had had a forward-mounted turret mounting a 1.46in (37mm) main gun and two machine guns. This vehicle appeared in 1929 and was reclassified as a medium tank.

Light tank type 98

By 1939 over 100 Type 95 light tanks were in service, and these were followed by an improved version, the Light Tank Type 98,

Above: The Type 95 Ha-Go was one of the better Japanese tanks produced in the 1930s. It saw action in China and in the early phases of the Pacific War, but by 1943 it was obsolete.

which entered service in 1942. The light tanks were used with some success in the early Pacific campaigns, especially against Allied infantry unsupported by tanks of their own, and were also employed in a defensive role with Japanese garrisons on the Pacific islands, notably Tarawa Atoll. By then, however, the light tank had had its heyday, and they proved extremely vulnerable to Allied anti-armor weapons such as the Bazooka.

Experiments in Armor
⚒ **1935 Russia**

BT-7 LIGHT TANK

Russia's BT-7 light tank was used in large numbers and saw considerable
action in border skirmishes between the Soviet Union and Japan.
However, it was obsolete by the summer of 1941.

Specifications

Armament: One 1.77in (45mm)
M–32 gun; two 0.3in (7.62mm)
DT MGs

Armor: 0.236–0.866in (6–22mm)

Crew: 3

Dimensions: Length 18ft 8in
(5.68m); Width 7ft (2.43m); Height
7ft 6in (2.28m)

Weight: 13.83 tons (14,050kg)

Powerplant: M-17T 12-cylinder
gasoline, 450bhp (335.8kW) at
1750rpm

Speed: 53.4mph (86km/h)

Range: 155 miles (250km)

The Soviet BT-7 light tank of 1935 was a logical development of the BT-5, incorporating various refinements as a result of the lessons learned during border conflicts in the Far East in the early 1930s. The BT-7 was fast, agile, and very popular with its crews, particularly as it was mechanically sound and simple to maintain. Both BT-5s and BT-7s were used in further border skirmishes with Japan in 1939, and were found to be superior to Japanese AFVs in their class. The BT-7 was the principal Soviet tank used in the occupation of eastern Poland in 1939, and large numbers were used in action against the invading Germans in 1941, suffering huge losses.

Above: The BT-7 light tank was very popular with its crews, but it was no match for German armor and suffered heavy losses. It fared much better during the Russian invasion of Manchuria in August 1945.

Varying usage

Most of the surviving BT tanks were shipped to the Far East, where they were employed in the Soviet invasion of Manchuria in 1945. Several versions of the BT-7 were produced; these included a close support variant armed with a 3in (76mm) main gun. The BT-7 could be fitted with tracks of varying width for use on different types of terrain. In action, the BT-7's biggest drawback was its lack of armor, which was sacrificed to achieve higher speed.

Below: The BT-7 was an agile tank, as demonstrated in this photograph. Although fast and maneuverable, its biggest problem was that it was too lightly armored, which made it very vulnerable in combat.

Experiments in Armor
⚔ **1935 UK**

VICKERS MARKS V AND VI LIGHT TANKS

The Vickers Light Tanks were initially intended to police Britain's extensive colonial possessions, but they lacked capability when they were used against German tanks early in World War II.

Specifications

(Mk VI)

Armament: One 0.303in (7.7mm) MG; one 0.5in (12.7mm) MG

Armor: 0.25–0.65in (4–14mm)

Crew: 3

Dimensions: Length 13ft 2in (4.01m); Width 6ft 10in (2.08m); Height 7ft 5in (2.26m)

Weight: 4.8 tons (4875kg)

Powerplant: Meadows 6-cylinder gasoline, 88bhp (65.6kW)

Speed: 35mph (56km/h)

Range: 125 miles (200km)

The Vickers Light Tanks of the 1930s were inspired by the Carden-Loyd series of light vehicles of the previous decade, and in fact the Carden-Loyd Mk VIII served as the prototype Vickers Light Tank Mk I. This was followed by the Mk 1A, with better armor, and the Mk II, with an improved turret design and modified suspension. The hull design was simple, with riveted armor. The early Vickers Light Tanks carried a two-man crew, but in the Mk V the turret was enlarged to accommodate two men, making a crew of three. The armament was also improved, the tank being fitted with a 0.5in (12.7mm) machine gun alongside the standard 0.303in (7.7mm) weapon.

MKVI

The next development was the fast and agile Mk VI, which incorporated numerous development. The Vickers Light Tanks proved excellent vehicles for policing Britain's vast colonial possessions, but they were virtually useless when they encountered German AFVs in the early campaigns of World War II. Their main application was in the Western Desert, where the Mk VI was successfully used in a scouting role

Right: With their totally inadequate armament, the early Vickers light tanks were not much use for anything other than armored scouting, and suffered serious losses when they were used in the infantry support role, to which they were unsuited.

Experiments in Armor
1935 USA

M1/M2 COMBAT CAR

These armored fighting vehicles were developed at a time when the emphasis was on light tanks in just about every army in the world. They had reasonable firepower and were speedy.

Above: *The M1 series of light tanks on parade. They laid the foundation for tank development in the USA.*

These American light tanks were developed in the early 1930s and made their appearance in 1935. The M1 was originally known as T2E1: It evolved from experimental prototypes, the T2 and T5, which underwent trials in April 1934. These had an improved suspension and were armed with twin machine guns in the turret, one 0.5in (12.7mm) caliber and one 0.30in (7.62mm), and another of 0.30in (7.62mm) in the forward hull. The vehicle went into production late in 1935 at the Rock Island Arsenal under the name of M2A1.

Variants

A further development, the T2E2, was fitted with twin turrets, each containing a machine gun; and went into production as the M2A2 in 1938. It was, perhaps predictably, nicknamed "Mae West" by its crews. Further variants were the M2A3, which also had twin turrets, with improved suspension, thicker armor, increased gear ratios, and better engine cooling, and the M2A4, which was armed with a hand-traversed 1.46in (37mm) gun and which was rushed into production on the outbreak of war in Europe. The M2A4 saw some action in the Philippines early in 1942, and surviving vehicles were used for training up to 1943.

Specifications

(M1)

Armament: One 0.50in (12.7mm) MG; one 0.30in (7.62mm) MG

Armor: 0.63in (16mm)

Crew: 4

Dimensions: Length 13ft 7in (4.14m); Width 7ft 10in (2.4m); Height 7ft 9in (2.3m)

Weight: 5.89 tons (5987kg)

Powerplant: Continental W-670 7-cylinder gasoline, 250hp (186.6kW)

Speed: 45mph (72km/h)

Range: 100 miles (161km)

Experiments in Armor
⚒ 1935 USA

M2 LIGHT TANK

The American M2 light tank was yet another design that was inspired by the Vickers six-ton light tank of the early 1930s, and its developments served in the Pacific.

Specifications

Armament: One 1.46in (37mm) gun; four 0.30in (7.62mm) MGs

Armor: 0.98in (25mm)

Crew: 4

Dimensions: Length 14ft 7in (4.45m); Width 8ft 4in (2.53m); Height 8ft 3in (2.52m)

Weight: 10.26 tons (10,432kg)

Powerplant: Continental 7-cylinder radial, 250hp (186.6kW)

Speed: 34mph (55 km/h)

Range: 130 miles (209km)

Inspired by the Vickers six-ton light tank, the M2 Light Tank was developed by Rock Island Arsenal as an infantry support vehicle in 1935. After only 10 units had been delivered, all with single turrets, the US Army changed the specification to a twin-turret configuration, with a 0.3in (7.62mm) machine gun in the second turret. Although it was inefficient, the twin-turret layout was

Below: The M2 light tank saw a good deal of service in the Pacific War, where it was used as an infantry support vehicle for the US Marines fighting on Guadalcanal.

favored by the light tank designers of the mid-1930s, especially those influenced by the Vickers designs.

Upgrades

The vehicle was progressively upgraded during its early years in service, but after the outbreak of war in Spain, closely followed by conflict in China and Europe, the US military realized that the M2 was no longer adequate and ordered the development of the M3. This was based on the M2 series but with heavier armor and a slightly longer hull. Production switched from the M2A4 to the M3 in 1941, and this later design served widely in the early campaigns in the Pacific, particularly in support of the US Marine Corps fighting for possession of Guadalcanal. Some M3s were also purchased by Britain, together with about 30 M2A4s.

Experiments in Armor
⚒ **1936 France**

AMC-35 LIGHT TANK

Although the AMC-35 cavalry tank was fairly widely available when
Germany invaded France in May 1940, it could not be deployed
immediately because of a shortage of trained crews.

The AMC-35 (Automitrailleuse de
Combat Renault Modèle 35) was, in
essence, an upgraded version of Renault's
earlier cavalry tank, the AMC-34. The AMC-
35 was first delivered to the French Cavalry
regiments in September 1938. It resembled
the earlier AMC-34, but had a slightly
lengthened hull to accommodate a
shortened version of the 180hp (134.2kW)
V-6 engine used in the Char B1. The AMC-
35's two-man turret was equipped with a
0.89in (25mm) gun with 120 rounds and a
0.295in (7.5mm) machine gun. Production
was excruciatingly slow, 12 vehicles from the

initial production run being supplied to
Belgium, but it accelerated in September
1939, on the outbreak of war. When
Germany invaded Belgium on May 10,
1940, eight of the Belgian AMC-35s went
into action; four were destroyed by antitank
guns and two more were abandoned after
breaking down. The French AMC-35s
remained idle due to a lack of trained crews,
and it was not until the Germans broke
through at Sedan, five days after the start of
the invasion, that they were sent into action.
Some captured examples were used for
patrol duty in occupied France.

Specifications

Armament: One 1.85in (47mm)
gun or one 0.89in (25mm) cannon;
one 0.295in (7.5mm) MG

Armor: Maximum, 0.89in (25mm)

Crew: 3

Dimensions: Length 14ft 11in
(4.55m); Width 7ft 2.5in (2.2m);
Height 7ft 6.5in (2.3m)

Weight: 14.27 tons (14,500kg)

Powerplant: Renault, 4-cylinder
gasoline, 180hp (134.2kW)

Speed: Road, 26mph (42km/h)

Range: Road, 99.4 miles (160km)

Left: *The AMC-35 was yet
another example of how France's
military strength was depleted
because of labor unrest and
changing government policies.
Production was accelerated just
before the outbreak of war, but it
came too late for the tanks to be
deployed in sufficient numbers to
meet the German attack.*

Experiments in Armor
✗ 1936 France

FCM-36 INFANTRY TANK

The FCM Company rushed to build a prototype of this new light tank

in competition with Renault and Hotchkiss. Many defects had to be

corrected before it was ready for service.

Below: The FCM-36 infantry tank was rushed into production because it was cheap and could easily be mass produced. Not all the problems encountered during trials had been rectified by the time it entered service.

Specifications

Armament: One 1.46in (37mm) gun; one 0.295in (7.5mm) MG

Armor: Maximum, 1.57in (40mm)

Crew: 2

Dimensions: Length 13ft 10in (4.22m); Width 6ft 4.75in (1.95m); Height 7ft 0.6in (2.15m)

Weight: 12.15 tons (12,350kg)

Powerplant: Berliet 8.4-litre, 4-cylinder diesel, 91hp (67.9kW)

Speed: Road, 14.9mph (24km/h)

Range: Road, 140 miles (225km)

The FCM-36 (Forges et Chantiers de la Méditerrannée) was designed as a cheap infantry tank that could easily be mass produced. After several prototype trials and numerous modifications, it was pronounced to be acceptable for service in July 1936. An order for 100 vehicles was placed with FCM, the French War Department also ordered similar tanks from Renault and Hotchkiss, and follow-on orders for batches of 100 were placed in 1938 and 1939.

Heavy losses

The FCM-36 was issued to two tank battalions, the 4e and 7e Bataillon de Chars de Combat, which received 50 vehicles each in March and April 1939. After the outbreak of war in September, these battalions were amalgamated with the 3e BCC (which was equipped with the Renault R-35) to form the 503e Groupement de Bataillons de Chars, the armored reserve of the French Second Army. This formation saw intense fighting during the German crossing of the Meuse. It was no match for the German Panzer IIIs and suffered heavy losses. After the Battle of France the Germans captured about 50 FCM-36s, 10 of which were later rebuilt as Marder tank destroyers and 12 as self-propelled guns. One FCM-36 is on display at the Musée des Blindés, Saumur.

Experiments in Armor
⚔ 1936 UK

MATILDA I INFANTRY TANK

The Matilda I infantry tank acquitted itself well in France, but the campaign showed that it was outdated and it was afterwards relegated to secondary duties such as training.

The first British requirement for an "infantry" tank was issued in 1934 and resulted in the A11 Infantry Tank Mk I (Matilda I). This was developed in 1935 by Vickers-Armstrongs, and emerged as a small two-man vehicle with a single turret-mounted Vickers 0.303in (7.7mm) machine gun. The Matilda I was intended to be produced quickly, and incorporated parts taken from other vehicles, such as a Fordson tractor gearbox and a Ford V8 engine.

The duck
One senior military observer, seeing the Matilda I in action, commented that it "waddled like a duck," so it was given its

Above: The Matilda I was designed to be produced quickly, and incorporated parts taken from tractors and other vehicles.

nickname after a popular cartoon duck of the time. The first order for the Matilda I was placed in April 1938, and production continued until 1940, by which time the vehicle had been deployed to France. Together with the later (and completely unrelated Matilda II), it fought in the Battle of Arras, and contributed to the near-annihilation of General Erwin Rommel's 7th Panzer Division. After the fighting in France, all these tanks were withdrawn from first-line service and relegated to training duties.

Specifications

Armament: One 0.303in (7.7mm) MG or 0.5in (12.7mm) Vickers MG

Armor: 0.39–2.36in (10–60mm)

Crew: 2

Dimensions: Length 15ft 11in (4.85m); Width 7ft 6in (2.286m); Height 6ft 1in (1.867m)

Weight: 10.98 tons (11,160kg)

Powerplant: Ford V-8 gasoline, 70bhp (52.22kW)

Speed: 7.95mph (12.8km/h)

Range: 80.11 miles (129km)

Experiments in Armor
⚒ 1937 Germany

PANZERKAMPFWAGEN III MEDIUM TANK

The Panzer III was produced in large numbers, and when Germany invaded the Soviet Union in 1941, it was the most widely produced German tank. Many of these tanks were later adapted as self-propelled guns.

Above: A Panzer III fording a river. The Mk III was instrumental in Rommel's early victories over the British Commonwealth forces in North Africa, being able to out-fight every type of British tank.

Left: The Panzer III was without doubt one of the best tanks to be produced during World War II, with several versions used for different tasks. It was originally designed as a tank destroyer.

Specifications

(Panzer III Ausführung F)
Armament: One 1.46in (37mm) gun; two 0.312in (7.92mm) MGs
Armor: Maximum, 1.18in (30mm)
Crew: 5
Dimensions: Length 17ft 4.5in (5.38m); Width 9ft 10.9in (2.91m); Height 7ft 11.75in (2.435m)
Weight: approx 19.2 tons (19,500kg)
Powerplant: Maybach HL120 TRM, V-12 gasoline, 300hp (223.7kW)
Speed: Road, 24.8mph (40km/h)
Range: Road, 102.5 miles (165km)

In the mid-1930s, the German Army decreed that each armored battalion should be equipped with three companies of relatively light medium tanks and one company of heavier and more powerful support tanks (the latter emerging as the Panzer Mk IV). The Panzer III medium tank was designed as a result of this. While the Panzer IV was designed for the infantry support role, the Panzer III was intended to fight and destroy other tanks. Mass production of the tank began in 1939.

Models A–G

The first three production models (Ausführungen A, B and C) were built in relatively small numbers, and were used during the invasion of Poland in September 1939. The next model (D) had thicker armor and a revised cupola, and in 1940 Ausführung F entered production. This last model was armed with a high-velocity 1.97in (50mm) gun and an uprated engine, and was fitted with only six roadwheels. The Ausführung G had a similar armament, but featured a still-more powerful engine. By mid-1941 the Panzer III was the most popular German tank, and most machines had been retro-fitted with the 1.97in (50mm) gun. It was used successfully against the British Army in North Africa in late 1941, when every type of British tank was outgunned.

Experiments in Armor
⚒ **1937 Germany**

PANZERKAMPFWAGEN IV MEDIUM TANK

The Panzer IV was one of the most famous tanks ever produced and became the workhorse of the German Panzer divisions in World War II, operating in many different roles.

Below: This Panzer IVG, depicted late in the war, has had extra armor plate added to its hull and turret to protect it against the latest Allied antitank projectiles. It was still a match for tanks such as the Sherman.

One of the most important armored fighting vehicles of World War II, the Panzer IV was intended for the infantry support role, leaving the Panzer III to deal with enemy armor. Krupp was the manufacturer, and the first Panzer IV came off the assembly line in October 1937. The driving force behind the development of Germany's new medium tanks—restricted to these two types by economic constraints—was Colonel Heinz Guderian. His plan was to concentrate these armored fighting vehicles in formations—the celebrated Panzer divisions—instead of splitting them up in packages between the field armies. It was a formula that worked with devastating effect.

Firing problems

The Panzer IV was armed with the short 2.95in (75mm) KwK L/24 low-velocity gun. This fired a high-explosive round and was effective against fortifications and infantry, but it lacked accuracy. In 1941, after the first encounters between the Panzer IV and the Russian T-34, the Panzer IV Ausführung F was equipped with a redesigned turret mounting a more powerful 2.95in (75mm) L/43 antitank gun. In this guise, it became the Panzer IVF2, later renamed the Panzer IVG. This variant became the workhorse of the German armored divisions and remained unchanged except for upgrades to its main armament and armor, as dictated by operational experience. These upgrades, particularly in guns and sighting systems, enabled the Panzer IV to hold its own with the Russian T-34 and the American Sherman, which it encountered for the first time in North Africa in 1942.

Specifications

(PzKpfw IV Ausführung F2)

Armament: One 2.95in (75mm) gun; two 0.312in (7.92mm) MGs

Armor: Maximum, 1.97in (50mm)

Crew: 5

Dimensions: Length 21ft 9in (6.63m); Width 9ft 5.5in (2.88m); Height 8ft 9.5in (2.68m)

Weight: approx 22 tons (22,350kg)

Powerplant: Maybach HL120 TRM, V-12 gasoline, 300hp (223.7kW)

Speed: Road, 24.8mph (40km/h)

Range: Road, 130 miles (209km)

Above: *Panzer IVs advancing across the Russian steppes in 1943. These tanks have been upgraded to carry a 2.95in (75mm) long-barrel high-velocity gun, but they lack the extra armor that would be a later feature.*

Successful operations

The Panzer IV remained in production throughout World War II, some machines being supplied to Germany's satellites. About 40 were converted to amphibious tanks, originally for the projected invasion of England, and were used in the invasion of the Soviet Union. Others, fitted with additional radio equipment, were used as command vehicles. The last variant was the Ausführung J, which appeared in March 1944. In all, production amounted to some 9000 vehicles. Many Panzer IV chassis were converted to specialized roles such as tank destroyers, self-propelled howitzers, and recovery vehicles. The Panzer IV continued to be used after 1945, notably in Syria, which purchased a number of these machines. They were then used to shell Israeli settlements from positions on the Golan Heights during the brief so-called "Water War" conflict of 1965. The surviving Panzer IVs were captured by Israel during the Six-Day War of 1967, to become museum pieces.

Below: *The Ausführung A was one of the earliest models of the Panzer IV. The turret design was substantially modified at a later date and most of the "A" models were used for training.*

Experiments in Armor
⚒ 1937 Germany

STURMGESCHÜTZ III SELF-PROPELLED ASSAULT GUN

The Germans were quick to recognize the importance of self-propelled guns as a means of concentrating the strength and speed of artillery. The Panzer III and IV tank chassis proved ideal for conversion.

Below: The Sturmgeschütz III employed the suspension and drive train of the PzKpfw tank combined with a well-armored carapace.

The Sturmgeschütz III and IV were self-propelled artillery versions of the well-tried Panzer III and IV models, and were intended primarily for the tank destroyer role. The StuG III, based on the chassis of the Panzer III, was the most widely produced German armored fighting tank of World War II, with as many 10,500 vehicles in production. The StuG III was originally intended as a mobile infantry support weapon, but as time went by, it was employed increasingly as a tank destroyer. Its origins lay in a 1935 proposal by Colonel Erich von Manstein, in which he suggested that so-called Sturmartillerie (storm artillery) units should be developed to lend fire support to infantry formations. As the war progressed, it was realized that the StuG III's L/48 gun was inadequate to cope with the latest additions to enemy armored forces, and so the StuG IV —based on the Panzer IV chassis—was developed to accommodate the more powerful L/70 2.953in (75mm) tank gun. The new vehicle was named the Jagdpanzer (tank hunter) IV, and became operational in October 1943. Most Jagdpanzer IVs served on the Eastern Front, where they inflicted great losses on Soviet armor.

Specifications

(StuG III Ausf G)

Armament: One 2.95in (75mm) antitank gun; two 0.312in (7.92mm) MGs

Armor: Maximum 1.97in (50mm)

Crew: 4

Dimensions: Length 22ft 2.5in (6.77m); Width 9ft 8.1in (2.95m); Height 7ft 1in (2.16m)

Weight: approx 23.52 tons (23,900kg)

Powerplant: Maybach HL120TRM, V-12 gasoline, 300hp (223.7kW)

Speed: Road 24.9mph (40km/h)

Range: Road 96.3 miles (155km)

Experiments in Armor
⚒ 1937 Japan

TYPE 97 TE-KE TANKETTE

The small Type 97 Te-Ke Tankette was used in China and the Pacific during World War II, and provided infantry support as well as reconnaissance.

Specifications

Armament: One 1.46in (37mm) gun

Armor: 0.63in (16mm)

Crew: 2

Dimensions: Length 12ft 1in (3.68m); Width 5ft 11in (1.80m); Height 5ft 10in (1.77m)

Weight: 4.67 tons (4750kg)

Powerplant: Ikega 4-cylinder diesel, 65bhp (48.5kW)

Speed: 26mph (42km/h)

Range: 155 miles (250km)

Two prototypes of the Type 97 Te-Ke Tankette were produced by Tokyo Motor Industries in 1937 in response to an Imperial Japanese Army requirement for a small armored reconnaissance vehicle. The original model had the engine and driver at the front and the small turret at the rear, but this was later moved forward to allow better crew communication. The engine then moved to the back. As was common with small and cramped reconnaissance vehicles, the interior was lined with asbestos to give the crew some protection from the heat. The hull was riveted and the driver sat on the left of the commander, who gained access to the turret via a hinged hatch at the rear.

Infantry support

The Type 97 Te-Ke was used on all fronts, but its principal application was in China, where it was sometimes used for infantry support. It could also be used to tow an ammunition trailer. Generally, the Type 97 Te-Ke was organized in companies of up to 17 vehicles. Some of these were salvaged from Pacific islands many years after World War II and have been restored for museum display.

Below: The Type 97 Te-Ke could hardly be called a success. Its gun was completely ineffective against all types of Allied armor, while its own riveted hull could be penetrated by small-arms fire.

Experiments in Armor
⚒ **1937 Japan**

TYPE 97 CHI-HA MEDIUM TANK

The Type 97 Chi-Ha medium tank was unusual in that it was fitted with
a diesel engine at a time when most other AFVs used gasoline engines.
As a result, it had a good firing range.

Specifications

Armament: One 6pdr
(2.24in/57mm) gun; two 0.303in
(7.7mm) MGs

Armor: 0.98in (25mm)

Crew: 4

Dimensions: Length 18ft (5.5m);
Width 7ft 8in (2.33m); Height 7ft
4in (2.23m)

Weight: 14.76 tons (15,000kg)

Powerplant: Mitsubishi Type 97
V-12 diesel, 170bhp (127kW)

Speed: 24mph (39km/h)

Range: Unknown

Left: *Tanks like the Type 97
generally performed well in Japan's
early campaigns in the Pacific and
Southeast Asia. From 1942
onward, however, they began to
encounter more effective Allied
armor and antitank weapons,
and suffered accordingly.*

The Japanese Type 97 Chi-Ha medium tank was developed in response to a mid-1930s requirement for a replacement for the Type 89B, which was approaching the end of its useful life. Two prototypes were built, one by Mitsubishi and the other by the Osaka Arsenal. The Mitsubishi design, which was heavier than the Osaka vehicle, was selected and the first of an eventual 3000 examples came off the assembly line in 1937. At a time when the tanks of other nations had gasoline engines, Japanese tanks—including the Type 97—were diesel-fueled. This increased their combat radius and also reduced the fire risk.

New turret
In 1942 a new version—the Type 97-Shinhoto—appeared. Shinhoto means "new turret." This variant was armed with a new high-velocity 1.85in (47mm) gun. Other variants included the Shi-Ki, a command tank with a 1.46in (37mm) gun, the Se-Ri armored recovery vehicle, and a series of self-propelled guns based on the Type 97 chassis. The Type 97 was replaced on the production line by the Type 1 Chi-He medium tank, followed by the Type 3 Chi-Nu. Only 60 Type 3 Chi-Nus were produced before the end of the war.

Left: *The Type 97 was probably
the best Japanese tank to see active
service in World War II, but
although its design compared well
with its western counterparts, it
suffered from an inadequate gun.*

Experiments in Armor
1938 Czechslovakia

CKD/PRAGA LT-H EXPORT TANK

The Czech arms industry was very conscious of the huge export market that existed for weapons of all kinds, and designed the LT-H specifically to meet this growing demand.

Specifications

(Swiss LT-H)

Armament:	One 0.94in (24mm) cannon; two 0.295in (7.5mm) MGs
Armor:	1.26in (32mm)
Crew:	3
Dimensions:	Length 14ft 9in (4.51m); Width 6ft 6in (2m); Height 7ft 6in (2.3m)
Weight:	7.5 tons (7620kg)
Powerplant:	Saurer 4-cylinder diesel, 125bhp (93kW)
Speed:	28mph (45km/h)
Range:	156 miles (250km)

Above: *The LT-H was a conventional prewar tank design, with riveted armor and rear engine.*

This light tank was developed in Czechoslovakia entirely for export purposes, and had already found a flourishing world market before the German occupation of Czechoslovakia in 1939. The tank was fast and reliable, and its armor plating would withstand most ammunition of the time. However, its armament left much to be desired, comprising a single 1.47in (37mm) main gun. The vehicle was built under license in Switzerland under the name of Panzer-39; the Swiss also bought 24 units "off the shelf." These were armed with a 0.94in (24mm) Oerlikon cannon and fitted with a diesel engine of Swiss design. The tank was also exported to Peru and other countries were showing an active interest in it when Germany invaded Czechoslovakia. Latvia had ordered a cannon-armed version; this was appropriated by the Germans and issued to the Slovak Army. Units of the LT-H under manufacture in Czechoslovakia were commandeered by the Germans and issued to the Wehrmacht as the LT-38.

Right: *The LT-H would almost certainly have achieved great success on the export market had Czechoslovakia not been overrun by the Germans. The export drive was only just beginning in 1939.*

Experiments in Armor
⚒ 1938 Czechoslovakia

LT-38 MEDIUM TANK

The LT-38 was another example of the excellence of the tanks designed in Czechoslovakia before World War II. It was widely used by Germany's allies on the Eastern Front from 1941 onward.

Below: *The LT-38 was a modified version of the Czech LT-H, produced for Germany and her allies. It saw considerable service with Germany's "satellite" countries, Hungary, Slovakia, Romania, and Bulgaria.*

The LT-38 medium tank, built in Czechoslovakia, was used by the German Army under the name of Panzerkampfwagen 38(t). It was designed in 1937 in response to an urgent requirement from the Czech Army for a new light tank, in the light of the rapidly deteriorating international situation. The LT-38 was a conventional pre-World War II tank design, with riveted armor and rear-mounted engine. The centrally located two-man turret housed the main armament, a Skoda A7 gun and a 0.312in (7.92mm) machine gun. A second machine gun of similar caliber, manned by the radio operator, was mounted in the forward hull next to the driver. The tank was an instant export success, 50 vehicles being purchased by Iran and 24 by Peru and Switzerland respectively. The Czech Army also ordered 150, but none had entered service before Czechoslovakia was overrun by the Germans in 1939.

Production of the LT-38 continued after the German occupation and the tank was used by the Wehrmacht and Germany's satellites—Hungary, Slovakia, Romania, and Bulgaria. The LT-38 chassis also served as the basis for assault guns, antiaircraft guns and antitank guns.

Specifications

Armament: One 1.46in (37mm) cannon (or 37mm KwK L/40 or L/45); two 0.312in (7.92mm) MGs

Armor: 0/59–0.98in (15–25mm)

Crew: 4

Dimensions: Length 15ft 1in (4.60m); Width 6ft 11in (2.12m); Height 7ft 10in (2.4m)

Weight: 9.25 tons (9400kg)

Powerplant: Praga EPA model I 6-cylinder gasoline, 125bhp (93kW) at 2000rpm

Speed: 26mph (42km/h)

Range: 155 miles (250km)

Experiments in Armor
✗ 1938   Germany

SDKFZ 251 APC

Below: *The SdKfz 251 was one of the most prolific armored personnel carriers ever produced.*

The SdKfz 251 was a key element of a Panzer division, enabling the infantry it carried to keep pace with the armor instead of bringing up the rear and being open to surprise attack.

Specifications

Armament: Two 0.312in (7.92mm) MGs

Armor: Maximum, 0.47in (12mm)

Crew: 2 plus 10 troops

Dimensions: Length 19ft (5.8m); Width 6ft 6.7in (2m); Height 5ft 8.9in (1.75m)

Weight: approx 8.37 tons (8500kg)

Powerplant: Maybach HL42 TUKRM, 6-cylinder gasoline, 100hp (74.5kW)

Speed: Road, 32.6mph (52.5km/h)

Range: Road, 112 miles (180km)

Right: *The Flammpanzerwagen version of the SdKfz 251 was fitted with two flame projectors and initially a rear-mounted flamethrower.*

The SdKfz 251 was an armored personnel carrier capable of carrying a full infantry section of 12 men. The first production models were issued to the 1st Panzer Division in 1939 and the APC was subsequently produced in four main models, A to D.

Numerous modifications

The SdKfz 251 underwent over 20 modifications, with many more carried out locally in the field. One variant, known as the "Uhu" (Owl) was fitted with an infrared searchlight and was used to illuminate targets for small groups of Panzer tanks operating at night; another, produced late in the war, was fitted out as an antiaircraft platform optimized to engage low-flying fighter bombers. Other variants were fitted with a 2.95in (75mm) short assault gun to provide local fire support, and one variant, known as the *Stuka zum Fuss* ("dive-bomber on foot" or "infantry Stuka") was fitted with a tubular frame on which rocket launcher tubes were mounted. The SdKfz 251 halftrack was produced in thousands– 14,500 units, in fact —and was used on all fronts, operating in conjunction with the Panzer formations.

Experiments in Armor
⚒ 1938 UK

CRUISER TANKS MARKS I–V

The concept of the cruiser tank was sound. In essence, it was designed to fill the traditional cavalry roles of reconnaissance and pursuit, but the requirement for speed meant that it also carried light armor.

Left: *The A9 Mk I was the first cruiser tank, and was designed to perform the roles of reconnaissance and pursuit. Completely outclassed by the Panzers, many were abandoned in France after the British evacuation.*

Specifications

Mk I Cruiser (A9) 1938
Armament: One 2pdr
(1.57in/40mm) gun; two 0.303in
(7.7mm) MGs
Armor: 0.23–0.55in (6mm–14mm)
Crew: 6
Dimensions: Length 19ft 3in
(5.79m); Width 8ft 4in (2.5m);
Height 8ft 4in (2.654m)
Weight: 12 tons (12,190kg)
Powerplant: AEC Type A A.179
developing 150bhp (111.9kW)
Speed: 24.84mph (40km/h)
Range: 149 miles (240km)

In the early 1930s the British Army took the decision to develop two separate types of armored fighting vehicle. One was an infantry tank (to operate in support of ground forces) and the other a "cruiser" tank (whose role was to seek and destroy other tanks and vehicles). In 1934 Vickers designed the Cruiser Tank Mk I (A9), which entered production in 1937. Its turret was power-traversed and the vehicle carried a six-man crew. Its main armament was a 1.757in (40mm) two-pounder gun, supplemented by three machine guns, two of which were mounted in small subsidiary turrets. Production of the Mk I ended with the 125th vehicle, the early model, seeing service in France and North Africa. It was followed by the Heavy Cruiser Tank Mk II, which had begun life as the A10 Infantry Tank based on the AS9.

Christie suspension

The next cruiser tank represented an important step forward in British tank development, as it used a suspension system based on one devised by American, J. Walter Christie. A prototype made its appearance in 1937 and proved to have an excellent performance, the Christie suspension making a huge difference. The A13 developed into the Cruiser Tank Mk III. Its armament was reduced to one 1.57in (40mm) gun and a single machine gun, which made it possible to eliminate two crew members. Its big drawback was its inadequate armor, which led to substantial losses when it encountered German Panzer IIIs in France and the Western Desert. This deficiency led to the development of the Cruiser Tank Mk IV (A13 Mk II) in which the thickness of the armor was increased to 0.79 or 1.18in (20 or 30mm). This was still not very substantial, nevertheless it acquitted itself well against Italian AFVs in the Western Desert, where it saw considerable action. The next British cruiser tank in the series was the Cruiser Tank Mk V (A13 Mk III), which had a redesigned turret, better armor and a higher top speed.

Below: *Mk I A9 cruiser tanks on maneuvers. Although these armored vehicles performed well on prewar exercises, their puny two-pounder guns were useless against the Panzers.*

Experiments in Armor
⚒ 1938 UK

MATILDA II INFANTRY

The Matilda II took the Germans by surprise during the fighting in France in 1940. Too few of them were available to have an appreciable effect on the campaign, however.

Specifications

Armament: One 2pdr (1.57in/40mm) gun; one 0.31in (7.92mm) Besa MG

Armor: 0.51–3.07in (13–78mm)

Crew: 4

Dimensions: Length 18ft 5in (5.613m); Width 8ft 6in (2.59m); Height 8ft 3in (2.515m)

Weight: 26.5 tons (26,925kg)

Powerplant: Two gasoline 6-cylinder AEC engines, 87bhp (64.8kW)

Speed: 15mph (24km/h)

Range: 160 miles (257km)

Below: The Matilda II was the only British tank with enough armor to withstand German antitank projectiles in the early years of World War II. After its brief moment of glory at Arras in May 1940, it fought in the Western Desert. The pictured tank is a German operated version.

Properly called the Tank, Infantry, Mk II, but more widely known as the Matilda II to distinguish it from the earlier (and unrelated) Matilda I, this was the best British tank in service at the outset of World War II. It was designed at the Royal Arsenal, Woolwich, built by the Vulcan Foundry, and finally produced in 1937, but only two were in service at the outbreak of war in September 1939. Over the next four years, some 2987 Matildas were built until production ceased in August 1943. Because of the thickness of its armor, the Matilda proved virtually immune to the fire of the German tanks encountered in France. In one memorable action at Arras on May 21, 1940, 16 Matildas, backed up by 58 of the smaller Mk Is (armed with machine guns) severely disrupted the advance of General Erwin Rommel's 7th Panzer Division. The British attack was only halted when the Matildas came up against 3.46in (88mm) antiaircraft guns, hastily turned into antitank weapons on Rommel's orders.

Above: A Matilda II being unloaded at a port on the Suez Canal. The Matilda served the British 8th Army well, but was armed only with the two-pounder gun, which had no effect on enemy tanks like the Panzer Mk III.

British-design success

Over 1000 Matildas were sent to the Soviet Union and were used from the winter of 1941. Others were used by the 4th Australian Armoured Brigade in New Guinea and Borneo until the end of hostilities. The Matilda was therefore the only British-designed tank in service from the start to the end of World War II.

T7037

Experiments in Armor
⚒ **1938 USA**

M3 HALFTRACK

The M3 Halftrack was perhaps the most widely recognized vehicle
in World War II, and appeared in every theatre of war.

*Below: The M3 was the most
widely used Allied halftrack of
World War II, serving with all
the Allied forces. This example is
shown complete with a canvas tilt,
and a forward-mounted winch.*

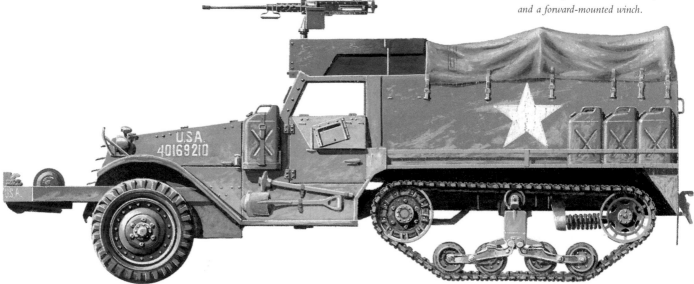

Widely used by the American and other Allied forces during World War II, the M3 Halftrack became a familiar sight, including an appearance on the Russian Front. In the 1920s, the American Army

Below: This photograph shows the M3's forward-mounted winch and the "pulpit" machine-gun mounting. The vehicle is armed with a 0.5in (12.7mm) Browning heavy machine gun.

purchased some Citroen Kegresse P17 halftracks, and was sufficiently impressed by their performance to order the development of a US vehicle, which emerged in prototype form as the T14 in 1931. Known as the M2 in US Army service, the halftrack formed the hull of a White M2 scout car with a Kegresse halftrack suspension. Four US manufacturers were involved in producing the halftracks, turning out 41,000 between 1941 (when the M2 entered production) and 1944.

M3 variants

Later, the M2 was supplemented by the Half-Track Personnel Carrier M3, which could also be used as a communications vehicle, an artillery towing vehicle and an armored ambulance. One of the disadvantages of the M3 was its lack of floor armor, making its passengers vulnerable to mines. M2 and M3 Halftracks were used by the US forces in the Korean War, by the French in Indo-China and by the Israelis in their early postwar conflicts.

Specifications

(M3A2)

Armament: One 0.50in (12.7mm) MG; two 0.30in (7.62mm) MGs

Armor: 0.512in (13mm)

Crew: 3 plus 10

Dimensions: Length 20ft 9in (6.34m); Width 7ft 4in (2.22m); Height 7ft 6in (2.28m)

Weight: 9.33 tons (9477kg)

Powerplant: White 160AX 6-cylinder inline, gasoline, 143hp (106.7kW)

Speed: 45mph (72km/h)

Range: 200 miles (322km)

Experiments in Armor
✖ 1939 France

HOTCHKISS H-39 LIGHT TANK

The Hotchkiss H-39 was the last in a series of light armored fighting vehicles developed by Hotchkiss in the 1930s. It was fast and agile, but no match for the guns of the Panzers.

Specifications

Armament: One 1.46in (37mm) gun; one 0.295in (7.5mm) MG

Armor: Maximum, 1.57in (40mm)

Crew: 2

Dimensions: Length 13ft 10in (4.22m); Width 6ft 4.75in (1.95m); Height 7ft 0.6in (2.15m)

Weight: 11.9 tons (12,100kg)

Powerplant: Hotchkiss 1938, 6-cylinder gasoline, 120hp (89.5kW)

Speed: Road, 22.7mph (36.5km/h)

Range: Road, 93.2 miles (150km)

Right: This H-39 was one of many used by the Free French forces after the French armistice with Germany.

Considered to be one of the best French tanks in service in May 1940, the H-39 was a straightforward development of the H-35 light tank series, with thickened armor and an improved high-velocity SA38 gun for better armor penetration. About 100 of the H-39 variant had been delivered to the French armored units at the time of the German invasion; total production of the H-38 and H-39 totaled 890 units, together with 400 of the earlier H-35 models. The two later variants could be distinguished

Above: Armed with the SA38 1.46in (37mm) L33 gun, the Hotchkiss H-39 had a respectable performance by 1930s standards. Its biggest disadvantage was that its commander also had to operate the gun.

from the H-35 by their raised rear decking, which was flat instead of sloped.

Brief encounters

Encounters between the Hotchkiss and German armor tended to be brief and one-sided; on May 14, 1940, for example, one Hotchkiss battalion lost 11 of its 15 tanks in a matter of minutes, during a counterattack on German forces crossing the Meuse. After the Armistice, many captured H-39s were taken into German service as the PzKpfw 39-H 735(f). Some had their turrets removed and were fitted out as tank destroyers, with German antitank guns installed. Others were used in the hands of Vichy French forces in Syria in 1941.

Chapter 3

THE ERA OF THE LIGHT TANK AND ARMORED CAR

Light tanks and armored cars outnumbered their heavier counterparts in the first two years of World War II. Scouting and fast pursuit (which had traditionally been the roles the cavalry) had become as important as the job of the infantry support tank. In the British Army, the so-called cruiser tank was most widely used, but paid the penalty for being weakly armed when it came up against the Panzers in the Western Desert.

Above: *The Humber scout car, which saw widespread use with the British Army, was a purposeful vehicle that proved to be thoroughly reliable. It was well liked by its crews.*

Left: *British Cromwell tanks assembling near the start line in readiness for the breakout from Normandy in 1944. The breakout, through strong German defenses, cost the British Army many AFVs.*

France's light tanks also stood little chance against the better-armored Panzer III and IV, which destroyed them with almost contemptuous ease. Italy's tanks, although adequate at the time of their conception in the 1930s, were obsolete by the time Italy entered the war in June 1940, and were never adequately updated or replaced. The same was true of Japan's armored fighting vehicles: They were adequate in combat against minimal opposition in China, Burma, and the Philippines, but were mostly ineffective later on. Outside Germany, the country that made the biggest advances in the development of tanks up to the end of 1941 was the Soviet Union. Here, a "no-frills" approach to tank design paid dividends. The fast light tanks that were developed in the 1930s became increasingly up-gunned and were fitted with heavier armor until they were transformed into medium tanks. These developments culminated in the superlative T-34/76 of 1940—the best tank of its kind.

The Era of the Light Tank and Armored Car
⚒ **1939 Germany**

SDKFZ 222 LIGHT RECONNAISSANCE VEHICLE

The German Army had virtually free rein in selecting their equipment in the 1930s, and the SdKfz 222 was a consequence of this.

Below: *This SdKfz was very popular, and remained in production right up to the end of the war.*

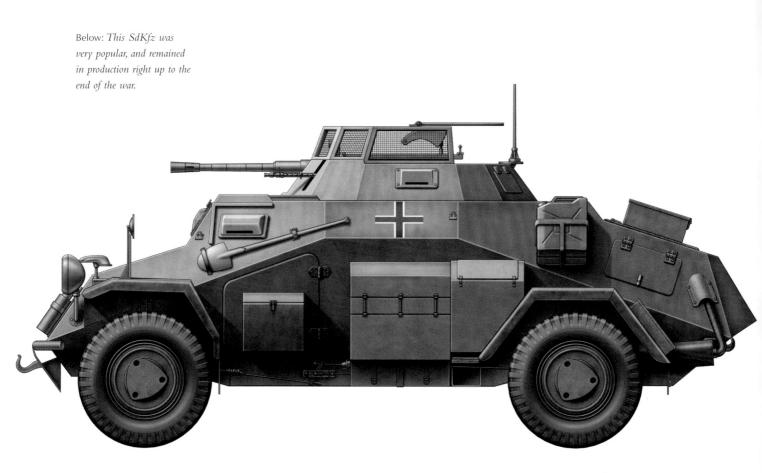

The SdKfz 222 was one of a series of light reconnaissance 4x4 armored cars developed by Eisenwerk Weserhütte between 1934 and 1944. The basic model was the SdKfz 221, which had a two-man crew and was armed with a single 0.312in (7.92mm) MG34 machine gun; the SdKfz 222 had a much more effective 0.79mm (20mm) cannon as well as the MG34 and carried a third crew member to operate it. Some vehicles were experimentally armed with a 1.97in (50mm) cannon to provide still greater hitting power. A third variant, the SdKfz 223, was a radio vehicle.

High speed

The SdKfz 222 proved to be a reliable and popular vehicle in action: Its high cross-country speed enabled it to scout ahead of advancing Panzer columns and extricate itself from trouble. Its main drawback was its radius of action, which was restricted by the amount of fuel its internal tanks would hold. This was not a major problem in the western and southern European campaigns, but in Russia it caused operational difficulties. The SdKfz 222 had a large export market to China prior to 1939.

Specifications

Armament: One 0.79in (20mm) or 1.1in/0.79in (28mm/20mm) cannon; one 0.312in (7.92mm) MG

Armor: Maximum, 0.57in (14.5mm)

Crew: 3

Dimensions: Length 15ft 9in (4.8m); Width 6ft 4.8in (1.95m); Height 5ft 11in (1.8m)

Weight: approx 4.72 tons (4800kg)

Powerplant: Horch, V-8 gasoline, 81bhp (60.4kW) or 90hp (67.1kW)

Speed: Road, 46.6mph (75km/h)

Range: Road, 174 miles (280km)

The Era of the Light Tank and Armored Car

⚒ **1939 Germany**

SDKFZ 250 ARMORED PERSONNEL CARRIER

Popular, reliable, and highly versatile, the SdKfz 250 remained in production until the end of World War II. It was expensive to produce, but proved itself to be excellent value for money.

Below: *This SdKfz is pictured in France in 1944.*

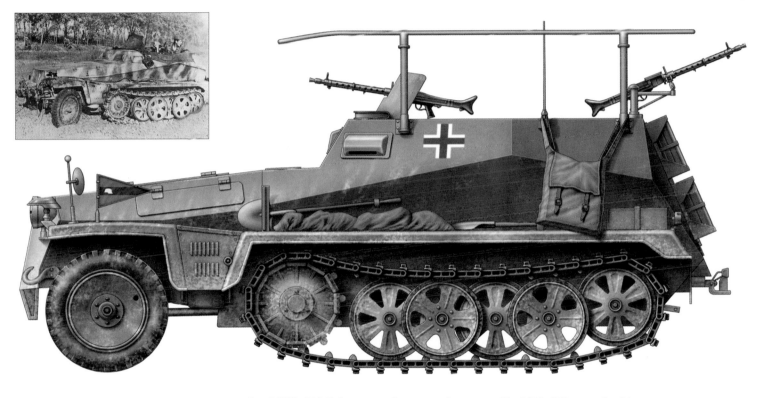

Specifications

(SdKfz 250/1)

Armament: Two 0.312in (7.92mm) MGs

Armor: Maximum, 0.57in (14.5mm)

Crew: 2 plus 4 troops

Dimensions: Length 14ft 11.5in (4.56m); Width 6ft 4.75in (1.95m); Height 5ft 5.4in (1.66m)

Weight: approx 5.61 tons (5700kg)

Powerplant: Maybach HL42 TRKM, 6-cylinder gasoline, 100hp (74.5kW)

Speed: Road, 40.4mph (65km/h)

Range: Road, 217.5 miles (350km)

The SdKfz 250 light armored personnel carrier stemmed from the same design that resulted in the SdKfz 251, which was a heavier vehicle. The design worked toward two types of APC, a one-tonner and a three-tonner, and it was the former that was produced as the SdKfz 250. The chassis was made by Demag AG of Wetter (in the Rühr) and was based on that of the SdKfz 10 truck. The armored body was made by Büssing-NAG. Production of the SdKfz 250/1 started in June 1941. This vehicle carried half a platoon (six men) and two machine guns. It was followed by various other models, which included versions armed with a variety of weapons ranging from an 3.19in (81mm) mortar to a 0.79in (20mm) cannon.

Above: *The SdKfz 250 was produced in many versions through the war and could be armed with a wide variety of weapons; this one has two MG34 machine guns.*

SdKfz 250/9

A much-improved model appeared in 1942 in the form of the SdKfz 250/9. Three prototypes were sent to Russia for operational trials, where they were found to be much more effective than the SdKfz 222. Production of the latter was therefore discontinued, and mass production of the SdKfz 250/9 began in May 1943. Some SdKfz 250s were converted to the role of tank destroyer, armed with a 1.46in (37mm) antitank gun.

The Era of the Light Tank and Armored Car
1939 Italy

CARRO ARMATO M11/39 MEDIUM TANK

Italy's M11/39 light tank was quickly deemed to be obsolete by the Italian Army. Nevertheless, they sent it to war in North Africa and used it in a role for which it was never intended.

Below: *A troop of Carro Armato M11/39 medium tanks on maneuvers.*

This light tank was produced by Fiat and appeared in prototype form in 1939. It suffered from weak armor and a poor 1.46in (37mm) gun. This was hull-mounted with a small two-man turret above, housing a pair of machine guns. Two principal models were built, with six and eight roadwheels respectively. Only 100 examples of the M11/39 were built, as the type was considered to be virtually obsolete by the time it entered service, but 70 were sent to North Africa after Italy entered the war in June 1940. Although it had been developed as a light infantry support AFV, the M11/39 was used as a medium tank in the Western Desert, and was consequently required to perform tasks that were far beyond its capabilities. Its shortcomings were revealed in the earliest skirmishes in Libya, when it came up against the British Matildas and Valentines, against which it stood little chance of survival.

Armor weakness

The weakness of the Italian armor was soon appreciated by the British commanders in the early stages of the Desert War: they exploited this and launched a series of crippling offensives against the Italian forces.

Specifications

Armament: One 1.46in (37mm) gun; two 0.315in (8mm) Breda MGs
Armor: 0.24–1.18in (6–30mm)
Crew: 3
Dimensions: Length 15ft 6in (4.73m); Width 7ft 2in (2.18m); Height 7ft 7in (2.30m)
Weight: 11 tons (11,175kg)
Powerplant: One SPA 8 T diesel, 105bhp (78.3kW)
Speed: 20.7mph (33.3km/h)
Range: 124 miles (200km)

Below: *This official photograph shows a Marmon Herrington Mk II armored car in its original configuration.*

The Era of the Light Tank and Armored Car
⚒ **1939 South Africa**

MARMON HERRINGTON MK I/II/III ARMORED CAR

Produced in South Africa, the Marmon Herrington armored cars were the only vehicles of their kind available in any numbers to the British Commonwealth forces in North Africa.

Specifications

(MKIII)

Armament: Two 0.303in (7.6mm) machine guns (but many vehicles fitted with enhanced weapons fit)

Armor: 0.47in (12mm)

Crew: 3

Dimensions: Length 17ft 5in (5.308m); Width 7ft 6in (2.286m); Height 8ft 2in (2.489m)

Weight: 13,440lb (6096kg)

Powerplant: Ford V-8 gasoline, 85bhp (63kW)

Speed: 50mph (80km/h)

Range: 200 miles (322km)

The development of armored cars was a bold venture for the South African armaments industry, which had no experience in producing armored fighting vehicles of any kind. When the South African Government ordered two of these vehicles to be developed in 1938, work proceeded slowly. The resulting vehicles used a Ford truck chassis imported from Canada and a four-wheel drive transmission from Marmon Herrington in the USA, with armament supplied by the United Kingdom and armor plating by the South African Iron & Steel Industrial Corporation.

Breakout of war

When war broke out in 1939, the armored cars were immediately ordered into production as the South African Reconnaissance Vehicle Mk I (which had a long wheelbase and a 4x2 drive configuration) and the South African Reconnaissance Vehicle Mk II (which had a shorter wheelbase and a 4x4 drive). It was known to the British as the Marmon Herrington, Mk II armored car. The Mk II armored cars formed the bulk of the reconnaissance vehicles available to the British Commonwealth forces in North Africa. The Mk Is were withdrawn after a poor performance against the Italians in East Africa. In mid-1941 the MkIII entered production; it had enhanced suspension and many other improvements to increase reliability.

Below: *A typical Marmon Herrington Mk II armored car in desert camouflage.*

The Era of the Light Tank and Armored Car
1939 Soviet Union

KV-1 HEAVY TANK

The KV-1 was the only type of Soviet tank capable of holding its own against the Panzers when Germany invaded the Soviet Union in June 1941. It was produced only in small numbers.

At the time of its appearance in 1941, the Klim-Voroshilov KV-1 was the most formidable tank in the world. It was developed in 1938 as a successor to the T-35, taking its name from Klimenti Voroshilov, who was then the Commissar for Defense. The tank was evaluated under operational conditions in the war with Finland, and ordered into production as the KV-1A (with a long-barrel 3in [76.2mm] gun) and the KV-2 (with a 4.8in [122mm] main armament, which made the tank very ponderous to use). The KV-2 had a tall, slab-sided turret that made a tempting target for enemy gunners and rendered the tank vulnerable. The KV-1, however, was a formidable vehicle that served the Red Army well during the most dangerous period of the war on the Eastern Front. Its biggest drawback was that it suffered from a lack of mobility, which caused problems on the vast open spaces of the Russian plain. It was at its most useful in forming the spearhead of an armored attack, when it was used as a battering-ram to break through enemy defenses, creating a gap that could then be exploited by T-34s.

Left: *This photograph gives a good impression of the size and bulk of the KV-1, which struck terror into its opponents.*

Specifications

(KV-I Model 1942)

Armament: One 3in (76.2mm) L/41 ZiS-5 gun; three or four 0.3in (7.62mm) DT MGs (bow, coaxial, turret rear, and occasionally commander's cupola)

Armor: 1.18–2.95in (30–75mm)

Crew: 5

Dimensions: Length 21ft 11in (6.68m); Width 10ft 11in (3.32m); Height 8ft 11in (2.71m)

Weight: 42.3 tons (43,000kg)

Powerplant: V2K V-12 diesel, 550bhp (410kW) at 2150rpm

Speed: 21.7mph (35km/h) (rarely achieved)

Range: 93 miles (150km)

Below: *The Soviet KV-1 heavy tank was the most powerful tank in the world when it first appeared, and was mainly used to break through strongly fortified positions. Its principal drawback was that it was slow and ponderous.*

The Era of the Light Tank and Armored Car

⚒ **1939 Sweden**

STRIDSVAGN M/38

In the years immediately before the outbreak of World War II, Sweden was producing very viable light tanks, and the Stridsvagn m/38 was an example of this. Export plans were thwarted by the war.

Specifications

Armament: One 1.46in (37mm) gun; one MG

Armor: 0.512in (13mm)

Crew: 3

Dimensions: Length 15ft 4in (4.67m); Width 6ft 9in (2.06m); Height 6ft 10in (2.09m)

Weight: 8.5 tons (8835kg)

Powerplant: Scania-Vabis 6-cylinder gasoline, 142bhp (106kW)

Speed: 28mph (45km/h)

Range: Not revealed

After the success of its L-60 tank (which had many advanced features that were to characterize the Swedish tank designs of the future) and of the L-100 (a scaled-down, faster version that carried the same benefits of a fine suspension and modern configuration), Sweden produced the Stridsvagn m/38. Swedish industry was intent on keeping the momentum going and making capital out of the market that existed for innovative light tanks. In September 1937 the Swedish Army placed an order for 17 of these vehicles, together with 48 examples of the Stridsvagn m/37 (or AH-IV-SV). These tanks were the only Swedish AFVs capable of engaging armored targets with any chance of success, as the weapons on other Swedish

Above: This Stridsvagn m/38, bearing the number 66, is now on permanent display at the Pansarmuseet (Tank Museum) at Axvall, Sweden. The m/38s first served at Göta Livgarde, but were transferred to two tank battalions of the 19th Regiment at Skövde and the 110th Regiment at Strängnäs in 1939.

vehicles were of insufficient caliber. The m/37 had a 1.46in (37mm) cannon, replacing the 0.79in (20mm) gun of earlier designs, and was powered by a Swedish engine. It had unusual features, such as a steering wheel instead of tillers, but was produced only in small numbers. This new generation of Swedish light tank might have enjoyed export success, had it not been for the outbreak of war in Europe.

The Era of the Light Tank and Armored Car
1939 USA

M3 SCOUT CAR

Armored scout cars like the White M3 were very widely used immediately before World War II, but when they came to be tested in action they were often found inadequate.

Specifications

Armament: One 0.5in (12.7mm) or 0.3in (7.62mm) MG
Armor: 0.512in (13mm)
Crew: 1 plus 7
Dimensions: Length 18ft 6in (5.63m); Width 6ft 8in (2.1m); Height 6ft 7in (2m)
Weight: 5.58 tons (5,670kg)
Powerplant: Hercules JXD 6-cylinder inline gasoline, 87hp (65kW)
Speed: 50mph (81km/h)
Range: 250 miles (403km)

Left: *The White M3 scout car was a favorite vehicle of the US military police during World War II. Originally used by reconnaissance units, it was not suited to crossing rough terrain.*

The White Motor Company M3 scout car was first produced in 1938 and was initially known as the T7. It had a relatively brief operational career: It was used mainly in the North African campaign and was progressively relegated to second-line duties thereafter. The vehicle was used mainly by reconnaissance units, but it was not really suitable for cross-country operations and was eventually replaced by the much more versatile halftrack. The vehicle could carry eight fully armed men and was itself well armed, fitted with one 0.5in (12.7mm) M2 heavy machine gun and two 0.30in (7.62mm) Brownings. The windscreen was made of shatterproof glass and a plate of 0.5in (12.7mm) armor with inbuilt vision slits could be brought down to cover it. Some M3s were used in the Philippines during the battle for the islands in 1942.

Command car

During its career the production M3A1 was used for a number of different purposes, one of which was as a command car. After it was relegated to second-line duties, it became one of the standard vehicles used by the American military police on road patrol work in the rear areas.

Left: *The top of the M3 could be removed, as seen in this photograph. The roller mounted in front of the vehicle was designed to prevent it from bogging down in soft ground.*

Above: *Like many other armored cars, the Autoblinda AB 40 had its origin in a requirement for a colonial policing vehicle. Its relatively small size is evident here.*

The Era of the Light Tank and Armored Car

⚒ 1940 Italy

AUTOBLINDA AB 40 ARMORED CAR

Italy faced a constant threat as a consequence of trouble in her African colonies. This brought an urgent need for modern armored cars to carry out secure policing in the late 1930s. The AB 40 was designed for this purpose.

The Autoblinda 40 of 1939 was the result of requests both by the Italian Colonial Police and the Army, both of whom needed a new high-performance armored patrol vehicle. The Colonial Police, in particular, were coming under increasing pressure from hostile dissident groups, while the Army needed to replace its obsolete equipment. The Italian Government decided that one vehicle would meet both requirements, and the result was the Autoblinda 40.

Phased out

The new vehicle, which entered production in mid-1940, had a rear-mounted engine and a turret (normally mounting twin machine guns) set well forward on the hull. A small

number of Autoblinda 40s had a 0.79in (20mm) cannon (taken from the Italian L/60 light tank) in place of the turret machine guns, and in this new guise it became the Autoblinda 41. This new combination of vehicle and weapon was far more efficient, and production of the AB 40 was phased out. Some AB 40s had their turrets replaced and were converted to AB 41s. By the end of September 1942, 298 Autoblinda 41s were deployed by the Italian Army in North Africa, Greece, and Yugoslavia.

Below. The armament configuration of the AB 40 is clearly seen in this image, comprising a turret-mounted 0.79in (20mm) cannon and a machine gun at the rear of the hull.

Specifications

Armament: One 0.79in (20mm) gun; two 0.315in (8mm) MGs

Armor: 0.354in (9mm)

Crew: 4

Dimensions: Length 17ft 1in (5.20m); Width 6ft 4in (1.92m); Height 7ft 11in (2.48m)

Weight: 7.38 tons (7500kg)

Powerplant: Ansaldo, 6-cylinder, gasoline, 80bhp (60kW)

Speed: 749mph (8km/h)

Range: 248 miles (400km)

The Era of the Light Tank and Armored Car

⚒ 1940 Italy

CARRO ARMATO L6/40 LIGHT TANK

The Italians placed a great deal of reliance on light cavalry tanks (like the L6/40) before and after their entry into World War II. Medium tanks would have been a much better proposition, however.

The Fiat L6/40 light tank was developed from the L3, and remained in service from Italy's entry into the war until the Armistice in September 1943. The vehicle was a conventional design of riveted construction, using a modified Carden-Loyd chassis. A centrally mounted one-man turret housed a Breda 0.79mm (20mm) cannon. The tank had a lengthy gestation period and several prototypes were produced in the late 1930s. All had different armament configurations. The first had a sponson-mounted 1.46in (37mm) gun, and another had twin 0.31in (8mm) machine guns. The turret-mounted Breda Modello 35 was selected, and the tank went into production as the Carro Armato L6/40. Several versions were produced, including flamethrower and command-tank variants. The most successful was a self-propelled gun version, the Semovente 47/32. The turret was removed and a 1.85in (47mm) antitank gun installed in the hull.

Operational disadvantage

In all, 283 examples of the light tank version were produced. Like many other light tanks of the period, the L6/40 had an operational disadvantage in that its commander also had to act as gunner and loader. When it first entered service, the L6/40 was roughly the equivalent of Germany's Panzer II.

Specifications

Armament: One 0.79in (20mm) Breda cannon; one 0.315in (8mm) Breda MG

Armor: 0.24–1.18in (6–30mm)

Crew: 2

Dimensions: Length 12ft 5in (3.78m); Width 6ft 4in (1.92m); Height 6ft 8in (2.03m)

Weight: 6.79 ton (s6900kg)

Powerplant: One SPA 18 D gasoline, 70bhp (52.2kW)

Speed: 26.1mph (42km/h)

Range: 125 miles (200km)

Below: *The L6/40 was based on the chassis of the British Carden-Loyd series of tankettes. The small turret was manually operated and was armed with a 0.79in (20mm) cannon and coaxial machine gun.*

The Era of the Light Tank and Armored Car
⚒ **1940 Italy**

CARRO ARMATO M13/40 MEDIUM TANK

Despite being outclassed by modern British tanks, the Carro Armato M13/40 was used widely—on both sides. Many abandoned examples were captured by the British and used against their former owners.

Specifications

Armament: One 1.85in (47mm) gun; four Modello 0.315in (38.8mm) MGs

Armor: 0.24–1.65in (6–42mm)

Crew: 4

Dimensions: Length 16ft 2in (4.92m); Width 7ft 3in (2.2m); Height 7ft 10in (2.38m)

Weight: 13.78 tons (14,000kg)

Powerplant: One SPA TM40 8-cylinder diesel, 125bhp (93kW)

Speed: 19.75mph (31.8km/h)

Range: 124 miles (200km)

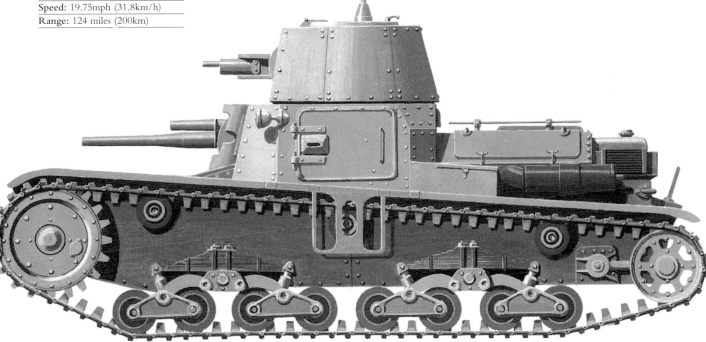

Above: Although quite a viable fighting machine at the outset of Italy's involvement in World War II, the M13/40 was soon outclassed by new types of British cruiser tank.

Right: Considered by many to be the best Italian tank of the war, the Carro Armato M13/40 was the primary medium tank of the Italian Army from 1940 to 1941.

The M13/40 was a progressive development of the M11/39, with revised armor and a 1.85in (47mm) gun. It was produced in substantial numbers, mainly by one contractor, Ansaldo-Fossati, and final production ran to 779 vehicles. The M13/40 was widely used in the Western Desert and in the Balkans. It also had the distinction of fighting on both sides. Many captured vehicles were issued to the 6th Royal Tank Regiment and the Australian 6th Cavalry Regiment early in 1941. This was a time when the Commonwealth forces in North Africa were desperately short of armored fighting vehicles of every kind.

White kangaroos

The Australian regiment had three squadrons of captured M13s, which they named Dingo, Wombat, and Rabbit. For identification purposes and to try to eliminate the danger of being hit by friendly fire, the captured tanks had large white kangaroos painted on their hulls and turrets. The tank's unreliability gave rise to many problems—not least its propensity to catch fire.

The Era of the Light Tank and Armored Car

1940 Italy

CARRO ARMATO P26/40

The Carro Armato P26/40 was the first Italian tank that could be compared to Allied medium AFVs. Various problems meant the Italians never used it in action, however.

Above: *The P26/40 was the best tank developed by the Italians in World War II, and would have been a match for similar Allied fighting vehicles but the lack of a suitable engine prevented it being used in combat.*

Ansaldo designed this tank in 1940. It is correctly named Carro Pesante P26/40 (Heavy Tank P26/40). It was developed in response to an Italian Army request for a 25-ton tank armed with a 2.95in (75mm) gun. The vehicles that had been in general use by the Italians were woefully inadequate in combat in the Western Desert. Some 1200 examples of this vehicle were ordered, and it promised to be very successful, but the project was hampered by the lack of a suitable engine and the Italian Army's wish to install a diesel rather than a gasoline engine. Consequently, it was not until 1942 that a prototype was completed, fitted with a 420hp gasoline engine, and only five pre-production vehicles had been produced by the time of the Italian surrender in September 1943. These were taken over by the Germans, who ordered production to continue. About 100 P26/40s were subsequently built, although only a few were used under the name of the Panzerkampfwagen P40 737 (i). These saw some success in countering the Allied landings at Anzio early in 1944.

Specifications

Armament: One 2.95in (75mm) gun; one MG

Armor: 1.97in (50mm)

Crew: 4

Dimensions: Length 19ft 1in (5.82m); Width 9ft 2in (2.80m); Height 8ft 3in (2.52m)

Weight: 26 tons (26,420kg)

Powerplant: V12 diesel, 275bhp (205kW)

Speed: 22mph (35km/h)

Range: 150 miles (240km)

The Era of the Light Tank and Armored Car
✗ 1940 Italy

SEMOVENTE L40 DA 47/32 ANTITANK VEHICLE

The Semovante L40 tank destroyer achieved some success in the Western Desert and also in Russia, where it was used by the Italian forces in action with the German Army Group South.

Specifications

Armament: One 1.85in (47mm) gun; one MG

Armor: 1.18in (30mm)

Crew: 3

Dimensions: Length 12ft 5in (3.78m); Width 6ft 4in (1.92m); Height 5ft 5in (1.63m)

Weight: 6.4 tons (6500kg)

Powerplant: Fiat 18D 4-cylinder gasoline, 70bhp (51kW) at 2500rpm

Speed: 26mph (42km/h)

Range: 125 miles (200km)

The Italians were early contenders in the race to produce an effective tank destroyer. In the late 1930s they mounted a 1.85in (47mm) antitank gun on the chassis of an L3 light tank. The gun was manned by a two-man crew who only had the benefit of minimal frontal protection, so a new vehicle was designed. This was the Semovente L40 Da 47/32 (the figure 32 denoting the length of the barrel, which was 32 calibers long). The gun itself was a license-produced version of the Austrian Böhler 1.85in (47mm) dual antitank and infantry support weapon—one of the best anti-armor guns then in existence.

Battle action

The L40 went into action in the Western Desert in 1942, 280 units being produced,

and it proved effective against British light tanks. Its poorly protected crew was still vulnerable to counter-fire, however. Some vehicles were provided with overhead protection at a later date and served with the Italian forces on the Russian Front. After the Italian surrender, many surviving L40s were taken over by the Germans, who used them as all-terrain-tracked vehicles during the fighting in Italy in 1944.

Below: *In designing the Semovente L40 the Italians attempted to mount an antitank gun on a light tank chassis. Although it was successful in trials, it suffered from a lack of crew protection in combat and was soon replaced.*

The Era of the Light Tank and Armored Car

✖ **1940 Soviet Union**

KV–II HEAVY TANK

The KV-II heavy tank was the result of an attempt to field a heavy bombardment tank, with a super-powerful gun based on the chassis of the earlier KV-I. It was not very effective in action owing to its poor mobility.

Specifications

Armament: One 5.98in (152mm) M–1938/40 L/20 howitzer; two 0.3in (7.62mm) DT MGs
Armor: 1.18–4.33in (30–110mm)
Crew: 6
Dimensions: Length 22ft 3in (6.79m); Width 10ft 11in (3.32m); Height 12ft (3.65m)
Weight: 53.1 tons (53,963kg)
Powerplant: V-2K 12-cylinder diesel
Speed: 15.9mph (25.6km/h)
Range: 87 miles (140km)

Left: *The Russian KV-II must surely take the prize for the ugliest tank ever built. Its vast turret made a tempting target for enemy gunners. The KV-II was mostly used for static bombardment.*

The KV-II heavy tank was developed as an attempt to produce a vehicle as effective as the KV-I, but with a more powerful gun. It was intended to provide fire support in breakthrough operations, and to this end a massive 4.8in (122mm) M1938 L22/7 howitzer was mounted in a newly designed turret. This turret was heavily armored, but its high, slab-sided shape, and sheer bulk made it a tempting target. It was practically immoveable except when the tank was stationary. The original howitzer was soon replaced by a 5.98in (152mm) weapon. This was able to fire both high explosive and armor-piercing rounds, 36 of which could be carried. The gun had a range of 13,565 yards (12,400m), which meant that the tank could adopt a bombardment position that was often outside the range of defensive weaponry.

Poor mobility

One of the KV-II's main drawbacks was its poor mobility. It was six tons heavier than the KV-I but it lacked any increase in engine power. Later production KV-IIs were based on the chassis of the KV-1B and were designated KV-IIB, some of which were adapted as flamethrower tanks.

Left: *The massive bulk of a KV-II towers over a BA-10 armored car. The latter's gun turret has been rotated through 180 degrees to point its gun rearward.*

The Era of the Light Tank and Armored Car

✗ 1940 Sweden

STRIDSVAGN M/39 LIGHT TANK

Sweden was neutral during World War II, but never felt secure from the threat of surprise attack. She therefore placed great emphasis on the development of "home-grown" weapons. The Strv m/39 tank was an example of this.

Below: The Stridsvagn m/39 was originally fitted with a steering wheel, but soon reverted to the more usual system of lever steering. A very mobile vehicle, it was designed for rapid deployment to any part of Sweden's lengthy frontier.

Specifications

Armament: One 1.46in (37mm) gun; two MGs

Armor: 0.512in (13mm)

Crew: 3

Dimensions: Length 15ft 4in (4.67m); Width 6ft 9in (2.06m); Height 6ft 10in (2.09m)

Weight: 9 tons (9335kg)

Powerplant: Scania-Vabis 6-cylinder gasoline, 142bhp (106kW)

Speed: 28mph (45km/h)

Range: Not revealed

A straightforward development of the Strv m/38, the Stridsvagn m/39 incorporated a number of new design features, but reverted to the usual system of lever steering. The new tank was armed with a 1.46in (37mm) main gun and two machine guns. When Germany invaded neighboring Norway, Sweden (although a firmly neutral country) became increasingly aware of the threat from Nazi Germany. In the fear the tanks might be called on to take on the powerful German Panzers, their armor protection was increased by an extra 1.37in (35mm), although the new armor plating was simply made available, rather than actually fitted. The m/39 was deployed with the Swedish Army's 19th and 110th Regiments, and later by K2 in Helsingborg. In the event of a sudden surprise attack by German forces from Norway, Sweden would have had a long frontier to protect, and so the Swedish Army placed great emphasis on speed and mobility, which is why it concentrated on the development of light, fast armored fighting vehicles. The lack of armor was a price that had to be paid for enhanced performance.

The Era of the Light Tank and Armored Car
1940 Soviet Union

T-34 TANK

Arguably, no tank in the history of warfare has come as a greater shock to the enemy, nor inflicted more terror, than did the T-34 when it first appeared on the Russian Front in the summer of 1941.

Specifications

(T-34/76 1941)

Armament: 3in (76.2mm) L/41.2 F-34 rifled gun; two 0.3in (7.62mm) Degtaryev DT MGs (one coaxial, one hull-mounted)

Armor: 1.89in (47mm) (hull front), 2.56in (65mm) (turret front)

Crew: 4

Dimensions: Length 20ft (6.09m), gun forward 21ft 7in (6.58m); Width 9ft 9in (2.98m), Height 8ft 5in (2.57m)

Weight: 30.9 tons (31,390kg)

Powerplant: V-2-34 4-stroke V-12 diesel, 500bhp (373kW) at 1800rpm

Speed: 25mph (40km/h)

Range: Road, 268 miles (432km); Cross-country, 228 miles (368km)

Above: *The business end of a T-34. Note the sloping armor, an innovation that made most German antitank projectiles ineffective when the T-34 first entered combat in the summer of 1941.*

The T-34 boasted a very advanced design for its day and was the result of the continual upgrading and refinement of the less-than-successful BT-7. This upgrading produced two designs known as the A-20 and A-30—both developments of the BT-1S. These were rejected in favor of the T-32—a cruiser tank with a more powerful gun and heavier armor. It appeared in 1939 and had most of the features of the T-34. The vehicle was designed by a group under the leadership of Mikhail Ilyich Koshkin. He was a sick man with less than two years to live, but embarked on updating the armor of the T-32. This became the T-34.

Common sense

The new tank was the product of robust common sense, and owed its existence to a team of men who could envisage a

Above: *The T-34 was not a tank for crew comfort; it was dirty, noisy, smelly, and very functional. The driver's hatch is shown in this photograph, together with the tank's main armament.*

Variants

The T-34 was produced in many variants and was the second most widely produced tank of all time. The most widely produced was its successor, the T-54/55. The T-34/8, appeared in 1943. It was an improved model and it was this version that opened the gates to the flood of Soviet armor which, after the battle of Kursk in July 1943, began to roll westward to the frontiers of Germany. By 1945, the T-34 had replaced nearly every type of Russian tank in production. After World War II, T-34s equipped the armies of many countries within the Soviet sphere of influence, and in 1950 a full brigade of 120 T-34s spearheaded the North Korean attack on South Korea. In all, 39 countries used the T-34, and production only ended in 1958 after many thousands had been issued. Most recently, the T-34 was used in the conflicts in the former Yugoslavia, and some T-34s acquired by Cuba saw action in Angola.

mid-20th-century battlefield much more clearly than any of their Western counterparts. The T-34 went into mass production in late 1940 as the T-34/76A. By the time of the German invasion of the Soviet Union in June 1941, it was already well established. The long and fluid nature of the front meant that it was initially used at the points of greatest danger, leaving older tanks to try to stem the German advance elsewhere.

Below: *Cutaway drawing showing the interior of the T-34/85. This later model of the T-34 was instrumental in turning the tide of war on the Eastern Front, and was a match for the formidable German Panzer. It remained in use long after the war with Soviet satellite countries and in Africa.*

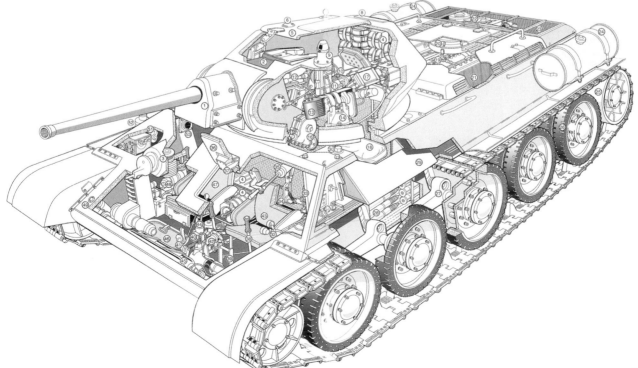

The Era of the Light Tank and Armored Car
1940 UK

MARK III VALENTINE INFANTRY TANK

The Valentine was one of the most successful pre-World War II tank designs. It was used widely, and proved a valuable asset in the desert, where it first saw action in 1941.

Specifications

Armament: One 2pdr (1.57in/40mm) gun; one 0.31in (7.92mm) Besa MG
Armor: 0.32–2.56in (8–65mm)
Crew: 3
Dimensions: Length 19ft 4in (5.89m); Width 8ft 8in (2.63m); Height 7ft 6in (2.273m)
Weight: 17 tons (17,272kg)
Powerplant: AEC 6-cylinder diesel 131bhp (97.73kW), or AEC 6-cylinder gasoline 135bhp (180.9kW), or GMS 6-cylinder diesel 135bhp (180.9kW)
Speed: 14.9mph (24km/h)
Range: 90 miles (145km)

In 1938, Vickers was asked to produce a new infantry tank based on the A10 design, and in July 1939 the new vehicle was ordered into production as the Infantry Tank Mk III Valentine. It carried heavier armor than the A10, and incorporated many improvements as a result of the problems that the earlier tank had experienced.

Mass production
The Valentine was rushed into mass production in 1940 in the aftermath of the loss of British armor during the fighting in France. It was first used in the Western Desert during Operation Crusader (the British offensive to relieve Tobruk) in November 1941, by which time it had become one of

the most important armored fighting vehicles in the British Army. By early 1944, when production ceased, 8375 units had been produced. The tank was also produced in Canada, although most of the Canadian output was sent to the Soviet Union. The Valentine proved readily adaptable to various roles and numerous variants were produced, ranging from bridge-layers to self-propelled guns. Many Valentines saw service in the Burma campaign, where they were superior to the Japanese types in service.

Right: *An early model Mk V Valentine receives a good deal of attention in Valletta as Malta celebrates the birthday of King George VI in 1943. The Valentine saw service worldwide.*

Above: *The Valentine Mk III was mass produced from 1940 and took part in all the campaigns in the Western Desert.*

The Era of the Light Tank and Armored Car

 1940 UK

MARK V TANK COVENANTOR (A13 MARK III)

The Mk V Covenantor cruiser tank was a promising design, evolving over a period of years from the design of earlier vehicles. It was let down by its engine, which had a difficult cooling system.

Specifications

Armament: One 2pdr (1.57in/40mm) gun; one 0.31in (7.92mm) Besa MG

Armor: 0.28–1.58in (7–40mm)

Crew: 4

Dimensions: Length 19ft (5.8m); Width 8ft 7in (2.61m); Height 7ft 4in (2.23m)

Weight: 18 tons (18,300kg)

Powerplant: Meadows-Flat "flat-12" gasoline, 300bhp (223.8kW)

Speed: 31.05mph (50km/h)

Range: 99.36 miles (160km)

Below: *The Covenantor cruiser tank showed a good deal of potential, but it suffered from an unreliable engine. Here, a troop of Covenantors is seen advancing through harvest fields on maneuvers in southern England.*

The A13 Mk III, otherwise known as the Cruiser Tank Mk V, was a progressive development of the earlier vehicles in the Nuffield cruiser tank series. Based on the A13 Mk II, although substantially reworked, it had a purpose-built Meadows-Flat 12 engine designed to give a higher speed. Armor was increased, and the tank was fitted with a low-silhouette turret. The tank itself could have been very successful; the problem lay with the engine, whose cooling system persistently failed to work. Four attempts were made to overcome the problem, but it was never put right.

Before the outbreak of war, some Covenantors were equipped with mine-clearing rollers and used for experimental purposes. Later on, many vehicles were stripped of their turrets and used as recovery vehicles. None of the 1771 Covenantors produced ever saw combat, although some were used as bridge-layers by the Australians in the Pacific. The armored recovery vehicles that were derived from the tank performed a useful role until the end of the war, however. The Covenantor developed into the Crusader, which was to see much service in North Africa.

The Era of the Light Tank and Armored Car
⚔ 1940 UK

MARK VI CRUISER TANK (CRUSADER) (A15)

The Mk VI Crusader played an important part in the Desert War, despite being outclassed by its German counterparts. Its main weakness, at least in its early deployment, was its lack of firepower.

Specifications

Armament: One 6pdr (2.24in/57mm) gun; one or two 0.31in (7.92mm) Besa MGs
Armor: 0.28–1.93in (7–49mm)
Crew: 5
Dimensions: Length 19ft 6in (5.994m); Width 8ft 8in (2.642m); Height 7ft 4in (2.235m)
Weight: 19 tons (19,300kg)
Powerplant: Nuffield Liberty V-12 gasoline, 340bhp (253.64kW)
Speed: 26.7mph (43km/h)
Range: 124.2 miles (200km)

The Mk VI Crusader tank was designed and built by Nuffield, who used the A13 Covenantor as the basis. The A15 was an improved design. Its prototype had two small auxiliary forward turrets, each fitted with a machine gun, but these were eliminated in the production version. The new tank also had five roadwheels on either side, against the Covenantor's four. The Crusader I entered service in 1941 and it was immediately apparent that its 2pdr (1.57in/40mm) main armament was inadequate, so plans were made to replace it with the new 6pdr (2.24in/57mm) gun. It was this version, designated Crusader III, which became the most important tank in the desert war, first seeing action at the Second Battle of Alamein in October 1942. An antiaircraft version of the Crusader Mk III was also produced, the 6pdr (2.24in/57mm) gun being replaced by a Bofors 1.57in (40mm) antiaircraft gun mounted in an open-topped turret.

Relegated

As more effective tanks such as the Churchill became available, the Crusader was gradually relegated to secondary duties and specialist roles, including those of a gun tractor and a bulldozer. Over 5300 Crusaders were built.

Above: *The Crusader was the first British tank to be armed with an effective gun, the six-pounder. Its other main asset was its suspension, which was so tough that the tank could often exceed its designed maximum speed.*

Left: *The Crusader had a well-designed turret, with sloping armor. Despite its various attributes, however, it was outclassed by its German opponents, and was gradually relegated to second-line duties.*

The Era of the Light Tank and Armored Car
⚒ **1940 UK**

A17 MARK VII TETRARCH

Initially rejected by the British Army as a light tank, the A17 Mk VII
Tetrarch found a new lease of life as a reconnaissance tank for the
newly formed airborne forces in 1941.

Specifications

Armament: One 2pdr
(1.57in/40mm) gun; one 0.31in
(7.92mm) Besa MG

Armor: 0.16–0.55in (4–14mm)

Crew: 3

Dimensions: Length 13ft 6in
(4.11m); Width 7ft 7in (2.31m);
Height 6ft 11in (2.10m)

Weight: 7.5 tons (7620kg)

Powerplant: Meadows Flat-12
gasoline developing 165bhp
(123kW) at 2700rpm

Speed: 39.74mph (64km/h)

Range: 139.73 miles (225km)

The A17 Tetrarch started life as a private
venture of the Vickers Company, and
was initially called the Purdah. The prototype
underwent a series of trials in 1938, and
despite the fact that it lacked adequate armor
and armament, it went into production in
1940 as a reconnaissance vehicle. However,
following an appraisal of the poor
performance of light tanks in action,
production was stopped until 1941, and the
A17 was adopted by the newly established
airborne forces. At the same time,
Specification (X.27/40) was issued for a large
glider capable of airlifting the tank, and this
resulted in the General Aircraft Hamilcar,

*Above: Designed to be carried into action in a
Hamilcar glider, the Tetrarch was deployed by British
airborne forces during the Normandy landings. This
example has an adaptor fitted to its two-pounder gun
to increase muzzle velocity.*

which first flew in March 1942. The vehicle
was given the name Tetrarch in 1943, and the
combination of Hamilcar and Tetrarch went
into action on the night of June 5, 1944,
when the gliders landed on the River Orne
with elements of the Airborne Armoured
Reconnaissance Regiment. The Tetrarch was
also used in Operation Varsity—the crossing
of the Rhine at Wesel in March 1944.

The Era of the Light Tank and Armored Car
⚒ **1940 USA**

LVT ASSAULT LANDING VEHICLE FAMILY

The tracked landing vehicle (LVT) brought a new dimension to amphibious warfare operations, and was indispensable in the Allies' Pacific campaigns, as one island after another had to be recaptured.

Above: *The LTV4, seen here, differed from earlier LTVs in having its loading ramp at the rear.*

Above: *An LVT at speed. In an assault, the LVTs would hit the beach in line abreast in order to discharge as many infantry as quickly as possible.*

The LVT (Landing Vehicle Tracked) had its origins in a civilian rescue vehicle called the Alligator, which had been developed in the USA in 1935 for use in the Florida Everglades. The idea caught the attention of the US Marine Corps, who improved the basic design and developed it into the military LVT. The initial version, the LVT1, was intended purely as a supply vehicle, and 200 were ordered. Subsequent models, however, were developed as amphibious assault vehicles, starting with the LVT2, whose rear-mounted engine was taken from the M3 light tank. To increase the size of the cargo compartment, the engine was moved forward and a loading ramp was installed at the rear. These modifications produced the LVT4. The first LVTs could carry 24 men or 4500lb (2000kg) of cargo, whereas the LTV4 could lift various cargo combinations, including a 4.13in (105mm) howitzer.

First action

The LVT first went into action during the landings by the US Marines on Guadalcanal in 1942. An armored fire support version, fitted with a turret and gun taken from the Stuart light tank, was known as an Amtank. A further variant, the LVT-3, had two Cadillac engines in side sponsons, allowing increased cargo space. Total production of the LVT family ran to 18,621 units.

Specifications

Armament: One 1.46in (37mm) cannon; one 0.50in (12.7mm) MG; three 0.30in (7.62mm) MGs

Armor: 0.512in (13mm)

Crew: 3 plus 24

Dimensions: Length 26ft 1in (7.95m); Width 10ft 8in (3.25m); Height 10ft 1in (3.01m)

Weight: 14.6 tons (14,878kg)

Powerplant: Continental W670-9A 7-cylinder radial, 250hp (186.6kW)

Speed: Road 25mph (40km/h); Water 7mph (11km/h)

Range: 125 miles (201km)

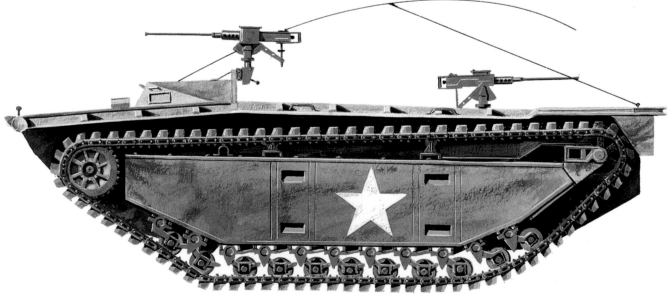

The Era of the Light Tank and Armored Car
⚒ **1940 USA**

Below: Built to replace the M2 light tank, the M3 was little more than an upgrade of that design. It quickly proved to be undergunned and underarmoured, but it was built in large numbers.

M3A1 STUART LIGHT TANK

The M3A1 light tank was the main combat version of the M2/M3 light tank series in service with the US Army when the United States entered the war in December 1941.

Specifications

(M5 model)

Armament: One 1.46in (37mm) M6 gun; three 0.30in (7.62mm) MGs

Armor: 2.5in (64mm)

Crew: 4

Dimensions: Length 14ft 3in (4.34m); Width 7ft 5in (2.25m); Height 7ft 7in (2.3m)

Weight: 14.7 tons (14,969kg)

Powerplant: Two Cadillac Series 42 V-8 110hp (82kW) each

Speed: 37mph (58km/h)

Range: 100 miles (161km)

Right: The M3A1 was used in all theaters of war. It was robust and reliable, performing well in all types of terrain. The British nicknamed it the "Honey."

After the fighting in France in 1940 had been assessed by neutral US observers, it was realized the M2 light tank was becoming rapidly obsolete, and steps were taken to improve it by adding thicker armor and incorporating a new suspension system to cope with the extra weight. The revised vehicle was designated M3A1. It entered production in 1941. The British Army was

the first to use it in combat and it fought widely during World War II.

Jeb Stuart

It was the British who named it the Stuart, after the Civil War General Jeb Stuart. About 170 Stuart tanks took part in Operation Crusader, the desert battle of November 1941, and although British tank crews complained about the weakness of its 1.46in (37mm) gun they praised its handling and reliability, which earned it the nickname "Honey." In American service, it first saw combat in the Philippines in 1942. The M3 was gradually replaced by an improved version with two Cadillac engines, the M5, from 1942, and in 1944 it was succeeded by the Light Tank M24. Many M3s were supplied to the Soviet Union, where, despite its deficiencies, it was superior to the equivalent Russian tanks then in service.

The Era of the Light Tank and Armored Car

1941 Italy

SEMOVENTE M41 SELF-PROPELLED GUN

The Semovente M41 was the most powerful of the Italian tank destroyers. It mounted a very effective 3.54in (90mm) antiaircraft gun on an M15/42 tank chassis.

Specifications

Armament: One 3.54in (90mm) cannon

Armor: Gun-crew protection only

Crew: 2

Dimensions: Length 17ft 9in (5.205m); Width 7ft 2in (2.20m); Height 7ft (2.15m)

Weight: 16.73 tons (17,000kg)

Powerplant: One SPA 15-TM-41 8-cylinder gasoline, 145bhp (108kW)

Speed: 22mph (35.5km/h)

Range: 124 miles (200km)

Above: *The Semovente M41 was a well-designed weapon, and its low profile made it well suited to combat in desert terrain, which was mostly flat. The Germans used M41s in a long-range artillery role after the Italian surrender.*

Although the M41 self-propelled gun was sometimes used against tanks, its primary function was as an assault gun. The weapon it carried, which was mounted at the rear of the M13 tank chassis, had much the same hitting power as the famous German 3.46in (88m). The two-man crew sat behind a gun shield which offered armored protection at the front and sides. In action, the M41 was intended to be used as "sniper" artillery, engaging targets at long range while staying outside the range of most counter-battery fire. Only 48 M41s were produced, the main reason being a shortage of the 90/53 cannons they used, most of which were diverted to meet antiaircraft requirements.

Desert terrain

The M41 was a very capable weapon, and was well suited to combat in the mostly flat desert terrain. Following Italy's armistice with the Allies in September 1943, the surviving Semovente M41s were seized by the Germans, who continued to use them until the end of World War II as long-range artillery, a role to which they were suited.

The Era of the Light Tank and Armored Car
✕ 1941 Japan

TYPE 1 CHI-HE MEDIUM TANK

The Japanese Type 1 Chi-He tank was the successor to the Type 97 Chi-Ha. It featured a more powerful engine, better armament, and improved armor protection.

Specifications

Armament: One 1.85in (47mm) gun, two 0.303in (7.7mm) MGs

Armor: 1.97in (50mm)

Crew: 5

Dimensions: Length 18ft 9in (5.5m); Width 7ft 8in (2.2m); Height 7ft 10in (2.38m)

Weight: 16.73 tons (17,000kg)

Powerplant: Mitsubishi Type 100 diesel V-12, 240bhp (179kW)

Speed: 27mph (43km/h)

Range: Unknown

The main improvement of this tank over the Type 97 Chi-Ha was its gun. This was a long-barrel 1.85in (47mm) weapon, which had a muzzle velocity of 888 yards (812m) per second, and double the penetrating power of the Type 97's low-velocity 2.24in (57mm). The turret was a new design, but Japan's industry was not equipped to produce the requisite number of hulls, so in most cases the new turret was mounted on a Type 97 chassis. Fifteen prototypes and evaluation models of the Type 1 were completed before the type went into mass production, but Japan's industrial capacity limited the output to 155 vehicles. The Type

1 Chi-He medium tank was followed by the Type 3 Chi-Nu, of which only 60 were built by the end of the World War II. In general, Japanese medium tanks were adequate for operations in the Pacific until they began to encounter the better armed and protected American types deployed from late 1942, but Japanese tank designers never seemed to match the expertise and development skill of their Western counterparts.

Below: *The Type I Chi-He medium tank was produced only in small numbers, and although it performed adequately in Japan's early Pacific campaigns it was never a match for improved American armor.*

The Era of the Light Tank and Armored Car
✷ 1941 Soviet Union

T-60 LIGHT TANK

Russia's T-60 light tank took part in a novel experiment in which, fitted with wings and tail unit, it was intended to be towed into battle as a glider. This concept was abandoned after one trial.

Below: Fitting the T-60 tank with flying surfaces so that it could be towed into battle like a glider was just one of many interesting experiments carried out by the Soviet military authorities before and during World War II.

The T-60 light tank was intended for the reconnaissance role, and was designed at the Moscow Factory No. 37, whose staff had already been responsible for the manufacture of two earlier AFVs, the T-30A and T-30B. The first of these was amphibious and was manufactured as the T-40; the second, designated the T-40S, was a dry-land version, which in the event proved too heavy and was abandoned. The combination of the T-30B prototype and the T-40 chassis, became the T-60. Production began in 1941, just after the German invasion. Armed with a 0.79in (20mm) cannon with a high muzzle velocity that enabled it to penetrate 0.58in (15mm) of perpendicular armor at 546.9 yards (500m), it was effective in its scouting role, but proved very vulnerable to tanks such as the Panzer III.

T60-A

The T-60A appeared in 1942. This was an improved version with better armor. One of the more interesting variants was intended to be converted into glider configuration by the addition of flying surfaces, and then towed into battle behind a large aircraft like the Tupolev TB-3. Only one trial was carried out, but the TB-3 had to cast the T-60 off as its weight and poor aerodynamics almost caused the tug aircraft to lose control. The T-60 made a safe landing.

Specifications

Armament: One 0.79in (20mm) ShVAK cannon; one 0.3in (7.62mm) DT MG

Armor: 0.275–0.98in (7–25mm)

Crew: 2

Dimensions: Length 13ft 6in (4.11m); Width 7ft 8in (2.3m); Height 5ft 8in (1.74m)

Weight: 6.3 tons (6400kg)

Powerplant: GAZ 203 gasoline, 70bhp (63kW) at 2800rpm

Speed: 28mph (45km/h)

Range: 280 miles (450km)

The Era of the Light Tank and Armored Car
✖ 1941 Sweden

STRIDSVAGEN M/40 LIGHT TANK

Sweden's Stridsvagen m/40 light tank was manufactured in large numbers in response to the potential threat from Germany, who had just invaded Norway and who coveted Sweden's natural resources.

Specifications

Armament: One 1.46in (37mm) gun; two MGs

Armor: 0.95in (24mm)

Crew: 3

Dimensions: Length 16ft 1in (4.9m); Width 6ft 11in (2.1m); Height 6ft 11in (2.1m)

Weight: 9.35 tons (9500kg)

Powerplant: Scania-Vabis 6-cylinder gasoline, 142bhp (106kW)

Speed: 30mph (48km/h)

Range: 125 miles (200km)

Below: Although it was never required to prove itself in combat, the Swedish m/40 light tank was more than capable of holding its own against similar fighting vehicles of other nations.

The Stridsvagn m/40 was the first Swedish tank to be manufactured in quantity and was ordered in substantial numbers by the Swedish Army. Several of its features showed that its designers had been influenced by a study of armored fighting vehicles being produced by the major powers.

Design features

The turret had a very modern design and the hull was well-proportioned, both welded and riveted with the engine at the rear. The tank had a hydraulic preselective gearbox combined with a high-low transfer box. Several different versions were produced, the last in 1944. There is no doubt that, had it been required to do so, the m/40 could have held its own in action against all but the most powerful German tanks. In late 1944, another perceived threat arose, this time from Russia, who had forced neighboring Finland to the armistice table and who would remain Sweden's principal cause for concern for decades to come. Over this time, Sweden would take even greater steps to ensure her neutrality remained intact.

The Era of the Light Tank and Armored Car

✖ **1941 UK**

CHURCHILL MARK IV INFANTRY TANK

The Churchill was without doubt the most important British tank to be produced in World War II, and gave rise to more variants than any other model. Its variations were crucial to the success of D-Day.

The Churchill tank was issued in 1939. It was the result of a request for a heavy AFV capable of breaking through obstacles, as the tanks of World War I were intended to do. During trials, however, it became apparent that a lighter tank would be needed, and so a revised specification was issued and allocated to Vauxhall Motors, who designed the Infantry Tank Mk IV, later to be named the Churchill. Starting from scratch, Vauxhall designed a well-armored tank with large, sturdy tracks. The design was completed by July 1940 and, with Britain in real danger of invasion following the collapse of France, the Churchill was ordered into production before its capability had been

Above: This artwork shows some of the Churchill's interior, including the driver's position, the gun breech, the engine compartment, and the suspension.

fully assessed. Many shortcomings were quickly revealed, including an engine that was underpowered and the same weak two-pounder gun that had been fitted to the earlier cruiser tanks. It put up a disastrous performance when it was first used in combat in support of the abortive and costly Dieppe landing operation in August 1942.

Variants

The tank was soon to vindicate itself with the Mk III version, however. Armed with a

Specifications

Armament: One 2pdr (1.57in/40mm) gun; two 0.31in (7.92mm) Besa MGs

Armor: 0.63–4.02in (16–102mm)

Crew: 5

Dimensions: Length 24ft 5in (7.442m); Width 11ft 4in (3.45m); Height 9ft (2.74m)

Weight: 39 tons (39,660kg)

Powerplant: Bedford Twin Six, 350bhp (261.1kW)

Speed: 14.9mph (24km/h)

Range: 88 miles (140km)

Right: *The Churchill was the most important British tank to go into production during World War II, and many different variants were produced. The specialized versions were to prove invaluable on D-Day.*

Below: *This photograph illustrates the Churchill's angular lines. It was a classic infantry tank, slow but heavily armored, and was more difficult to knock out than the American Sherman.*

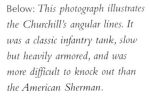

six-pounder gun, this was deployed to the Western Desert in time to take part in the decisive Battle of El Alamein in October 1942. The success of the Churchill continued, and a 2.95in (75mm) gun was introduced in the Mk VI version. The addition of more armor produced the Mk VII, which first went into action in support

of the Normandy landings in June 1944, and it was at this time that the special versions of the Churchill came into their own. These included the Churchill Mk III AVRE (Armoured Vehicle Royal Engineers, designed to knock out pillboxes and blockhouses at short range with its "flying dustbin" mortar bombs), the Churchill Mk III "Bobbin" (which could lay down a canvas mat 109 yards [100m] long to provide a road for vehicles over a soft beach surface), the Churchill Mk III bridge layer, and, most horrific and spectacular of all, the Churchill Mk VIII "Crocodile" (a flamethrowing tank that carried 400 gallons [1818 litres] of flame-gun fuel in a towed trailer). Compressed nitrogen forced the fuel from trailer to flame-gun, which was mounted in the normal machine-gun position, giving a range of about 120 yards (131m). The Churchill remained in first-line service with the British Army until 1952, and second-line recovery vehicles were not retired until 1965.

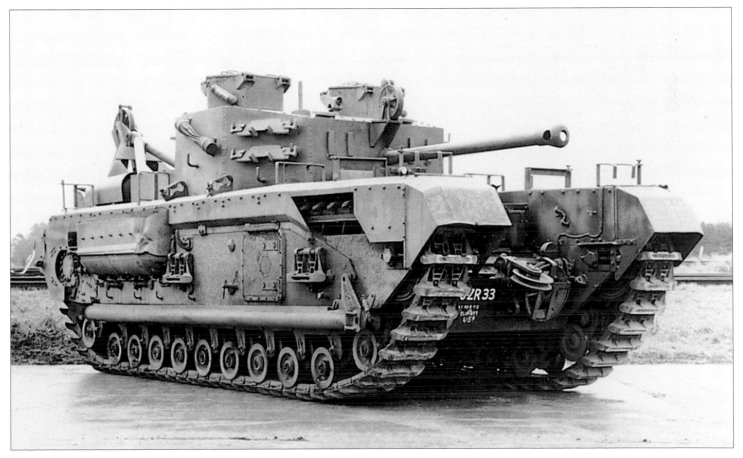

The Era of the Light Tank and Armored Car

✘ 1941 UK

HUMBER SCOUT CAR

Scout cars were in great demand in World War II and were used for all manner of duties. The British Army used two principal models, one produced by Daimler, the other by Humber.

At the outbreak of World War II, the principal producer of armored scout cars for the British Army was Daimler, but the increasingly pressing need for such vehicles could not be met by this company alone, and so other companies became involved. One of these was the Rootes group, which in 1942 produced a vehicle similar in layout to the Daimler Dingo. This was the Humber Scout Car, which carried a two-man crew, was fitted with a No. 19 radio set, and was armed with a Bren 0.303in (7.7mm) light machine gun. This was mounted on the roof and could be operated from inside the vehicle.

Vehicle usage

Between 1942 and 1945, when production ended, over 4000 Humber Scout Cars were delivered, being used for scouting and liaison by British armored units. The vehicles were also used by the Polish II Corps and the 1st Czechoslovakian Armored Brigade in Italy, and a few were used by the Italian Co-Belligerent Forces, who fought on the side of the Allies after Italy's surrender in 1943. The Humber, which was slightly larger and heavier than the Dingo, was generally considered to be less reliable than the Daimler vehicle.

Specifications

Armament: One 0.59in (15mm) Besa HMG (one 1.46in/37mm gun on the Mk 4); one 0.31in (7.92mm) Besa MG

Armor: 1.18in (30mm)

Crew: 3 (Mks 1 and 2); 4 (Mks 3 and 4)

Dimensions: Length 15ft (4.57m); Width 7ft 2in (2.18m); Height 7ft 10in (2.38m)

Weight: 6.85 tons (6960kg)

Powerplant: Rootes 6-cylinder gasoline, 90bhp (67.1kW) at 3200rpm

Speed: 45mph (72km/h)

Range: 250 miles (400km)

Left: *The angular little Humber Scout Car gave sterling service during World War II, especially in Italy, where they were used by British, Polish, and Czech forces. Some were also used by Italian Co-Belligerent forces after the Italian armistice.*

The Era of the Light Tank and Armored Car
✠ 1941 UK

MARK VII CRUISER TANK (CAVALIER)

The Mk VII Cavalier was one of Britain's unsuccessful cruiser tank ventures. It suffered from its American engine, which was underpowered. Later tanks had a version of the Rolls-Royce Merlin.

Specifications

Armament: One 6pdr (2.24in/57mm) gun; one or two Besa 0.312in (7.92mm) MGs

Armor: 0.79–2.99in (20–76mm)

Crew: 5

Dimensions: Length 20ft 10in (6.35m); Width 9ft 6in (2.88m); Height 8ft (2.428m)

Weight: 27 tons (27,432kg)

Powerplant: Nuffield Liberty gasoline V-12, 340bhp (253.64kW)

Speed: 24.22mph (39km/h)

Range: 164.57 miles (265km)

In 1941 the British General Staff issued a specification for a new tank to replace the Crusader, which was fast becoming obsolete and suffering unacceptable casualties. Nuffield produced a design, the Cavalier, which was ordered into production even before prototype trials had begun. This was unfortunate, because the tank was fitted with an American-made Liberty engine that was to give nothing but trouble throughout the vehicle's career, mainly because it was underpowered. The first choice for the Mk VII had been the Rolls-Royce Merlin, but in 1941 the entire production of this splendid powerplant was allocated to the RAF, and it would be some time before the manufacturing system could cope with the demands of the Army as well.

Above: Throughout its operational career, the Mk VII Cavalier cruiser tank suffered from the fact that it was fitted with an American Liberty engine, instead of the far superior Rolls-Royce Merlin that had originally been intended for it.

Variants

Variants of the Cavalier included an artillery observation post (where the gun was removed and replaced by radio equipment installed in the turret) and an armored recovery vehicle. In fact, most of the Cavaliers that were built ended up being either being converted to the recovery role, or they were used for training. All in all, the Cavalier was not really deemed a success.

Chapter 4

THE CHALLENGE OF TOTAL WAR

In October 1942 on the Leningrad front, Russian antitank gunners came face to face with the latest addition to the German tank arsenal. This was the formidable Tiger I, whose 3.94in (100mm) frontal armor defended against the Russians' 3in (76.2mm) antitank guns, and whose 3.15in (80mm) side armor could only be penetrated from the closest range. Fortunately for the Russians (and the British and Americans in North Africa—some Tigers were deployed to Tunisia in December 1942), the massive new Panzers were few in number.

Above: *The M5 Stuart VI tank, seen here, was powered by two Cadillac engines. Fitted with an M3A3 turret, it was the major variant in US service by 1943. Some 6800 examples were produced.*

Left: *The mighty Tiger tank, seen here in Russia in the summer of 1943, made a huge impact on the development of armored warfare. It was respected and feared right up to the end of World War II.*

Production only started in August, and the Tiger Mk I was plagued by technical problems. Nevertheless, the appearance of the Tiger, together with the Panther, another excellent German tank, precipitated a race that would see huge advances in armor and gunnery.

This was first put to the test in the Battle of Kursk, one of the truly decisive battles of the war, in July 1943. In 1944, when the latest Soviet T-34/85s and IS-2 tanks fought in Russia, the Sherman and Churchill tanks—as well as many lesser AFVs that fell into the medium category—confronted the same German tanks. They defeated them by numbers rather than technological mastery. The midwar years of 1943–44 brought about a revolution in tank design whose legacy remains today.

The Challenge Of Total War
1941 USA

M22 LOCUST LIGHT TANK

The M22 Locust was one of the smallest tanks used by the Allies in World War II. It was designed for airborne operations, providing firepower on and around a dropping zone until ground forces arrived.

Below: *Although development of the M22 light tank began in 1941, it was not deployed operationally until the closing months of Word War II, mainly because there was no aircraft big enough to airlift it into battle.*

Right: *The M22 served postwar with the Egyptian armed forces, and some were still in use in 1956, when Israel launched its attack toward the Suez Canal through the Sinai Peninsula.*

Designed to be airlifted into battle, the M22 faced an immediate problem: The only Allied transport aircraft capable of lifting it was the Douglas C-54, and this was only if the turret was removed and placed inside the fuselage, and the tank hull suspended below the wing. The solution to the problem was Britain's General Aircraft Hamilcar transport glider, which had been designed around the Mk VII Tetrarch light tank. The British Airborne forces took over the M22 and, towed into action inside the Hamilcar, it operated in support of the airborne landings by the 6th Airborne Division during Operation Varsity, the crossing of the Rhine at Wesel in March 1945. It was the British who gave the M22 the name Locust. Of 1900 Locusts ordered, only 830 were delivered. Some were issued to the Egyptian Army after the end of the World War II and used until 1956, when the Egyptian armed forces were re-equipped with Soviet material. The Locust carried a crew of three; the commander and gunner in the turret, and the driver in the hull. The vehicle was designed and built by the Marmon Herrington Corporation.

Specifications

Armament: One 1.46in (37mm) M6 cannon; one 0.30in (7.62mm) MG

Armor: 0.98in (25mm)

Crew: 3

Dimensions: Length 12ft 11in (3.94m); Width 7ft 4in (2.23m); Height 5ft 8in (1.74m)

Weight: 7.3 tons (7439kg)

Powerplant: Lycoming O-435T 6-cylinder radial, 162hp (121kW)

Speed: 40mph (64km/h)

Range: 135 miles (217km)

The Challenge Of Total War

⚔ 1941 USA

M3 GRANT/LEE MEDIUM TANK

The M3 medium tank was a hurried design, but it was armed with a powerful 2.95in (75mm) gun. It finally gave the Allies a fighting chance in combat against the Panzers.

Above: *This photograph clearly shows the position of the M3's 2.95in (75mm) gun in its sponson mounted on the right of the hull. This example has a modified turret.*

Specifications

(M3 medium tank [Lee Mk I])

Armament: One 2.95in (75mm) M2 or M3 cannon; one 1.46in (37mm) M5 or M6 cannon; four 0.30in (7.62mm) MGs

Armor: 2.24in (57mm)

Crew: 6

Dimensions: Length 18ft 6in (5.64m); Width 8ft 11in (2.72m); Height 10ft 3in (3.12m)

Weight: 26.7 tons (27,216kg)

Powerplant: Continental R-975-EC2 or E1 radial gasoline, 340hp (253.5kW)

Speed: 26mph (42km/h)

Range: 120 miles (193km)

The action of the German Panzers in France rendered the existing American tanks obsolete.

As a result of this, the American Army issued a specification for a new tank armed with a 2.95in (75mm) gun. This eventually materialized as the M4 Sherman, but in the interim they took the existing M2 and modified it, retaining the 1.46in (37mm) turret but adding a new 2.95in (75mm) main armament mounted in a sponson on the right-hand side of the hull. The redesigned tank was ordered into mass production. The British Army ordered it in large numbers to replace lost armor.

Above: *Designed to fill the gap until deployment of the M4 Sherman, the M3 Grant gave a massive boost to British Commonwealth forces in the Western Desert.*

General Grant

In British service the vehicle, which was fitted with a modified turret with a lower profile, was named the General Grant, while unaltered vehicles were named General Lee. The M3 went into action for the first time in the Western Desert in 1942, bringing much improved firepower to the Commonwealth armored divisions. Production of the M3 ended in December 1942, by which time 6258 units had been produced.

The Challenge Of Total War

🔨 1942 **Australia**

SENTINEL AUSTRALIAN CRUISER MARK I

Although it was produced hastily as a "panic measure," the Australian AC1 Sentinel, based on the American M3, was an effective AFV and would have acquitted itself well in combat.

The Sentinel Australian Cruiser Mk I was designed mainly in response to the outbreak of war in Europe. The war not only deprived Australia of defense materials normally shipped from England, but also made northern Australia vulnerable to the threat of a Japanese invasion. Attacks on Darwin and other targets in 1942 made this threat very real.

Left: *The Sentinel's original two-pounder gun was too puny to be effective, so successive models were armed with the 25-pounder and, ultimately, the 17-pounder antitank weapon.*

Specifications

Designs were drawn up following orders for a cruiser tank armed with a two-pounder (1.57in/40mm) gun and using as many components as possible of the American M3. The tank, first known as Australian Cruiser I (ACI), had an all-cast hull and was powered by three Cadillac engines. The first models were ready by January 1942, and received the name Sentinel. A follow-on version (the Sentinel AC3) was armed with a 25-pounder (3.45in/87.6mm) gun in place of the inadequate two-pounder (1.57in/40mm). However, this would clearly be ineffective against armor and so production switched to the Sentinel AC4, armed with a 17-pounder (3in/76.2mm) antitank gun in 1943. The Sentinel was never used in combat, but some vehicles, masquerading as Panzers, featured in the film *The Rats Of Tobruk*.

Specifications

Armament: One 2pdr (1.57in/40mm) gun; two 0.3in (7.62mm) MGs

Armor: 2.6in (65mm)

Crew: 5

Dimensions: Length 20ft 9in (6.4m); Width 9ft 1in (2.8m); Height; 8ft 5in (2.59m)

Weight: 28 tons (28,489kg)

Powerplant: Three Cadillac V-8 gasoline engines, 117bhp (87kW), in cloverleaf layout

Speed: 30mph (48km/h)

Range: 198 miles (319km)

Left: *Despite the fact that it was rushed into productiion, the Sentinel was a remarkably effective design with many innovations. This is the AC4, which had a 17-pounder gun.*

RAM I/II CRUISER TANK

Although Canada had no armored forces in 1939, its army was expanding rapidly. A cruiser tank was built to provide infantry support, resulting in Ram I/II. This was never actually issued in combat.

Above: *The Ram Mk I, seen here, was originally equipped with a two-pounder gun, but this was soon replaced by a much more effective six-pounder.*

Specifications

(Ram Mk II)

Armament: One 6pdr (2.24in/57mm) gun; three 0.3in (7.62mm) MGs

Armor: 3.42in (87mm)

Crew: 5

Dimensions: Length 19ft (5.791m); Width 9ft 1in (2.768m); Height 8ft 9in (2.667m)

Weight: 29 tons (29,484kg)

Powerplant: Continental R-975 9-cylinder air-cooled radial gasoline engine, 400bhp (298kW) at 2400rpm

Speed: 25mph (40.23km/h)

Range: 144 miles (232km)

Canada had to start from scratch with the manufacture of tanks, and this task was assigned to the Montreal Locomotive Works (now known as the Canadian Tank Arsenal). The original tank, based on the American M3, was designed to take a two-pounder (1.57in/40mm) gun, but experience abroad proved this to be inadequate. Its turret was redesigned to take a larger gun when one became available. The prototype Ram Mk I appeared in June 1941 and production began in November. In February 1942 production switched to the improved Ram Mk II, which was armed with a six-pounder (2.24in/57mm) gun. Work continued until July 1943, when the decision was taken to equip British and

Above: *The Ram I used the chassis of the American M3, but mounted its main armament in a turret rather than in a sponson as on the original US vehicle.*

Canadian armored units with the M4 Sherman tank.

Use of the Ram I/II

Although the Ram cruiser tank was never used in the role for which it was intended, some Ram conversions saw combat in Europe. After the war, about 100 Rams were taken over by the Dutch Army, which formed its first armored units with them.

ELEFANT HEAVY TANK DESTROYER

The Elefant was extremely heavy and slow. This meant that in practice it was better suited to the role of assault gun than that of tank destroyer. Most models were used in Russia.

Above: *The Elefant had a powerful 3.46in (88mm) antitank gun.*

Two German firms, Porsche and Henschel, vied for the production contract that was issued for the Tiger tank (then still in the design stage). In the event it was the Henschel design that was selected to become the PzKpfw VI Tiger, but the Porsche design was used in production as a tank destroyer. The 3.46in (88mm) dual antitank/antiaircraft gun was mounted in a large armored superstructure. Porsche received a contract to build 90 units under the name of Panzerjäger Tiger (P), although the tank became better known as either the Ferdinand or the Elefant. The (P) denoted Porsche, the company of origin.

Battle of Kursk
Most Elefant production took place in the

Above: *The Elefant was one of the failures of the German Panzerjäger designers. Despite its excellent main armament, it was far too cumbersome and, more importantly, the first examples lacked any kind of self-defense armament, making them vulnerable to infantry attack. In general, it was much too complex and unreliable.*

first half of 1943, so that the vehicles were ready for the great summer offensive of that year, which began in July with the Battle of Kursk. The Elefants' participation in the battle ended in disaster. The vehicles were too heavy and cumbersome and lacked any means of self-defense. Most were put out of action by specially trained Russian tank-killer squads, who blew off their tracks with explosive charges.

Specifications

Armament: One 3.46in (88mm) antitank gun; one 0.312in (7.92mm) MG

Armor: Maximum, 7.87in (200mm)

Crew: 6

Dimensions: Length 26ft 8.4in (8.14m); Width 11ft 1in (3.38m); Height 9ft 8.9in (2.97m)

Weight: approx 64 tons (65,000kg)

Powerplant: Two Maybach HL120TRM, V-12 gasoline, each developing 300hp (223.7kW)

Speed: Road, 18.6mph (30km/h)

Range: Road, 93.2 miles (150km)

Above: *The Marder II was numerically one of the most important German tank-destroyers, but its profile was rather high and it lacked protection.*

The Challenge Of Total War
⚒ **1942 Germany**

MARDER TANK DESTROYERS

The first of the Marder (Marten) series of tank destroyers, the Marder I, was built on the chassis of the Lorraine armored vehicle, hundreds of which were captured after the fall of France.

The Wehrmacht needed a powerful, mobile tank destroyer, and this assumed a new urgency toward the end of 1941, particularly on the Eastern Front. The appearance of the T-34 had come as an unpleasant surprise. As an interim measure, antitank guns were mounted on the bases of vehicles such as the obsolete Panzer II and captured vehicles like the Tracteur Blindé 37L Lorraine (a French artillery mover and armored personnel carrier). The result was the Marder series, whose vehicles were armed either with the 2.95in (75mm) PaK (Panzer Abwehr Kanone) 40 or the captured Russian 0.3in (7.62mm) F22 field gun. The Marder I, developed in May 1942, carried the PaK 1.57in (40mm) gun that was mounted in an open-topped crew compartment on a Lorraine chassis. About 170 Marder Is were built, some being conversions of French Hotchkiss and FCM light tanks.

Conversions

The Panzer II conversion was known as the Marder II, while the Marder III was a conversion of the Panzerkampfwagen PzKpfw 38 (t). Unlike the Marder I and II, which were used mainly in Russia, the Marder III was deployed on all fronts.

Below: *This Marder III was captured in North Africa in April 1943. The tank was armed with an effective 2.95in (75mm) gun, and was a very simple conversion of a Czech-produced tank chassis.*

Specifications

(Marder II 1942)
Armament: One 2.95in (75mm) antitank gun; one 0.312in (7.92mm) MG

Armor: Maximum, 1.38in (35mm)

Crew: 3

Dimensions: Length 20ft 10.4in (6.36m); Width 7ft 5.75in (2.28m); Height 7ft 2.6in (2.2m)

Weight: approx 10.63 tons (10,800kg)

Powerplant: Maybach HL62 TRM, 6-cylinder gasoline, 140hp (104.4kW)

Speed: Road, 24.8mph (40km/h)

Range: Road, 118 miles (190km)

The Challenge Of Total War
🔧 **1942 Germany**

PANZERKAMPFWAGEN V PANTHER

The Panther was intended as a counter to the T-34. Although it was probably the best German tank to emerge during World War II, it was too complex to build quickly enough.

Specifications

(PzKpfw V Ausführung G)

Armament: One 2.95in (75mm) gun; three 0.312in (7.92mm) MGs

Armor: Maximum, hull, 3.15in (80mm)

Crew: 5

Dimensions: Length 29ft 1in (8.865m); Width 11ft 3in (3.43m); Height 9ft 9in (2.97m)

Weight: 44.75 tons (45,465kg)

Powerplant: Maybach HL230P30, V-12 gasoline, 700hp (522kW)

Speed: Road, 34mph (54.7km/h)

Range: Road, 110 miles (177km)

By the end of 1941 it had become clear to the German General Staff that something had to be done to redress the armored balance with Russia. This was tilting in the Russians' favor thanks to the deployment of the T-34, which was more than a match for the Panzer IV. Two German companies—Daimler-Benz and MAN of Augsburg—were given the task of designing a powerful new tank, and the MAN design was accepted in May 1942. By September 1942 a prototype was being tested, and the vehicle, designated Panzerkampfwagen V Panther (SdKfz 171) was ordered into immediate production.

Below: *Cutaway showing the interior of the Panther V. Without doubt the best German tank of World War II, the Panther was hampered by its complexity, which created many problems on operations. The complicated nature of the vehicle is apparent in this illustration.*

Above: *The Panther was rushed into production without proper trials, and numerous faults soon became apparent. In its early days, more Panthers were lost through technical failure than enemy action.*

Combat

The Panther was first used in the Battle of Kursk in July 1943 and did not perform well. It was plagued with a number of problems. On July 10, only 38 Panthers were serviceable out of 200 deployed with XLVIII Panzer Korps. Once these early problems were solved, however, the Panther became a formidable fighting machine. It was widely used in Normandy in the weeks after D-Day as well as on the Russian Front. Some vehicles were used by the French Army for some time after World War II.

Right: *This photograph shows an early model Panther. In later models, armored skirts were added to offer some protection to the wheels, and the tank was covered in antimagnetic paste as a protection against magnetic mines.*

The Challenge Of Total War
1942 Germany

PANZERKAMPFWAGEN VI TIGER I

The Tiger I tank was developed in some haste in 1941. It was designed to combat the Russian KV-1, and was first used in the fall of 1942. It was so impressive that it tended to dominate the enemy whenever it appeared.

Although it was a brilliant, robust design, featured a 700hp (514.3kW) engine, and had a gearbox with eight forward and four reverse gears, the Tiger I showed serious deficiencies under operational conditions. It had a range of only 70 miles (112.7km) and despite the ingenious interleaving of bogies in the torsion bar suspension to enhance mobility, it was incompatible with the fast-moving Panzer divisions. This meant that it was rejected by the German tank leaders, who preferred the more mobile, smaller tanks which could be manufactured in greater quantity. Despite this, the Tiger I could easily afford to exchange shots with most enemy tanks at long range, and it had a deep-wading capability, which was unique among German tanks.

Above: *It is easy to see why the Tiger spread terror among its opponents wherever it appeared. The whole configuration of the tank exudes menace, and its enemies must have despaired of finding the means to counter it.*

Specifications

Armament: One 3.46in (88mm) gun; two or three 0.312in (7.92mm) MGs

Armor: Maximum, hull, 3.94in (100mm)

Crew: 5

Dimensions: Length 27ft 8.675in (8.45m); Width 11ft 3.8in (3.56m); Height 9ft 10in (3m)

Weight: Combat, approx 56 tons (56,900kg)

Powerplant: Maybach HL230P45, V-12 gasoline, 700hp (514.3kW)

Speed: Road, 23mph (37km/h)

Range: Road, 121 miles (195km)

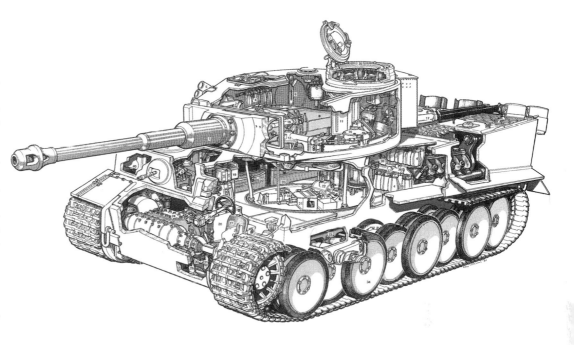

Right: *Cutaway showing the internal workings of the Tiger I. The Tiger I represented a new approach that emphasized firepower and armor at the expense of mobility, but this was not critical as it could knock out most Allied tanks while remaining outside the range of their guns.*

Below: *A Tiger I advancing along a typical dirt road in Russia. When the dirt turned to mud, and the mud froze like concrete to the tracks, the Tiger was always in danger of becoming immobilized.*

Geographical use

The Tiger I was originally named as the PzKw VI Ausführung H, although it was commonly known simply as the Tiger. The Tiger I—despite a number of technical problems that combined to reduce its operational efficiency—performed very well on the Eastern Front and in Tunisia. Comparatively few, however, were used in North Africa, as a result of air and submarine attacks from Malta on the Axis supply convoys.

Design

The Tiger I had frontal armor up to 4.72in (120mm) thick, with 3.15in (80mm) on the sides and back, and this proved very effective at stopping rounds from most antitank guns. The Tiger could knock out its most common opponents (the T-34, Sherman, and Churchill IV) at ranges exceeding 1600 yards, whereas the T-34 could not penetrate the frontal armor at any range, although it could penetrate the Tiger's side armor at a range of 500 yards or less. This was also true of the M4 Sherman. Wherever possible, this tank engaged a Tiger in units of four or more to get in close enough for a kill. In the later stages of World War II, the biggest threat to the Tiger was the rocket-armed fighter bomber. Even then, this was not sufficiently accurate to be sure of a kill against a single vehicle, but was reasonably effective against concentrations of tanks.

Withdrawal

The Tiger I was phased out from January 1944, with the introduction of the Panzerkampfwagen VI Tiger II Ausführung B. By this time, 1355 models had been built.

NASHORN TANK DESTROYER

Initially known as the Hornisse (Hornet), the Nashorn (Rhinoceros) tank destroyer was intended as an interim measure. It proved to be one of the most successful vehicles of its kind, however.

Left: *The soldier posing on this captured and rather battered Nashorn gives a good idea of the size of the vehicle's powerful 3.46in (88mm) gun. The rear decking and side armor appear to have been removed.*

Below: *The Nashorn was very much one of the interim tank-destroyer designs, for although the gun was mounted behind armor at the front and sides, the armor was relatively thin and the top and rear were open, making the crew vulnerable.*

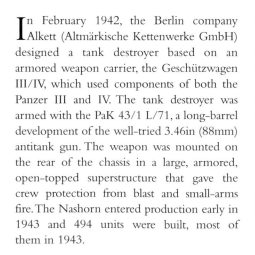

In February 1942, the Berlin company Alkett (Altmärkische Kettenwerke GmbH) designed a tank destroyer based on an armored weapon carrier, the Geschützwagen III/IV, which used components of both the Panzer III and IV. The tank destroyer was armed with the PaK 43/1 L/71, a long-barrel development of the well-tried 3.46in (88mm) antitank gun. The weapon was mounted on the rear of the chassis in a large, armored, open-topped superstructure that gave the crew protection from blast and small-arms fire. The Nashorn entered production early in 1943 and 494 units were built, most of them in 1943.

Use of Nashorn

The Nashorn was first used in the Battle of Kursk, where, unlike the Elefant, it acquitted itself very well, mainly because of its ability to engage enemy targets at long ranges. The Nashorn served on all fronts for the remainder of World War II, and one commander, Hauptmann Albert Ernst, destroyed 14 Russian tanks in a single day in December 1943. Two Nashorns survive as museum pieces—one in the United States Ordnance Museum and the other in the Kubinka Tank Museum, Moscow.

Specifications

Armament: One 3.46in (88mm) antitank gun; one 0.312in (7.92mm) MG

Armor: Maximum, 1.18in (30mm)

Crew: 4

Dimensions: Length 27ft 8.3in (8.44m); Width 9ft 4.6in (2.86m); Height 8ft 8.3in (2.65m)

Weight: approx 23.62 tons (24,000kg)

Powerplant: Maybach HL120TRM, V-12 gasoline, 300hp (223.7kW)

Speed: Road, 26mph (42km/h)

Range: Road, 133.6 miles (215km)

The Challenge Of Total War
✗ 1942 Italy

CARRO ARMATO M15/42 MEDIUM TANK

The M15/42 of 1943 was the latest tank in the Fiat medium AFV series, incorporating various improvements as a result of experience gained in the Desert War.

Specifications

Armament: One 1.85in (47mm) gun; two MGs
Armor: 0.24–1.65in (6–42mm)
Crew: 4
Dimensions: Length 16ft 2in (4.92m); Width 7ft 3in (2.20m); Height 7ft 10in (2.4m)
Weight: 14.37 tons (14,600kg)
Powerplant: SPA 8TM41 V8 diesel, 145bhp (108kW) at 1900rpm
Speed: 22mph (35km/h)
Range: 25 miles (200km)

The Fiat Carro Armato M15/42 medium tank first appeared in January 1943 and was essentially an upgrade of the M13/40. It was fitted with a more powerful diesel engine, as well as air filters to cope with desert sand conditions. The engine gave the tank a higher top speed than its predecessor, and also gave extra armor protection with an associated performance penalty. The M15/42 was distinguishable from its predecessor, the M14/41, in being slightly longer, with a crew access door in the side of the hull.

Geographical location

Most of the M15/42s built were issued to the Ariete Division, which had been evacuated from Africa and was resting and refitting in Italy. After the Italian surrender in September 1943 the division was moved to central Italy and the M15/42s took part in the defense of Rome against German Panzergrenadier and paratroop units intent on occupying the city. The Italians lost the battle and many of their tanks were taken over by the Germans, who ordered the construction of 28 more M15/42s.

Below: *The dejected appearance of this M15/42, with its gun drooping, rather sums up the history of the tank, whose performance in combat was far less effective than that of its Allied opponents.*

The Challenge Of Total War
⚒ 1942 Japan

TYPE 2 KA-M1 AMPHIBIOUS TANK

The Japanese led the way in the development of amphibious AFVs, experimenting with a prototype in 1928. They never made proper use of the concept, however, and too few of these vehicles were produced.

Below: The Type 2 amphibious landing craft was a very good design. It was simple and robust, and in 1942 it compared well with anything the Allies had to offer. Its problem was that it was not produced in sufficient quantity.

The Japanese Army pioneered the development of amphibious AFVs in the early 1930s. They tested the concept with a prototype halftrack, but the project was abandoned when the vehicle demonstrated a lack of cross-country mobility. However, further experiments were carried out with a Type 95 Ha-Go light tank, in which the AFV was fitted with kapok-filled floats, and the resulting combination was driven by two outboard motors.

Pacific campaigns

In 1940 the Imperial Japanese Navy took over the amphibious vehicle development program, and in 1942 devised the Type 2 Ka-Mi. This was intended for use by the Navy's Special Naval Landing Forces in the invasion of Pacific islands, where port facilities were lacking. The hull had built-in buoyancy chambers, and extra buoyancy was provided by steel pontoons fitted fore and

aft, the rearmost being fitted with steering rudders. Only 184 Type 2 Ka-Mi craft were built and these were used with some success, providing support for invading troops in Japan's early Pacific campaigns. Later on, however, the tank was used most often in a static defense role, dug in as part of beach defenses.

Below: The Ka-Mi was an ingenious adaptation of a light tank for the amphibious role in a similar fashion to some Duplex Drive M4 Shermans, which were used in the invasion of Normandy.

Specifications

Armament: One 1.46in (37mm) cannon; two 0.303in (7.7mm) MGs

Armor: 0.51in (13mm)

Crew: 5

Dimensions: Length 24ft 4in (7.42m); Width 9ft 3in (2.79m); Height 7ft 8in (2.34m)

Weight: 12.3 tons (12,500kg)

Powerplant: Mitsubishi 6-cylinder diesel, 115bhp (86kW)

Speed: road 23mph (37km/h); water 6mph (10km/h)

Range: Road, 125 miles (200km); Water, 94 miles (150km)

The Challenge Of Total War
⚒ 1942 Japan

TYPE 3 KA-CHI AMPHIBIOUS TANK

The Type 3 Ka-Chi amphibious tank showed off the ingenuity of Japanese designers again, but they lacked sufficient industrial resources to produce these tanks in any quantity.

Specifications

Armament: One 1.85in (47mm) gun; two 0.303in (7.7mm) MGs

Armor: 1.97in (50mm)

Crew: 5–7

Dimensions: Length 33ft 9in (10.3m); Width 9ft 9in (3m); Height 12ft 6in (3.82m)

Weight: 28.25 tons (28,700kg)

Powerplant: Mitsubishi Type 100 V-12 diesel, 240bhp (179kW)

Speed: Road, 20mph (32km/h); Water, 6mph (10km/h)

Range: 198 miles (319km)

The Type 3 Ka-Chi amphibious AFV was a heavier equivalent of the Type 2 Ka-Mi and was based on the Type 1 Chi-He chassis (although it was heavily modified and incorporated front and rear flotation pontoons). The forward pontoon had a curved bow shape, and both could be jettisoned after the vehicle had gone ashore. The turret retained the Che-He Type 1's 1.85in (47mm) main armament, but had a circular cupola designed to keep the hatch above water. Behind the turret, a vertical exhaust tower served a similar purpose. The Type 3 Ka-Chi was first used in action in the battle for Kwajalein Atoll in January 1944, where it was used in a static role as part of

Above: The Ka-Chi was based on a successful tank design, so it was still a capable fighting machine when it was ashore.

the beach-line defense system. Only 19 Type 3 Ka-Chi AFVs were produced, being scattered piecemeal with Japanese forces throughout the Pacific.

Capture by the Americans

The Americans captured one Type 3 Ka-Chi vehicle and found it to be viable in its intended role. It gave impetus to the development of amphibious tanks by the Americans that would be used to good effect in the invasion of Normandy.

The Challenge Of Total War

1942 Soviet Union

SU-76 ASSAULT GUN

The SU-76 was a hurried wartime conversion of the T-70 light tank, fitted with a 3in (76.2mm) gun. It was produced in large numbers and proved its success on the Eastern Front in 1943.

The SU-76 was something of an expedient. It was ordered into production at a time when the Soviet Army, having suffered massive losses in the second half of 1941, was in desperate need of AFVs. It was produced to help the Russian forces stem the German advance. One weapon to do this was the Zis-3 3in (76mm) artillery piece, which also had an excellent antitank capability. As the fighting so far had shown that Russian light tanks were virtually useless in combat, the T-70 light tank (already on the production line) was converted as a vehicle for the Zis-3 gun. The end product was the SU-76. "SU" denoted Samokhodnaya Ustanovka, or self-propelled mounting.

Above: *A conversion of the T-70 light tank, the SU-76 was rushed into production as a desperate attempt to find some means of engaging the latest German Panzers.*

Use of SU-76

Some necessary modification to the T-70 chassis meant that the SU-76 did not enter production until late 1942, and it was mid-1943 before it was issued to the Red Army. An early batch had been rebuilt with a different engine drive system. It subsequently performed very well, although it was completely lacking in comfort and disliked by its crews. The SU-76 was supplied to several Soviet satellite countries after the war.

Specifications

Armament: One 3in (76.2mm) Zis-3 L/41 gun

Armor: 0.39–1.37in (10–35mm)

Crew: 4

Dimensions: Length 16ft 5in (5m); Width 8ft 10in (2.7m); Height 6ft 11in (2.1m)

Weight: 10 tons (10,200kg)

Powerplant: Two GAZ-203 6-cylinder gasoline engines, 138bhp (103kW) at 3400rpm

Speed: 28mph (45km/h)

Range: 199 miles (320km)

The Challenge Of Total War
☭ **1942 Soviet Union**

T-70 LIGHT TANK

The T-70 was already an anachronism by the time it entered service.

The emphasis had switched to heavier tanks with better armor.

Specifications

Armament: One 1.77in (45mm) L/46 gun; one 0.3in (7.62mm) DT MG

Armor: 0.39–1.77in (10–45mm)

Crew: 2

Dimensions: Length 14ft 1in (4.29m), Width 7ft 7in (2.32m); Height 6ft 8in (2.04m)

Weight: 9 tons (9200kg)

Powerplant: Two GAZ 202 6-cylinder gasoline engines, 85bhp (104kW) at 3600rpm

Speed: 28mph (45km/h)

Range: Unknown

The T-70 light tank was produced in an attempt to combine the roles of the T-60 reconnaissance tank and the T-50 infantry support tank. Armed with a 1.77in (45mm) L/46 gun with 45 rounds of ammunition, the tank was operated by a crew of two—the driver and the commander, who also loaded and fired the gun. Commanding a tank platoon was virtually impossible: The commander had to devote his time to acquiring targets and loading and firing both the main armament and the machine gun, as well as issuing orders to the driver.

Production

Production of the T70 took place between March 1942 and October 1943, by which time 8226 vehicles had been completed. The first batch of T-70s had a GAZ-202 automotive engine on either side of the hull, one driving each track. The tank was soon redesigned with the engines in line on the right-hand side of the tank, with normal transmission and differential. A development, the T-80, featuring a two-man turret, was produced in small numbers. Its run was terminated when all light tank production was canceled in October 1943.

Below: *The T-70 light tank was a useful reconnaissance vehicle that was let down by its main armament. The 1.77in (45mm) gun with which it was armed was virtually useless against most German tanks. In action it was adequate, but far from outstanding.*

The Challenge Of Total War
⚔ 1942 Sweden

STRIDSVAGN M/42 LIGHT TANK

This was one of the last in the line of Sweden's light tanks, remaining

in first-line service until it was replaced by a British tank, the

Mk III Centurion.

The Stridsvagn m/42 of 1942 was developed from a succession of Swedish tanks that were the products of the Landswerk company. These included the L/60, which had welded construction and some sloped armor, and was armed with a 0.79in (20mm) cannon. The L/60 was adopted by Hungary and became known as the Toldi light tank. With its 0.79in (20mm) gun it was roughly comparable to the German Panzer II or Soviet T-60. The L/60 was also the chassis on which the Lanswerk Anti self-propelled 1.57in (40mm) gun was built. The immediate antecedent of the Strv m/42 was the Strv m/40, although the m/42 was longer and featured a redesigned turret and a larger mantel. It had six roadwheels on

Above: *This photograph depicts a four-wheeled armored personnel carrier version of the Stridswagen m/42, one of the most important AFVs in the Swedish Army's inventory during and after World War II.*

either side, and two spare roadwheels were suspended at the back of the turret.

Service
The m/42 was issued to the heavy tank companies of the Swedish Army's armored brigades, and remained in service until it was replaced by the Swedish version of the British Centurion Mk III. A four-wheel armored personnel carrier version of the m/42 was also developed. This was not fitted with a main gun, and was faster and more agile.

Specifications

Armament: One 2.9in (75mm) gun; three MGs

Armor: 3.15in (80mm)

Crew: 4

Dimensions: Length 16ft 1in (4.90m); Width 7ft 4in (2.20m); Height 5ft 3in (1.61m)

Weight: 22.14 tons (22,500kg)

Powerplant: Scania-Vabis, 320bhp (239kW)

Speed: 27mph (45km/h)

Range: 124 miles (200km)

The Challenge Of Total War
1942 USA

M10 TANK DESTROYER

The American M10 was produced in greater numbers than any other US AFV of its kind. It was the main armament of the US Army's tank destroyer battalions, and was also used by the British, French, and Italians.

Right: *The M10 was intended to be the principal weapon in the armory of the US Army's Tank Destroyer Command. Although relatively lightly armored, the M10 was fast and agile. In British Army service the M10 was called the Wolverine.*

Specifications

Armament: One 3in (76mm) M7 gun; one 0.50in (12.7mm) MG
Armor: 1.46in (37mm)
Crew: 5
Dimensions: Length (with gun) 19ft 7in (5.97m); Width 10ft (3.05m); Height 8ft 2in (2.49m)
Weight: 28.6 tons (29,028kg)
Powerplant: Two GMS6-71 diesels
Speed: 30mph (48km/h)
Range: 200 miles (322km)

The M10 was the result of a very sound tactical concept developed in the 1930s by the US Army. This planned for a tank destroyer force comprising both towed and self-propelled antitank guns. It was intended to be deployed *en masse* to disrupt an armored attack, leaving tanks to perform an infantry support role. One of the first vehicles to meet this requirement was the 3in (76mm) Gun Motor Carriage M10, which used the main chassis of the M4A2 Sherman medium tank, surmounted by an M7 3in (76mm) gun in a turret with a 360-degree traverse.

Production

The M10 went into production in September 1942. America's production capacity was large enough that 4993 units came off the assembly line before the end of the year, when production ceased. Most of these vehicles were issued to the US Army's 106 tank destroyer battalions. The tank was also used by the British Army (who named it the Wolverine) and later by the Free French and Italian Co-Belligerent forces. The British fitted the excellent 17-pounder antitank guns to some of their M10s, which were then named Achilles.

Below: *Late in the war the M10 was supplemented by a developed version, the M36, seen here. The M36 mounted a 3.54in (90mm) gun, still mounted in an open-topped turret.*

The Challenge Of Total War

⚒ 1942 USA

M4 SHERMAN COMBAT TANK

The M4 Sherman was the first truly effective combat tank produced by

the United States, and was greatly superior to its predecessor, the M3.

It proved to be a match for the Panzer IVF.

Armed with an excellent dual-purpose 2.95in (76mm) gun, the Sherman M4A1 finally gave the Allies a tank that could outmatch the German 3.46in (88mm) antitank gun, which had proved deadly when engaging earlier AFVs. Several different versions were produced: Some Shermans had very reliable diesel engines, while others had gasoline radial engines, originally made for aircraft. The gasoline-engined variants were

Above: *A Sherman Crab in action. Serving with the 79th Armored Division, these tanks were an enormous asset during the D-Day landings.*

unpopular. They were prone to catching fire after being hit. The Germans nicknamed them "Tommy Cookers," after a portable stove used in the previous war, or "Ronsons," after the famous brand of lighter. Another problem was that the Sherman could be very difficult to evacuate, especially if the main gun turret came to rest at the wrong angle and prevented one or the other of the forward hatches from being opened.

Production

Using the same basic hull and suspension as the M3, the first M4 was produced in September 1941. It was first known as the Medium Tank T6, and went into mass production as the M4. The first standard production model of this extremely important fighting vehicle was the

Specifications

Armament: One 2.95in (75mm) gun; one 0.5in (12.7mm) MG; two 0.30in (7.62mm) MGs

Armor: 2.44in (62mm)

Crew: 5

Dimensions: Length 19ft 4in (5.88m); Width 8ft 7in (2.68m); Height 9m (2.74m)

Weight: 74.5 tons (75,705kg)

Powerplant: Wright R-975-C1, radial, 9-cylinder

Speed: 24mph (39km/h)

Range: 100 miles (160km)

Below: *The Sherman Crab was the most widely used mine-clearance flail tank of World War II. Other tanks were also fitted with flails, but the Sherman was the preferred carrier.*

Right: *Shermans disembarking from a Landing Ship (Tank). The name Sherman was bestowed on the M4 by the British, who used large numbers, from the desert to the final battles in northwest Europe.*

M4A1 (Sherman II) with a fully cast rather than a cast/welded hull; other main variants were the M4A2 (Sherman III) with a welded hull, the M4A3 (Sherman IV) and the M4A4 (Sherman V). Some of the later versions mounted a 2.99in (76mm) gun. All versions had different engines, all progressively more powerful. The British Army acquired large numbers of Shermans, and took them into action for the first time at the Battle of El Alamein in October 1942. As they had done with the Churchill tank, the British modified numbers of Shermans for special tasks, such as flamethrowing and clearing paths through minefields.

Shortcomings

Although the Sherman had the edge over the Panzer IV, it stood little chance in a one-to-one encounter with later German AFVs like the Tiger and Panther, which had strengthened armor and formidable firepower. The Sherman-equipped units suffered heavy losses when they came up against Tigers for the first time in Tunisia. This scenario was repeated in Normandy a year later, following the D-Day landings. What the Sherman lacked in armor and firepower, however, was made up by sheer weight of numbers; over 40,000 had been produced when production ceased in 1945.

The Challenge Of Total War
1942 USA

M5 (GENERAL STUART) LIGHT TANK

The M5 proved that the light tank could no longer hope to survive in a battlefield environment dominated by Panzer IVs and Tiger tanks.

Specifications

Armament: One 1.46in (37mm) M6 gun; three 0.30in (7.62mm) MGs

Armor: 2.5in (64mm)

Crew: 4

Dimensions: Length 14ft 3in (4.34m); Width 7ft 5in (2.25m); Height 7ft 7in (2.3m)

Weight: 14.7 tons (14,969kg)

Powerplant: Two Cadillac Series 42 V-8, 110hp (82kW) each

Speed: 37mph (58km/h)

Range: 100 miles (161km)

The M5 was the last version of the M3 light tank series. It was powered by twin Cadillac engines, which gave a slightly different appearance to its rear decking and distinguished it from the earlier vehicles. The M5A1 had an improved turret with radio equipment installed in its rear, creating a bulge. In British service the M5 was called the Stuart VI. It gradually replaced the M3 from 1942 and continued to be the principal American light tank until 1944, when it was replaced by the M24. The M5 was used most widely in the Pacific and Burma, where Japanese infantry were poorly equipped with antitank weapons. The inadequacy of the light tank was revealed with disastrous consequences at the Battle of the Kasserine

Above: Although the M5 light tank was a great asset in the Pacific Theater, it was no match for the Panzers it encountered in North Africa early in 1943.

Pass, where M3s and M5s came up against Panzer IVs and Tigers and were completely annihilated.

Disbanding light tank batallions

After the Battle of the Kasserine Pass, the Americans disbanded their light tank battalions and deployed the vehicles in companies. These were attached to medium tank battalions for scouting purposes. Some ex-British M5s were used in combat by Indian and Pakistani forces in the Independence War of 1947.

Above: The Stuart light tank was widely used as a reconnaissance vehicle, being attached to medium tank battalions for scouting purposes. Many were used by the Red Army under lend-lease arrangements.

The Challenge Of Total War
✗ 1942 USA

M6 HEAVY TANK

Design of the M6, with a planned weight of 50 tons, was initiated in 1940 as part of the US Army re-equipment program. This had assumed high priority following the outbreak of the war in Europe.

Specifications

Armament: One 3in (76mm) gun; one 1.46in (37mm) gun; three 0.50in (12.7mm) MGs and two 0.30in (7.62mm) MGs

Armor: 5.23in (133mm)

Crew: 5

Dimensions: Length 27ft 8in (8.44m); Width 10ft 2in (3.1m); Height 10ft 7in (3.23m)

Weight: 44.6 tons (45,360kg)

Powerplant: Wright Whirlwind G-200 9-cylinder radial, 925hp (690kW)

Speed: 22mph (35km/h)

Range: 100 miles (161kms)

The trouble with the M6 was that it was outdated in concept, following the design of British and French tanks of the 1920 and 1930s. The original M6 proposal had variants with four turrets, the two main ones carrying 2.95in (75mm) guns, and the secondary turrets armed with 1.46in (37mm) and/or machine guns. In addition, four more machine guns were to be installed on ball mountings at various points of the hull, and this resulted in a very heavily armed AFV. The project, now known as Heavy Tank T1, was approved on June 11, 1940. Within three months, the multi-turret concept had been abandoned in favor of a single turret mounting a 3in (76mm) gun and a coaxial 1.46in (37mm), plus six machine guns.

Above: The M6 was a promising heavy tank design that came to nothing because the Americans concentrated their considerable production facilities on medium tanks. This M6 is flanked by an M3 light tank and an M3 Grant.

Prototypes and production

Three prototypes were built between 1941 and 1942, one with electric transmission and the other two with torque converter transmission. The former was known as the M6A2 and the latter as the M6 and M6A1. Forty units were manufactured, but they never left the USA and consequently were never used. A sole surviving example is on display at the United States Army Ordnance Museum, Aberdeen, Maryland.

The Challenge Of Total War
✕ 1942 USA

T17E1 STAGHOUND ARMORED CAR

The Staghound was a sturdy and popular armored car that performed well for the British and Commonwealth forces during and after World War II.

The T17 Staghound resulted from a US Army ordnance specification for two new armored cars, one heavy, the other medium. The heavy armored car became the T18 Boarhound, while the medium design, produced by the Ford Motor Company, became the T17 Deerhound. This was a 6x6 prototype; the production version (the T17E1), a 4x4 configuration, was named the Staghound. The ASFV was armed with a 1.46in (37mm) gun in a rotating turret, a coaxial machine gun, and a bow machine gun. The armored car never served with the US forces, but it was snapped up by the British, who ordered an initial batch of 300. In addition to the British Army, the Staghound was issued to Australian, Canadian, Indian, New Zealand, and Belgian units. It first saw action in Italy in 1943.

Variants

The Staghound appeared in several guises. One was the Staghound Mk II, with a 2.95in (75mm) howitzer in the turret in place of the 1.46in (37mm) gun; another was the Staghound Mk III, which was fitted with a Crusader tank turret mounting a 2.95in (75mm) gun. The Staghound Command was a variant with the turret removed. The AFV continued in service with the several armies long after 1945.

Below: *The Staghound was a large and well-armored fighting vehicle that was easy to operate and maintain. It was also fast and had a good operational range. It first saw action in Italy in 1943, where it proved well able to cope with often difficult terrain.*

Specifications

Armament: One 1.46in (37mm) gun; two or three 0.30in (7.62mm) MGs

Armor: 2in (51mm)

Crew: 5

Dimensions: Length 18ft (5.49m); Width 8ft 10in (2.69m); Height 7ft 9in (2.36m)

Weight: 13.48 tons (13,700kg)

Powerplant: Twin GMC 270, 194hp (144.8kW) total

Speed: 55mph (89km/h)

Range: 450 miles (724km)

Below: *The Staghound continued to serve in the British Army for several years after 1945, one version being converted to mount a Crusader tank turret.*

The Challenge Of Total War
⚒ 1943   Canada

GRIZZLY I CRUISER

Although it was planned to manufacture the M4A1 Sherman tank in large quantities under the name Grizzly, the program was cut short.

Specifications

Armament: One 2.95in (75mm) gun; two 0.3in (7.62mm) MGs; one 0.5in (12.7mm) MG

Armor: 2.95in (75mm)

Crew: 5

Dimensions: Length 19ft 1in (5.816m); Width 8ft 7in (2.626m); Height 9ft 10in (2.997m)

Weight: 29.91 tons (30,391kg)

Powerplant: Continental R975-C1 gasoline, 353bhp (263kW) at 2400rpm

Speed: 24mph (38.64km/h)

Range: 120 miles (193km)

The Grizzly was a Canadian-built M4A1 Sherman with some modifications, the most notable of which was the fitting of CDP tracks. The initial intention was to produce 1200 units of the Canadian version by February 1944, but the program was shortlived. By June 1943, tanks were becoming available from US production in such quantities that the requirements of the Canadian Army were fulfilled. By September 1943, an agreement had been reached with the War Office whereby all four Canadian armored brigades and two armored reconnaissance regiments would be equipped with US-built Shermans.

Above: *A Canadian version of the Sherman, the Grizzly was produced in small numbers.*

Discontinuation

The firm producing the Grizzly, the Montreal Locomotive Works, was instructed to discontinue production as soon as practicable and devote its resources to the manufacture of the 25-pounder SP gun instead. Production of the Grizzly began in August 1943, and the first delivery of 23 tanks was made in the following October. By mid-January 1944, 188 tanks had been built, and it was at this point that the program was discontinued.

The Challenge Of Total War
⚒ 1943 Germany

JAGDPANTHER TANK DESTROYER

Originally known as Panzerjäger Panther, this excellent tank destroyer

so impressed Adolf Hitler that he ordered the name to be changed to Jagdpanther.

Left: *The Jagdpanther's powerful main gun could knock out any Allied tank, including the heavy Soviet IS-2s, although in their case a side shot was usually necessary.*

The Jagdpanther was a successful purpose-built tank destroyer rather than a hastily built conversion constructed by mounting a partly armored gun box on top of a tank chassis. Admittedly, the chassis in this case was the Panther's, but it was virtually unaltered and surmounted by a well-designed armored superstructure containing a 3.46in (88mm) PaK 43 antitank gun, with an MG34 or MG42 machine gun for self-defense. The Jagdpanther performed exceptionally well, and was popular to use. It could destroy virtually any Allied tank, and it was not unknown for single Jagdpanthers to hold up an Allied armored advance for a considerable period of time.

Above: *The Jagdpanther was a superlative fighting vehicle and was destined to become one of the most famous armored fighting vehicles of its kind. Small groups could hold up much larger armored formations for lengthy periods.*

Allied bombing

Planned production of the Jagdpanther was 150 units per month, this figure was never achieved, largely due to Allied bombing. By the time the production facilities at Braunschweig and Brandenburg were overrun in April 1945, only 383 Jagdpanthers had been completed. The one fault of the Jagdpanther was that it was underpowered, and this meant that it could only be used in a defensive role.

Specifications

Armament: One 3.46in (88mm) antitank gun; one or two 0.312in (7.92mm) MGs

Armor: Maximum, mantlet, 3.94in (100mm); front, 3.15in (80mm)

Crew: 5

Dimensions: Length 32ft 5.7in (9.9m); Width 11ft 2.6in (3.42m); Height 8ft 11in (2.72m)

Weight: approx 45.27 tons (46,000kg)

Powerplant: Maybach HL230P30, V-12 gasoline, 700hp (522kW)

Speed: Road, 28.6mph (46km/h)

Range: Road, 99.4 miles (160km)

Specifications

Armament: One 2.95in (75mm) antitank gun; one or two 0.312in (7.92mm) MGs

Armor: Maximum, 2.36in (60mm)

Crew: 4

Dimensions: Length 22ft 5.7in (6.85m); Width 10ft 4.8in (3.17m); Height 6ft 0.8in (1.85m)

Weight: approx 23.62 tons (24,000kg)

Powerplant: Maybach HL120TRM, V-12 gasoline, 265hp (197.6kW)

Speed: Road, 24.8mph (40km/h)

Range: Road, 130.5 miles (210km)

Below: *The Jagdpanzer IV was a tank-killer variant of the well-proven Panzer Mk IV and housed its 2.95in (75mm) gun in a superstructure formed from well-sloped armored plates, as is apparent in this photograph. This is a later example without the muzzle brake.*

The Challenge Of Total War

1943   Germany

JAGDPANZER IV TANK DESTROYER

The Jagdpanzer IV was a tank-hunting version of the PzKpfw IV. It was armed with a 2.95in (75mm) gun housed in a low-profile superstructure formed from well-sloped armored plates.

Germany's military planners became convinced that the guns of existing close support artillery AFVs needed to be radically improved if they were to be effective. This decision was taken in the light of combat experience gained during the campaigns of 1942, particularly in the Soviet Union, where German armor was coming up against increasing numbers of T-34 tanks. The gun that was selected was the 2.95in (75mm) long-barrel weapon, and was the same that had been produced to arm the Panther tank. To install this gun in carriers such as the Panzer III would, however, require much modification and consequent delay, so the Panzer IV's larger chassis was used as the basis of the new Jagdpanzer IV. This became operational in October 1943 and immediately found favor with its crews, not least because of its effective armor protection and the low silhouette of its hull, making it a difficult target.

Early and later versions

Early production Jagdpanzer IVs were still fitted with the muzzle brake. Later versions used a much longer 2.95in (75mm) gun (although this had the effect of overloading the chassis) and also used side armor plating.

145

TIGER II (PANZERKAMPFWAGEN VI)

The Tiger II, sometimes called the King Tiger or Royal Tiger, was the most formidable tank used in World War II. Its main problem was that it was slow and cumbersome, and lacked mobility.

Specifications

Armament: One 3.46in (88mm) gun; two 0.312in (7.92mm) MGs

Armor: Maximum, hull, 5.9in (150mm)

Crew: 5

Dimensions: Length 33ft 8.9in (10.286m); Width 11ft 10.7in (3.625m); Height 10ft 0.9in (3.075m)

Weight: approx 66.93 tons (68,000kg)

Powerplant: Maybach HL230P30, V-12 gasoline, 700hp (514.3kW)

Speed: Road, 21.75mph (35km/h)

Range: Road, 105 miles (170km)

The Tiger II (PzKpfw VI) combined the heavy armor of the Tiger I with the sloped armor of the Panther and was, in effect, a completely different vehicle from the Tiger I. It first went into action in Normandy in July 1944, and was used on the Eastern Front the following month. The Tiger II, sometimes called the King Tiger, was the most powerful tank to be deployed anywhere during World War II, and together with the Panther it formed the spearhead of the German offensive in the Ardennes in December 1944. This drove a dangerous wedge between the Allied armies. Fortunately, the offensive petered out for lack of fuel and many Tigers were abandoned by their crews.

Above: *The Tiger II was a formidable fighting machine, but its weak points were that it could be rendered immobile by freezing mud clogging its suspension.*

Problems

Despite its success in combat, the Tiger continued to experience many problems, not least of which were caused by its overlapping wheel suspension, which became easily clogged with mud. This had the potential for dire consequences, especially in the Russian winter, when the mud froze and had to be chipped away before the tank was ready for action. The Tiger II chassis was used as the basis for the Jagdtiger B, 48 of which were built. This was armed with a 5.04in (128mm) gun.

Above: *A King Tiger battalion preparing to move off. These Tigers are fitted with Porsche turrets; some had turrets developed by Henschel. The long-barreled 3.46in (88mm) gun could fire both armor-piercing and HE ammunition.*

The Challenge Of Total War
1943 Germany

SDKFZ 234 PUMA ARMORED CAR

The German industry produced the best armored cars to be used in World War II, and the fast vehicles of the SdKfz 234 series were considered by many to be the best of all.

Specifications

Armament: One 1.97in (50mm) gun; one 0.312in (7.92mm) MG
Armor: Maximum, 1.18in (30mm)
Crew: 4
Dimensions: Length 19ft 8.2in (6m); Width 7ft 7.7in (2.33m); Height 7ft 9.6in (2.38m)
Weight: approx 11.5 tons (11,700kg)
Powerplant: Tatra 103, V-12 diesel, 210hp (156.6kW)
Speed: Road, 55.5mph (90km/h)
Range: Road, up to 559 miles (900km)

The SdKfz 234 armored car was first deployed in 1943 on the Eastern Front. The vehicles in this series were all eight-wheel drive and similar in appearance to the SdKfz 233 series, which they replaced.

Further models

The original model was the SdKfz 234/1, which was armed with a 0.79mm (20mm) cannon and a coaxial MG34 machine gun, but it was the 234/2 variant that was the first to see active service. The SdKfz 234/2, arguably the best armored car to be produced in World War II, was armed with a 1.97in (50mm) gun, and although it was heavily armored (weighing nearly 12 tons), it had a top speed of over 50mph and its gun gave it the ability to engage light tanks. It was named the Puma. The next model, the SdKfz 234/3, was nicknamed "Stummel" (Stumpy) because of its short 2.95in (75mm) L/24 gun, mounted in a raised open superstructure. The final variant, the SdKfz 234/4, mounted a 2.95in (75mm) PaK 40 antitank gun. The SdKfz 234s were often used to carry out fast raids on enemy communications across open country.

Above: *The SdKfz 234 armored car was well suited to making surprise attacks on Soviet communications in the rear areas, being fast and well-armed.*

The Challenge Of Total War

⚒ 1943 Hungary

TURAN II LIGHT TANK

The Hungarian Army had only one tank division during World War II. It was equipped with the Turan Mks I and II, which were variants of the Czech T22 light tank.

Below: A Turan I tank fording a river in Russia. The Hungarian Army remained loyal to the Germans to the bitter end, unlike other Axis allies such as Romania, which changed sides when the Russians gained the upper hand.

The Hungarian Turan series of AFVs was based on the Skoda T22, a light tank produced in Czechoslovakia. The Turan was produced in two variants, the I and II, the first being armed with a 1.57in (40mm) gun and the latter with a 2.95in (75mm) weapon in a redesigned turret. The Turan I formed the main equipment of the Hungarian Army's sole armored division from 1942, but its 1.57in (40mm) gun proved completely ineffective against Soviet armor and losses were high.

Weapons

It was decided that a bigger gun was needed, and the weapon selected was the 2.95in (75mm) M41, developed from the Austro-Hungarian Bohler 2.95in (75mm) 18M field gun. Turans armed with this weapon were known as 41M Turan II Nehez Harckocsi (Heavy Tank), although they were not, in fact, heavy tanks. The name was later changed to 41M Turan 75 Rovid Nehez Harckocsi (Short Heavy Tank), and these were issued to the armored division in May 1943. An improved version, the Turan II 43M, mounted a 1.70in (43mm) (L/43) tank gun, which was a Hungarian development of the German PaK 40 antitank weapon. This tank was known as the Hasszu Nehez Harckocsi (Long Heavy Tank). Production of the Turan II ran to 139 units, together with 230 Turan Is. A proposed heavier variant, the Turan III, was never produced.

Specifications

Armament: One 2.95in (75mm) gun; two 0.315in (8mm) MGs

Armor: 0.55–1.97in (14–50mm)

Crew: 5

Dimensions: Length 18ft 8in (5.68m); Width 8ft 4in (2.54m); Height 7ft 8in (2.33m)

Weight: 18.2 tons (18,500kg)

Powerplant: Weiss V-8 gasoline, 260bhp (194kW) at 2200rpm

Speed: 29mph (47km/h)

Range: 103 miles (165km)

The Challenge Of Total War
☭ 1943 Soviet Union

IS-1 HEAVY TANK

The Iosif Stalin (IS) tank was named after the leader of the Soviet Union.
It was developed from the KV-85, which was a version of the KV-1. The IS
tanks were the most powerful to serve in the Red Army in World War II.

Above: *The IS-2 tank, which
supplanted the IS-1 in service
during 1944, was the heaviest
Soviet wartime tank of all, and
spearheaded the breakthrough
into Berlin in April 1945.*

Specifications

(IS-1, 1943)
Armament: One 3.35in (85mm)
gun; two 0.3in (7.62mm) DT MGs
Armor: 1.18–5.2in (30–132mm)
Crew: 4
Dimensions: Length 27ft 3in
(8.32m); Width 10ft 8in (3.25m);
Height 9ft 6in (2.9m)
Weight: 45.3 tons (46,000kg)
Powerplant: V-2-IS 12-cylinder
diesel, 510bhp (380kW)
Speed: 24.8mph (40km/h)
Range: 155 miles (250km)

The IS-1 was developed from the KV
series of heavy tanks to combat German
AFVs such as the Tiger and Panther. Its
design was named KV-13. Marshal Kliment
Voroshilov had fallen out of political favor,
however, and so the new design was named
Iosif (Joseph) Stalin instead. The first batch,
used for evaluation, was called IS-85. The IS-
1 retained the 3.34in (85mm) gun of the
KV-85, but production models were fitted
with the long 4.8in (122mm) gun. This had
greater penetrating power and also enough
strength to blow off a tank's turret even if it

failed to penetrate the armor. With this
modification the tank became the IS-2, the
first examples of which appeared in 1944. A
further variant, the IS-3, retained the 4.8in
(122mm) gun but had a redesigned, more
rounded turret that resembled an upturned
soup bowl.

Assault on Berlin

The IS tanks were the spearhead of the final
assault on Berlin in April 1945, their power
and protection enabling them to break
through the enemy defense barriers.

The Challenge Of Total War

1943 Soviet Union

KV-85 HEAVY TANK

The heavy KV-85 was produced as a stop-gap measure to counter the German Panther. Although it was produced in limited numbers, it formed the basis of future war-winning designs.

Above: *The KV-85 was used virtually as a battering-ram during its early operations in 1944 and suffered heavy losses, but this led to the development of its highly successful successor, which was the Iosif (Joseph) Stalin.*

Heavy tanks had fallen out of favor with the Soviet General Staff in 1942, following disappointing performances in combat and a lack of mobility, and the following year there were serious proposals to abandon the development of heavy tanks altogether. However, the arrival of the German Panther tank in 1943 caused a reappraisal of the heavy tank concept. As an interim measure, the development of the KV series of heavy tanks continued with the KV-85. This was a KV-1S with a redesigned turret, and had been intended for the latest in the KV line, the KV-13. The KV-85 mounted the same 3.35in (85mm) DT-5 gun as the SU-85 (hence its name) but the gun was in high demand and consequently production of the KV-85 was slow. Only 130 units were built before production switched to other developments. The KV-85 was produced in the fall and winter of 1943 and 1944, and most were destroyed during the intense fighting that took place as the Russians launched their 1944 offensives. It was the KV-85, however, that became the prototype of the heavy tank that would take the Red Army to the gates of Berlin, the IS-1.

Specifications

Armament: One 3.35in (85mm) D-5T gun; three 0.3in (7.62mm) DT MGs

Armor: 1.18–4.3in (30–110mm)

Crew: 4

Dimensions: Length 28ft 3in (8.6m); Width 10ft 8in (3.25m); Height 9ft 6in (2.9m)

Weight: 45.3 tons (46,000kg)

Powerplant: V-2 12-cylinder diesel, 600bhp (448kW) at 1900rpm

Speed: 25mph (40km/h)

Range: 155 miles (250km)

The Challenge Of Total War
⚒ **1943 UK**

CHALLENGER CRUISER

The Challenger cruiser was one of the ugliest tanks produced during World War II. Its was basically a Cromwell armed with a 17-pounder (2.98in/76mm) gun, stripped of much armor to reduce weight.

Top: *The Challenger's large turret is clear in this photograph.*

Specifications

Armament: One 17pdr (2.98in/76mm); one 7.62mm (0.3in) MG

Armor: 0.79–4.02in (20–102mm)

Crew: 5

Dimensions: Length 26ft 4in (8.147m); Width 9ft 7in (2.9m); Height 8ft 9in (2.66m)

Weight: 31.5 tons (32,000kg)

Powerplant: Rolls Royce Meteor V-12, 600bhp (447.6kW)

Speed: 14.90mph (24km/h)

Range: 119.85 miles (193km)

In 1941, the British Army was in desperate need of a tank armed with a gun that could tackle even the heaviest German tank, and the 17-pounder (3in/76mm), then under development, was selected to meet the requirement. It was decided to mount the gun on an A27 Cromwell/Centaur chassis, which was lengthened to accommodate the extra weight and larger turret. The new design, the A30 (later to be known as the Challenger) began its trials in March 1942, and revealed many inadequacies, not the least that the lengthened suspension did not cancel out the extra weight of the new turret. In addition, the mounting of the heavy gun made the turret traverse so slow that a new mechanism had to be designed.

Above: *The Challenger was in effect a stretched Cromwell armed with a 17-pounder gun, the tank's armor being reduced to save weight. It was just as well that the similarly armed Sherman Firefly was adopted by the British Army instead.*

Delays

Despite its troubles, the Challenger was ordered into production on the strength of its gun power, but the first tanks were not delivered until March 1944, too late for them to undergo the waterproofing trials necessary for them to take part in the D-Day landings. In the end, the M4 Sherman, fitted with the 17-pounder (2.98in/76mm) gun, was adopted to meet the army's requirement, and the Challenger was relegated to the sidelines.

CROMWELL CRUISER (A27M) AND CENTAUR CRUISER TANKS

The Cromwell and Centaur were contemporary cruiser tank designs, but with different engines. It was the Cromwell's Meteor engine (a derivative of the famous Rolls-Royce Merlin) that gave it the edge.

Specifications

(Cromwell)
Armament: One 6pdr (2.24in/57mm) or 75mm (2.95in) gun; two 0.31in (7.92mm) Besa MGs
Armor: 0.315–2.99in (8–76mm)
Crew: 5
Dimensions: Length 20ft 10in (6.35m); Width 9ft 8in (2.91m); Height 9ft 4in (2.83m)
Weight: 27.5 tons (27,970kg)
Powerplant: Rolls Royce Meteor V-12, 600bhp (447.6kW)
Speed: 31.67mph (51km/h)
Range: 172.64 miles (278km)

Specifications

(Centaur)
Armament: One 6pdr (2.24in/57mm) or one 3.74in (95mm) howitzer; one or two 0.31in (7.92mm) Besa MGs
Armor: 0.79–2.99in (20–76mm)
Crew: 5
Dimensions: Length 20ft 10in (6.35m); Width 9ft 6in (2.896m); Height 8ft (2.49m)
Weight: 27 tons (27,432kg)
Powerplant: Nuffield Liberty gasoline, 395bhp (294.67kW)
Speed: 26.70mph (43km/h)
Range: 164.57 miles (265km)

In 1941 the British Army issued specification A27, calling for a tank to replace the Crusader. Two tenders were offered, one for a tank designed around a Liberty engine and the other equipped with a version of the Rolls-Royce Merlin (named Meteor). The first design (the A27L) became the Cruiser Tank Mk VIII Centaur, the main version of which was the Centaur IV, used by the Royal Marines Armoured Support Group in the battle of Normandy. Because of its inadequate engine, the Centaur never reached its full combat potential.

Cromwell Mark IV
The second design, the contemporary Cruiser Tank Mk VIII Cromwell (A27M),

Above: The Cromwell proved to be an effective tank when it went into action in Normandy. Its 2.95in (75mm) gun gave it a reasonable chance against German armor. The tank entered service in 1943 and many crews were trained on it before it saw combat.

proved to be an extremely reliable fighting machine, especially when the six-pounder (2.24in/57mm) gun that formed its original armament was replaced by the harder-hitting 2.95in (75mm). The Cromwell Mk IV used the latter gun and it was issued to the British armored regiments in October 1943. Although production of the Sherman had started by mid-1944, the Cromwell saw action in Normandy with the 7th Armoured Division and acquitted itself well.

Specifications

Armament: One 17pdr
(2.98in/76mm) gun; one 7.62mm
(0.3in) MG
Armor: 0.47–2.95in (12–75mm)
Crew: 5
Dimensions: Length 19ft 4in
(5.89m); Width 8ft 7in (2.62m);
Height 9ft (2.75m)
Weight: 29.69 tons (30,164kg)
Powerplant: Continental 9-
cylinder radial, 400bhp (298.2kW)
Speed: 25mph (40.2km/h)
Range: 120 miles (193km)

The Challenge Of Total War
⚔ **1943 UK**

SHERMAN FIREFLY

The Sherman Firefly was developed to counter Germany's latest Tiger and Panther tanks, with their excellent guns and heavy armor. It proved very effective in its assigned task.

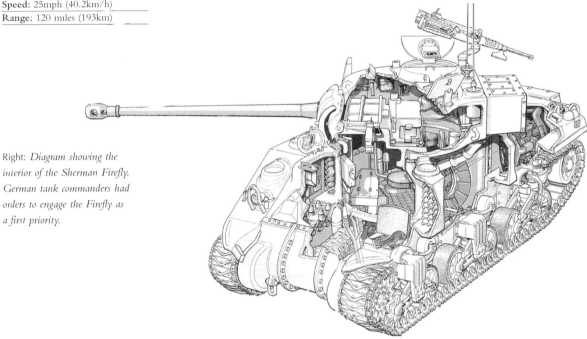

Right: *Diagram showing the interior of the Sherman Firefly. German tank commanders had orders to engage the Firefly as a first priority.*

Below: *The Sherman Firefly was one of the best-known of the Sherman variants. It was armed with a very effective 17-pounder gun that could get the better of most types of Panzer.*

One of the best-known Sherman variants, the Sherman Firefly was a British version of the M4 armed with a 17-pounder (2.98in/76mm) gun. The Firefly was issued to the British armored divisions in 1944, in time for the Normandy landings. The original intention had been to concentrate the Fireflies, which were among the few Allied AFVs capable of taking on the German Tigers and Panthers. This was done in special troops and squadrons, but it was then decided to attach one or more Firefly to each troop of a tank battalion.

Effectiveness

The 17-pounder (2.98in/76mm) gun, fired a regular APC round and penetrated a Tiger's armor at over 1094 yards (1000 metres), and this distance was increased twofold when more effective armor-piercing ammunition came into use in the latter months of World War II. Because of the Sherman Firefly's effectiveness, German tank crews had orders to engage and destroy it as a first priority, and since the Firefly was no better armored than other M4 variants, it was vital that its crew responded quickly. About 600 Fireflies were produced, most of them M4A4 conversions.

The Challenge Of Total War

1943 USA

M18 HELLCAT TANK DESTROYER

The M18's low silhouette, high speed, and high firepower gave it the ability to destroy every German tank except the Tiger II. It was an ideal vehicle for picking off enemy tanks from ambush.

Above: *The M18 was designed as a tank destroyer from the outset, but it was used more as an assault gun and conventional self-propelled artillery.*

Specifications

Armament: One 3in (76mm) M1 gun; one 0.50in (12.7mm) MG

Armor: 0.47in (12mm)

Crew: 5

Dimensions: Length over gun 21ft 10in (6.7m); Width 9ft 9in (2.97m); Height 8ft 5in (2.6m)

Weight: 17.9 tons (18,142kg)

Powerplant: Continental R-975, 9-cylinder, radial, 400hp (298.5kW)

Speed: 50mph (80km/h)

Range: 150 miles (240km)

In December 1941, the US War Ordnance Department issued a specification that called for the design of a fast tank destroyer using a Christie suspension (the Wright Continental R-975 engine) and armed with a 1.46in (37mm) gun. In the course of development the Christie was replaced by a torsion bar suspension, and the inadequate 1.46in (37mm) main armament was replaced by a 2.24in (57mm) gun, which was fitted to the prototypes. During evaluation, this caliber also proved inadequate, so the 2.24in (57mm) was replaced in turn by a 3in (76mm) weapon. Production of the M18, (unofficially) nicknamed Hellcat, began in July 1943 and the tank became operational in Italy in the summer of 1944.

Success

Although the M18 was not sufficiently well armored to trade blows with the latest German tanks, its speed made it an excellent vehicle for hit-and-run operations. In July 1944, for example, the 630th Tank Destroyer Battalion destroyed 53 Tigers and Panthers, plus 15 self-propelled guns, losing only 17 M18s. About 2500 Hellcats were produced up to October 1944, when production ceased. Surplus M18s, however, were used by the former Yugoslavia until the early 1990s.

Left: *M18s moving up to the front in the winter of 1944–45. The Hellcat had the distinction of being the fastest armored fighting vehicle of World War II. It was an ideal tank destroyer, but lacked armor and was fitted with an open-topped turret, as is evident in the photograph.*

The Challenge Of Total War

1943 USA

M8 GREYHOUND LIGHT ARMORED CAR

This was one of the longest-serving vehicles of its kind in military history. Widely used during World War II, some of these tanks were still being used in various parts of the world in the early 21st century.

Specifications

Armament: One 1.46in (37mm) gun; two 0.30in (7.62mm) MGs

Armor: Unknown

Crew: 4

Dimensions: Length 16ft 5in (5.01m); Width 8ft 4in (2.54m); Height 7ft 5in (2.26m)

Weight: 7.68 tons (7802kg)

Powerplant: Hercules JXD 6-cylinder inline gasoline, 110hp (82kW)

Speed: 60mph (100km/h)

Range: 350 miles (563km)

Above: *The M8 Light Armored Car was widely used, although it was considered too lightly armored by the British. It was originally designated T22.*

A product of the Ford Motor Corporation, the M8 Greyhound was ordered to a specification that was drawn up to include design lessons learned by US observers who had been following the war in Europe and North Africa in 1940 and 1941. Ford's design, the T22, was judged to be the best of four submissions, and the vehicle was ordered into production as the Light Armored Car M8. With production totaling 11,667 vehicles by the time it ended in April 1945, the M8 had by far the highest production of all US armored car types. The M8 proved to be a superb fighting vehicle, with an excellent cross-country performance.

Left: *US M8s advance along a road in Tunisia after the Allied landings in North Africa. The crew had to strap their kit to any convenient parts on the hull or turret as internal space was limited.*

Usage

The M8 was considered to be too lightly armored by the British Army, although in 1943 it was issued to the British and Commonwealth Armies, who named it the Greyhound. War surplus M8s were greatly prized by smaller nations, and some were still being used by developing countries in Africa and Latin America in the early 21st century. A variant of the M8, the M20 Utility Car, was basically an M8 with the turret removed.

Chapter 5

FROM WORLD WAR TO COLD WAR

The decade between 1944 and 1954 saw a revolution in armor and firepower. An earlier lack of engine power had made this impossible. By 1944 tanks of British design were powered by the Rolls-Royce Meteor, a derivative of the superlative Merlin aero-engine. At the end of World War II, just as this new technology was reaching perfection, the western Allies embarked on a program to scrap the bulk of their AFVs.

Above: *The T-54/55 was an ongoing development of the famous T-34/85 and was used by many armies throughout the world. It saw a great deal of action in the many limited conflicts since World War II.*

Left: *A Saracen APC on exercise. The commander has a roof-mounted machine gun. The Saracen was widely used in Northern Ireland during antiterrorist operations against the IRA.*

It was a path the Soviet Union did not choose to follow; instead, the USSR continued to build tanks on a massive scale, filling their armored divisions with heavy monsters like the IS series and excellent medium tanks like the T-54/55. It was not long before the threat to western Europe became apparent. Allies of an emerging NATO rushed to build comparable AFVs that would be capable of stemming a Soviet armored onslaught. Had the Russians chosen to launch an armored thrust toward the Rhine in the late 1940s they might have achieved their aim with comparative ease, but America had the atomic bomb, and they did not. Thwarted in western Europe, the Russians turned elsewhere to explore communist expansion, and in 1950 it was the T-34 tank that spearheaded the attack on the Republic of Korea. For the first time, American and British tanks engaged their Soviet counterparts in battle; the stage was set for the development of armored technology.

From World War to Cold War

✗ **1944   Germany**

HETZER TANK DESTROYER

The Hetzer was the best German tank destroyer to be used in World War II. It was a powerful vehicle for its size, and was also much cheaper to manufacture and operate than other Panzerjäger.

Left: The small size and low profile of the Jagdpanzer Hetzer can be readily appreciated when compared with the height of the US soldier in this photograph. Note the "Saukopf" (pig's head) gun mantle, which provided extra frontal protection, and the lack of a muzzle brake.

Below: This Jagdpanzer 38 (t) Hetzer has a roof-mounted machine gun for local defense.

In the war on the Eastern Front, the Wehrmacht used various Stürmgeschutz assault guns. These proved far more adept at destroying enemy armor than did the tank destroyers that were little more than large and unwieldy guns mounted on a tank chassis. The German High Command therefore decided to develop a light tank destroyer on the lines of an assault gun, and used the chassis of the PzKpfw 38 (t) as its basis. The result was the Panzerjäger 38 (t) Hetzer (Baiter), which turned out to be the most successful German tank destroyer of World War II.

Production

The Hetzer was produced from 1943 at the Skoda works in Prague, but subsidiary plants in other parts of Czechoslovakia were also involved. Before the factories were overrun by Soviet forces in 1944, 1577 units had been built. In combat, the Hetzer was very effective. Its very small size and low silhouette made it a difficult target to engage. It was manufactured in Czechoslovakia after the war. Some vehicles were exported to Switzerland between 1947 and 1952, where the Swiss Army continued to use them until the 1970s.

Specifications

Armament: One 2.95in (75mm) antitank gun; one 0.312in (7.92mm) MG

Armor: Maximum, 2.36in (60mm)

Crew: 4

Dimensions: Length 20ft 11.1in (6.38m); Width 8ft 7.5in (2.63m); Height 7ft 1.4in (2.17m)

Weight: approx 15.5 tons (15,750kg)

Powerplant: Praga AC/2, 6-cylinder gasoline, 160hp (119.3kW)

Speed: Road, 26mph (42km/h)

Range: Road, 110 miles (177km)

From World War to Cold War

1944 Germany

JAGDTIGER HEAVY TANK DESTROYER

The massive Jagdtiger with its 5in (128mm) gun was a powerful weapon. However, it was underpowered and too heavy to be used as anything other than a defense weapon.

Right: *This Jagdtiger is fitted with the Henschel suspension, one of two types fitted to this AFV. The other was manufactured by Porsche and was distinguished by larger roadwheels. The Jagdtiger was the heaviest AFV to see service in World War II.*

Based on the Tiger II (King Tiger), the Jagdtiger was the heaviest and most powerful armored fighting vehicle of World War II. With all its equipment, its weight was 76 tons, much of which was accounted for by armor. It was hardly surprising, therefore, that it needed a lot of power to move it, and the necessary power was not provided by its 700hp (522kW) Maybach engine. The Jagdtiger's main armament was a 5.04in (128mm) PaK 44 antitank gun or a PaK 80, which was similar. However, many vehicles were fitted with an 3.46in (88mm) weapon, as Allied bombing had disrupted production of the bigger guns.

Defensive role

It was hardly appropriate to describe the Jagdtiger as a tank hunter: It was so heavy that it had to wait for enemy tanks, which placed it in a purely defensive posture. The Jagdtiger was produced at the Niebelungenwerke at St. Valentin in Austria, which only managed to turn out 70 examples before the end of the war.

Below: *Although its heavy frontal armor made it a difficult vehicle to destroy, the Jagdtiger was too heavy and too underpowered to be used as anything other than a defensive weapon.*

Specifications

Armament: One 5.04in (128mm) antitank gun; two 0.30in (7.92in) MGs

Armor: Maximum, 9.84in (250mm)

Crew: 6

Dimensions: Length 34ft 11.3in (10.65m); Width 11ft 10.9in (3.63m); Height 9ft 8.1in (2.95m)

Weight: approx 68.9 tons (70,000kg)

Powerplant: Maybach HL230P30, V-12 gasoline, 700hp (522kW)

Speed: Road, 23.6mph (38km/h)

Range: Road, 105.6 miles (170km)

Above: *Now relegated to museums, the T-34 was the most advanced tank of its kind when it was first deployed in 1941.*

From World War to Cold War
1944 Soviet Union

T-34/85 TANK

When the T-34/85 went into production in the winter of 1943 and 1944, it was the most formidable tank in service anywhere. It was to be the spearhead of the Red Army's drive to Berlin.

Specifications

Armament: One 3.35in (85mm) ZiS-S-53 gun; two 0.3in (7.62mm) DT MGs

Armor: 3.54in (90mm)

Crew: 5

Dimensions: Length 26ft 7in (8.15m); Width 9ft 7in (2.99m); Height 9ft (2.74m)

Weight: 31.5 tons (32,000kg)

Powerplant: V-2-34 12-cylinder diesel, 500bhp (373kW) at 1800 rpm

Speed: 34mph (55km/h)

Range: 190 miles (300km)

During 1942, Soviet factories produced more than 5000 units of the T-34/76 tank, but it became clear that extensive changes had to be made to the existing design if the T-34 was to keep up with the new generation of German AFVs. The existing T-34 chassis was adapted to take a cast, three-man turret, fitted with a much more powerful gun. This was the long 3.35in (85mm) which, like the German 3.46in (88mm), was adapted from an antiaircraft gun. Its performance was roughly similar to that of the 3.46in (88mm) fitted in the Tiger I; the 3.35in (85mm) fired a 21.5lb (9.75) shot at a muzzle velocity of 2600 ft (792m)/sec, compared with the 3.46in (88mm) gun's 22.25lb (10.09kg) shot at 2657 ft (810m)/sec. For the T-34/85 of course, a

Above: *Cutaway showing the interior of the T-34/85. A very advanced design for its time, the tank was produced in thousands and proved robust, agile, and very effective in combat.*

heavier gun, coupled with increased armor, added up to a heavier tank, which meant a certain loss of operational flexibility. Nevertheless, the vital statistics of the T-34/85 were a tribute to the efficiency of the amended design. Its overall weight rose from 27 tons (27,430kg) to 32 tons (32,510kg), and its effective range dropped from 280 miles (450 km) to about 190 miles (306km). Its speed was a little below 30mph (48.28 km/h), about the same as the Panther. When it entered production in the winter of 1943, it was the most formidable tank in the world.

From World War to Cold War

🔨 1944 UK

KANGAROO ARMORED PERSONNEL CARRIER

The Kangaroo APC was devised by a Canadian officer as a means of reducing casualties in the field—which, in 1944, were becoming alarmingly high.

Specifications

Armament: One 7.7mm (0.303in) Browning MG

Armor: 3.56in (90mm)

Crew: Sherman 2 plus 11 (Priest 2 plus 20)

Dimensions: Length 19ft 9in (6.02m); Width 8ft 6in (2.59m); Height 8ft 4in (2.54m)

Weight: Unavailable

Powerplant: Continental R 975-EC2 9-cylinder radial developing 400bhp (298.2kW) at 2400rpm

Speed: 25mph (40.2km/h)

Range: 120 miles (195km)

The Kangaroo APC was the brainchild of Lieutenant-General Guy Simonds. He commanded the 2nd Canadian Corps, and, having become concerned about the losses suffered by his men in the weeks following the D-Day landings, he sought a means of providing them with better protection. He ordered the conversion of 102 M7 Priest self-propelled guns (all of which had become nonoperational due to worn gun barrels) into armored personnel carriers capable of carrying 12 troops each (although in the event, they carried 20). Other conversions involved Canadian Ram tanks or Shermans, all of which became known as Kangaroos. In Normandy, Kangaroos were operated by the 49th Armored Personnel Carrier Regiment, which was part of the 79th Armored

Above: The Canadian Cruiser Tank Ram Mk I was used only for training, but as the tanks were withdrawn from service, their turrets were removed and the vehicles converted into the Ram Kangaroo APC.

Division. They were used for the first time in the fighting around Caen, and later in attacks on the Channel ports, which were holding out on Hitler's orders long after the Allied invasion forces had swept inland.

Forerunner of today's APC

The Kangaroo, which provided infantry with full armored protection for the first time, as well as the means of remaining at the forefront of an armored advance, was the forerunner of today's armored personnel carrier

From World War to Cold War

1944 USA

M26 PERSHING HEAVY TANK

The M26 Pershing Heavy Tank entered operational service in 1945, just too late to have any impact on World War II, but in time to take part in the latter stages of the Pacific War.

Above: *An M26 Pershing about to cross the Rhine. This excellent tank entered service too late to make an impact on the war in Europe, but it saw some action in the Pacific.*

Named after General John "Black Jack" Pershing, who commanded the American Expeditionary Force in France during World War I, the M26 heavy tank was developed primarily to counter the German Panther. This was in widespread operational service in France and outmatched the M4 Pershing—the tank that formed the bulk of the Allied armored forces at the time of the campaign in Normandy. Prior to this, the development of heavy tanks had been accorded low priority in the United States, the main effort being concentrated on medium tanks, in particular the M3/M4 series. When the formidable power of the latest Panzers was assessed in the weeks after D-Day, heavy tank development was given higher priority. Following trials with various

Right: *A group of D Company First Marine Division soldiers, standing on a M-26 tank to spearhead a patrol in search of guerrillas.*

Specifications

Armament: One 3.54in (90mm) M3 gun; one 0.50in (12.7mm); two 0.30in (7.62mm) MGs

Armor: 4in (102mm)

Crew: 5

Dimensions: Length 28ft 3in (8.66m); Width 11ft 6in (3.51m); Height 9ft 1in (2.78m)

Weight: 41.2 tons (41,891kg)

Powerplant: Ford GAF, 500hp (373kW)

Speed: 30mph (48km/h)

Range: 100 miles (161km)

Below: *The Pershing influenced US tank development up to the M60 series.*

saw little action before the end of World War II. Ten tanks assigned to the 3rd Armored Division, however, in one encounter, destroyed two Tigers and a Mark IV from a range of about 1000 yards (914m). One or two examples of so-called "Super Pershings," fitted with a 3.54in (90mm) T15E1 high-velocity gun, also arrived in Europe at a very late stage of the war. One of these took part in an action near Dessau on April 4, 1945, destroying a King Tiger and a Panther. Some also deployed to the Pacific, where they were used in the invasion of Okinawa. Five years later, Pershings saw action in Korea, where they were the only American tank capable of matching the T-34/85s being used by the North Koreans and Chinese. According to official US history, some M26s were removed from museums, being hastily refurbished and returned to service for use in Korea. The bulk of vehicles that were still operational were deployed in Europe.

prototypes the first of a new generation of US heavy tanks emerged. This was the Heavy Tank T26E3, selected for production as the Heavy Tank M26.

Geographical use

The first M26 vehicles reached northwest Europe early in 1945. They were assigned to the 3rd and 9th Armored Divisions, but they

NATO armored forces

The Pershing formed a valuable addition to NATO's armored forces in the dangerous early years of the Cold War, which could easily have developed into a shooting war over issues such as the Berlin blockade. The tank was the first in a series that led to the M60 of today.

From World War to Cold War
1944 USA

M36 TANK DESTROYER

The M36 was developed to counter the latest generation of German tanks such as the Panther and Tiger. It could engage and destroy these tanks with a high-kill probability factor.

Specifications

Armament: One 3.54in (90mm) M3 gun; one 0.50in (12.7mm) MG
Armor: 1.97in (50mm)
Crew: 5
Dimensions: Length (excluding gun) 20ft 2in (6.14m); Width 10ft (3.04m); Height 8ft 11in (2.71m)
Weight: 27.7 tons (28,123kg)
Powerplant: Ford GAA V-8, 500hp (373kW)
Speed: 30mph (48km/h)
Range: 150 miles (240km)

Above: *The M36 was a very successful and potent tank destroyer, and was more than a match for all types of enemy armor. It was armed with a powerful 3.54in (90mm) gun.*

The M36 tank destroyer was developed as a replacement for the standard M10, whose 3in (76.2mm) gun was not powerful enough for the latest generation of German tanks like the Tiger and Panther. The new AFV comprised the hull of an M10A1 with a new turret mounting a 3.54in (90mm) M3 gun, plus a machine gun in an antiaircraft mounting. As a weight-saving measure the turret was open-topped, but it was fitted with a folding armored roofkit to protect from shrapnel. A large bulge at the rear of the turret was a counterweight to the heavy gun, and provided additional stowage for ammunition. About 1400 M36s were produced during World War II. The first models were deployed to Europe in the fall of 1944 in time to help counter the German Ardennes offensive. About 300 Sherman hulls were also converted to take the 3.54in (90mm) gun. These were known as the M36B1.

Success

The M36 was one of the few armored fighting vehicles able to engage and destroy the latest Panzers with any success, and was also used against the T-34 in Korea.

Left: *The M36 saw action in Korea and continued to serve with the armies of foreign countries for many years after the end of World War II.*

From World War to Cold War

1944 USA

M24 LIGHT TANK (CHAFFEE)

The M24 Chaffee was introduced too late to make a significant contribution to World War II, but it fought in later conflicts, including the Korean War and the Indo-Pakistan conflict.

Specifications

Armament: One 2.95in (75mm) M6 gun; one 0.50in (12.7mm) MG; two 0.30in (7.62mm) MGs
Armor: 1.5in (38mm)
Crew: 4 or 5
Dimensions: Length 18ft (5.49m); Width 9ft 8in (2.95m); Height 8ft 1in (2.46m)
Weight: 18 tons (18,371kg)
Powerplant: Two Cadillac 44T24 V-8, 110hp (82kW)
Speed: 34mph (55km/h)
Range: 175 miles (281km)

The M24 light tank (later known as the Chaffee) was a joint venture between the US Ordnance Committee and Cadillac. In March 1943, Cadillac set about developing a new AFV which would eradicate the shortcomings that had become apparent in the M3/M5 series. One of these was the weak 1.46in (37mm) armament, so the new design featured a light tank based on the M5A1, but armed with a 2.95in (75mm) gun. This new vehicle was called the T24, this being changed to M24 when it was accepted for service. Its gun was a derivative of the 2.95in (75mm) weapon developed for the B-25H, the anti-ship version of the North American Mitchell bomber. Production of the Light Tank M24 began in 1944, and 4731 vehicles were eventually produced, some of which were allocated to the British Army.

Above: *The M24 was a good-looking design and was well-armed for its size and weight. This small tank carried a surprisingly large crew of five men—commander, gunner, loader, driver, and radio operator.*

Geographical use

The first M24s were deployed to Europe in December 1944, but did not play an important part in the last months of World War II. They were only available in relatively small numbers and were vulnerable to German tank and antitank guns. They were used in a reconnaissance role during the Korean War, however, with the French in Indo-China and with the Pakistani Army in the 1971 conflict with India.

Below: *The M24 Chaffee light tank, armed with a 2.95in (75mm) gun, was introduced into service in late 1944, and formed the basis of a new family of armored fighting vehicles in the postwar years.*

From World War to Cold War
✗ 1945 Soviet Union

T-44 MEDIUM TANK

The T-44 medium tank was intended to be a replacement for the
splendid T-34, but its progress was dogged by mechanical problems.
It formed the basis of the later, very successful T-54.

Produced in the closing months of World War II, the T-34 medium tank was intended to be the successor to the famous T-34. It was the result of a design project known as the T-34M. This was abandoned at the outset of the war but picked up once more in late 1943. With further developments, the T-34M became the T-44, which, although it resembled the T-34, was in fact a new design with heavier armor for better protection against large antitank guns. Production of the T-44 began in August 1944 and in September the tank was issued to three Soviet Army tank brigades. They used it for training purposes before re-equipping with T-34/85s prior to the final assault on Berlin.

Above: *The T-44 was not a successful tank, and was an intermediary between the excellent T-34 and the very effective T-54, the standard Soviet tank of the postwar era.*

About 150 T-44s were completed by the end of World War II, but continued technical problems meant that this tank was not used in combat. Production ended in late 1945 after 965 units had been produced, some of which were used during the Soviet invasion of Hungary in 1956. Although the T-44 was unsuccessful, its design formed the basis of the very effective T-54, one of the principal tanks of the Cold War.

Specifications

Armament: One 3.35in (85mm)
D-5T gun; two 0.3in (7.62mm)
DT MGs

Armor: 4.72in (120mm)

Crew: 4

Dimensions: Length 25ft 1in
(7.65m); Width 10ft 4in (3.15m);
Height 8ft (2.45m)

Weight: 31.4 tons (31,900kg)

Powerplant: V-2-44, 12-cylinder
diesel, 512bhp (382kW) at 2000rpm

Speed: 31.7mph (51km/h)

Range: 186 miles (300km)

Above: The Centurion was arguably the best tank to see service in the Korean War. Its biggest asset was the renowned L7 4.124in (105mm) gun, on which many of today's tank guns are based.

CENTURION (A41) MAIN BATTLE TANK

Originally designed to withstand a direct hit from a 3.46in (88mm) antitank round, the Centurion went on to become one of the most successful battle tanks of the Cold War era.

Right: The Centurion main battle tank incorporated all the lessons learned in the design of earlier generations of British tanks. It was hugely successful, thousands being built for service with armies all over the world.

Specifications

Armament: One 17pdr (3in/76mm); one coaxial 0.31in (7.92mm) Besa MG or one 0.79in (20mm) Polsten cannon

Armor: 0.75–4in (17–127mm)

Crew: 4

Dimensions: Length 24ft 6in (7.82m); Width 11ft 2in (3.39m); Height 9ft 11in (3.01m)

Weight: 42.5 tons (43,182kg)

Powerplant: Meteor V-12 gasoline, 650bhp (484.7kW)

Speed: 22mph (35km/h)

Range: 120 miles (192km)

Development of the Centurion main battle tank started in 1943, in response to a War Office requirement for a new heavy cruiser tank. One of the principal requirements was that the new AFV should be able to withstand a direct hit from an 3.46in (88mm) gun, but at an early stage of the development program the 40 ton (40,640kg) weight limit (imposed by the capacity of existing transport trailers) had to be increased to fulfill this requirement. The War Office decided to build new trailers rather than hamper the design of what promised to be an excellent tank, so work proceeded on a heavier version. By this time, construction of the first 40-ton prototypes

was well advanced, and these were completed as the Centurion Mk I. Only a few of these were produced before production switched to the more heavily armored Centurion Mk II. This was followed by the Mk III, which featured a fully automated stabilization system for its 20-pounder gun. The latter was used only for a short time before it was replaced by an effective 4.13in (105mm) weapon.

Success

The Centurion became one of the world's most successful tanks. It was supplied to many armed forces, and was used in Korea, the Middle East, and Vietnam. When production ended in 1962, 4423 units had been built.

From World War to Cold War

1945 UK

COMET CRUISER (A34)

The Comet cruiser tank went into action during the closing phase of World War II. It was the result of an attempt to smooth out the defects of earlier AFVs in this category.

Below: *Entering service with the British Army in 1945, the Comet was still being used in the United Kingdom until the early 1960s, and by other armies as late as the mid-1970s.*

The Comet was an attempt by the British Army to remedy the problems in the design of earlier cruiser tanks during combat in the Western Desert. The first attempt at redesign resulted in the Challenger, comprising a 17-pounder (3.03in/77mm) antitank gun mounted on a Cromwell chassis. The mounting of this larger gun created its own problems, the biggest of which was a reduction in armor protection. Ultimately the Challenger was not a success. The Comet design used a 3.03in (77mm) version of the 17-pounder (3.03in/77mm) gun. It had a lower muzzle velocity, the engine was uprated, and the armor welded rather than riveted. The prototype Comet was completed in February 1944 and the first examples were delivered in September, in time to take part in the British XXX Corps' dash to the Rhine at Arnhem. The Comet was also used during the crossing of the Rhine at Wesel in March 1945, and served alongside the Centurion during the Korean War. Production by the end of World War II totalled 1200 units, some of which were supplied to foreign armies.

Specifications

Armament: One 17pdr (3.03in/77mm); two 0.31in (7.92mm) Besa MGs

Armor: 0.98–4.02in (25–102mm)

Crew: 5

Dimensions: Length 21ft 6in (6.55m); Width 10ft 1in (3.07m); Height 8ft 8in (2.67m)

Weight: 32.7 tons (32,223kg)

Powerplant: Rolls-Royce Meteor V-12, 600bhp (447.6kW)

Speed: 32mph (50km/h)

Range: 125 miles (200km)

From World War to Cold War
✗ 1947 USA

M46 MEDIUM TANK

A development of the M26, the M46 medium tank was used very
successfully in Korea, where it proved more than a match
for the T34/85.

Specifications

Armament: 3.54in (90mm) M3A1
gun; one 0.50in (12.7mm) MG;
one 0.30in (7.62mm) MG

Armor: 3.94in (100mm)

Crew: 5

Dimensions: Length 23ft (7.04m);
Width 11ft 5in (3.48m); Height
(over MG) 9ft 10in (3m)

Weight: 43.3 tons (44,000kg)

Powerplant: Continental AV-1790-
5 V-12, 704hp (525.4kW)

Speed: 30mph (48km/h)

Range: 80 miles (130km)

The M46 was a direct descendant of the
M26 Pershing. This had been reclassified
as a medium tank shortly after the end of
World War II. The M26 was not sufficiently
mobile to meet this classification, however, so
in 1948 the decision was taken to fit the tank
with a better engine (the Continental AV-
1790-3) and an Allison CD-850-1 cross-
drive transmission. With these improvements
the tank was renamed M26E2. As further
modifications were incorporated, the US
Ordnance Department decided that it
merited a new name, and so it became
the M46.

China and Korea
The M46 fought in Korea and played its part

*Above: In Korea, the M46 Patton was more than a
match for the T-34/85, which was to be expected, as
the American AFV was a newer design and fell more
into the category of the heavier Iosef Stalin series.*

in the defense of the Pusan perimeter
following the North Korean offensive. This
almost drove South Korean and hastily
assembled American forces from the
peninsula in the last half of 1950. It was also
used in September in support of the landings
at Inchon by the US Marines, and covered
the fighting retreat of UN forces following
the massive intervention by Communist
China in the final weeks of the year. The
M46 was the first in the series of the famous
US General George S. Patton.

From World War to Cold War
⚒ **1948   Soviet Union**

T-54/55 MAIN BATTLE TANK

The T-54/55 series of main battle tanks has seen more combat than any other post-World War II tank. It was also produced in the largest numbers, many thousands being built.

No other tank in the world has been produced in such quantity as the T-54/55 series. It was developed as the Soviet Union's main battle tank in 1947 and was still serving with some developing-world (and former Soviet-friendly) countries 60 years later. The T-54 was based on the T-44, but with a 3.94in (100mm) gun instead of an 3.34in (85mm) weapon. In service, the tank was progressively updated, the T-54A model being fitted with gun-stabilization and night-vision equipment. The T-55B was the first model to incorporate infrared night-vision equipment and two-axis stabilization for the main gun.

Design and use

The T-55 was a T-54 modified for operations on the nuclear battlefield. It had a thicker turret casting, more powerful engine, and primitive NBC protection. Production of the T-54/55 continued in the former Soviet

Above: *The T-54/55's main armament was originally the D10T 3.9in (100mm) rifled gun, a very large caliber weapon for its time, but long since made obsolete by its inability to penetrate modern armor with the types of armor-piercing ammunition it used.*

Specifications

Armament: One 3.94in (100mm) D-10T gun; two 0.3in (7.62mm) DT MGs; one 0.5in (12.7mm) DShK AA MG

Armor: Maximum, 8in (203mm)

Crew: 4

Dimensions: Length (hull) 21ft 2in (6.45m); Width 10ft 9in (3.27m); Height 7ft 10in (2.4m)

Weight: 35.42 tons (36,000kg)

Powerplant: V-54 12-cylinder diesel, 520bhp (388kW) at 2000rpm

Speed: 30mph (48km/h)

Range: 250 miles (400km)

Above: East German T-54 training tanks in operation. Like many Warsaw Pact forces, the East German army continued to rely on the T-54/55 rather than convert entirely to the T-62.

Below: The T-55 was a version of the T-54, upgraded for operations on a battlefield where tactical nuclear weapons were expected to be used, and feared an early form of NBC protection.

Union into the 1980s, and was also undertaken in China (where it was produced as the Type 69), Czechoslovakia, Romania, and Poland. The T-54/55 has been used very widely, particularly in the Middle East during the 1967 Six-Day War and the Yom Kippur War of 1973. During these two conflicts, Israel captured over 1000 T-54/55s and retained many of them for the Israeli Army. They replaced the Soviet 3.94in (100mm) gun with a 4.13in (105mm) L5 or M68 and the Russian engine with a General

Motors diesel. In Israeli service the T-54/55 was known as the Tiran-5. After their retirement from reserve units in the 1990s many were sold on to Latin-American countries, while others were modified as armored personnel carriers.

Export

The T-54/55 was exported to over 40 countries, while China exported thousands of her Type 69 variant. Many of these were delivered to Iran and Iraq, and fought during the long "oil war" between those two countries in the 1980s. Most of the Iraqi tanks were destroyed during the Gulf War of 1991, where their encounters with American M1 Abrams and British Challenger main battle tanks were short, brutal, and one-sided. Some of Iraq's surviving Type 69s were still in service during the second Gulf War in 2003, when they were used in a static artillery role. The T-54/55 was also used in the Balkan wars that accompanied the dissolution of the former Yugoslavia, and before that in Vietnam. The series was produced in at least 12 different versions, and was continually modified during its service life.

From World War to Cold War
⚒ 1948   France

AMX-13 LIGHT TANK

The AMX-13 was France's first postwar light tank design and was a huge
success. It was exported to 24 countries, as well as being used by the
French Army themselves.

In the post-World War II years, the French
Army urgently needed to re-arm
themselves and drew up a requirement for
three new armored fighting vehicles. One of
these was a light tank, which was
subsequently developed by Atelier de
Construction d'Issy-les-Moulineaux under
the name of AMX-13. The tank went into
production in 1953 and proved to be one of
the most successful vehicles of its kind ever
to be manufactured. An estimated 7700 units
were produced between 1945 and 1985, and
about half of these were used for export. The
2.95in (75mm) gun of the original AMX-13
production model was modeled on the
German L/71 Panther gun, and this
was replaced by a 3.54in (90mm) weapon
in 1966.

Geographical use

The AMX-13 was phased out of service with
the French Army in the 1970s, but the
vehicle was exported to 24 countries, and
continues to be used by some of these. The
biggest export customer was Singapore,
which purchased 350 units. Some of the
export variants are armed with a 4.13in
(105mm) gun. The AMX-13 was used by the
Israeli Army in the Six-Day War of 1967, but
this version's 2.95in (75mm) gun was
ineffective against the amor of the T-54 and
T-55 main battle tanks used by Egypt and
Syria, so the tank was phased out, with some
being sent to Singapore.

*Below: Diagram showing an AMX-13 fitted with an
FL-10 two-man turret and armed with the original
2.95in (75mm) gun.*

*Above: Later versions of the
AMX were armed with a 3.54in
(90mm) or 4.13in (105mm) gun,
the latter pictured here.*

Specifications

Armament: One 2.95in (75mm),
3.54in (90mm), or 4.13in (105mm)
gun; one or two 0.295in (7.5mm)
or 0.30in (7.62mm) MGs

Armor: Maximum, 0.98in (25mm)

Crew: 3

Dimensions: Length, overall 16ft
(4.88m); Width 8ft 2.8in (2.51m);
Height 7ft 6.5in (2.3m)

Weight: 14.76 tons (15,000kg)

Powerplant: Sofam Model 8Gxb,
8-cylinder gasoline, 250hp
(186.4kW)

Speed: Road, 37.3mph (60km/h)

Range: Road, 21.7–248.5 miles
(350–400km)

From World War to Cold War
⚒ 1950 France

AMX VCI INFANTRY COMBAT VEHICLE

The AMX VCI was a versatile infantry combat vehicle that was later
adapted to other roles. It was still in service in the 21st century.

Specifications

Armament: One 0.50in (12.7mm)
MG or one 0.30in (7.62mm) MG

Armor: Maximum, 1.18in (30mm)

Crew: 3 plus 10 troops

Dimensions: Length 18ft 8.4in
(5.7m); Width 8ft 9in (2.67m);
Height 7ft 10.8in (2.41m)

Weight: 14.76 tons (15,000kg)

Powerplant: Detroit Diesel 6V-
53T, 6-cylinder diesel, 280hp
(208.8kW)

Speed: Road, 39.8mph (64km/h)

Range: Road, 310–341 miles
(500–550km)

The AMX VCI infantry combat vehicle was one of the three armored vehicles ordered by the French Government straight after World War II (the others being the AMX-13 light tank and the Panhard armored car). All used the same chassis. The AMX VCI was very popular with armies in the developing world. The VCI was a better design than similar types of AFV of that era, as it was fitted with a machine-gun turret and its infantry could use their weapons from within the vehicle. Its main drawback was that it had no amphibious capability. The VCI was produced in several different versions. These included the AMX VCI Toucan (a standard AMX VCI personnel

Above: This French Army AMX VCI is fitted with a cupola-mounted machine gun. Note the firing ports in the troop compartment, seen just below the gunner.

carrier with a Toucan turret mounting a 0.79in [20mm] automatic cannon) and the AMX Cargo (a cargo carrier based on the VCI chassis). The rear area of this latter model was open-topped, and some of the armor was removed to make the vehicle lighter. The AMX TB was an armored ambulance version of the AMX VCI. In this role, the vehicle was unarmed and carried medical supplies, stretchers, a respirator, and a refrigerator.

From World War to Cold War

⚔ **1950 France**

PANHARD EBR ARMORED CAR

The Panhard EBR served the French Army well for nearly 40 years.

Four of its eight wheels were raised for road travel and could be

lowered for cross-country operations.

The design of the Panhard EBR dated back to the late 1930s, when Panhard et Levassor was one of the French Army's prime manufacturers of wheeled armored fighting vehicles. After the end of World War II, Panhard received a contract for the construction of a prototype 8x8 armored car, while the rival firm Hotchkiss was asked to produce a 6x6 vehicle. The prototypes of both vehicles were evaluated by the French Army, and the Panhard et Levassor submission was selected for production as the EBR (Engin Blindé de Reconnaissance, or armored reconnaissance vehicle). The first production vehicles were completed in 1950, and 1200 units were built until production ceased in 1960. The vehicle was exported to Mauritania, Morocco, and Tunisia.

EBR VTT

The EBR VTT was an armored personnel carrier version, some of which were exported to Portugal for use by the security services.

Some vehicles were fitted with the FL-10 turret of the AMX-13 light tank, armed with a 2.95in (75mm) gun. The EBR was phased out of service by the French in 1987.

Above: *The center pairs of roadwheels had steel rims, and were lowered when the vehicle was traveling across country to give better traction in muddy conditions.*

Below: *The Panhard EBR was the French Army's standard armored car from 1950, and was based on a prewar design.*

Specifications

Armament: (EBR-75) one 2.95in (75mm) gun; one or three 0.295in (7.5mm) MGs; (EBR-90) one 3.54in (90mm) gun; one 0.295in (7.5mm) MG

Armor: Maximum, 1.57in (40mm)

Crew: 4

Dimensions: Length, (EBR-75) 20ft 2.4in (6.157m), (EBR-90) 24ft 0.6in (7.331m); Width (both models) 7ft 11.2in (2.42m); Height, (EBR-75) 7ft 6.6in (2.327m), (EBR-90) 8ft 5.7in (2.582m)

Weight: (EBR-75) 12.3 tons (12,500kg); (EBR-90) 14.66 tons (14,900kg)

Powerplant: Panhard 12 H 6000 S, 12-cylinder gasoline, 149.1kW (200hp)

Speed: Road, 65.25mph (105km/h)

Range: Road, 354 miles (570km)

From World War to Cold War

✖ 1951 Soviet Union

ASU-57 TANK DESTROYER

The ASU-57 was the result of a requirement by the Soviet airborne forces for an effective tank-killer that could be dropped into action alongside the paratroops and deployed immediately.

Specifications

Armament: One 2.24in (57mm) M 55 gun

Armor: Maximum, 0.59in (15mm)

Crew: 3

Dimensions: Length 12ft 3in (3.73m); Width 7ft 3in (2.2m); Height 4ft 8in (1.42m)

Weight: 7.3 tons (7400kg)

Powerplant: ZIL-123 6-cylinder gasoline, 110bhp (82kW)

Speed: 40.4mph (65km/h)

Range: 189 miles (320km)

When the Soviet airborne forces were removed from the direct control of the Soviet Army in 1946, they were placed under the direct orders of the Defense Ministry. This reorganization prompted a call for various types of specialized armored vehicle to be used by the airborne forces. Since these forces had always been vulnerable to enemy armor, an airborne tank destroyer was high on the list of priorities. After much experimentation with various prototypes, the ASU-57 was accepted for production in 1951. This tank was a light vehicle constructed from aluminum and steel. This made the vehicle as lightweight as

Above: Designed to be dropped in support of Soviet airborne forces, the ASU-57 was a good example of the priority assigned to airborne operations in postwar USSR.

possible, enabling it to be mounted on a pallet and air-dropped from small cargo aircraft. Special braking rockets were often fitted to the pallet to help soften the impact on landing, a technique that was later adopted to cushion the landing of Soviet space capsules. The ASU-57 was armed with a 2.24in (57mm) gun developed from the ZIS-2 antitank gun of World War II vintage.

M41 WALKER BULLDOG LIGHT TANK

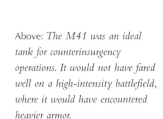

The M41 Walker Bulldog light tank was developed in response to a requirement from the US Army for an armored fighting vehicle to replace the M24 Chaffee, which lacked powerful main armament.

Following trials with a series of prototypes designated T37, the vehicle that was accepted for production was known as the Light Tank T41. In 1950 its name changed to Light Tank M41 Little Bulldog, and again to Walker Bulldog in honor of General Walton Walker (who was killed in a road accident in Korea in 1950). Production of the M41 started in 1951 at Cadillac's Cleveland Tank Plant, and by 1953 the new tank had completely replaced the M24 in US Army service. The Walker Bulldog was well-armed and agile, but it was noisy and heavy, which caused problems when transported by air.

Geographical use

The M41 was never used by the US Army, but it was exported to the Army of the Republic of Vietnam (ARVN), who used it against North Vietnamese T-54s. The M41 was exported to Brazil, Chile, Denmark, Dominican Republic, Guatemala, New Zealand, Somalia, Taiwan, Thailand, and Tunisia. Many of these tanks incorporated various improvements to prolong their active life, and were still in service in the early 21st century.

Above: The M41 was an ideal tank for counterinsurgency operations. It would not have fared well on a high-intensity battlefield, where it would have encountered heavier armor.

Specifications

Armament: One 3in gun (76mm); one 0.3in (7.62mm) MG; one 0.50in (12.7mm) MG

Armor: 1.23in (32mm)

Crew: 4

Dimensions: Length (over gun) 26ft 11in (8.21m); Width unknown; Height 8ft 11in (2.72m)

Weight: 23.13 tons (23,495kg)

Powerplant: Continental AOS-95-3 6-cylinder gasoline, 500hp (373kW)

Speed: 45mph (72.4km/h)

Range: 100 miles (161km)

Left: A cheap but effective tank, the M41 was an attractive proposition for many of America's "third world" allies, to whom it was widely exported.

PT-76 LIGHT AMPHIBIOUS TANK

Above: The PT-76 continues in use with armies that were once allied to the former Warsaw Pact.

Developed in the late 1940s, the Russian PT-76 has proved itself to be an excellent design. It is still in service in many parts of the world.

Specifications

Armament: One 3in (76.2mm) D056T gun; one 0.3in (7.62mm) SGMT MG; sometimes one 0.5in (12.7mm) DShKM antiaircraft MG

Armor: 0.197–0.67in (5–17mm)

Crew: 3

Dimensions: Length 22ft 8in (6.91m); Width 10ft 4in (3.14m); Height 7ft 5in (2.255m)

Weight: 13.78 tons (14,000kg)

Powerplant: One V-6 6-cylinder diesel, 240bhp (179kW) at 1800rpm

Speed: land 28mph (45km/h), water 6.2mph (10km/h)

Range: Road, 174 miles (280km); Water 40.4 miles (65km)

Development of the PT-76 light amphibious tank began in 1949, and the type was accepted for service in 1952. Production started in 1953 at the Stalingrad (later Volgograd) Tank Factory, and the vehicle was adopted as the standard reconnaissance tank of the Soviet and Warsaw Pact armed forces. PT-76 is an abbreviation of Plavayushchy Tank (literally "swimming tank"). About 7000 PT-76s were built before production ended in 1963; 2000 vehicles were exported to 24 countries under Soviet influence. This production total includes an improved variant, the PT-76B, which appeared in 1958. The type was also produced in China as the Type 63, and many of these

Above: A PT-76 rolling ashore from a Soviet landing craft during an amphibious warfare exercise. The tank has seen a good deal of action around the world.

were exported to Pakistan, Sudan, Tanzania, and Vietnam. India acquired large numbers of PT-76s, and these were used in the Indo-Pakistan wars of 1965 and 1971. The PT-76 has also been used in the Arab–Israeli wars, and in the counterinsurgency role in countries such as Indonesia.

Continued use

The PT-76 was still in widespread use in the early part of the 21st century: Russia was reported to have used it in Chechnya.

From World War to Cold War

1952 USA

M103 HEAVY TANK

The M103 heavy tank was intended to outgun the latest Soviet types in its class, the IS and T-10. It was never used in action and its size and weight made operations difficult.

Below: *An M103 prototype. The turret is traversed to the rear and the travel lock, used to secure the gun when the vehicle is in transit, is open.*

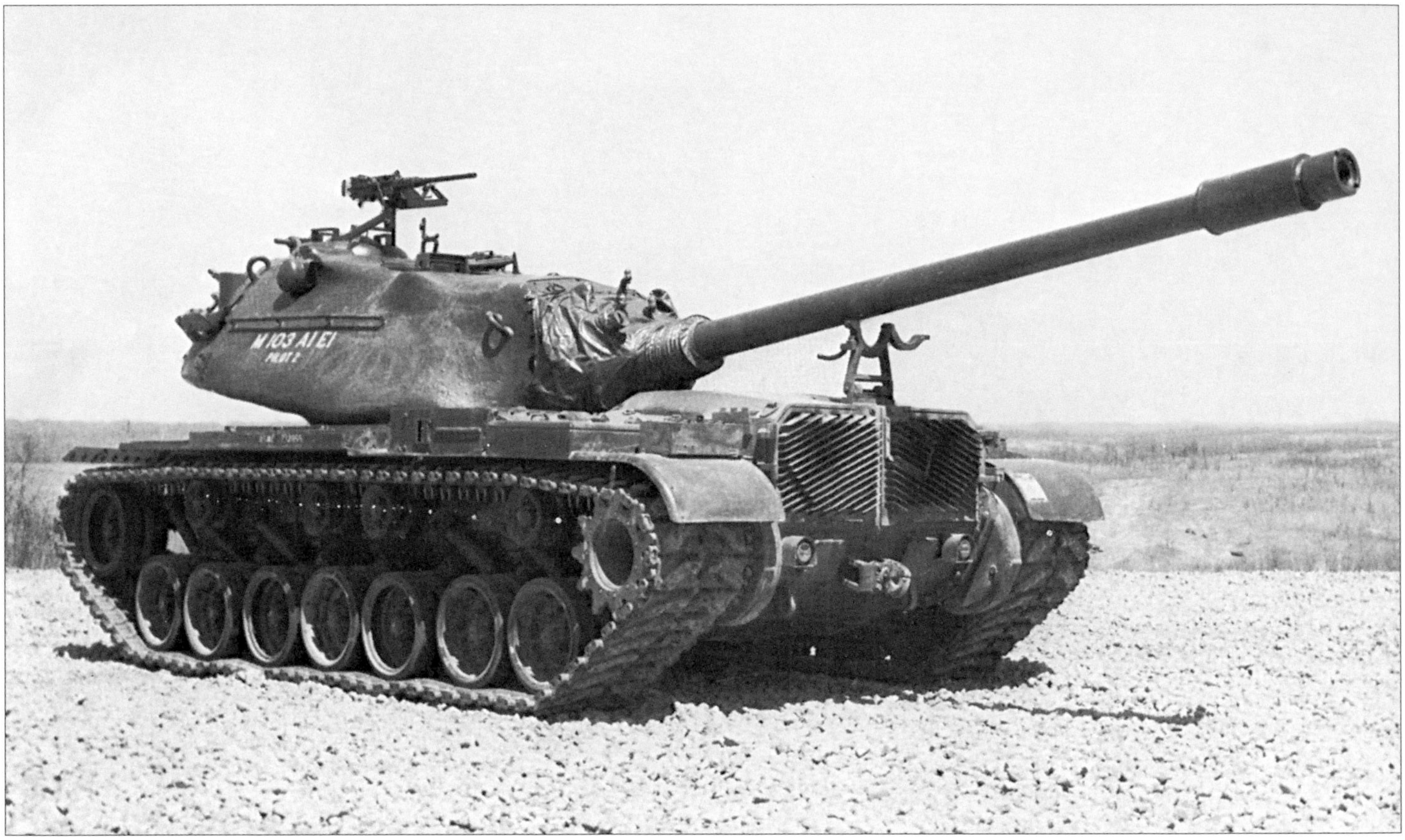

The M103 heavy tank (or Tank, Combat, Full Tracked 120mm M103) was a product of the early years of the Cold War. This time also saw the appearance of the M41 and M47 light and medium tanks.

The M103 was originally known as the T43, and went through protracted initial designs. Several prototypes were evaluated, and trials showed up many defects; 100 modifications were required before the type was accepted for service as the M103. The type entered production in 1952 at the Chrysler Tank Plant in Detroit, and over the next two years 200 units were built and deployed to Europe for service with the US 7th Army. The tank was never popular; it was heavy and underpowered, and suffered from fragile drive systems.

Different versions

The successive versions of the M103 had much in common with the M47, M48, and M60, although the turret was larger to accommodate the massive 4.72in (120mm) gun, its two loaders, the gunner, and commander. The number of M103s in service was progressively reduced during the 1960s and the last examples were withdrawn in 1974. Several M103s still exist as museum pieces in America.

Specifications

Armament: One M58 120mm (4.72in) gun; one 0.30in (7.62mm) MG; one 0.50in (12.7mm) MG

Armor: 7in (178mm)

Crew: 5

Dimensions: Length 33ft 1in (10.11m); Width 12ft 4in (3.76m); Height 11ft 8in (3.56m)

Weight: 55.8 tons (56,700kg)

Powerplant: Continental AV-1790-5B gasoline, 810hp (604kW)

Speed: 21mph (34km/h)

Range: 80 miles (129km)

From World War to Cold War
 1952   USA

M47 PATTON I MEDIUM TANK

The M47 was one of the oldest members of a family of medium tanks that

began with the M26 and extended right through to the modern-day M60.

It was widely used by armies throughout the world.

Specifications

Armament: One M36 3.54in (90mm) gun; two 0.50in (12.7mm) MGs; one 0.3in (7.62mm) MG

Armor: 4.53in (115mm)

Crew: 5

Dimensions: Length (over gun) 28ft in (8.56m); Width 10ft 6in (3.2m); Height 11ft (3.35m)

Weight: 45.4 tons (46,165kg)

Powerplant: Continental AVDS-1790-5B V-12 gasoline, 810hp (604.5kW)

Speed: 30mph (48km/h)

Range: 80 miles (129km)

Below: The M47 Patton was rushed into production to meet the needs of the Korean War, although it did not fight there.

The requirement that produced the M47 Patton tank originated in the Korean War. At that time, the principal American medium tank was the M46, but this had never been seen as anything other than an interim vehicle, to be replaced in due course by the T42, then under development. With rearmament assuming high priority following the outbreak of hostilities in Korea, however, it was realized that the continuing development of the T42 would take too long, and so yet another interim AFV came into being. This was the M47,

made up of a T42 turret on an M46 chassis. Named Patton after the flamboyant commander of the US 3rd Army in World War II, the tank was produced by the Detroit Arsenal and was very successful. Although it was soon replaced in US service by the M48, it was widely used by many of America's NATO allies and by 18 other countries. Although it arrived too late to be used in the Korean War, it was used in combat in other parts of the world, including the former Yugoslavia.

Below: The M47 medium tank was developed too late to see action in Korea, but it has since seen combat in many other parts of the world.

From World War to Cold War
⚒ 1953 Soviet Union

T-10 HEAVY TANK

The prototype T-10 appeared in 1955, although development plans had been underway since 1948. The tank remained in production until 1966, when the Soviet Union dispensed with most of its heavy tanks.

Below: *A T-10 heavy tank with a 0.5in (12.7mm) DshKM heavy antiaircraft machine gun mounted on the commander's cupola. The T-10 became operational in 1955.*

The T-10 was Russia's last heavy tank, and the final development of the KV and IS series. When it was first accepted for production in 1952 it was known as IS-10, but when Stalin fell from favor, the tank was renamed T-10. The type differed from its predecessor, the IS-3, in having a longer hull, seven pairs of roadwheels (instead of six), a larger turret mounting a new main gun, and an uprated engine. The T-10A and T-10B were improved models, the former having two-axis gun stabilization and the latter improved gunnery optics. The final version was the T-10M, which was equipped with a longer M-62-T2 (L/43) gun with a five-baffle muzzle brake, a two-axis gun stabilizer, heavier caliber machine guns, infrared night-vision equipment, and NBC protection. About 2500 examples of all models were built before production ended in 1966. T-10 production ceased in 1966 after the manufacture of further heavy tanks was cancelled by the Soviet Government. Heavy AFVs had been completely removed from service by 1993. The T-10 was used by Egypt, North Vietnam, and Syria as well as by the Soviet Army.

Left: *The T-10 was armed with an extremely powerful 4.8in (122mm) gun. Some former Egyptian T-10s were used by Israel for static defense on the Suez Canal.*

Specifications

Armament: One 4.8in (122mm) D-74 gun; two 0.57in (14.5mm) KPV MGs; optional 0.5in (12.7mm) DShK AA MG

Armor: Maximum, 10.63in (270mm)

Crew: 4

Dimensions: Length 24ft 4in (7.41m); Width 11ft 8in (3.56m); Height 7ft 11in (2.43m)

Weight: 51.18 tons (52,000kg)

Powerplant: V2 -IS, 12-cylinder diesel, 690bhp (515kW) at 2000rpm

Speed: 26mph (42km/h)

Range: 155 miles (250km)

From World War to Cold War
🔧 1953 UK

SARACEN ARMORED PERSONNEL CARRIER

The Saracen was the first British armored personnel carrier to be developed after the end of World War II, and remained the only one of its kind in service for many years.

Below: The Saracen armored personnel carrier was just one of a family of effective AFVs. It entered service in 1953.

Specifications

Armament: One Browning 7.62mm (0.3in) MG; one Bren 0.3in (7.62mm) LMG

Armor: 0.32–0.63in (8–16mm)

Crew: 2 plus 10

Dimensions: Length 17ft 2in (5.233m); Width 8ft 4in (2.539m); Height 8ft 1in (2.463m)

Weight: 10 tons (10,170kg)

Powerplant: Rolls-Royce 8-cylinder gasoline developing 160bhp (119.3kW) at 3750rpm

Speed: 45mph (72.5km/h)

Range: 248.5 miles (400km)

Right: The 6x6 Saracen was widely used by the British Army and was ideal for counterinsurgency operations in 1950s trouble spots such as Cyprus and Malaya.

Built by the Alvis Company of Coventry, the Saracen 6x6 armored personnel carrier was one of a family of wheeled armored vehicles designed by the Fighting Vehicles Research and Development Establishment. This family was known as the FV600 series and also included the FV601 Saladin armored car (which shared many parts in common with the Saracen). Because of the escalating emergency in Malaya, where thousands of British Commonwealth troops were locked in a bitter struggle with communist guerrillas, priority was given to the production of the Saracen, the first examples coming off the assembly lines in December 1952. Production continued until 1972, by which time 1838 vehicles had been completed.

Geographical use

The Saracen served throughout the world wherever British forces were deployed, from Germany to Hong Kong, and it was there, in 1993, that the last examples were used. Several versions of the Saracen were produced, all with relatively minor variations. Despite its widespread use, it was only actually used in combat in Malaysia. It was replaced in service in Germany by the FV432 fully tracked APC, which had a better cross-country performance, improved armor protection, and a greater action radius.

From World War to Cold War
1953 USA

M48 MAIN BATTLE TANK

One of the most widely used medium tanks in the world, the M48 was a successful design from the outset, and went on to perform well in conflicts around the world.

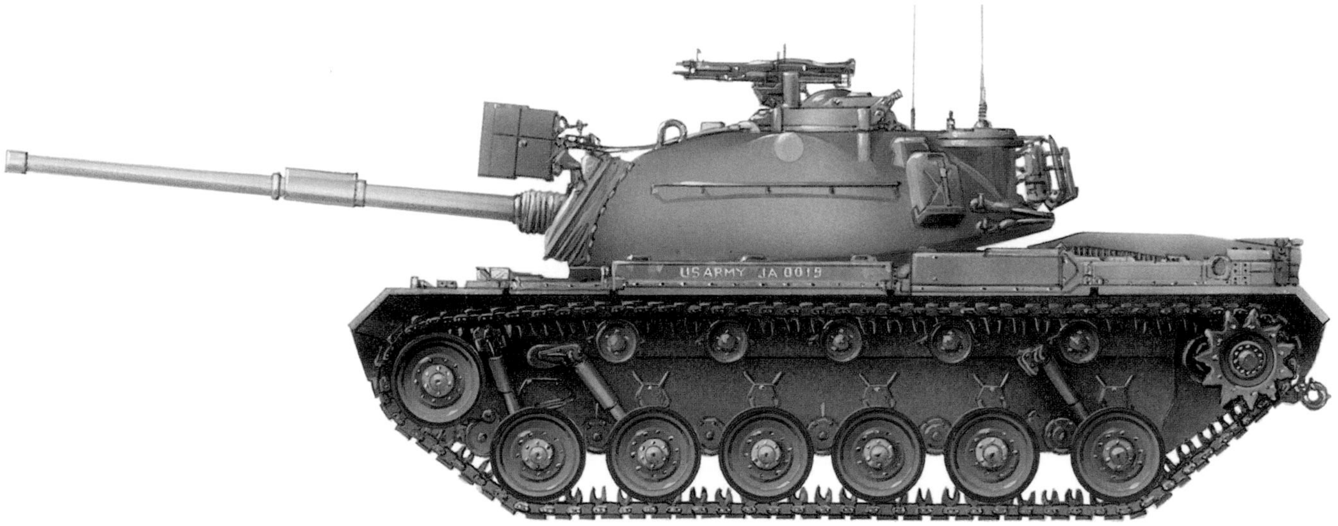

The M47 had been in service for only a year when the US Army decided to replace it with another product of the Patton series, the M48. This had a new turret, redesigned hull and improved suspension. It entered production in 1952 at Chrysler's Delaware Tank Plant. The early versions of the M48 used gasoline engines, but combat experience in the Arab-Israeli war of 1956 showed that it readily burst into flames when hit, just as the early Shermans had done in World War II. In 1959, Chrysler upgraded existing tanks to produce the M48A3 model, which featured a diesel powerplant. Production of the M48 ended that year, by which time over 11,700 units had been built.

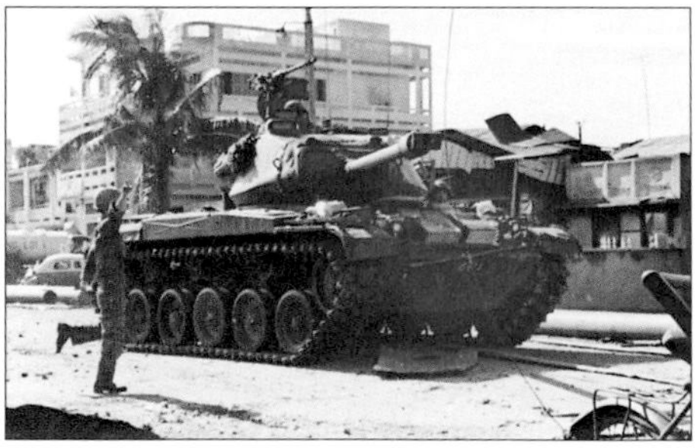

Above: *An M48 advances during street fighting in Saigon in May 1968. The M48 was intended for long-range engagements, and in Vietnam a gunner often had to be carried on the rear deck for close-in protection.*

Upgrades

In the mid-1970s the M48 was upgraded and fitted with a 4.13in (105mm) gun, making it more compatible with the M60 (alongside which it operated). This variant was designated M48A5. By this time, most of the

Specifications

(M48A5)

Armament: One 4.13in (105mm) L7 gun, three 0.3in (7.62mm) MGs
Armor: 7in (180mm)
Crew: 4
Dimensions: Length (over gun) 30ft 6in (9.31m); Width 11ft 11in (3.63m); Height 10ft 1in (3.01m)
Weight: 48.2 tons (48,987kg)
Powerplant: Continental AVDS-1790-2 12-cylinder supercharged diesel, 750hp (559.7kW)
Speed: 30mph (48km/h)
Range: 310 miles (499km)

Left: *Israel's M48s have 3.94-in (105mm) guns, diesel engines, and low-profile commander's cupolas. Many have been retrofitted with the same explosive reactive armor (ERA) fitted to the IDF's M60 tanks.*

Below: *US Marines ride ashore on an M48 during an exercise. The M48 was very effective in American hands, but less so in the service of other armies whose tactics left much to be desired. It was outfought by the British-built Centurion.*

M48s had been relegated to National Guard and Reserve formations, but it continued to be used by frontline formations, and the Americans allowed other operators them to upgrade their M48s to M48A5 standard. In Germany, the Federal German Army upgraded 650 M48s by replacing the US M68 41.3in (105mm) gun with the British L7A3 weapon and other equipment. In this guise it became known as designation M84A2GA2.

Combat

The M48 was used in combat during the Vietnam War, where it was used in an infantry support role. It was first used in tank-versus-tank combat during the Indo-Pakistan war of 1965, where it suffered heavy losses, particularly against the Indian Army's Centurions. At the Battle of Asal

Uttar, during an assault on Indian positions, the Pakistanis lost 100 M48s, although losses decreased after the Pakistanis revised their tactics. Poor tactics were largely responsible for the losses inflicted by Israeli M48s on Egyptian T-54s and T-55s in the Sinai desert during the Six-Day War of 1967, but on the West Bank, Jordanian M48s were outfought by Israeli M4 Shermans. Again, this was due to better Israeli tactics. Many Jordanian M48s were captured and put into Israeli service.

Continuing service

Many foreign countries are still using the M48 in the early part of the 21st century and it remains a viable fighting vehicle, although it is becoming increasingly vulnerable to portable antitank weapons.

From World War to Cold War
1955 USA

M50 "ONTOS" TANK DESTROYER

The ugly Ontos was designed as a tank destroyer, but it never operated in that role. Instead, it was used as a fire support vehicle by the US Marines in Vietnam.

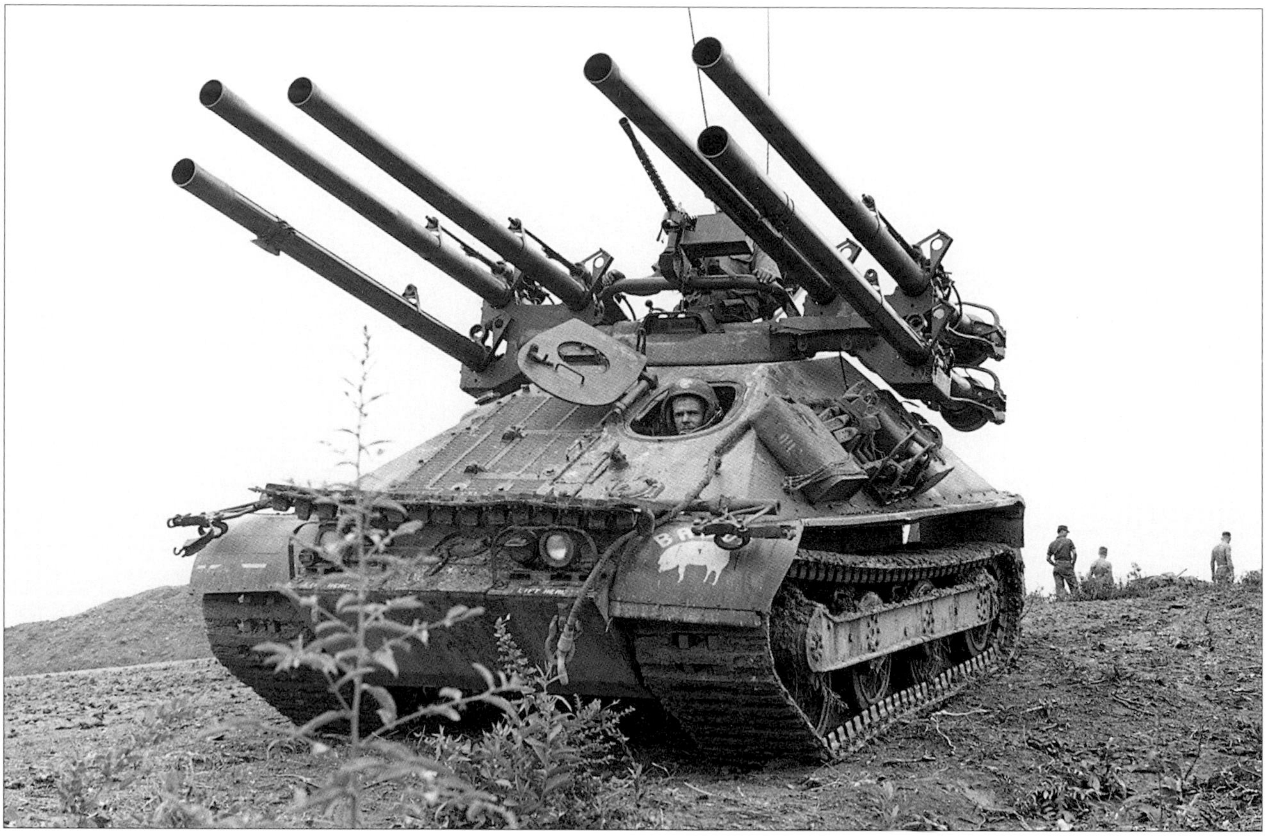

Above: *Although the M50 was useful as a fire support vehicle in Vietnam, it would have been less effective against a full-scale Soviet armored assault in Europe.*

Cold War threats were escalating around the world in the 1950s. The US Army initiated the development of a light, air-transportable antitank missile system, intended for rapid overseas deployment. The result was the Rifle Multiple 4.17in (106mm) Self-Propelled M50—an extremely ugly vehicle whose appearance earned it the name Ontos (meaning "The Thing" in Greek). Its main armament comprised six 4.17in (106mm) recoilless rifles, which could be fired in rapid succession to break up a massed armored assault of the kind favored by the Russians. The prototype, built by Allis-Chalmers in 1952, was based on the chassis of the M56 Scorpion light antitank vehicle.

Trials and production

Exhaustive trials were carried out, but almost as soon as these were completed in 1955 the US Army canceled its order. The US Marine Corps, on the other hand, saw some merit in the AFV and ordered a run of 297 units. The first vehicle was delivered in October 1956 and production was completed in 1957. Ontos was used extensively by the USMC in Vietnam as a fire support vehicle. The survivors were cut up for scrap when they were shipped back to America in 1970.

Specifications

Armament: Six 4.17in (106mm) recoilless rifles; one 0.30in (7.62mm) MG
Armor: 0.15in (13mm)
Crew: 3
Dimensions: Length 12ft 5in (3.83m); Width 8ft 6in (2.60m); Height 6ft 10in (2.13m)
Weight: 8.5 tons (8641kg)
Powerplant: General Motors 302 V6 gasoline, 145hp (108.2kW)
Speed: 30mph (48km/h)
Range: 150 miles (241km)

From World War to Cold War

⚒ **1956 UK**

CONQUEROR HEAVY TANK

The Conqueror tank was intended to combat Soviet heavy armor such as the IS-3, and was armed with a powerful 4.72in (120mm) main gun. Its key problem was its weight, which made it unwieldy.

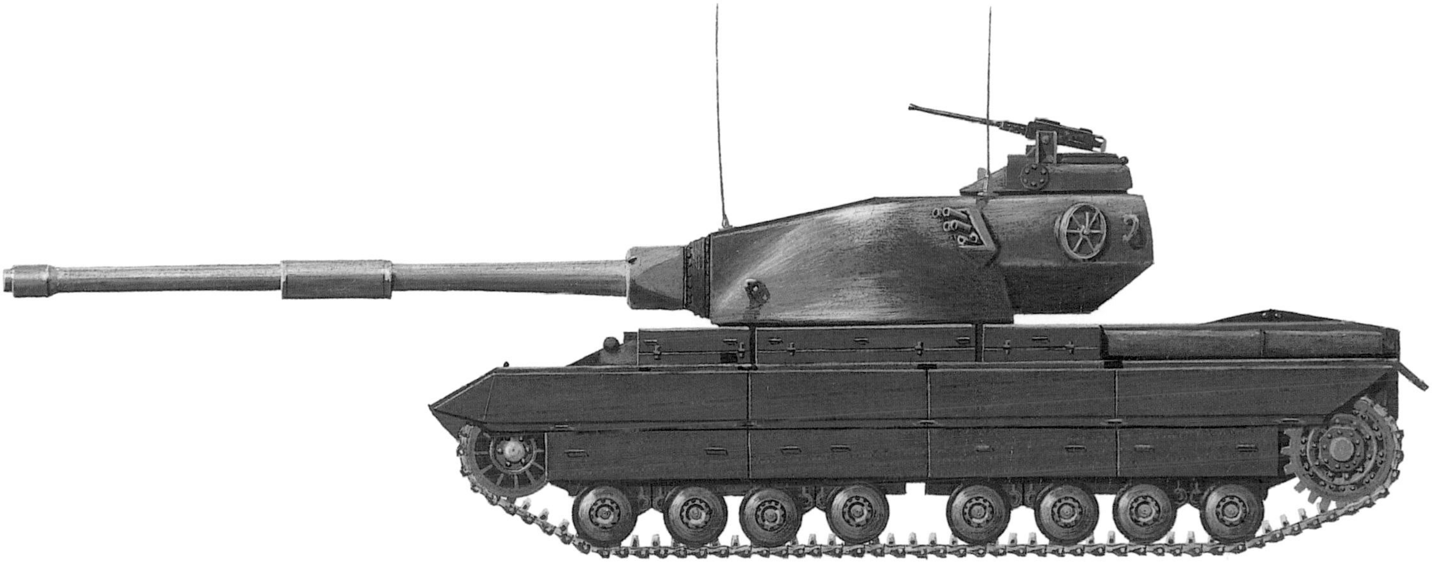

Specifications

Armament: One 4.72in (120mm) L1 gun; two 7.7mm (0.303in) MGs

Armor: 7.12in (178mm) max

Crew: 4

Dimensions: Length 38ft (11.58m); Width 13ft (3.987m); Height 11ft (3.352m)

Weight: 65 tons (66.045kg)

Powerplant: Rover Meteor M120 Mk1A 12-cylinder gasoline developing 810bhp (604kW) at 2800rpm

Speed: 21.3mph (34km/h)

Range: 95 miles (153km)

The western Allies assessed the Soviet tank threat in Europe in the late 1940s. One of their principal concerns was that the latest IS-3 heavy tank was so well protected that its armor would not be penetrated by the NATO tank guns then coming into use. The Americans and British both designed new heavy tanks in response to this threat. The American AFV was the M103; the British equivalent was the FV214 Conqueror. Production of this tank began in 1955 and continued until 1958, during which time 200 units were built and deployed to the British Army of the Rhine.

Drawbacks

Problems quickly began to manifest themselves, however. Although the Conqueror possessed very heavy armor (it was 7in [178mm] thick at the front) this contributed to the tank being overweight. The large turret fitted with a rotating cupola for the commander also contributed to this problem, although this was necessary to house the 4.72in (120mm) gun. The weight of the Conqueror made it very slow, and many river bridges in Germany were incapable of supporting it. Apart from its hitting power, it offered no advantage over the Centurion, and the last examples were withdrawn in 1966.

Above: *The Conqueror heavy tank was produced to counter the threat posed by the USSR's IS-3. In service, it lacked the mobility essential for rapid deployment in the face of an enemy armored attack.*

From World War to Cold War
1956 USA

LANDING VEHICLE TRACKED (LVT)-5

The LVTP5 tracked landing vehicle served the US Marine Corps for two decades, but was never especially popular owing to its maintenance problems and lack of sufficient combat radius.

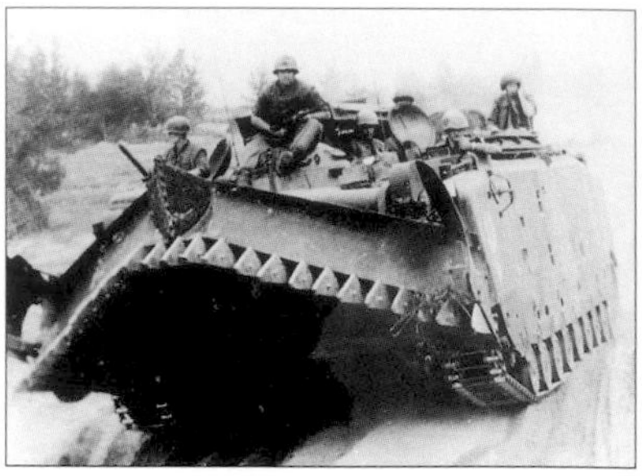

Above: *The LVTP5 had excellent amphibious capabilities, and it served as the US Marine Corps' APC in Vietnam.*

Below: *The LVTP5 was based on the same tactical concepts as the previous "Buffalo" LVTs.*

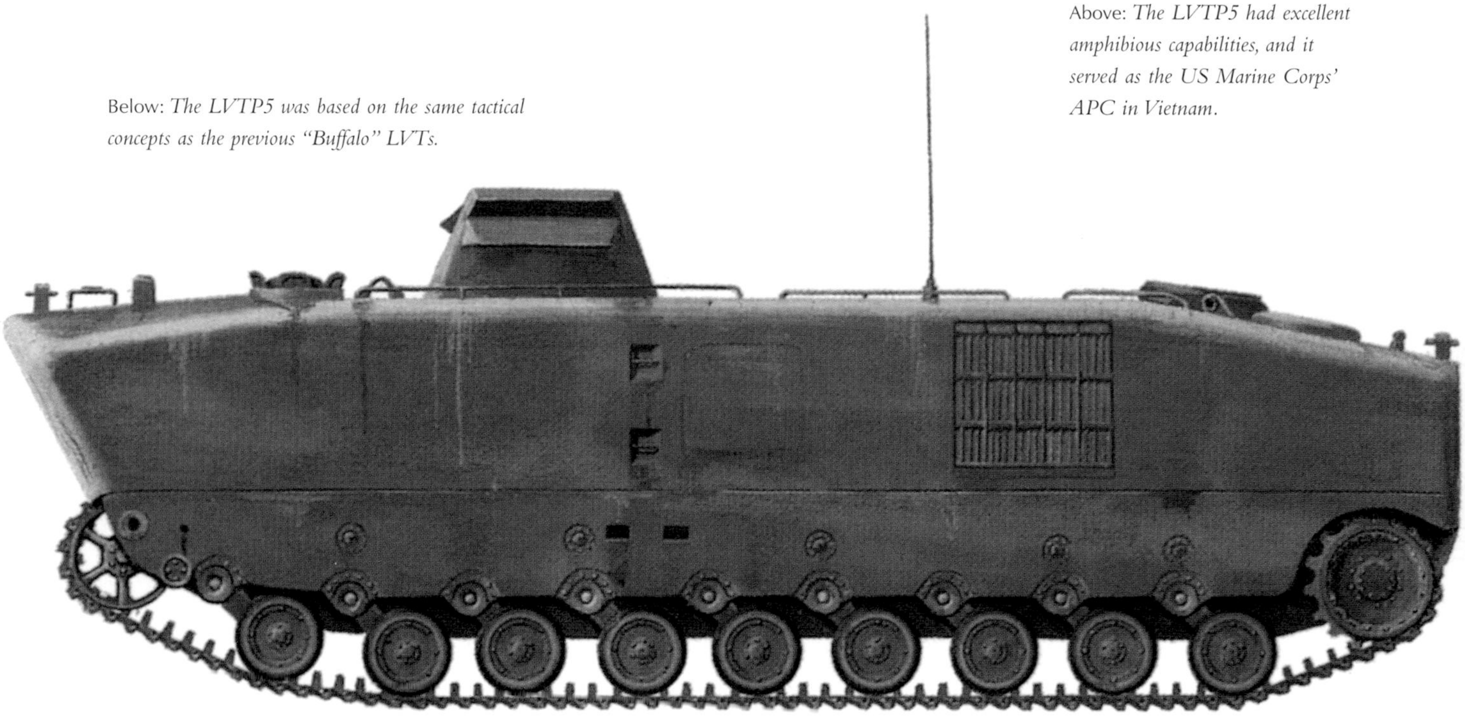

Accepted into service with the US Marine Corps in 1956, the LVTP5 (Landing Vehicle Tracked Personnel Model 5) was a large, tracked landing vehicle with an inverted V-shaped bow designed for efficient performance in the water. Over 1100 units were produced in the space of a year, replacing the USMC's vehicles of World War II vintage. The basic design underwent some minor modifications, including the fitting of a snorkel over the engine compartment, and the new name of LVTP5A1 was then adopted. The vehicle could carry 34 fully equipped marines, 32 on four-man seats and the other two on the gunner's platform. In an emergency, 45 men could be carried standing up. The LVTP5 could carry 5.36 tons (5,443 kg) of cargo when afloat, and 8.04 tons (8,165 kg) when on land. It could also accommodate a 4.13in (105mm) towed howitzer, its crew, and 90 rounds of ammunition.

Drawbacks

Although the LVTP5 was an intelligent design, it never proved adequate owing to its short operating range and its complexity of maintenance. The vehicle was phased out by 1974, some vehicles being acquired by Taiwan and the Philippines, and Chile.

Specifications

Armament: One 0.30in (7.62mm) MG

Armor: 0.63in (16mm)

Crew: 3 plus 25

Dimensions: Length 29ft 8in (9.04m); Width 11ft 8in (3.57m); Height 9ft 6in (2.92m)

Weight: 36.8 tons (37,400kg)

Powerplant: Continental AV-1790-1, V-12, gasoline

Speed: land 30mph (48km/h); water 6.6mph (11km/h)

Range: Road, 190 miles (306km); Water, 57 miles (92km)

From World War to Cold War
✖ 1956 USA

M113 ARMORED PERSONNEL CARRIER

Below: The Norwegian army's fleet of upgraded M113A1 vehicles are fitted with a Hägglunds one-man turret armed with a Rheinmetall 20mm MK Rh 202 cannon.

The M113 is the world's most widely used armored personnel carrier. By 1992 production totaled 75,000 units, and further production runs have brought the figure to over 80,000.

Specifications

(M113A1)

Armament: Various, but minimum usually one 0.50in (12.7mm) MG	
Armor: 1.77in (45mm)	
Crew: 2 plus 11	
Dimensions: Length 8ft 3in (2.52m); Width 8ft 10in (2.69m); Height (to hull top) 6ft 1in (1.85m)	
Weight: 11.16 tons (11,343kg)	
Powerplant: General Motors 6V53 6-cylinder diesel, 212hp (158.2kW)	
Speed: 38mph (61km/h)	
Range: 298 miles (480km)	

With production exceeding 80,000 units, the M113 is the most widely used armored fighting vehicle of all time. Introduced in 1960, it was developed to transport airborne troops in transport aircraft like the Lockheed C-130 Hercules, as well as to perform its primary role as a battlefield APC. The original M113 model was powered by a gasoline engine, and this was replaced in 1964 by the diesel-powered M113A1. The M113A2 entered service in 1979. This was essentially the same model as the A1 but had an improved cooling system and suspension. It was followed by the M113A3, which was fitted with a more powerful turbocharged diesel engine. The M113 was only lightly armored: it was designed to provide protection from shrapnel for its 11 troops before they disembarked in the forward battle area.

ACAV version

More armor protection was added to produce an ACAV (Armored Cavalry) version, which was transformed into a true armored fighting vehicle by the addition of shields for its machine guns.

Above: The M113 has been used by 50 countries and has been produced in several versions to perform different tasks, such as that of command vehicle.

Chapter 6

POSTWAR DEVELOPMENT

By the end of the 1950s, tank designers had to factor in a new issue, namely the threat of tactical nuclear exchange. This actually gave a new lease of life to the tank: An AFV seemed to offer the best protection against the effects of a nuclear weapon's heat, blast, and radiation. To a large extent, armor would resist the physical effects of a nuclear blast, while mobility would help land forces to avoid nuclear strikes by passing rapidly through irradiated or devastated areas.

Above: *Chinese infantry debouching from a Type 63 light tank. The Type 63, among other defensive measures, can inject diesel into the exhaust to make its own smokescreen.*

Left: *Germany's Leopard tank formed an important part of NATO's frontline defense during the dangerous years of the Cold War. It incorporated all the best aspects of early tanks, like the Panther.*

The later development of enhanced radiation weapons (commonly known as neutron bombs) would put a different slant on the situation, for armor was no protection against massive blasts of radiation, and tank crews were at risk of being killed immediately. By tacit agreement on both sides, however, neutron bombs were never used operationally.

The 1960s saw the emergence of the armored personnel carrier in huge numbers, and, over time, this became the infantry combat vehicle. It was armed with its own guns so that it could provide valuable fire support to the infantry it had just disgorged. Sometimes it carried its own antitank missiles, which were becoming the biggest threat to the AFV. At this stage they were large and relatively unwieldy, but they had soon developed so that they could be transported and fired by a single infantryman. Soon, every soldier would become a potential tank destroyer.

Postwar Development
⚒ **1958 Sweden**

STRIDSVAGN (STRV) 74 LIGHT TANK

The Strv 74 light tank of 1957 was a further development in a long line of indigenous Swedish armored fighting vehicles, dating back to World War II.

The Strv 74 was a modified version of the Strv m/42, which in turn had been developed from the Strv m/40. The development of tanks in this series can be traced back to the development of the 16 ton (16,256kg) Lago tank by Landsverk AB, produced for the Hungarian Army, and an improved version of the L-60. The m/42 had a longer chassis than the m/40, as well as two extra roadwheels. The tank had a revised, rounded turret placed forward on the hull which incorporated a more powerful gun. The m/42 and Strv 74 were both maneuverable, well protected designs, and

Above: The Stridsvagn 74 light tank was an effective fighting vehicle and served the Swedish Army for many years, production only ending in 1981.

had an effective main armament. The Strv 74 was the result of a series of revisions and rebuilding that began with the Strv m/40. Production of the Strv 74 began in 1957 and continued at intervals until 1981. The tank was subject to numerous updates involving the installation of new equipment. With its angular turret and high profile, the Strv 74 was a functional rather than an aesthetic vehicle.

Specifications

Armament: One 2.95in (75mm) gun; three MGs

Armor: 3.15in (80mm)

Crew: 4

Dimensions: Length 16ft (4.9m); Width 7ft 4in (2.2m); Height 5ft 3in (1.61m)

Weight: 22.14 tons (22,500kg)

Powerplant: Scania-Vabis, 320bhp (239kW)

Speed: 27mph (45km/h)

Range: 125 miles (200km)

Postwar Development

🔧 **1959 China**

TYPE 59 MAIN BATTLE TANK

Since the early 1960s, China's Type 59 main battle tank has formed the bulk of the Chinese Army's armored strength. It is a direct copy of the Soviet T-54A.

Specifications

Armament: One 3.94in (100mm) gun; one 0.5in (12.7mm) MG; two 0.3in (7.62mm) MGs

Armor: 8in (203mm)

Crew: 4

Dimensions: Length 29ft 6in (9m); Width 10ft 8in (3.27m); Height 8ft 6in (2.59m)

Weight: 35.43 tons (36,000kg)

Powerplant: Type 12150L V-12 diesel, 523bhp (390kW)

Speed: 31mph (50km/h)

Range: 373 miles (600km)

In 1956, the Soviet Union supplied China with a quantity of T-54As, and a production facility was subsequently set up (with Soviet help) at the Inner Mongolia Machinery Building Factory in Baotou, Inner Mongolia. The first Chinese-assembled T-54A was rolled out in 1958, using kits supplied by the Soviet Union. Small numbers of T-54As built with Chinese components were being produced by 1959, and the vehicle was known as Type 59. Series production of the Type 59 began in 1963, and 10,000 units were built with a number of different variants before production stopped in the late 1980s. The People's Liberation Army (PLA) took about 6,000 Type 59 tanks, most of which were still in service at the end of the 1990s.

Above: China's Type 59 main battle tank leaped into the world headlines in 1989, when it was used against student demonstrators in Beijing's Tiananman Square. The picture of a lone student confronting one became legendary.

Upgrades

The tank underwent some significant upgrades in its later period of service; the improved Type 59-I was fitted with a primitive fire control system and a laser rangefinder, while the Type 59-II was fitted with a British L5 4.13in (105mm) rifled gun and a more powerful diesel engine. Some Type 59 tanks were also upgraded to Type 59D standard in the 1990s.

Postwar Development
⚒ 1959 Germany

JAGDPANZER KANONE (JPK)

The Jagdpanzer Kanone was one of the first combat vehicles to be issued to the reborn Federal German Army. It was designed to share many features with other tanks in its family.

Above: The Jagdpanzer Kanone's design goes back to tank destroyers such as the Hetzer of World War II, relying on its low silhouette and high speed for survival.

When the Federal German Army came into existence in the 1950s, priority was given to the development of a family of combat vehicles with much in common, including the use of the same basic chassis. One of these vehicles was a tank destroyer, the Jagdpanzer Kanone (JPK), armed with a 3.54in (90mm) gun. A variant on this was the Jagdpanzer Rakete, of which 163 units were built; it was armed with French SS.12 antitank missiles, which were later replaced by HOT (Haute subsonique Optiquement Téleguidé) missiles. Like the best of its predecessors, the Jagdpanzer Kanone relied on high speed (both forward and reverse) and a low silhouette for survival. The vehicle was

very reminiscent of the wartime Sturmgeschutz IV. Production, which began in 1959, ran to 750 vehicles, some of which were supplied to Belgium. The Marder infantry combat vehicle was also a member of this family.

Use by German Army

The JPK was introduced into the German Army in 1966. Many of these vehicles had their main armament removed and became observation vehicles.

Specifications

Armament: One 3.54in (90mm) gun; two 0.30in (7.62mm) MGs

Armor: Maximum, 1.97in (50mm)

Crew: 4

Dimensions: Length 20ft 5.6in (6.238m); Width 9ft 9.3in (2.98m); Height 6ft 10in (2.085m)

Weight: approx 25.3 tons (25,700kg)

Powerplant: Daimler-Benz MB837, 8-cylinder diesel, 500hp (372.9kW)

Speed: Road, 43.5mph (70km/h)

Range: Road, 248.5 miles (400km)

Specifications

(BRDM-1 Scout car 1959)

Armament: One 0.3in (7.62mm) SGMB MG

Armor: 0.394in (10mm)

Crew: 5

Dimensions: Length 18ft 8in (5.7m); Width 7ft 3in (2.25m); Height 6ft 3in (1.9m)

Weight: 5.5 tons (5600kg)

Powerplant: GAZ-40P 6-cylinder gasoline, 90bhp (67.2kW) at 3400rpm

Speed: Road, 50mph (80km/h); Water 5.6mph (9km/h)

Range: 311 miles (500km)

Below: Maneuverable and cheap to produce, the BRDM amphibious armored scout car was one of the most effective AFVs produced by the Soviet Union during the Cold War era. It was widely exported to armies around the world.

Postwar Development
1959 Soviet Union

BRDM SERIES

Russia's BRDM amphibious fighting vehicles were widely used by Soviet and Soviet-aligned forces during the Cold War era. They were used in many wars during that period.

The BRDM-1 was the first of the BRDM series of amphibious armored scout cars and entered service in 1959. The vehicle was fully amphibious and was propelled by a single rear-mounted water jet. It was produced in several versions, some of which were adapted to carry the Sapper, Snagger, and Swatter antitank guided weapons. In the early 1960s, the BRDM-1 was replaced by the BRDM-2; this had better road and cross-country performance, a heavier armament in a fully enclosed turret, a more powerful rear-mounted engine, night-vision equipment, and an NBC (nuclear-chemical-biological) warfare system.

BRDM-2s armed with the Sagger antitank missiles were used by the Egyptian and Syrian armies in the 1973 Yom Kippur War with Israel. The six-round Sagger launcher was raised above the roof of the vehicle when engaging a target; the missiles could be cable-launched from up to 262.47 ft (80m) outside the vehicle. The latest development in the line is the BRDM-3, which went into production for the Russian forces in the 1990s.

Usage

The BRDM vehicles, complete with their various antiarmor systems, have been widely used by many Soviet-friendly nations and have proved very popular, being both cheap and effective.

Above: The basic BRDM reconnaissance version is armed with a variety of antitank and surface-to-air guided missiles. This one is carrying the AT-11 Sniper laser-guided antitank weapon.

Postwar Development
⚔ **1959 UK**

SALADIN ARMORED CAR

The long-serving Saladin armored car was popular with the armed forces of several countries, and proved to be an excellent vehicle for patrol duty by the United Nations.

The Saladin (FV601) 6x6 armored car was developed for the British Army in 1959 by Alvis (then based in Coventry). It had much in common with the Alvis Saracen 6x6 armored personnel carrier. Production began in 1959 and ended in 1972, totaling 1177 vehicles. The Saladin was also used by Indonesia, Jordan, the Federal German Police, Yemen, and Lebanon. It was widely used in various UN police operations, and in 1974 Saladins were used in defense of Nicosia airport when Turkish forces invaded Cyprus.

No variants

No variants of the Saladin were produced, although some vehicles had their gasoline engines replaced by a more fuel-efficient Perkins diesel for sale to Indonesia, and the Saladin turret was fitted to some Australian Army M113A1 armored personnel carriers for fire support. The British Army replaced the Saladin with the Alvis Scorpion light tank, which was also issued to units of the Royal Air Force Regiment.

Specifications

Armament: One 3in (76mm) gun; two 0.3in (7.62mm) MGs

Armor: 0.31–0.63in (8–16mm)

Crew: 3

Dimensions: Length 16ft 2in (4.93m); Width 8ft 4in (2.54m); Height 8ft 7in (2.92m)

Weight: 11.4 tons (11,590kg)

Powerplant: Rolls-Royce gasoline developing 170bhp (126.7kW) at 3570rpm

Speed: 44.7mph (72km/h)

Range: 248.5 miles (400km)

Left: *The hull of the Saladin is of all-welded steel armor construction. The driver had the benefit of excellent vision and the vehicle was generally popular with all its users.*

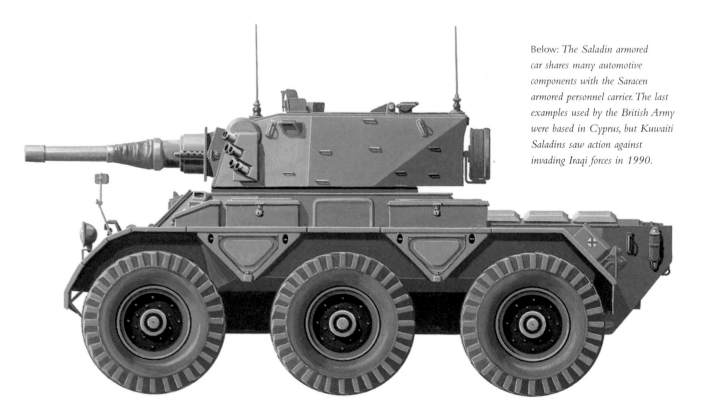

Below: *The Saladin armored car shares many automotive components with the Saracen armored personnel carrier. The last examples used by the British Army were based in Cyprus, but Kuwaiti Saladins saw action against invading Iraqi forces in 1990.*

Postwar Development
⚒ **1960 France**

CHAR AMX-30 MAIN BATTLE TANK

Below: The AMX-30, seen here negotiating an obstacle, was designed by the Atelier de Construction d'Issy-les-Moulineaux.

The AMX-30 main battle tank is probably the most successful of all France's modern armored fighting vehicles, and has been exported to 12 countries. Spain was the leading export customer, taking 120 vehicles.

Specifications

Armament: One 4.13in (105mm) gun; one 0.79in (20mm) cannon; one 0.30in (7.62mm) MG

Armor: Maximum, 3.15in (80mm)

Crew: 4

Dimensions: Length overall 31ft 1in (9.48m); Width 10ft 2in (3.1m); Height 7ft 6in (2.29m)

Weight: 35.43 tons (36,000kg)

Powerplant: Hispano-Suiza HS 110, 12-cylinder multi-fuel, 700hp (522kW)

Speed: Road, 40.4mph (65km/h)

Range: Road, 248.5–280 miles (400–450km)

Development of the AMX-30 started in the mid-1950s in response to a requirement by the French Army for a new battle tank to replace the ageing AFVs of American origin and World War II vintage. The design of the tank was developed by the Atelier de Construction d'Issy-les-Moulineaux and made no attempt at heavy armor protection. Instead, plans developed for a vehicle with lighter armor, higher speed and maneuverability, and armament that was sufficiently accurate to kill on its shot. The first prototypes were completed in 1960 and series production began in 1966. Since then, over 3500 AMX-30s and variants have been produced for the home and export markets.

Above: A French Army AMX-30 camouflaged for desert operations. The primary antitank round of its 4.13in (105mm) gun is the OCC (HEAT) type, which can penetrate 15.75in (400mm) of armor and has a muzzle velocity of 3280ft (1000m) per second.

Export

The French Army accepted 387 AMX-30s and 659 AMX-30B2s. The latter introduced improvements including an integrated fire control system (incorporating a laser rangefinder and a low-light TV system), and an upgraded automotive system (including new transmission). The AMX-30 was used by the 6th Light Armored Division on the left flank of the Coalition invasion during the Gulf War of 1991.

Postwar Development
⚔ 1960 France

PANHARD AML LIGHT ARMORED CAR

This excellent French armored car has been in continuous production

for nearly half a century. It has been supplied to over 40 countries

worldwide and used regularly in combat.

Specifications

Armament: One 3.54in (90mm) low-recoil gun; one 0.30in (7.62mm) MG

Armor: Maximum, 0.47in (12mm)

Crew: 3

Dimensions: Length, hull 12ft 5.2in (3.79m); Width 6ft 5.5in (1.97m); Height 6ft 9.5in (2.07m)

Weight: 5.41 tons (5500kg)

Powerplant: Panhard Model 4 HD, 4-cylinder gasoline, 90hp (67.2kW) or Peugeot XD 3T, 4-cylinder diesel, 98hp (73kW)

Speed: Road, 56mph (90km/h)

Range: Road, 373 miles (600km)

Left: *The Panhard AML armored car has been one of the most successful wheeled armored fighting vehicles produced since the end of World War II, with over 4000 manufactured in France and South Africa.*

The Panhard AML (Automitrailleuse Legère) was developed to meet a request to replace the Daimler Ferret, which had been used in large numbers. The AML prototypes were produced in 1959 and the first production vehicles were issued to the French light armored units in 1961. Since then, over 4800 units have been built both for the French Army and for export purposes. The armored car has been built in two versions, the AML 60 and AML 90—the latter being armed with a Hispano 3.54in (90mm) gun. The Eland 60 and Eland 90 are license-produced versions for the South African Army. The Panhard AML has been used in Angola and the Falklands, where it was used by the Argentine forces, and in the Lebanese Civil War between 1975 and 1990. Its export to over 40 countries is some indication of its success.

Weapons

The AML 60 carries a number of weapons, including a 2.36in (60mm) breech-loading mortar and various machine-gun combinations. Some of the later vehicles are armed with a 0.79in (20mm) cannon.

Left: *The Panhard AML has seen a good deal of action around the world, from the Falkland Islands (where it was used by Argentinian forces) to the Lebanon. It is used by over 40 countries.*

Postwar Development

⚒ **1960 Japan**

TYPE 60 TRACKED PERSONNEL CARRIER

The wintry climate of Hokkaido, Japan's northern island, prompted
the need for tracked personnel carriers that could be used in the snow.
One of these vehicles was the Type 60.

Specifications

Armament: One 0.5in (12.7mm)
MG; one 0.3in (7.62mm) MG

Armor: Not available

Crew: 4 plus 6

Dimensions: Length 15ft 10in
(4.85m); Width; 7ft 10in (2.4m);
Height 5ft 7in (1.7m) to hull top

Weight: 11.61 tons (11,800kg)

Powerplant: Mitsubishi Model 8
HA 21 WT V-8 turbocharged
diesel, 220bhp (164kW)

Speed: 28mph (45km/h)

Range: 144 miles (230km)

The Komatsu Type 60 tracked personnel carrier was developed for use on the northernmost Japanese island of Hokkaido, where there are often heavy snowfalls. Two vehicles were actually developed at the request of the Japanese Ground Self-Defense Force—the other being the Type 61, which was designed and built by the Ohara Ironworks. The Komatsu Type 60 was also referred to as the Medium Snow Mobile. It was designed to carry 10 men (including the driver) over any kind of snowfield, and also had the capability to tow a trailer of weapons weighing 3307lb (1500kg). The Type 60's front-mounted Mitsubishi diesel engine is coupled to a manual gearbox with four forward and one reverse gears. Suspension is

based on the use of torsion bars and bogies with eight dual roadwheels, track-return rollers, drive sprockets, and an idler. The cargo compartment is behind the cab and features a drop tailgate.

Type 61

The other oversnow vehicle, the Type 61 (sometimes known as the Large Snow Mobile) is similar in appearance to the Type 60, but is larger and fitted with a more powerful engine.

Below: *The Komatsu Type 60 oversnow vehicle was developed from the civilian KC-20 and was designed specifically for operations in the northern Japanese island of Hokkaido.*

Postwar Development

⚒ **1960 USA**

M60 MAIN BATTLE TANK

The M60 main battle tank was developed in the late 1950s to counter the threat from Russia's new T-62 medium tank. It did not meet the T-62 in combat for another 30 years, however.

The M60 was the last in the line of US main battle tanks that began with the M46. Its development began in response to intelligence in 1957. This suggested that the Russians were developing a new medium tank, the T-62, which was armed with a 4.53in (115mm) gun that would make it superior to the American M48. The simplest solution was to fit the existing M48 with a more powerful engine and the British 4.13in

(105mm) L7. With these improvements, the modified tank (originally designated the M68) went into production in 1959 and was deployed operationally in 1960. Renamed the M60, its production run eventually totalled 15,000 units. The first prototypes and

Below: *The M60 is one of the world's most successful main battle tanks, and has seen service with some 20 armies since it was first deployed in 1960. It was used in large numbers during the 1991 Gulf War.*

Specifications

M60A1

Armament: One M68 4.13in
(105mm) gun; one 0.3in (7.62mm)
MG; one 0.50in (12.7mm) MG

Armor: 5.63in (143mm)

Crew: 4

Dimensions: Length (over gun)
31ft (9.44m); Width 11ft 11in
(3.63m); Height 10ft 8in (3.27m)

Weight: 51.8 tons (52,617kg)

Powerplant: Continental AVDS-
1790-2A V-12 turbocharged diesel,
750hp (559.7kW)

Speed: 30mph (48km/h)

Range: 311 miles (500km)

early production machines were completed at the Chrysler Corporation's Delaware Defense Plant, but from 1960 onward, production switched to the Detroit Tank Plant, also operated by Chrysler (although later taken over by General Dynamics). Production ceased in 1987.

Upgrades

The M60 underwent various upgrades during its operational life. The first took place in 1963, when the M60A1 appeared with a larger and better designed turret, improved armor, and more efficient shock-absorbers. The next variant, the M60A2, featured a redesigned low-profile turret with a commander's machine-gun cupola on top, giving the commander a good view and field of fire while remaining protected. It was also armed with a 5.98in (152mm) caliber main gun similar to that of the M551 Sheridan, which was able to fire the Shillelagh gun-launched antitank missile as well as normal rounds. The M60A2 was abandoned after a relatively short time, and most units were rebuilt to the standard of the next variant, the

Above: The M60's main 4.13in (105mm) gun was fitted with a thermal sleeve, which was designed to prolong the useful life of the barrel before it needed to be changed. The tank was progressively upgraded during its service career.

M60A3. This incorporated a number of technological advances, such as a new rangefinder and ballistic computer and a turret stabilization system. All American M60s were upgraded to this standard.

Geographical use

The M60 was widely exported and was first used during the Arab–Israeli Yom Kippur War of October 1973, as well as in the invasion of the Lebanon in 1982. M60s operating with the US Marine Corps and the Royal Saudi Army were also used in Operation Desert Storm in 1991, where they led the attack on Iraqi forces in Kuwait and subsequently the drive to Kuwait City. It proved effective against all types of Iraqi armor—including the T-62, which it had been developed to counter many years earlier.

Postwar Development
⚒ 1960 USA

M551 SHERIDAN LIGHT TANK

The Sheridan light tank had a poor operational record, and was only retained in service because of its air-portable capability. Some of these vehicles were used in the US invasion of Panama in 1989.

Specifications

Armament: One 5.98in (152mm) gun/missile system; one 0.3in (7.62mm) MG

Armor: Not available

Crew: 4

Dimensions: Length 20ft 8in (6.30m); Width 9ft 3in (2.82m); Height 9ft 8in (2.95m)

Weight: 15.6 tons (15,830kg)

Powerplant: Detroit Diesel 6V-53T, 6-cylinder turbocharged diesel, 300hp (224kW)

Speed: 45mph (72km/h)

Range: 373 miles (600km)

In 1959, the US Army issued a request for a new air-portable light tank to replace the M41 light tank and the M56 self-propelled gun that were then in service with the US airborne forces. The new vehicle was developed under the name of Armored Reconnaissance/Airborne Assault Vehicle (AR/AAV) and then designated XM551. The development contract was awarded to the Allison Division of General Motors, which produced 12 prototypes. Evaluation of these was still incomplete in 1965, when the company was awarded a four-year production contract. The vehicle was accepted for service in 1966 and given the name M551 General Sheridan, after Civil War General Philip Sheridan. It was used by the US Army in Europe, South Korea, and

Vietnam. Between 1966 and 1970, 1700 Sheridans were produced.

Problems

Several faults came to light during the Sheridan's operational service. This was mostly in Vietnam, where the vehicle proved to be vulnerable to mines because of its light belly armor. In fact, the armor was light all round, and could be penetrated by heavy machine-gun rounds. Some Sheridans were equipped to carry the Shillelagh gun-launched antitank missile, but firing of the 5.98in (152mm) gun upset the missile's circuitry. The Sheridan was withdrawn from first-line service in the 1980s, although one battalion of the 82nd Airborne Division used the AFV until the mid-1990s.

Above: *About 1700 M551 Sheridan light tanks were built. The last operational unit to use it was the 82nd Airborne Division.*

Below: *The Sheridan had to be light in order to be air-portable, but this made it vulnerable, as its armor could be penetrated by heavy machine-gun rounds.*

Postwar Development

1961 Germany

MARDER I INFANTRY COMBAT VEHICLE

The Marder I was NATO's first infantry fighting vehicle. It combined the qualities of an armored personnel carrier with those of a light tank. It will be replaced by a lighter and cheaper AFV in due course.

Specifications

(Marder 1A3)

Armament: One 0.79in (20mm) cannon; one 0.30in (7.62mm) MG

Armor: Maximum, 1.18in (30mm)

Crew: 3 plus 6 or 7 troops

Dimensions: Length 22ft 6.8in (6.88m); Width 11ft 1in (3.38m); Height 9ft 10.7in (3.015m)

Weight: Combat, 32.97 tons (33,500kg)

Powerplant: MTU MB 833 Ea-500, 6-cylinder diesel, 447.4kW (600hp)

Speed: Road, 40.4mph (65km/h)

Range: Road, 310 miles (500km)

In the 1960s three German companies were asked to submit proposals for a new infantry combat vehicle—in the same family as the one including the Jagdpanzer Kanone and the Jagdpanzer Rakete. Many different prototypes were built and trialed, and the Bundeswehr adopted the Marder (Marten) Schützenpanzer Neu M-1966. Rheinstahl was selected as the prime contractor, with MaK of Kiel as the principal subcontractor. Both companies now form part of Rheinmetall Landsysteme. The Marder entered service with the Federal German Army in 1971, and was the first AFV of its type to be used by NATO. For the first time, infantry traveling in an armored personnel carrier were able to carry effective fire support, as the Marder was equipped with a two-man power-operated turret mounting a 0.79in (20mm) cannon and a 0.30in (7.62mm) machine gun. The latest version of the Marder is the Marder 1A5, and is equipped with very effective anti-mine protection features.

Delays

The introduction of the Marder I into service was delayed because priority was given to the production of the Jagdpanzer Kanone and the Jagdpanzer Rakete.

Below: *The Marder was the first Mechanized Infantry Combat Vehicle to enter service in the West, and was one of NATO's most effective ICV's for many years.*

Postwar Development
1961 Germany

RAKETENJAGDPANZER 1

The Raketenjagdpanzer (meaning "rocket-hunting tank") was developed as an attempt to extend the range and accuracy of the Federal German Army's tank-killing power. It was armed with French missiles.

Above: *A Raketenjagdpanzer showing the mounting of the Milan antitank missile launcher. The Raketenjagdpanzer represented a breakthrough in military technology and greatly enhanced the capability of the Bundeswehr.*

The Raketenjagdpanzer 1 was first used by the Bundeswehr in 1961. It was a missile-armed tank destroyer based on the chassis of the Hispano-Suiza HS-30. The vehicle was armed with the French SS-11 wire-guided antitank missile and carried 10 rounds. The missile was guided by radio pulses transmitted through the wire by the operator, who kept the SS-11 in sight through a periscope. The tank was powered by two Rolls-Royce B81 Mk 80F engines, giving it a speed of about 30mph (50km/h). It was built by Henschel and Hanomag, who produced 318 units for the Bundeswehr. Most of the vehicles were later upgraded with additional armor and a new missile system, and the AFV was then renamed Raketenjagdpanzer Jaguar 1. This upgrade took place between 1978 and 1982, and at a later date, new optics and a thermal imaging system were added. The Jaguar 1 used HOT (Haut-subsonique Optiquement Téléguidé Tiré d'un Tube), a heavy missile with a range of between 250 and 13,200ft (76.2 and 4023.36m). This was developed by Euromissile.

Specifications

(Jaguar 1)

Armament: One HOT antitank missile launcher; two 0.30in (7.62mm) MGs

Armor: Maximum, 1.98in (50mm)

Crew: 4

Dimensions: Length 21ft 8.2in (6.61m); Width 10ft 2.8in (3.12m); Height, hull top, 6ft 5.9in (1.98m)

Weight: approx 25.1 tons (25,500kg)

Powerplant: Daimler Benz MB 837, 8-cylinder diesel, 500hp (372.9kW)

Speed: Road, 43.5mph (70km/h)

Range: Road, 248.5 miles (400km)

Postwar Development
✖ **1961 Soviet Union**

BTR-60P ARMORED PERSONNEL CARRIER

The BTR-60P is one of the most widely used armored personnel carriers in the world, and is used in some unexpected places. American forces encountered it in Grenada in 1984.

BTR stands for Bronetransporter (Armored Transport). This series of armored personnel carriers was introduced into service with the Red Army in 1960 as a replacement for the BTR-152, which had revealed a number of shortcomings. The first BTR-60P to be issued to the Soviet motorized infantry divisions had an open roof, but the next variant, the BTR-60PA, had an armored roof, although this meant that vehicle's capacity was reduced from 14 to 12 men. The next model, the BTR-60PB, had a more refined sighting system for its gun. All versions of the series were fully amphibious and were propelled by a single water-jet mounted at the rear. The BTR-60P remained in production until 1976, when it was superseded by the BTR-70.

Geographical use

It was used in combat by Egyptian and Syrian forces during the Yom Kippur War of 1973, and by the Russians in the invasion of Afghanistan, where many were lost to antitank rockets used by the insurgents. The vehicle has been used in over 40 countries, including Cuba, during its intervention in Angola.

Below: *The BTR-60PA variant has a fully enclosed troop compartment and can carry a maximum of 16 troops, although its usual complement is 12. It is normally armed with a pintle-mounted 0.3in (7.62mm) machine gun.*

Specifications

BTR-60PB

Armament: One 0.57in (14.5mm) KPV MG; one coaxial 0.3in (7.62mm) PKT MG

Armor: 0.55in (14mm)

Crew: 2 plus 14

Dimensions: Length 24ft 10in (7.56m); Width 9ft 4in (2.85m); Height 7ft 7in (2.31m)

Weight: 10.1 tons (10,300kg)

Powerplant: Two GAZ-49B 6-cylinder gasoline, 90bhp (67.16kW) each at 3400rpm

Speed: land 50mph (80km/h); water 6.2mph (10km/h)

Range: 310 miles (500km)

Postwar Development
⚔ 1961   Soviet Union

T-62 MAIN BATTLE TANK

The T-62 was innovative in mounting the world's first smoothbore tank gun, but proved something of a disaster in combat. It was poorly armored and prone to catching fire.

Specifications

Armament: One 4.57in (115mm) smoothbore U5TS (2A20 Rapira) gun; one 0.3in (7.62mm) PKT MG

Armor: 0.55–9.53in (14–242mm)

Crew: 4

Dimensions: Length (hull) 21ft 9in (6.63m); Width 10ft 10in (3.3m); Height 7ft 10in (2.39m)

Weight: 39.37 tons (40,000kg)

Powerplant: V-55 12-cylinder diesel, 580bhp (432.8kW) at 2000rpm

Speed: 31mph (50km/h)

Range: 280 miles (450km)

The T-62 main battle tank was a straightforward development of the T-55 and was armed with a 4.57in (115mm) smoothbore gun. Some 20,000 T-62s were manufactured in the Soviet Union between 1961 and 1984, and the tank was also made in Czechoslovakia and North Korea. Most of the Czech production was intended for export. The T-62's main gun—the first smoothbore tank weapon in the world— allowed for much greater velocity and hitting power than the 3.54in (90mm) and 4.13in (105mm) weapons used by the western powers at that time. The T-62 was put to the test during the Yom Kippur War of 1973, and revealed its tendency to catch fire when penetrated. The Israelis captured several

Above: *A T-62 during operations in Afghanistan. The T-62 was not particularly effective in combat, showing a tendency to catch fire when penetrated. Egyptian T-62s suffered heavily in the Yom Kippur War of 1973.*

hundred T-62s from the Egyptians and Syrians and pressed them into service. They added thermal imaging equipment and laser rangefinders, improved the armor, and replaced the unreliable Soviet diesel engines with reliable American ones. In Israeli service, the T-62 was known as the Tiran-6, and many vehicles were sold on to developing countries. This tank suffered heavily in Chad during the Libyan invasion of 1982, when scores were knocked out by the Army of Chad supported by French special forces.

Postwar Development
1961 Switzerland

PZ 61 AND PZ 68 MAIN BATTLE TANKS

The Pz 61 and Pz 68 were an attempt by the Swiss Army to produce their own tank. Traditionally, they had bought foreign tanks, such as the British Centurion.

Specifications

(Pz 68)

Armament: One 4.13in (105mm) gun; two MGs
Armor: 4.72in (120mm)
Crew: 4
Dimensions: Length 22ft 7in (6.88m); Width 10ft 4in (3.14m); Height 9ft (2.75m)
Weight: 39.07 tons (39,700kg)
Powerplant: MTU MB-837 V8 diesel, 660bhp (492.5kW) at 2200rpm
Speed: 34mph (55km/h)
Range: 215 miles (350km)

In 1959, the Federal Construction Works in Thun, Switzerland produced the first prototypes of a new main battle tank, the KW30. This was followed by 10 preproduction examples designated Pz 58. The Swiss Army placed an order for 150 production vehicles, designated Pz 61. These were armed with the excellent British 4.13in (105mm) L7 gun and were delivered in 1965–66. Further development of the Pz 61 resulted in the Pz 68, the first prototype of which was completed in 1968. Major differences were a stabilization system for the 4.13in (105mm) gun, a more powerful engine, modified transmission, wider tracks with replaceable rubber pads, and greater length of track in contact with the ground.

Variants

The Swiss Army accepted 170 Pz 68s (later designated Pz 68 Mk 1) between 1971 and 1974. These were followed in 1977 by 50 Pz 68 Mk IIs, which had a thermal sleeve for the 7.09in (180mm) gun and a carbon-monoxide extractor. The next variant, the Pz 68 Mk 3, had all the refinements of the Mk 2 plus a larger turret. The last production model was the Mk 4, 60 of which were delivered between 1983 and 1984.

Below: *A Pz 68 main battle tank of the Swiss Army on maneuveres. The Pz 68 was not the most successful tank design, reportedly suffering from some 50 faults, including cracking fuel tanks, a short track life, and a defective gun stabilizing system.*

Postwar Development
⚒ 1962 China

TYPE 62 LIGHT TANK

China is the last country in the world to use large numbers of light tanks in a combat rather than a reconnaissance role. This makes its Type 62 something of an anachronism.

It remains a mystery why China continued to produce large numbers of light and medium tanks in a nonreconnaissance combat role long after other nations had ceased to do so. It is equally puzzling why the little 21-ton Type 62 should be classed as a medium tank. The Type 62 resembles a scaled-down version of the Type 59 main battle tank, and its design appears to be based on this. It has a cast-and-welded turret that is smaller, but otherwise identical to that of the Type 59. The Type 62 mounts an 3.25in (85mm) gun, but its armor protection is limited and inadequate against modern antitank weapons. By today's standards the

Above: The Type 62 is virtually a scaled-down version of the Type 59 MBT, and was optimized for operations in rugged terrain, such as in southern China.

Type 62 is obsolete, although it continues to be used in substantial numbers by the PLA in training establishments and second-line defense units. The Type 63, an amphibious version, has the same turret and main gun as the Type 62, mounted on a Chinese copy of the Russian PT-76 light amphibious tank hull. Both types have been exported to China's clients in Africa and Asia, and were used by the North Vietnamese Army in the closing stages of the Vietnam War.

Specifications

Armament: One 3.35in (85mm) gun; two 0.3in (7.62mm) MGs; one 0.5in (12.7mm) MG

Armor: Unknown

Crew: 4

Dimensions: Length 25ft 11in (7.9m); Width 9ft 5in (2.86m); Height 7ft 5in (2.25m)

Weight: 20.67 tons (21,000kg)

Powerplant: Diesel, 430bhp (320kW)

Speed: 37mph (60km/h)

Range: 311 miles (500km)

Specifications

Armament: One Type 61 3.54in (90mm) gun; one 0.5in (12.7mm) MG; one 0.3in (7.62mm) MG

Armor: 2.52in (64mm)

Crew: 4

Dimensions: Length 26ft 10in (8.19m); Width 9ft 8in (2.95m); Height 8ft 3in (2.49m)

Weight: 34.45 tons (35,000kg)

Powerplant: Mitsubishi Type 12 HM 21 WT diesel, 600bhp (447kW)

Speed: 28mph (45km/h)

Range: 124 miles (200km)

Postwar Development
1962 Japan

TYPE 61 MAIN BATTLE TANK

The Type 61 was Japan's first postwar tank. It was considered by many to be seriously undergunned; it was slow to enter service and soon became obsolete.

Design of Japan's first postwar tank was initiated in 1954 under the direction of the Ground Armaments Directorate at the Technical Research and Development HQ of the Japanese Self-Defense Force. The first prototypes were completed in 1957, comprising two Model ST-A1s and two Model ST-A2s. These were followed by two ST-A3 and 10 ST-A4 vehicles for evaluation; the production version, named Type 61, started coming off the assembly line at the Maruko works of Mitsubishi Heavy Industries in 1962. Production was initially very slow. Only 10 tanks were completed in the first year, but 250 units had been delivered by 1970.

Design features

The hull of the Type 61 is of all-welded steel construction. The driver is seated at the front of the hull on the right, and is provided with a single-piece hatch that has three periscopes mounted forward. The turret is made of cast steel with an overhanging bustle (similar to that of the US M47 medium tank) and a light sheet steel stowage box at the rear. The Type 61 was replaced in first-line service by the Type 74.

Below: *Japan's first indigenous postwar main battle tank, the Type 61 suffered from a slow production rate. It was approaching obsolescence by the time it entered service and was eventually replaced by the Type 74.*

Postwar Development

⚒ 1962   UK

FV432 ARMORED PERSONNEL CARRIER

The FV432 armored personnel carrier has served the British Army very well for many years, and its planned replacement has been postponed several times. It has been produced in a number of different versions.

Below: This FV432 is armed with a 0.30in (7.62mm) General Purpose Machine Gun, a gun that was very effective against Argentine aircraft during the Falklands War.

The FV432 was developed in the late 1950s and is the armored personnel carrier version of the FV340 series of British armored fighting vehicles. The first prototype was completed in 1961. Production was undertaken from 1962 by GKN Sankey (later known as Alvis Vehicles). Deliveries to the British Army began in 1963, and some 3000 vehicles had been built by the time production was completed in 1972. The construction of the FV432 is entirely of steel. The chassis is a conventional tracked design with the engine at the front and the driving position to the right. The vehicle commander's hatch is situated directly behind the driver's position. There is a large split-hatch round opening in the passenger compartment roof and a side-hinged door in the rear for loading and unloading. Many FV432s have a one-man turret mounted above the rear troop compartment, mounting a 0.30in (7.62mm) General Purpose Machine Gun (GPMG).

Variants

Variants include an ambulance model (with accommodation for both seated and stretcher patients), a command vehicle fitted with extensive communications equipment, a maintenance carrier, mortar carrier, minelayer, recovery vehicle, and an artillery command vehicle (equipped with Field Artillery Computer Equipment).

Specifications

Armament: One 0.3in (7.62mm) MG

Armor: 0.23-0.47in (6-12mm)

Crew: 2 plus 10

Dimensions: Length 17ft 3in (5.251m); Width 9ft 2in (2.8m); Height 7ft 6in (2.286m)

Weight: 15.04 tons (15,280kg)

Powerplant: Rolls-Royce 2-stroke 6-cylinder multi-fuel engine developing 240bhp (18.9kW) at 3750rpm

Speed: 32mph (52.2km/h)

Range: 360 miles (580km)

Specifications

Armament: One 3.35in (85mm)
gun; one 0.3in (7.62mm) MG; one
0.5in (12.7mm) MG

Armor: 0.55in (14mm) steel

Crew: 4

Dimensions: Length 27ft 8in
(8.44m); Width 10ft 6in (3.2m);
Height 8ft 4in (2.52m)

Weight: 18.11 tons (18,400kg)

Powerplant: Model 12150-L V-12
diesel, 400bhp (298kW)

Speed: Road 40mph (64km/h);
Water 7mph (12km/h)

Range: 230 miles (370km)

Postwar Development
⚒ **1963 China**

NORINCO TYPE 63 AMPHIBIOUS LIGHT TANK

Although the hull design of the Type 63 amphibious light tank is based
on that of the Russian PT-76, its automotive components are adapted
from the Chinese Type 77 armored personnel carrier.

*Above: The Type 63 tank is still
very much a frontline fighting
vehicle in the Chinese Armed
Forces, being deployed mainly in
support of Marine Infantry units.
It saw combat in Vietnam.*

*Right: Chinese troops debouching
from a Type 63 during an exercise.
A Type 63 can create its own
smokescreen by injecting diesel
fuel into the exhaust.*

This Chinese light amphibious tank has a
hull similar to that of the Russian PT-
76, but it is fitted with a more powerful
engine that is derived from the powerplant
of the Type 77 series armored personnel
carrier. The vehicle is fully amphibious, being
propelled in water by two water jets

mounted at the rear of the hull. During the
1960s China continued to use large numbers
of light and medium tanks as part of its main
armored forces, and consequently went to
great lengths to increase armament and
armored protection. For this reason, the Type
63 is a scaled-down version of a main battle
tank, carrying an 3.35in (85mm) gun. The
Type 63 remains in first-line service with
the People's Liberation Army and has been
exported to a number of countries friendly
to China, including Vietnam. The tank
was used with the North Vietnamese
Army during the closing stages of the
Vietnam War. The Type 63's predecessor, the
Type 62, was a Chinese–Russian hybrid and
now serves only with second-line and
training units.

LEOPARD I MAIN BATTLE TANK

The Leopard I main battle tank was an extremely important element of NATO's landwarfare defense during the most dangerous years of the Cold War. It was originally intended to be a joint Franco–German collaborative project, but France withdrew and Federal Germany proceeded alone.

Right: A Leopard Mk 1 sporting the red maple leaf insignia of the Canadian Armed Forces. The first production Leopard 1 was delivered to the Bundeswehr in 1965 and was produced in several versions.

The Leopard project was initiated in 1956. Its aim was to develop a new AFV to replace the Bundeswehr's M47 and M48 tanks, which were becoming obsolete. The requirement called for a vehicle that would withstand hits from a 0.78in (20mm) antitank gun and be able to operate in an environment contaminated by nuclear, chemical, or biological warfare. The gun selected for its main armament was the British L7A3 4.13in (105mm) weapon. In June of 1957, Germany and France signed an agreement to develop the new tank. This was known initially as the Standard-Panzer. Two German and one French design teams were invited to submit proposals, each team producing two prototypes. Italy joined the development program in 1958.

Original design

Testing of the various prototypes began in 1960, and it was the design submitted by Porsche that was selected, although some changes to the original design were made before it was accepted for production. These included a new cast turret and several hull changes to raise the rear deck in order to make a roomier engine compartment. An optical rangefinder system was also added.

Specifications

Armament: One 105mm (4.13in) L7A3 rifled gun; two 7.62mm (0.30in) MGs

Armour: Maximum, 70mm (2.75in)

Crew: 4

Dimensions: Length 9.543m (31ft 3.5in); Width 3.25m (10ft 8in); Height 2.61m (8ft 7in)

Weight: approx 40,400kg (39.76 tons)

Powerplant: MTU 10-cylinder diesel developing 619kW (830hp)

Speed: Road, 65km/h (40.4mph)

Range: Road, 600km (373miles)

Right: *When it was first produced, the Leopard 1 was a very capable main battle tank, offering a high level of agility and excellent firepower, thanks to its 4.2in (105mm) L7 gun of British design.*

Below: *The fact that the Leopard 1 is still operational with armies around the world in the early years of the 21st century is proof of the tank's excellent capability.*

Upgrades

The first batch of production Leopard 1 tanks was built by Krauss-Maffei of Munich between September 1955 and June 1966. The next three batches comprised the Leopard 1A1 model, which included a new gun stabilization system. The Leopard 1A1 was subjected to various upgrades in the 1970s. Follow-on models were the Leopard 1A2, with a more heavily armored turret; the 1A3, with a new welded turret; the 1A4, with a new computerized fire control system; the 1A5, with a completely new turret; and the 1A6, with additional armor and a 4.72 in (120mm) gun.

Exports

The Leopard 1 was exported to (or sometimes manufactured in) 12 countries. Italy was the biggest customer, acquiring 920 units. The other customers were Australia (90), Belgium (132), Brazil (240), Canada (114), Chile (unspecified), Denmark (330), Greece (335), the Netherlands (unspecified), Norway (172), and Turkey (307). The Bundeswehr employed 724 units, which were progressively replaced by the Leopard 2. During the Cold War, the Leopard and the British Chieftain would have borne the brunt of any tank battle that might have developed on the North German plain, and would have played a decisive part in blunting any Soviet offensive. The commonality between the armies using the Leopard in this sector—German, Belgian, and Dutch—would have been an important factor.

Postwar Development
⚒ 1963 UK

CHIEFTAIN MARK 5 MAIN BATTLE TANK

Until the introduction of the Leopard 2, the Chieftain was arguably the best main battle tank in service with any of the NATO forces during the 1960s and 1970s. It secured large export orders.

Specifications

Armament: One 4.72in (120mm) L11A5 gun; two 0.3in (7.62mm) MGs; one 0.5in (12.7mm) MG

Armor: Not available

Crew: 4

Dimensions: Length 24ft 8in (7.518m); Width 11ft 6in (3.50m); Height 9ft 6in (2.895m)

Weight: 54.13 tons (55,000kg)

Powerplant: Leyland L60 multi-fuel developing 750bhp (559.2kW) at 2100rpm

Speed: 30mph (48km/h)

Range: 248.5–280 miles (400–500km)

Left: *A British Chieftain main battle tank armed with a 4.72in (120mm) L11A5 rifled tank gun. The latter is fitted with a thermal sleeve to reduce barrel distortion and prolong its useful life before a change is needed. Several special-purpose variants of the Chieftain have been produced.*

The Chieftain, designed by Leyland, was intended to replace the Centurion as the main British battle tank, as the Centurion was becoming increasingly vulnerable to the latest generation of Soviet tanks and antitank weapons. The British decided to sacrifice lightness and mobility for effective armor protection, and to equip the new tank with a powerful 4.72in (120mm) rifled gun, which was very accurate. The prototype Chieftain appeared in 1959 and was followed by six more units, these being evaluated between 1961 and 1962.

Export

Nine hundred Chieftains were built for the British Army and the type attracted large export orders. Kuwait was an early customer, ordering 165 Chieftain Mk 5TKs. Twelve ex-British tanks were supplied to the Sultanate of Oman, who also took delivery of 15 new-build vehicles. The largest export order, however, came from Iran, who ordered 707 units in addition to a further 187 units of an upgraded model, the Improved Chieftain. The Iranian Chieftains were used in the Iran–Iraq war during the 1980s. Jordan also ordered 274 Chieftains. The Chieftain's one drawback was its engine, which was a multi-fuel type that never reached its planned power output.

Left: *The Chieftain is an extremely successful tank and attracted large export orders from countries in the Middle East.*

Postwar Development

🛠 **1964 UK**

VICKERS MARK 1 AND MARK 3 MAIN BATTLE TANKS

The Vickers MBT was developed as a private venture for countries requiring a simple, powerful MBT at minimum cost. It used many components of the Chieftain and Centurion vehicles.

Specifications

(Vickers Mark 1 1964)

Armament: One 4.13in (105mm) L7A1 gun; two 0.3in (7.62mm) MGs; one 0.5in (12.7mm) RMG

Armor: 0.75–3.16in (17–80mm)

Crew: 4

Dimensions: Length 26ft (7.92m); Width 10ft 6in (3.168m); Height 8ft (2.44m)

Weight: 37.99 tons (38,600kg)

Powerplant: Leyland L60 6-cylinder multi-fuel developing 650bhp (484.7kW) at 2670rpm

Speed: 30mph (48km/h)

Range: 300 miles (480km)

The Vickers main battle tank was developed purely for export. It used the standard 4.13in (105mm) L7 rifled tank gun and the automotive components of the Chieftain. The tank was produced as a private venture, but when India issued a requirement for a tank very similar in concept and design, Vickers offered the MBT and it was accepted. The first two prototypes were completed in the spring of 1963 and series production began the following year. An agreement had been reached in the meantime whereby India would also manufacture the AFV under the name Vijayanta (Victorious). Over 2200 Vijayantas were produced, and these were used in combat against Pakistani forces in 1965 and 1971.

Export

Kuwait ordered 70 Vickers MBT Mk 1 tanks in 1968, and these were delivered between 1970 and 1972. Meanwhile, Vickers continued to develop the basic Mk 1 design, installing a more powerful engine and improving the turret design to produce the Mk 3. Kenya ordered two batches of 38 Mk 3s between 1977 and 1978, and Nigeria ordered 36 units in 1981. Both countries also acquired small numbers of the armored recovery vehicle variant.

Below: *Developed as a private venture, the Vickers Mk 1 main battle tank became a major export success, the biggest customer being India, which produced over 2200 examples under the name Vijayanta (Victorious).*

Postwar Development
⚒ 1965 Austria

STEYR SK 105 LIGHT TANK

The Austrian Steyr SK 105 light tank and tank destroyer has seen widespread service, not only with the Austrian Army, but also with the armies of six countries.

D evelopment of this Austrian light tank, also known as the Kürassier, was begun in 1965 by Saurer-Werke (later taken over by Steyr-Daimler-Puch) to meet a requirement by the Austrian Army for a fast anti-armor vehicle. The prototype was tested in 1967 and preproduction vehicles were evaluated in 1971. The Austrian Army has only used 286 units, but the tank has enjoyed a healthy export market, 112 vehicles having been supplied to Argentina, 34 to Bolivia and Botswana respectively, 17 to Brazil, 111 to Morocco, and 42 to Tunisia. Variants of the SL 105 include the Greif (Griffin) armored recovery vehicle, the Pionier combat engineer vehicle, and the Fahrschulpanzer driver training vehicle.

Above: *This photograph of an SK 105 light tank negotiating a steep incline clearly shows the French TCV 29 laser rangefinder mounted on the roof of the turret at the rear, with an infrared/white light searchlight above it.*

Design features

The SK 105 is fitted with an improved version of the French FL-12 in which the gun is positioned in the upper part, with the commander on the left and the gunner on the right. The 4.13in (105mm) gun is fed by two revolver-type magazines, each holding six rounds. The vehicle is protected from ammunition of up to 0.78in (20mm) over its frontal arc, and the remainder of the vehicle is protected against small-arms fire.

Specifications

Armament: One 4.13in (105mm) GIAT-Cn-105-57 rifled gun; one 0.3in (7.62mm) MG74 coaxial MG

Armor: Not revealed

Crew: 3

Dimensions: Length 18.31ft (5.582m); Width 8.20ft (2.50m); Height 8.30ft (2.53m)

Weight: 38,580lb (17,500kg)

Powerplant: Steyr 7FA diesel, 320bhp (238kW)

Speed: 40.6mph (65.3km/h)

Range: Not available

Specifications

T-64 MAIN BATTLE TANK

The T-64 main battle tank was never deployed outside the boundaries of the Warsaw Pact countries. It was fitted with the latest explosive reactive armor and other advanced features.

(T-64B)

Armament: One 4.92in (125mm) D-81TM (2A46 Rapira 3) smoothbore gun; one coaxial 0.3in (7.62mm) PKT MG; one 0.5in (12.7mm) NSVT AA MG

Armor: Maximum, 7.87in (200mm)

Crew: 3

Dimensions: Length (hull) 24ft 3in (7.4m); Width 11ft 11in (3.64m); Height 7ft 3in (2.2m)

Weight: 41.34 tons (42,000kg)

Powerplant: 5DTF 5-cylinder opposed diesel, 750bhp (560kW)

Speed: 47mph (75km/h)

Range: 248 miles (400km)

Introduced in the late 1960s, the T-64 Soviet Main Battle Tank was designed to complement the T-72 series. Unlike the T-72, however, which was exported to Soviet-friendly armies, the T-64 was only used by the Soviet armed forces. The first operational model, the T-64A, made its first appearance outside the Soviet Union in 1976, when it was issued in 1976 to the Guards Armored Divisions of the Group of Soviet Forces in Germany (GSFG), and some time later in Hungary's Southern Group of Forces (SFG). The only known variant of the T-64A was the T-64AK command vehicle, which carried additional radio equipment and a telescopic mast. The next model, the T-64B, made its appearance in East Germany and Hungary in 1981. As well as having new hull and turret armor, the T-64B was equipped to fire the Kobra (AT-8 Songster) gun-launched antitank missile, a radio command-guided

Above: T-64s being transported on railroad flat cars. The T-64 was deployed with the Soviet Group of Forces in Germany from 1976, and later models were deployed to the Warsaw Pact countries from 1981.

weapon. Six rounds could be carried in the automatic loader, as well as 36 conventional rounds. About 8000 T-64s were built, some 2000 of which were handed over to the Ukraine after the breakup of the Soviet Union.

Below: The T-64 was only ever intended to be used by the Soviet armed forces, and was designed to complement the T-72 series. The tank was widely used, some 8000 being built, about a quarter of which were handed over to the Ukraine after the breakup of the USSR.

PANSARBANDVAGN (PBV) 302 ARMORED PERSONNEL CARRIER

Sweden's Pbv 302 APC has been in service for many years, and has been adapted to perform a variety of different tasks. The vehicles have served with UN forces in the former Yugoslavia.

Left: *Sweden's Pansarbandvagn 302 has proved a well-designed and effective armored personnel carrier, able to cope with most types of terrain, and has been produced in several different versions. It is in service only with the Swedish Army.*

The Swedish Army's Pbv 302 was first issued in 1966, the prototype having been completed in 1962. It has been produced in several different versions, the main one being the Pbv 302A tracked armored personnel carrier. The combat command and control variant is the Stripbv 3021, which has radio communications equipment and four antennae; the fire control version is the Epvb 3022, in which the commander's hatch is replaced by a cupola with rangefinding devices, three radio antennae, and additional buoyancy aids. The Bplpbv 30023 is an armored fire direction post with four antennae, and fire control and communications equipment, while the Pbv 3024 is a radio relay version.

Armament

The Pbv 302A can carry eight infantrymen, it is armed with a 0.79mm (20mm) automatic cannon. This has a rate of fire of 20 rounds per minute. The cannon is fed by magazines which hold 30 rounds each. The firepower can be supplemented by the infantrymen themselves, who can open fire through roof hatches. The main armament is effective against targets at a range of 1 mile (1.6km).

Specifications

Armament: One 0.79in (20mm) cannon

Armor: 0.79in (20mm)

Crew: 2 plus 10

Dimensions: Length 17ft 7in (5.35mm); Width 9ft 5in (2.86m); Height 8ft 2in (2.49m)

Weight: 13.29 tons (13,500kg)

Powerplant: Volvo-Penta 6-cylinder turbocharged diesel, 280bhp (209kW) at 2200rpm

Speed: 41mph (66km/h)

Range: 186 miles (300km)

Postwar Development
1966 Sweden

STRIDSVAGN (STRV) 103 S-TANK

The Bofors Stridsvagn 103 S-Tank originated in a request by the Swedish Army to replace its fleet of 300 Centurions (among other armored fighting vehicles) with a homegrown product.

Specifications

Armament: One 4.13in (105mm) gun; three MGs
Armor: Not revealed
Crew: 3
Dimensions: Length 27ft 7in (8.42m); Width 11ft 10in (3.62m); Height 8ft 3in (2.50m)
Weight: 39.07 tons (39,700kg)
Powerplant: Rolls-Royce K60 multi-fuel, 240bhp (179kW) at 3750rpm and Boeing 553 gas turbine, 490bhp (365kW) at 38,000rpm
Speed: 31mph (50km/h)
Range: 242 miles (390km)

When the requirement for this tank was first issued, a heavy tank designated KRV was already under development. This was abandoned, however, and the emphasis switched to completing the Strv 103. The S-Tank tested a number of new design features, the most obvious of which was the absence of a turret. This layout was adopted so that the tank could keep a low profile in action, and this was further enhanced by its bulldozer blade, so that it could dig itself in if a static defense was required. The disadvantage of a turretless design was that the entire vehicle had to be turned for aiming purposes. Although the tank could be slowed on its tracks as fast as a turret could be turned, this aspect was not attractive to potential customers. Although the design generated a high level of interest it did not attract any overseas customers. The S-Tank has a Rolls-Royce multi-fuel engine (later replaced by a Detroit diesel in the modernized Strv 103C) and a Boeing gas turbine.

Left: *This photograph shows the S-Tank's bulldozer blade in the retracted position. The last S-Tanks were withdrawn from service with the Swedish Army in 2001.*

Below: *The Stridsvagn 103 S-Tank was a bold design concept. The box at the rear of the hull is for external stowage of equipment. Novel though it was, the S-Tank did not attract overseas customers.*

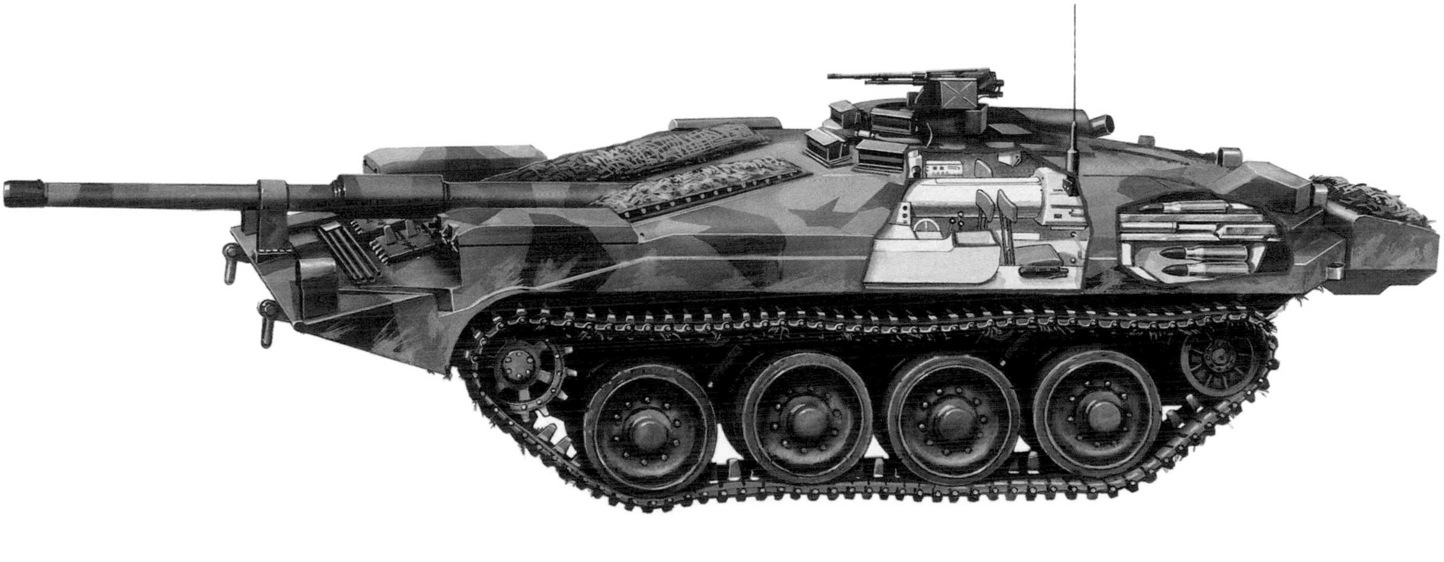

Postwar Development
⚒ 1967 Soviet

BMP-1 INFANTRY COMBAT VEHICLE

First seen in public in November 1967, the BMP-1 is believed to be the world's first infantry fighting vehicle. Its steeply-sloped hull can withstand heavy (0.50in/12.7mm) machine-gun fire.

Specifications

Armament: One 2.87in (73mm) 2A28 Grom low-pressure gun; one 0.3in (7.62mm) PKT MG; one AT-3 Sagger ATGW system
Armor: Maximum, 1.3in (33mm)
Crew: 2 plus 9
Dimensions: Length 22ft 2in (6.75m); Width 9ft 8in (2.94m); Height 7in 1in (2.15m)
Weight: 13.28 tons (13,500kg)
Powerplant: One Model 5D20 6-cylinder diesel, 300bhp (223.9kW) at 2000rpm
Speed: Road, 50mph (80km/h); Water, 5mph (8km/h
Range: 310 miles (500km)

The primary role of the BMP series of infantry fighting vehicles is to safely transport troops to the battle area, disembark them, and then provide them with fire support. The vehicle's smoothbore 2.87in (73mm) gun fires a HEAT (High Explosive AntiTank) round, and the original BMP-1 was also armed with the AT-3 Sagger antitank missile, this being operated by a two-man infantry team. With a range of up to 320 yards (300 metres) the missile was guided by command line-of-sight and its warhead could penetrate up to 15.7in (40cm) of armor. In 1970 an air-portable version of the BMP, the BMD-1, was issued to the Soviet airborne forces. The BMP-1 was designed to replace the BTR-50P series of tracked armred personnel carriers. The BMP-1 was replaced in due course by an

improved version, the BMP-2. Both variants have been widely exported.

Geographical use
The BMP-1 was first used in combat by Arab forces during the Yom Kippur War of 1973, and later saw action with the Russians in Afghanistan, with Iraq in various Middle East conflicts and with Libyan forces fighting in Chad.

Above: *The very effective BMP-1 was issued to many armies throughout the world. The example seen here is in service with the Finnish Army.*

Left: *The BMP-1 was the first infantry combat vehicle to enter service.*

Specifications

Armament: One 0.98in (25mm)
cannon; one 0.30in (7.62mm) MG

Armor: Not released

Crew: 3 plus 8 troops

Dimensions: Length 19ft 4.3in
(5.9m); Width 9ft 3.4in (2.83m);
Height 9ft 0.25in (2.75m)

Weight: 15.06 tons (15,300kg)

Powerplant: Baudouin 6 F11,V-8
diesel, 300hp (223.7kW)

Speed: Road, 40.4mph (65km/h);
Water, 6.2mph (10km/h)

Range: Road, 310.7 miles (500km)

Postwar Development
1968   France

AMX-10P INFANTRY COMBAT VEHICLE

The AMX-10P is a useful infantry combat vehicle. Despite belonging to a fairly early generation, it is still combat-effective and could be made still more so by the use of a one-man turret armed with a 0.98in (25mm) gun.

Above: Although designed a long time ago, the AMX-10P remains an effective infantry combat vehicle and is still in service with a number of countries, particularly in the Middle East.

Right: The AMX-10P infantry combat vehicle has a crew of three and can carry eight fully armed troops.

The AMX-10P infantry combat vehicle was developed from 1965 to meet the requirements of the French Army. The first prototype was completed in 1968 and production vehicles were delivered from 1973, replacing the AMX-VCI in service. Production ended in 1994, by which time over 1800 vehicles had been completed for the French Army and for export to countries such as Greece, Indonesia, Qatar, Saudi Arabia, Singapore, and the United Arab Emirates. The AMX-10P is fully amphibious (propelled in the water by jets at the rear of the hull) and is fitted with an NBC system and night-vision equipment. The AMX-10P forms the basis of a complete family of vehicles including command post, HOT anttank, mortar tractor, fire control, artillery observation, repair, ambulance, radar, and fire support variants.

The AMX-10P has a two-man power-operated turret armed with a 0.30in (7.62mm) machine gun and a dual-feed 0.78in (20mm) cannon. The latter will possibly be replaced by a 0.98in (25mm) weapon, offering improved penetration capabilities against a new generation of armored fighting vehicles.

Chapter 7

THE ARMOR REVOLUTION

It takes up to 15 years from the initial design of a new tank to its entry into service, and so the tanks that began to be used in the 1970s and early 1980s were the fruits of 1960s technology. One of the most radical improvements, manifest in main battle tanks such as the British Challenger, the US Abrams, the German Leopard, and the Israeli Merkava, was the introduction of composite armor. Tanks began to take on a different appearance.

Above: *Germany's excellent Leopard 2 tank has been a huge success story, and is in service with several NATO armies, as well as those of Sweden and Switzerland. The tank's capability is constantly being upgraded.*

Left: *The LVTP7 amphibious assault vehicle had a much different design from that of its predecessors, featuring a fully-enclosed troop compartment offering much greater protection.*

Composite and reactive armor reduced the likelihood of penetration by an enormous factor, while well-designed sloped armor was proof against most antitank guided weapons with hollow charge warheads. The 1970s and 1980s saw a subtle switch from traditional antitank methods to more revolutionary ones. Helicopters, for example, became armed with "fire and forget" antitank missiles (designed to penetrate the turret of a target from above), while belly attack mines with special fuses, capable of disabling any armored fighting vehicle, opened a new arena of danger. All this compelled AFV designers to rethink the distribution of armor, and in some cases to devise vehicles that were very nearly mine-proof. Another improvement took place in gunnery, as well as in the sighting and stabilizing systems that turned the tank gun into a highly accurate weapon capable of hitting a target with the first shot from ranges of 9843ft (3000m).

The Armor Revolution
⚒ 1968   Germany

SPÄHPANZER LUCHS (LYNX) ARMORED RECONNAISSANCE VEHICLE

The Henschel Wehrtechnik Luchs armored reconnaissance vehicle was developed specifically for the German Army in the mid-1960s, but the reason for its existence largely vanished with the demise of the Cold War.

The Spähpanzer Luchs 8x8 armored reconnaissance vehicle originated in a requirement by the German Army in the mid-1960s. Two companies submitted designs and Daimler-Benz emerged the winner. The production contract (for 408 vehicles) was awarded in 1973 to Rheinstahl Wehrtechnik (later Henschel Wehrtechnik). The first vehicle was delivered in 1975 and production lasted until 1978. The Luchs is fully amphibious, driven by two propellers mounted at the rear. The steering is power-assisted and all eight wheels can be steered. When it was first used, the Luchs had infrared night-vision equipment for all crew members, but this was replaced by Therma

Above: The Spähpanzer Luchs, designed in the mid-1960s, continued a long tradition of German 8x8 armored reconnaissance vehicles. The Luchs carries a four-man crew and is fully amphibious.

night-vision equipment. The driver sits at the front left-hand side of the vehicle, with the two-man turret to his rear. The engine is mounted at the rear of the vehicle on the right, and the radio operator (who also acts as second driver) has a rearward-facing position on the left. The turret has full power traverse through 360 degrees, and manual controls are provided for emergency use. The Luchs was not developed further and no variants have been produced.

Specifications

Armament: One 0.79in (20mm); one 0.30in (7.62mm) MG

Armor: Not released, estimated 0.79in (20mm)

Crew: 4

Dimensions: Length 25ft 4.8in (7.743m); Width 9ft 9.3in (2.98m); Height 6ft 11.6in (2.125m)

Weight: Combat, approx 19.19 tons (19,500kg)

Powerplant: Daimler-Benz OM 403, V-10 multi-fuel; diesel, 390hp (290.8kW), gasoline 320hp (238.6kW)

Speed: Road, 56mph (90km/h); Water, 6.2mph (10km/h)

Range: Road, 453.6 miles (730km)

The Armor Revolution

1968 Soviet Union

MTLB MULTIPURPOSE TRACKED VEHICLE

The MTLB was one of the most successful tracked vehicles ever built, and has a number of track options to make it suitable for operations in almost every kind of terrain.

Above: *The MTLBs here are two of the 900 examples purchased from stocks held in the former German Democratic Republic for service with the Swedish Army.*

Specifications

Armament: One 0.3in (7.62mm) PKT MG

Armor: 0.275–0.55in (7–14mm)

Crew: 2 plus 11

Dimensions: Length 21ft 2in (6.454m); Width 9ft 4in (2.85m); Height 6ft 2in (1.865m)

Weight: 11.7 tons (11,900kg)

Powerplant: YaMZ 238 8-cylinder diesel, 240bhp (179kW) at 2100rpm

Speed: 38.5mph (62km/h)

Range: 310 miles (500km)

The MTLB multipurpose tracked vehicle was developed in the late 1960s to replace the ATP armored tracked artillery tractor. It can accommodate 11 infantrymen seated on canvas seats along each side of the troop compartment, which has two large exit doors at the rear and two hatches in the roof. A manually operated turret, armed with a 0.30in (7.62mm) machine gun, is mounted at the front of the hull on the right-hand side. The MTLB is fully amphibious and is propelled in the water by its tracks. The basic version is normally fitted with 13.8in (350mm) wide tracks which give a ground pressure of 0.46kg/cm², but these can be replaced by much wider 22.24in (565mm) tracks, which lower the ground pressure and give the vehicle improved mobility in snow or swamp. The standard version of the vehicle is the MTLBV; others include the MTLB artillery tractor, the MTLBU command vehicle and the TTLB artillery director, which has a "Big Fred" artillery/mortar locating radar mounted on the roof.

Export

After the demise of the Cold War many MTLBs were sold to overseas customers; Sweden, for example, acquired 900 vehicles from East German stocks.

Below: *The MTLB is one of the most successful and widely used tracked vehicles in the world, and examples that were made surplus by the disintegration of the Warsaw Pact were eagerly snapped up by other nations.*

The Armor Revolution
⚒ 1970 Israel

MAGACH MAIN BATTLE TANK

In the 1960s Israel purchased large numbers of surplus M48 tanks from West Germany. This was kept secret from the Israeli public, who were against links of any kind with the Germans.

Specifications

Armament: One 4.13in (105mm) gun; three 0.30in (7.62mm) MGs

Armor: Not revealed

Crew: 4

Dimensions: Length 22ft 10in (6.95m); Width 11ft 11in (3.63m); Height 10ft 9in (3.27m)

Weight: Not revealed

Powerplant: General Dynamics Land Systems AVDS-1790 series diesel engine

Speed: Not revealed

Range: Not revealed

Left: *This picture of a Magach 7 shows considerable departures from the original M60 profile, including additional armor and a stowage area at the rear of the turret.*

The Magach series of main battle tanks was the Israeli Defense Force's name for the American M48/M60. In Hebrew, it means Chariots of the War Heroes (Merkavot Giborei Hamilchama). The first M48A2 tanks were purchased from West Germany in the 1960s. These were armed with a 3.54in (90mm) gun and were used during the Six-Day War of June 1967. This conflict saw more M48s (in this case captured from Jordan) added to the IDF's inventory of armor. The Magach was progressively upgraded by the Israelis. As a first step, the 3.54in (90mm) gun was replaced by the British 4.13in (105mm), which had performed well in the Centurion. The tanks were also fitted with "Blazer" reactive armor blocks to defeat. Despite the added protection, many M48s were lost in combat during the 1973 Yom Kippur War. These losses were made good by the delivery

of American M60s, which then became the latest additions to the Megach series. Upgraded M60s were used in the Israeli invasion of the Lebanon in 1982. The older vehicles in the Megach series were gradually withdrawn and rebuilt as heavy armored personnel carriers.

Below: *The Magach 7's revised turret outline was created by the addition of modular appliqué armor and large blocks of reactive armor. This one has additional frontal armor, producing pronounced "wedges."*

The Armor Revolution
1972 USA

LANDING VEHICLE TRACKED LVTP7/AAVP7

Below: *Thanks to its sandwich-plated steel armor with a layer of Kevlar underneath, the AAVPZ is extremely well protected against fire from heavy caliber weapons. It is also highly seaworthy, a watertight engine compartment making it capable of negotiating rough water during the landing phase.*

The LVTP7 amphibious assault vehicle was developed as a replacement for the LVTP5, which was used in Vietnam and suffered from a short range. The new vehicle had sufficient range to penetrate inland.

Specifications

Armament: One 1.57in (40mm) grenade launcher; one 0.50in (12.7mm) MG
Armor: 1.77in (45mm)
Crew: 3 plus 25
Dimensions: Length 26ft (7.94m); Width 10ft 8in (3.27m); Height 10ft 8in (3.26m)
Weight: 22.48 tons (22,838kg)
Powerplant: Detroit Diesel 8V-53T turbo-charged diesel, 400hp (298.5kW)
Speed: Road 40mph (64km/h); Water 9mph (14km/h)
Range: 300 miles (482km)

Now known as the AAVP7, the LVTP7 entered production in 1972 for the US Marine Corps. It is a fully tracked armored amphibious assault landing vehicle, designed to transport marines from landing ship to shore and then inland. Its name was changed to AAVP7 in 1985. The AAVP7A1 Amtrack provides protected transport of up to 25 combat-equipped marines through all types of terrain. The engine compartment can be completely water-sealed, making it seaworthy in rough water conditions. The vehicle is fitted with sandwich-plated steel armor with a layer of Kevlar underneath, designed to protect the occupants from heavy-caliber weapons fire. The vehicle's own firepower comprises an M2.50 machine gun, an MK-19 1.57in (40mm) grenade launcher, and a line charge with C4 explosives for use in clearing mines. It can travel at speeds of up to 40mph (64km/h) on land and 9mph (14 km/h) at sea.

Upgrades

The LVTP7 replaced the shorter-ranged LVTP5, which saw much active service in Vietnam. It will eventually be replaced by a new AFV, the advanced assault amphibious vehicle.

The Armor Revolution
☭ 1972   Soviet Union

T-72 MAIN BATTLE TANK

Fast and reliable, yet relatively cheap to construct, the T-72 was the
first Russian main battle tank to be exported to countries outside the
Warsaw Pact area.

The T-72 main battle tank entered production in 1972 and remained the principal Russian AFV until the collapse of the Soviet Union. First seen in public at a May Day parade in 1977, the T-72 was built under license in Czechoslovakia, India, Iran, Iraq, Poland, and the former Yugoslavia, where the tank was designated M-84. At least 50,000 of these vehicles have been built and the tank is in service with 30 armies around the world. The original version of the T-72 was the T-72A. This had a laser rangefinder and improved armor, while the T-72B had additional front-turret armor. The T-72BM

Specifications

Armament: One 4.92in (125mm) D-81TM (2A46M) smoothbore gun; one coaxial 0.30in (7.62mm) PKT MG; one 0.50in (12.7mm) NSVT AA MG

Armor: 9.84in (250mm)

Crew: 3

Dimensions: Length 31ft 3in (9.53m) (gun forward), 21ft 8in (6.67m) (hull); Width 12ft 9in (3.59m); Height 7ft 3in (2.22m)

Weight: 44.78 tons (45,500kg)

Powerplant: V-46 12-cylinder diesel, 780bhp (582kW) at 2000rpm

Speed: 40mph (65km/h)

Range: 250 miles (400km)

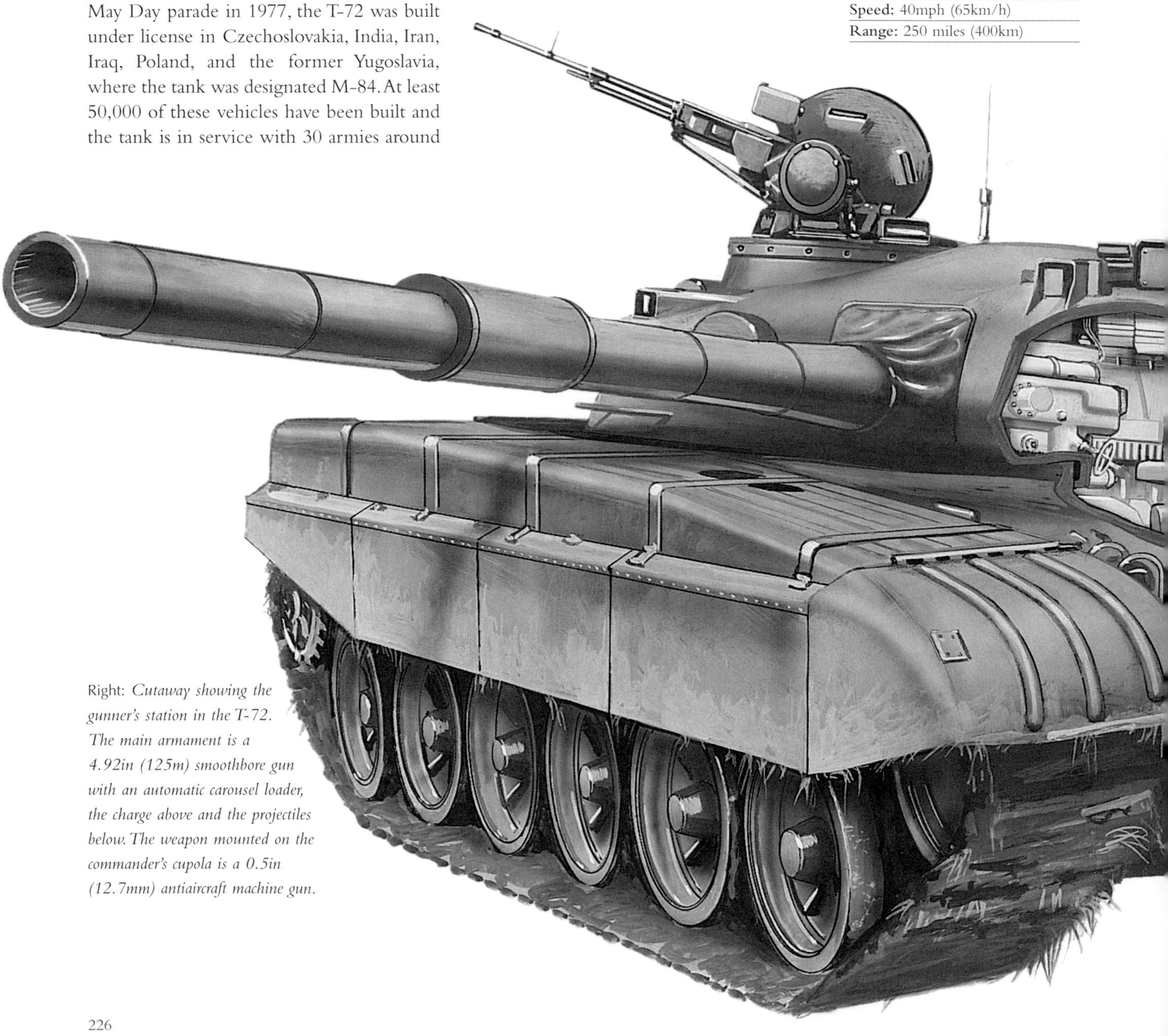

Right: Cutaway showing the gunner's station in the T-72. The main armament is a 4.92in (125m) smoothbore gun with an automatic carousel loader, the charge above and the projectiles below. The weapon mounted on the commander's cupola is a 0.5in (12.7mm) antiaircraft machine gun.

Above: *A T-72 of the Iraqi Army's Republican Guard, abandoned after the 1991 Gulf War. Note the infrared searchlight to the right of the gun, which is fitted with a thermal sleeve and fume extractor. The T-72 was widely exported, at least 50,000 having been built.*

was the first upgrade to incorporate Kontakt-5 explosive reactive armor; the export version of this is the T-72S. The T-72BK is a command vehicle with additional communications equipment.

Gulf War

The T-72 had the dubious distinction of fighting on both sides during the Gulf War of 1991. The Kuwaiti Army accepted the first of 200 tanks (the M-84 version) to be ordered from Yugoslavia. Iraq's Republican Guard is thought to have taken about 1000 T-72s, although these proved no match for the American M1 Abrams and the British Challenger.

The Armor Revolution
⚒ 1973 France

PANHARD M3 ARMORED PERSONNEL CARRIER

Although the Panhard M3 is one of the ugliest APCs in service anywhere, it is nonetheless extremely functional and has been widely exported, as well as adapted to different roles.

The Panhard M3 4x4 APC began life as a private venture. The first prototype was completed in 1969 and the first production vehicles appeared in 1971. Since then, the vehicle has been exported widely, for use both by the military and the police. Some police vehicles are fitted with a one-man turret armed with a machine gun. The hull of the M3 is constructed from all-welded steel armor. The troop compartment, with accommodation for 10 people, has twin doors at the rear and a single door on each side of the hull.

Variants

The antiaircraft version is known as M3VDA and is fitted with a power-operated turret mounting twin 0.79in (20mm) cannons. The M3VAT carries a full range of tools for repairs in the field and has a jib for hoisting engines. The M3VPC is a command vehicle, with extensive communications equipment; the M3VTS is an ambulance model; and the M3VLA is an engineer vehicle, fitted with a hydraulically operated dozer blade for clearing obstacles. The M3 can be fitted with night-vision equipment for the drive, and export vehicles have air conditioning.

Specifications

Armament: Various, typically one or two 0.30in (7.62mm) MGs

Armor: Maximum, 0.47in (12mm)

Crew: 2 plus 10 troops

Dimensions: Length 14ft 7.2in (4.45m); Width 7ft 10.5in (2.4m); Height, hull top 6ft 6.7in (2m)

Weight: 6 tons (6100kg)

Powerplant: Panhard Model 4 HD, 4-cylinder gasoline, 90hp (67.1kW)

Speed: Road, 55.9mph (90km/h); Water, 2.5mph (4km/h)

Range: Road, 372.8 miles (600km)

Left: *This Panhard M3 has the driver's hatch open and its commander is protected by Creusot-Loire STB shield behind his 0.30in (7.62mm) machine gun. More than 4000 M3s were built before production ceased.*

Below: *The Panhard M3 is a very workmanlike APC and is in service with many countries, particularly those that were once part of France's colonial empire in Africa. It is no longer in production.*

The Armor Revolution
⚒ 1973 France

RENAULT VAB ARMORED PERSONNEL CARRIER

The Renault VAB armored personnel carrier has been highly successful since 1976, and is used by many armed forces worldwide. It is an effective peacekeeping machine, and has been used in many trouble spots.

Above: *This infantry combat version of the VAB features a turret armed with a 0.787in (20mm) cannon. The VAB was a major export success, having been sold to the armies of at least 16 countries.*

The VAB (Vehicule de l'Avant Blinde) frontline armored vehicle is an Infantry Corps tactical armored vehicle produced by the Euro Mobilite Division of Giat Industries, who have headquarters at Versailles in France. A joint venture company, Satory Military Vehicles, was set up by Giat and Renault Trucks with responsibility for the VAB series amongst others, including the AMX-10RC and the French Army's new VBCI wheeled infantry fighting vehicle. In September 2003, however, Giat was given the position of prime contractor as well as responsibility for marketing of the VBCI, the AMX 10P and AMX 10RC. Renault Trucks Defense, meanwhile, was the prime contractor for the VAB, and they also held marketing responsibilities. The first

production vehicles were completed at St. Chamond in 1976, and since then more than 5,000 VABs have been produced in 30 different versions. Large numbers of VABs were used in Operation Desert Storm, and this tank has been deployed in United Nations peacekeeping missions in Bosnia, Cambodia, Croatia, Lebanon, Rwanda, and Somalia. In addition to the 4000 VABs in service with the French Army, the AFV also serves with the armed forces of 15 other countries.

Below: *All versions of the VAB have a similar layout, with the driver front left, the commander/machine gunner on the right, the engine compartment to the rear of the driver, a small passageway on the right, and the troop compartment to the rear.*

Specifications

Armament: One 0.50in (12.7mm) MG or one 0.30in (7.62mm) MG

Armor: Estimated, 0.98in (25mm)

Crew: 2 plus 10 troops

Dimensions: Length 19ft 7.4in (5.98m); Width 8ft 2in (2.49m); Height, hull top, 6ft 9in (2.06m)

Weight: 4x4 version 12.8 tons (13,000kg); 6x6 version 13.98 tons (14,200kg)

Powerplant: Renault MIDS 06.20.45, 6-cylinder diesel, 220hp (164kW)

Speed: Road, 57.1mph (92km/h); Water, 5mph (8km/h)

Range: Road, 621.4 miles (1000km)

The Armor Revolution
⚒ 1973 UK

SCORPION/SCIMITAR RECONNAISSANCE VEHICLES

Although the last Scorpion reconnaissance vehicles were withdrawn in 1994, some of their chassis remained in use as the Sabre, which mounted a 1.18in (30mm) cannon turret taken from other AFVs.

Manufactured by Alvis Vickers, the Scorpion light tank (or Combat Vehicle Reconnaissance Tracked Fire Support) was first used by the British Army in 1973. Designed to be a fast, air-transportable reconnaissance vehicle, it featured aluminum armor and mounted a 3in (76mm) L23A1 gun. The original model was fitted with a Jaguar 0.9 gallon (4.2 litre) gasoline engine, which had a very good power/weight ratio, although some models were fitted with the Perkins diesel engine. The Scorpion was an extremely compact AFV, and ideal for the reconnaissance role. The FV107 Scimitar was similar in appearance to the Scorpion, but mounted a 3.54in (30mm) Rarden cannon in place of

Above: The original Scorpion was armed with a 3in (76mm) main gun, but this was later replaced by a 1.18in (30mm) Rarden cannon.

the 3in (76mm) gun. Both the Scorpion and the Scimitar were used in the battle for the Falkland Islands in 1982, their light weight and tracks making it possible for them to cross the marshy Falklands terrain with ease. During the final assault on Port Stanley, they acted in support of 2 Para. The Scorpion was used by the British Army, the Royal Air Force Regiment, and 12 other countries. The largest user outside the UK was Belgium, who set up an assembly line for the production of 700 vehicles. The last Scorpions were withdrawn in 1994.

Specifications

Armament: One 3in/3.54in (76mm/90mm) gun; one 0.30in (7.62mm) MG

Armor: Not available

Crew: 3

Dimensions: Length 14ft 5in (4.38m); Width 7ft 2in (2.18m); Height 6ft 10in (2.09m)

Weight: 7.94 tons (8073kg)

Powerplant: Jaguar 0.9 gallon (4.2 litre) gasoline, 190bhp (141.6kW) at 4750rpm

Speed: 50mph or 45mph (80.5km/h or 72.5km/h)

Range: 644km or 756km (400 or 470 miles)

The Armor Revolution
✗ 1974 Brazil

ENGESA EE-11 URUTU ARMORED PERSONNEL CARRIER

Like Sweden, Brazil has taken care to avoid reliance on imported military equipment. One of their own designs is the EE-11 armored personnel carrier.

Right: *The Engesa Urutu is armed with a single 0.5in (12.7mm) M2HB heavy machine gun. Production is complete and the Engesa company is no longer trading, having gone into bankruptcy in 1993.*

Specifications

Armament: One 0.78in (20mm) cannon (typical)

Armor: Not available

Crew: 1 plus 12

Dimensions: Length 20ft (6.1m); Width 8ft 8in (2.65m); Height 9ft 6in (2.9m)

Weight: 13.78 tons (14,000kg)

Powerplant: Detroit Diesel 6V-53T 6-cylinder water-cooled diesel, 260bhp (193kW) at 2800rpm

Speed: 65mph (105km/h)

Range: 528 miles (850km)

The Engesa EE-11 Urutu 6x6 armored personnel carrier was developed in response to a request made by the Brazilian Army. The first prototype was completed in 1970 and production vehicles appeared in 1974. The EE-11 shares much in common with the Engesa EE-9 Cascavel armored car, which was under development at the same time. The EE-11 has seven variants, the main differences between them being the engine, which can be either a Mercedes-Benz or Detroit diesel. The MkVII has a supercharged diesel in place of the standard 6V-53 (as installed in the Mk III). The vehicle is fully amphibious and is propelled by its wheels. Before entering the water a trim vane is erected at the front of the vehicle.

Variants

The variants of the EE-11 include an 3.19in (81mm) mortar carrier, an ambulance with a higher roof, a cargo carrier, an armored fire support vehicle with a 3.54in (90mm) turret as fitted to the EE-9 Cascavel armored car, an antiaircraft vehicle with twin 0.78in (20mm) cannons, and an internal security vehicle with a blade for clearing obstacles. About 20 countries have purchased the EE-11.

Below: *The Urutu—here demonstrating its amphibious qualities—is in widespread service around the world. It can be maintained by using commercial vehicle parts.*

The Armor Revolution
✷ 1974 Brazil

ENGESA EE-9 CASCAVEL ARMORED CAR

The São Paulo company Engesa had a long experience of manufacturing trucks. During the late 1960s they developed two 6x6 armored vehicles for the Brazilian Army. One of these was the EE-9 armored car.

Specifications

Armament: One 3.54in (90mm) gun; one 0.30in (7.62mm) coaxial MG; one 0.3in (7.62mm) AA MG

Armor: Not available

Crew: 3

Dimension: Length 17ft 1in (5.2m); Width 8ft 8in (2.64m); Height 8ft 10in (2.68m)

Weight: 13.19 tons (13,400kg)

Powerplant: Detroit Diesel 6V-53N 6-cylinder water-cooled diesel, 212bhp (158kW) at 2800rpm

Speed: 62mph (100km/h)

Range: 547 miles (880km)

Left: *Later production versions of the EE-9 armored car feature a laser rangefinder mounted externally above the 3.54in (90mm) gun and also a 0.30in (7.62mm) machine gun mounted at the commander's station. Iran captured a number of these vehicles during the long-running war with Iraq.*

The EE-9 Cascavel (Rattlesnake) 6x6 armored car was developed in tandem with the EE-11 armored personnel carrier, with which it shares many features. The first prototypes of the EE-9 were completed in November 1970. A batch of preproduction vehicles followed between 1972 and 1973 and the first production vehicles were delivered to the Brazilian Army in 1974. The initial production model was the Cascavel II. This had the same 1.46in (37mm) gun as the M3 Stuart light tank, which was then still in service with the Brazilian Army. All early models were eventually rebuilt with an Engesa turret armed with a 3.54in (90mm) gun. The Cascavel was an export model, featuring a French Hispano-Suiza H-90 turret armed with a 3.54in (90mm) GIAT gun. The Cascavel Mks IV–VII have a two-man Engesa ET-90 turret armed with a 3.54in (90mm) Cockerill Mk III gun manufactured under license in Brazil. Later production variants of the EE-9 carry a laser rangefinder mounted externally over the 3.54in (90mm) gun, and have a 0.30in (7.62mm) gun mounted externally at the commander's station. This AFV has been widely exported, and was used in the Iraq and Iran war.

Above: *The AMX-10RC was well suited to desert conditions. It was first issued to the 2nd Regiment of Hussars, based at Sourdon, in 1981, and was subsequently used in Chad and Iraq.*

AMX-10RC RECONNAISSANCE VEHICLE

France's AMX-10RC was developed primarily for the French Army and did not attract large export orders, as other preceding French AFVs had done. The high cost of each unit was one factor in this.

The AMX-10RC 6x6 reconnaissance vehicle was developed as a replacement for the Panhard EBR 8x8 armored car. The first prototype appeared in 1971 and the first deliveries were made to the French Army in 1978. The French Army accepted 337 units up to 1978, when production ended. Unlike many other French AFVs, this tank did not export widely, probably because the unit cost was high and the vehicle was too sophisticated. The only export customers were Morocco, who took delivery of 108 units, and Chad, who received 12. The AMX-10RC was used by the French Army in the 1991 Gulf War, where it served with the French 6th Light Armored division, and in Chad, where it played its part in routing Libyan forces. The vehicle has an advanced fire control system that includes a laser rangefinder, a computer, and a low-light thermal imager that engages stationary and moving targets by day and night.

Plans to upgrade

It was anticipated that the AMX-10RC would receive a number of upgrades, but these plans were abandoned, although a battlefield management system has been installed.

Below: *Cutaway showing the interior of the AMX-10RC. A highly effective reconnaissance vehicle, the AMX-10RC might have enjoyed more export success had it not been so expensive.*

Specifications

Armament: One 4.13in (105mm) gun; two 0.30in (7.62mm) MGs

Armor: Not released

Crew: 4

Dimensions: Length 30ft (9.15m); Width 9ft 8.1in (2.95m); Height 8ft 8.725in (2.66m)

Weight: 15.63 tons (15,880kg)

Powerplant: Baudouin Mode 6F 11 SRX diesel, 280hp (208.8kW)

Speed: Road, 52.8mph (85km/h); Water, 4.47mph (7.2km/h)

Range: Road, 621.4 miles (1000km)

The Armor Revolution
⚒ **1974   Germany**

LEOPARD 2 MAIN BATTLE TANK

The Leopard 2 is an extremely powerful tank and is one of the finest of

its generation, offering a unique blend of firepower, protection, and

mobility. First delivered in 1978, it is still being radically upgraded.

As the successor to the Leopard 1, the Leopard 2 made its appearance in 1979 and is in service with the armies of Austria, Denmark, Germany, the Netherlands, Norway, Switzerland, Sweden, and Spain. Over 3200 units have been produced. The Finnish Army is buying 124 units and the Polish Army acquired 128 surplus Leopard 2A4 tanks from Germany. In August 2005, Greece placed an order for 183 surplus Leopard 2A4 and 150 Leopard 1A5 tanks from German Army reserves. In November 2005, an agreement was signed for the sale of 298 German Army Leopard 2A4 tanks to

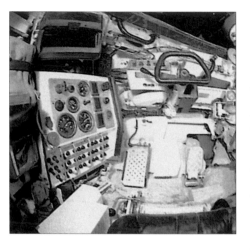

Above: *The computerized interior of the Leopard 2 is a far cry from those of the tank's World War II ancestors, the Tiger and the Panther. The layout is conventional, with the driver seated front right, the commander on the right of the turret, the gunner to his front, and the loader on the left.*

Specifications

(Leopard 2A5)
Armament: One 4.72in (120mm) smooth-bore gun; two 0.30in (7.62mm) MGs

Armor: Multilayer, thickness not released

Crew: 4

Dimensions: Length 32ft 8.4in (9.97m); Width 12ft 3.25in (3.74m); Height 8ft 7.9in (2.64m)

Weight: approx 58.75 tons (59,700kg)

Powerplant: MTU MB 873 Ka501, 12-cylinder diesel, 1500hp (1118.5kW)

Speed: Road, 44.75mph (72km/h)

Range: Road, 310 miles (500km)

Above: *The Leopard 2 commander's low-profile cupola is on the right with the periscope sight to his front. The 4.72in (120mm) gun is fitted with a thermal sleeve and fume extractor, and the gunner's sight is immediately to the right of the mantlet.*

Turkey, with deliveries planned over 2006 and 2007. The Leopard 2A6 includes a longer L55 gun, an auxiliary engine, improved mine protection, and an air conditioning system.

Upgrades

The 2A6 configuration has been developed for the German Army, and 225 2A5 tanks are being upgraded. The first of these was delivered in March 2001. A similar upgrade is also being carried out on behalf of the Royal Netherlands Army. The Leopard 2A6EX is a next-generation variant, 170 of which have been ordered by Greece. Other Leopard 2 customers are Spain and Sweden.

Left: *The Leopard 2 relies for survival on its very advanced armor, which is of the spaced multilayer type and provides effective protection against most types of modern antitank weapon. Other vulnerable areas, such as the suspension, are protected by steel-reinforced rubber.*

The Armor Revolution
⚒ 1974 South Africa

LAND SYSTEMS OMC RATEL

The South African Land Systems OMC Ratel was developed as an

insurance against supplies of equipment being cut off as a result of UN

arms embargos during the apartheid regime.

For many years, the British 6x6 Saracen had been the South African Army's standard armored personnel carrier, but the South African Government now decided to produce their own infantry fighting vehicle to meet their army's future requirements. The first vehicles were produced by Sandock-Austral (now Land Systems OMC). More than 1350 examples were built for the home market and for export to Morocco. The South African Army's Ratels were used to mount frequent deep-penetration

raids into Angola (for instance in May 1978). The Moroccans have used their Ratels against Polisario guerrillas in the Sahara Desert.

Variants

The basic vehicle is the Ratel 20. One variant, the Ratel 60, has a two-man turret armed with a mortar and machine gun, while the Ratel 90 is a fire support vehicle, with a two-man turret equipped with a 3.54in (90mm) gun.

Below: *The Land Systems OMC Ratel has proved an ideal vehicle for use by the South African Army, whose deep-penetration raids into Angola were reminiscent of these carried out by the British Long Range Desert Group in World War II.*

Specifications

Armament: One 3.54in (90mm) gun; three 0.30in (7.62mm) MGs

Armor: 0.78in (20mm)

Crew: 3 plus 7

Dimensions: Length 23ft 4in (7.212m); Width 8ft 3in (2.526m); Height 9ft 7in (2.915m)

Weight: 41,887lb (19,000kg)

Powerplant: 6-cylinder in-line diesel, 282bhp (210kW) at 2200rpm

Speed: 65mph (105km/h)

Range: 534 miles (860km)

The Armor Revolution
1975 Japan

TYPE 74 MAIN BATTLE TANK

An unusual feature of this battle tank is its hydro-pneumatic suspension. This enables the driver to adjust the height of the suspension to suit the type of terrain, and also improves the gun's elevation arc.

Specifications

Armament: One 4.13in (105mm) gun; one 0.50in (12.7mm) MG; one 0.30in (7.62mm) MG
Armor: Unknown thickness steel
Crew: 4
Dimensions: Length 30ft 10in (9.42m); Width 10ft 5in (3.18m); Height 8ft 2in (2.48m) to hull top
Weight: 37.4 tons (38,000kg)
Powerplant: Mitsubishi 10ZF 22 WT, 10-cylinder diesel, 720bhp (536kW)
Speed: 38mph (60km/h)
Range: 250 miles (400km)

In 1972, Mitsubishi Heavy Industries and the Japanese Ground Self-Defense Force (JGSDF) began to develop joint plans for a new main battle tank to replace the Type 61. The design was finalized in 1964 and the first two prototypes were completed in September 1969. These were evaluated under the name of STB-1. They incorporated many features that were common to other main battle tanks of the period, for example the hydro-pneumatic suspension system of the MBT-70, the hull of the Leopard 1, and the British 4.13in (105mm) L7 series rifled gun. The turret was similar in design to that of the French AMX-30. The STB-1 had an automatic loader for the British L7A1 gun, which was subsequently built under license by the Japan Steel Works. The first production model, known as STB-6, appeared in 1973, and deliveries started in 1975. The JGSDF received 870 units of the Type 74, as the tank was now renamed. The fire control system includes a ballistic computer and laser rangefinder. Two specialized variants are the Type 78 armored recovery vehicle and the Type 87 mobile antiaircraft vehicle.

Below: *One unusual feature about the Type 74 is its hydro-pneumatic suspension, which allows the driver to adjust the height of the vehicle to suit the nature of the terrain it has to cross. This arrangement also improves the gun's elevation arc.*

The Armor Revolution
✶ 1975 UK

SAXON ARMORED PERSONNEL CARRIER

The Saxon armored personnel carrier was a useful addition for the British Army during the Cold War, and has since been used in troubled areas such as Bosnia.

Left: *The Alvis Saxon APC has proved an ideal vehicle for the internal security role and can be fitted with a variety of equipment to suit a particular mission, including a mast-mounted TV camera. This example is armed with a General Purpose Machine Gun.*

The Saxon armored personnel carrier started as a private venture by GKN Defence (which merged with Alvis Vehicles in 1998). The first prototype was completed in 1976 and the vehicle was adopted by the British Army in 1983. It was intended for issue to infantry battalions based in the United Kingdom, but liable to be deployed rapidly to Germany as reinforcements in a time of crisis. The vehicle, which can be best described as a battlefield taxi, is designed around truck parts and does not require the huge maintenance of track and running gear normally associated with APC/AIFVs. The value of the Saxon was its ability to protect troops from shell splinters and machine-gun fire while in transit in Europe. It is more of a mineproof lorry, rather than an armored personnel carrier, and the vehicle has been used successfully by British Mechanized Battalions serving with the UN in Bosnia. The British Army retains a number of Saxon IS (Patrol) vehicles for service in counterinsurgency operations. Saxon Patrol comes in two versions—a troop-carrier and an ambulance.

Export
The Saxon has been exported to Bahrain, Hong Kong, Malaysia, Nigeria, Oman, and the United Arab Emirates.

Specifications

Armament: One 0.30in (7.62mm) MG

Armor: Not available

Crew: 3 plus 4

Dimensions: Length 16ft 11in (5.13m); Width 7ft 4in (2.24m); Height 7ft 6in (2.26m)

Weight: 8.04 tons (8128kg)

Powerplant: Jaguar 0.9 gallon (4.2-litre) gasoline developing 190bhp (144.6kW) at 4750rpm

Speed: 50mph (81km/h)

Range: 300 miles (485km)

The Armor Revolution
✖ **1976 Argentina**

TAMSE TAM MEDIUM TANK

The TAM medium tank gave the Argentine Army its first modern

armored fighting vehicle, and has had limited use in counterinsurgency

operations.

Below: *Developed by Thyssen Henschel for the Argentine Army, the TAM was based on the well-proven Marder chassis. This example has its main gun in the locked position for transit.*

Specifications

Armament: One 4.13in (105mm); two 0.30in (7.62mm) MGs

Armor: Not available

Crew: 4

Dimensions: Length 22ft 3in (6.77m); Width 10ft 10in (3.29m); Height 8ft 11in (2.71m)

Weight: 29.53 tons (30,000kg)

Powerplant: MTU MB 833 Ka-500 6-cylinder diesel, 720bhp (537kW) at 2400rpm

Speed: 46.6mph (75km/h)

Range: 584 miles (940km)

In 1974, the German firm Thyssen Henschel was awarded a contract by Argentina to design and develop a new medium tank. This was known as TAM (Tanque Argentino Mediano) and was intended to replace Argentina's ageing Shermans. Also in question was the development of an infantry combat vehicle known as VCI (Vehiculo Combate Infanteria) to replace its M9s. Three prototypes of each were built, based on the very successful TH-301 light/medium tank design, and these were shipped to Argentina after trials had taken place in Germany. Production began at a new purpose-built factory. The Argentine Army had ordered over 500 vehicles of both types, but for economic reasons this was reduced to 350. Variants of the TAM were the VCA 155 (comprising a lengthened TAM chassis fitted with the turret of an Italian Palmaria 6.10in (155mm) self-propelled howitzer) and the VCRT (an armored recovery vehicle that was built in prototype form only). Some TAMs were converted into rocket launchers, the launchers (of Israeli manufacture) added to a TAM chassis. The TAM could have its operational range extended by fitting auxiliary fuel tanks at the rear of the hull.

The Armor Revolution
1976 Soviet Union

BTR-70 ARMORED PERSONNEL CARRIER

Like its predecessors, the BTR-70 armored personnel carrier has been used widely by the former Warsaw Pact countries and their Cold War allies. It saw frequent action during the Soviet invasion of Afghanistan.

Below: *The BTR-70 armored personnel carrier has been widely used in an internal security role.*

The BTR-70 is a further development of the BTR-60, and was first seen at the May Day parade in Moscow in 1980. It closely resembles a BTR-60PB, although it has a longer hull and an improved means of accessing the vehicle with doors on each side of the vehicle (replacing the dangerous and unpopular roof hatches of the earlier model). Other improvements include heavier armor plating and tyres less prone to puncture. In other respects, the vehicle is very similar to the BTR-60PB, with a more powerful engine configuration and armament comprising a primary heavy machine gun and secondary PKT machine gun on a roof-mounted turret.

Variants

The BTR-70 armored personnel carrier was used by the Soviet forces in Afghanistan, and some of the vehicles operating at this time were fitted with a 1.18in (30mm) AGS-12 grenade launcher mounted on the roof to the rear of the driver. Other variants of the basic design are the BTR-70MS (a turretless communications vehicle); the BTR-70KShM command/staff vehicle; the BREM (another turretless BTR-70 with a bow-mounted jib crane); the BTR-70Kh chemical reconnaissance vehicle; and the SPR-2 radar jammer.

Specifications

Armament: One 0.57in (14.5mm) KPVT MG; one coaxial 0.30in (7.62mm) PKT MG

Armor: Unknown

Crew: 2 plus 9

Dimensions: Length 24ft 9in (7.54m); Width 9ft 2in (2.8m); Height 7ft 4in (2.23m)

Weight: 11.3 tons (11,500kg)

Powerplant: Two ZMZ-4905 8-cylinder gasoline, 120bhp (89kW) each

Speed: 50mph (80km/h)

Range: 373 miles (600km)

The Armor Revolution
⚒ **1976 Switzerland**

Specifications

Armament: Various	
Armor: 0.39in (10mm)	
Crew: 1 plus 13	
Dimensions: Length 19ft 6in (5.97m); Width 8ft 2in (2.50m); Height 6ft 1in (1.85m)	
Weight: 10.3 tons (10,500kg)	
Powerplant: MOWAG V6 gasoline, 300bhp (223.9kW) at 2800rpm	
Speed: 62mph (100km/h)	
Range: 370 miles (600km)	

MOWAG PIRANHA ARMORED PERSONNEL CARRIERS

The Piranha family of armored personnel carriers has proved a huge success for the Swiss MOWAG company. It has been manufactured in four countries and has attracted large exports.

Below: A variety of armament options is available for the Piranha, depending on the role for which the vehicle is intended, and can range from a single machine gun to a 4.13in (105mm) low-recoil gun mounted in a power-operated turret. The 8x8 version of the Piranha is used by the United States Marine Corps.

In the early 1970s the Swiss company MOWAG started developing a range of multiwheeled armored vehicles that had many common features and were able to undertake a wide variety of tasks. The first prototype of this family, subsequently called Piranha, was completed in 1972 and the first production vehicles came off the assembly lines in 1976. As well as being manufactured in Switzerland, production lines were opened in Canada (Diesel Division, General Motors of Canada), Chile (FAMAE), and the United Kingdom (Alvis Vehicles). All the UK-produced vehicles have been exported to Kuwait, Oman, and Saudi Arabia. The Piranha can undertake a number a roles, including those of ambulance, antitank armed with ATGWs, cargo, command, internal security, mortar carrier, recovery, reconnaissance, and radar carrier. The vehicles are fully amphibious, propelled through the water by two propellers at the rear of the hull.

Layout

All Piranhas have a similar layout, with the driver at front left, the Detroit diesel on the right, and a rear troop compartment with roof hatches and twin doors in the rear. The troop compartment has provision for firing ports and vision devices.

The Armor Revolution
🔨 1977 Israel

MERKAVA MAIN BATTLE TANK

Israel's Merkava main battle tank was developed to avoid dependence on imports. It was first used during Israel's invasion of the Lebanon in 1982.

Below: *The Merkava Mk 3 featured many improvements over early production models, including a 4.72in (120mm) smoothbore gun, a more powerful 1200hp (895kW) engine coupled to a new transmission, and new armor.*

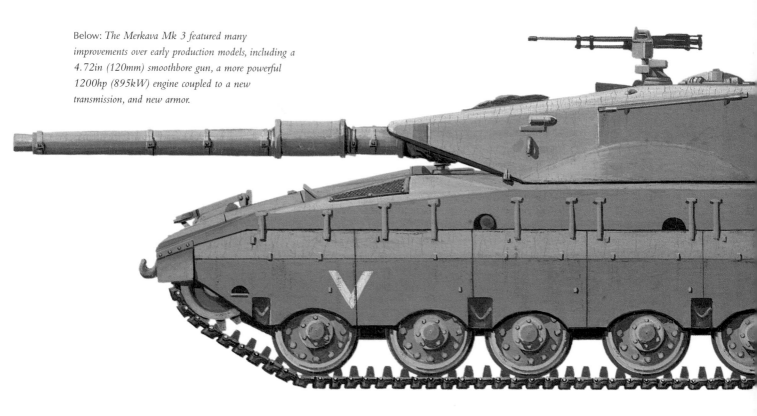

Prior to the Six-Day War in 1967, Israel's main source of modern weapons was France, but when the French placed an embargo on weapons following the 1967 conflict, Israel was forced to look elsewhere. One of the principal requirements was for a new main battle tank, and for a short time the Israeli Defense Force became involved in the British Chieftain tank development program, only to be asked to withdraw after Britain was subjected to political pressure from clients in the Arab world. With little prospect of assistance from elsewhere, the Israeli Government decided that their only alternative was to launch a series of their own weapon-production programs. The

development of a main battle tank was given high priority. The urgent need for a new MBT was reinforced during the Yom Kippur War of October 1973. Potential disaster for the Israelis was only averted by the

Left: *The Merkava is equipped with an identification friend/foe system, mounted on either side of the turret, for the identification of friendly fighting vehicles. It also has a threat warning system.*

Right: *A Merkava Mk 2 shrouded in exhaust smoke. Note the "kill" markings around the barrel, presumably registered against Syrian tanks during the fighting in Lebanon.*

Specifications

Armament: One 4.72in (120mm)
gun, three 0.30in (7.62) MGs

Armor: Not revealed

Crew: 4

Dimensions: Length 24ft 11in
(7.6m); Width 12ft 2in (3.7m);
Height 8ft 8in (2.64m)

Weight: 61.02 tons (62,000kg)

Powerplant: Teledyne AVDS 1790-
9Ar V12 turbo-charged diesel,
1200bhp (895kW)

Speed: 34mph (55km/h)

Range: 310 miles (500km)

*Above: The Merkava's main armament is fully
stabilized. The fire control system incorporates a
ballistic computer and laser rangefinder. The basic
ammunition load is 62 rounds.*

Americans, who sent M60 tanks into battle.

Design

The first prototype of the new Israeli MTB,
named Merkava (Chariot), was completed in
1974 and the first production vehicles were
issued in 1979. The tank is designed for
operations in the rough terrain of northern
Israel and the Golan Heights. It is unusual in
layout, with the engine at the front and the
fighting compartment to the rear. This gives
enhanced frontal protection, while the
ammunition (at the back) is not only in the
safest place but is also easily stowed through
a rear door. This makes replenishment in the

combat zone much safer. The turret, of cast
and welded construction, is well sloped to
give the maximum degree of protection, and
has a small cross-section that makes it a
difficult target.

Use and development

The Merkava I was first used in Lebanon in
1982, where it performed well against Syrian
T-72s. An improved version, the Merkava 2,
entered service in 1973. This incorporated
several improvements, including better armor
protection and fire control system. The next
production version, revealed in 1989, was the
Merkava Mk 3; this introduced a new
suspension and transmission system and a
new 4.72in (120mm) smoothbore gun. A
1995 version, the Mk 3B (also known as
Merkava Baz), has an improved fire control
system and a built-in NBC protection and
air-conditioning system. A modular armor
package (called "Kasag") was added to this
version, making the Merkava 3 Baz Kasag
one of the best-protected tanks in the world.

Current Mk 3 tanks

The current generation of Mk 3 tanks is
Dor-Dalet (4th generation) which includes
modular add-on armor, improved tracks, an
improved machine gun, and integral air
conditioning and NBC protection systems.
The latest model is the Merkava Mk 4,
which was introduced in 2004.

The Armor Revolution
⚒ **1978 France**

PANHARD VBL SCOUT CAR

Panhard continued their long tradition of producing excellent armored fighting vehicles for the French Army as well as for many overseas customers with the VBL. The 1000th VBL was completed in 1995.

The Panhard 4x4 Véhicule Blindé Leger (VBL) was developed by the Société de Constructions Mécaniques Panhard et Levassor in the late 1980s, in response to the French Army's requirement for a new light reconnaissance/antitank vehicle. The vehicle was approved in February 1985, although at this time it was already in production for Mexico. The first production vehicle for the French Army was completed in 1990. There are two basic versions of the VBL, a combat/antitank model (with a three-person crew and armed with one 0.30in [7.62mm] machine gun) and an intelligence/scout model (with a two-person crew and armed with one 0.30in [7.62mm] and one 0.50in [12.7mm] machine gun). The standard VBL has a wheelbase of 8.04ft (2.45m), but the vehicle can also be built with a wheelbase of 8.86ft (2.7m), which increases the vehicle's internal volume. The VBL is fully amphibious and has a single propeller mounted under the rear of the hull.

Export

Panhard has proposed over 20 models of the VBL for the export market, each to perform a specific role (such as battlefield and air defense radar, antiaircraft, antitank, internal security).

Specifications

Armament: One 0.30in (7.62mm) MG; MILAN antitank missiles

Armor: Maximum, 0.45in (11.5mm)

Crew: 2 or 3

Dimensions: Length 12ft 1.7in (3.7m); Width 6ft 7.5in (2.02m); Height 5ft 6.9in (1.7m)

Weight: 3.53 tons (3590kg)

Powerplant: Peugeot XD 3T, 4-cylinder diesel, 95hp (70.8kW)

Speed: Road, 123.9mph (95km/h)

Range: Road, 373 miles (600km)

Left: A French Army VBL on patrol in Afghanistan. This photograph gives a good impression of the vehicle's low profile, an enormous asset in the reconnaissance role, where concealment is imperative.

Below: *The Panhard VBL was designed to carry both a machine gun and a Milan antitank guided weapons platform, the configuration in which it is seen here. This variant carries six missiles. The vehicle can also mount a TOW or a HOT missile launcher, making it a formidable opponent for its size.*

The Armor Revolution

1978 South Africa

BUFFEL ARMORED PERSONNEL CARRIER

The Buffel APC was one of the workhorse vehicles of the South African Army from 1978 to the late 1990s. It was one of the most mine-resistant vehicles in the world.

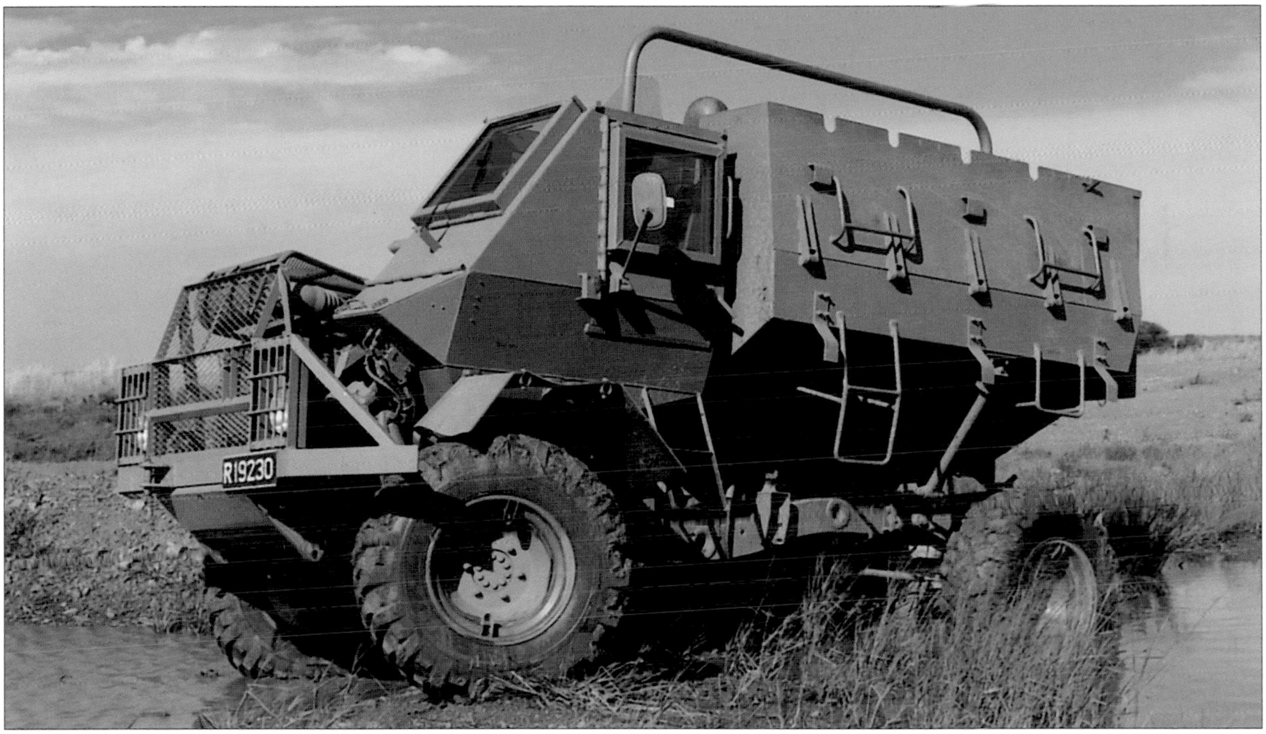

Specifications

Armament: Two 0.30in (7.62mm) MGs

Armor: Classified

Crew: 1 plus 10

Dimensions: Length 16ft 9in (5.1m); Width 6ft 9in (2.05m); Height 9ft 10in (2.995m)

Weight: 6.04 tons (6140kg)

Powerplant: Mercedes-Benz OM-352 diesel, 125bhp (93kW) at 2800rpm

Speed: 60mph (96km/h)

Range: 620 miles (1000km)

The Buffel (meaning "Buffalo" in Afrikaans) 4x4 armored personnel carrier was designed by Armscor, using the Mercedes-Benz Model 416/162 Unimog high-mobility truck. The Buffel was designed to be mine-resistant, and has remained the standard mine-protected APC in the South African Army since it appeared in 1978. The Buffel has the driver's cab and engine at the front of the vehicle on the left and right respectively, and the V-shaped belly helps to deflect the blast of any mine detonation upward and outward. The Buffel can offer protection against small-arms fire, the detonation of one Russian TM57 antitank mine (or its equivalent) anywhere underneath the vehicle, and the detonation of two TM57 mines under any wheel.

Above: *The Buffel armored personnel carrier was designed with maximum occupant protection in mind, especially against the mines that were strewn liberally throughout its area of operations. The V-shaped armored belly is designed to deflect the blast of a mine upward and outward, leaving the occupants unscathed.*

Geographical use

The Buffel was used widely and successfully by the South African forces in Angola, but by the late 1990s it was being phased out of service and replaced by the Mamba APC series. The Buffel was exported to Sri Lanka and Uganda. Specialized variants include a mortar carrier and a tractor with an armored cab.

The Armor Revolution
1978 Taiwan

CM-21 ARMORED INFANTRY FIGHTING VEHICLE (AIFV)

The American M113 armored personnel carrier had served Taiwan's army—
as well as many other armies—well for many years, but by the late 1970s
there was room for improvement. The result was the CM-21 AIFV.

The Taiwanese armored infantry fighting vehicle (AIFV) was developed in the late 1970s in response to a request issued from the Army of the Republic of China for a substantial upgrade of the American M113 APC. This was known as the CM-21. It was fitted with additional steel-laminate armor plates with foam spacers. These were fixed to the upper portions of the hull, which gave them a sloped appearance. The vehicle was equipped with a new Perkins diesel engine and firing ports were incorporated at the sides and rear of the infantry crew compartment. Otherwise there was little difference between the CM-21 and its predecessor. In all, 300 CM-21s were produced.

Variants

One variant mounts the Kung Feng IV 4.96in (126mm) multiple rocket launcher, while another (the CM-25) carries the TOW antitank guided weapon; another is armed with the indigenous Kuen Wu ATGW, and there are two mortar-carrying versions. A command-post version has extra communications equipment for artillery-fire direction.

Below: *A CM-21 armored personnel carrier on parade. With a relatively long coastline to defend against the threat of an invasion from the Chinese mainland, the rapid deployment of troops remains a high priority for the Taiwanese Army.*

Specifications

Armament: One 0.50in (12.7mm) MG

Armor: Unknown thickness aluminum and steel

Crew: 2 plus 11

Dimensions: Unknown

Weight: 11.7 tons (11,900kg)

Powerplant: Perkins TV8 640, diesel, 215bhp (160kW)

Speed: 42mph (68km/h)

Range: Unknown

The Armor Revolution
✖ 1979 Germany

TRANSPORTPANZER 1

The Transportpanzer 1 is still used in large numbers by the German armed forces. It carries out a wide variety of specialist roles in addition to its primary task of troop transport.

Specifications

Armament: One 0.79in (20mm) cannon or 0.30in (7.62mm) MG

Armor: Maximum, 0.39in (10mm)

Crew: 2 plus 10 troops (up to 14 on export models)

Dimensions: Length 22ft 4.9in (6.83m); Width 9ft 9.3in (2.98m); Height, hull, 7ft 6.5in (2.3m)

Weight: approx 18.7 tons (19,000kg)

Powerplant: Mercedes-Benz OM 402A, V-8 diesel, 320hp (238.6kW)

Speed: Road, 65.25mph (105km/h); Water, 6.5mph (10.5km/h)

Range: Road, 500 miles (800km)

The Transportpanzer 1 was one of a family of wheeled armored vehicles developed at the request of the Federal Germany Army in the mid-1960s The intention was to develop vehicles with as many common features as possible. The 8x8 design emerged as the Spähpanzer Luchs (Lynx) (of which 408 units were built between 1975 and 1978), while the 6x6 design was developed into the Transportpanzer 1 armored personnel carrier by Rheinstahl (later to become Rheinmetall Landesysteme). The company received orders for 1125 vehicles, the first of which was completed in 1979, and in 1983 10 units were delivered to Venezuela, which asked for them to be fitted with one 0.50in (12.5mm) and one 0.30in (7.62mm) machine gun. When used as an APC, the Transportpanzer 1

Above: *The Transportpanzer 1 has proved adaptable to a wide variety of roles. For example, the Spurpanzer Fuchs (Fox) is an NBC reconnaissance vehicle, while the TPz-1 Eloka is an electronic warfare version.*

(TPz1) can carry 10 troops as well as its two-man crew, but there are a number of models with specialized roles.

Variants
The TPz 1A3/ABC Spurpanzer Fuchs (Fox), of which 140 vehicles were built, is a reconnaissance vehicle fitted with NBC detection equipment. There is also an engineer version, whose task is to transport mines and demolition equipment, an electronic warfare version, a command and control model, and an ambulance.

The Armor Revolution
1979 Germany

WOLF GENERAL PURPOSE VEHICLE

The Mercedes-Benz-Wolf general purpose vehicle has proved a huge success story, with the German Army alone accepting over 10,000 units. It has been used by UN and by NATO police operations.

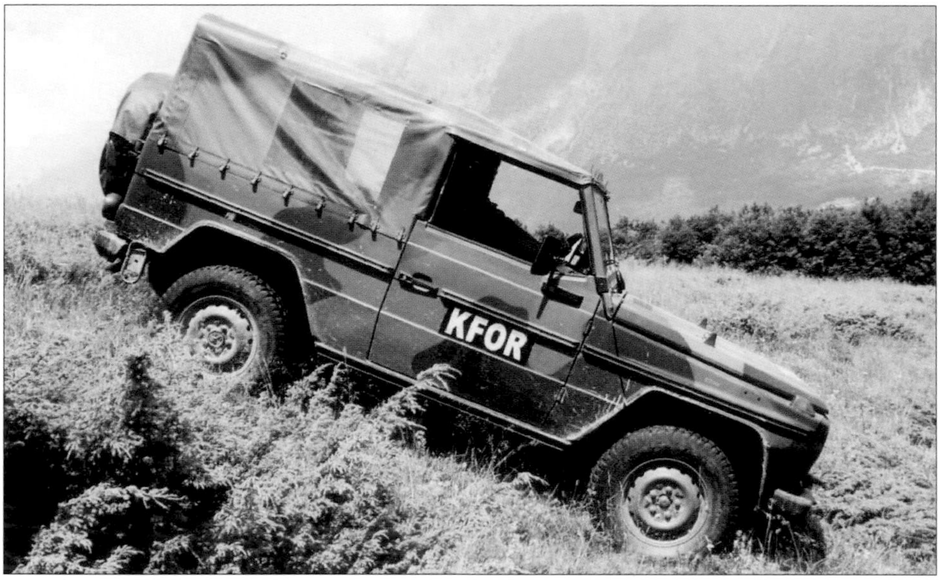

Above: *The Wolf general purposes vehicle seen here in camouflage.*

Specifications

Armament: n/a
Armor: n/a
Crew: 2 plus 11
Dimensions: Length: 14 ft 2in (4.32m); Width: 3 ft 3in (1.69m): Height: 6 ft 3in (1.92m)
Weight: 2.66 tons (2,700 kg)
Powerplant: Mercedes-Benz Diesel 91bhp (68 kW)
Speed: 65mph (105km/h)
Range: 373m (600 km)

Since production began in 1979, the German Army has taken delivery of over 10,000 Mercedes-Benz all-terrain G-class vehicles. This is only part of a total of 60,000 vehicles supplied to military customers in 26 countries. In Germany the vehicle is known as the Wolf, and the latest version, the G 270 CDI, has been equipped with special protection features developed by DaimlerChrysler. A small number of these vehicles have been produced since initial production in 2002, destined for military police units in Kosovo and elsewhere. The Wolf SSA has already proved its effectiveness in active operations.

Design features

In accordance with Bundeswehr specifications, the driver's cab and the build-on are protected against small-arms fire (3x2in [7.62x51mm] cal. Nato ball), while the driver's cab also provides protection against 0.22x1.77in (5.56x45mm) Nato SS109 and M193 rounds. The floor of the vehicle is reinforced against hand-grenade attacks. The focal point of the vehicle is the new 270 CDI engine. This is a five-cylinder straight-type motor featuring common rail diesel technology which, with a piston-swept volume of 2,685 cm^3, produces an output of approximately 156 HP (115 kW).

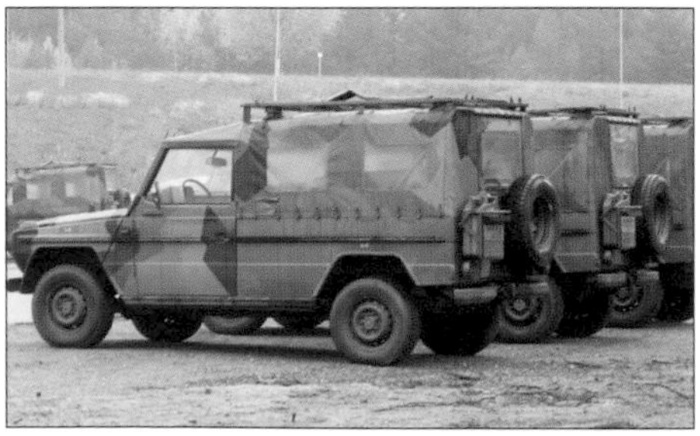

Below: *A convoy of Wolf vehicles which have been used by numerous armed forces around the world.*

The Armor Revolution

1979 Spain

BMR 600

The BMR 600 was designed for a battlefield role. To this end, it has a forward-mounted gun turret in addition to its embarked infantry, who can fire their weapons from inside the troop compartment.

Specifications

Armament: One 0.30in (7.62mm) MG

Armor: Not revealed

Crew: 2 plus 11

Dimensions: Length 20ft 2in (6.15m); Width 8ft 3in (2.50m); Height 7ft 9in (2.36m)

Weight: 13.78 tons (14,000kg)

Powerplant: Pegaso 6-cylinder diesel, 310bhp (231kW) at 2200rpm

Speed: 65mph (105km/h)

Range: 620 miles (1000km)

The BMR-600 (Blindado Medio Ruedas) was designed by the Spanish Army and Pegaso. The first prototype was completed in 1975 and first production vehicles delivered in 1979. It shares many features with the VEC. The company name for the BMR-600 was the BMR 3560.50. The driver sits front left, with the machine-gun cupola to his immediate rear and the engine compartment to his right. The troop compartment extends to the rear and is provided with roof hatches and a rear ramp.

Amphibious

The BMR-600 is fully amphibious, propelled by waterjets, one each side at the rear of the hull. Standard equipment includes power steering, engine compartment fire-extinguishing systems, run-flat tires, and winches. Optional equipment includes different tires, communications equipment, firing ports and vision blocks, night-driving equipment, and air-conditioning systems. Spanish Army BMR-600s feature a cupola with an externally mounted 0.50in (12.7mm) M2 HB MG which can be aimed and fired from inside. A wide range of weapon stations are available, including a turret-mounted 0.79in (20mm) cannon. This tank has been exported to Egypt, Peru, and Saudi Arabia.

Below: *The BMR 600 is a very functional, no-frills armored fighting vehicle and is part of a family of AFVs that have been developed since the original requirement was issued in the early 1970s.*

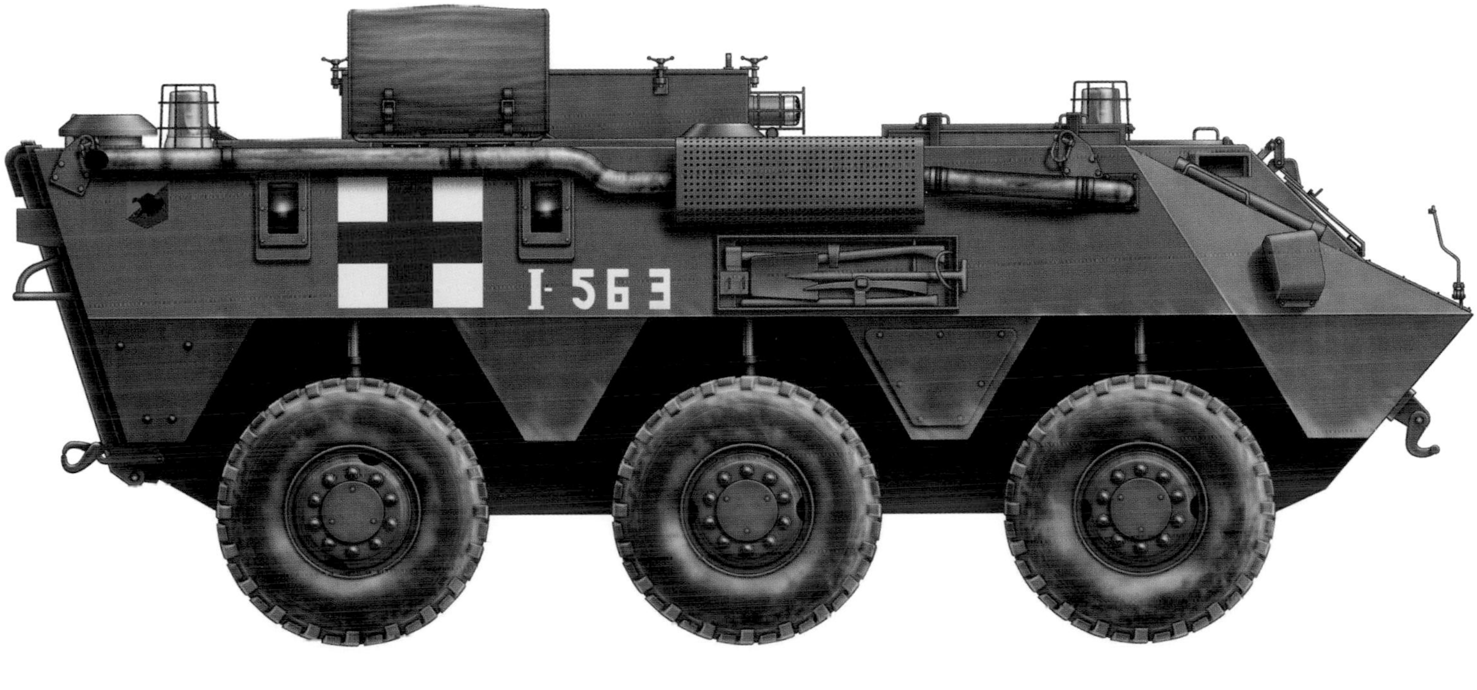

The Armor Revolution
1980 China

TYPE 69 AND 79

The Chinese Army was not satisfied with the performance of its Type 69 MBT, but it sold well on the export market. The biggest customer was Pakistan, which acquired 1300 vehicles.

Above: *The tank seen here is a Type 69II, armed with a 4.12in (105mm) main gun and a heavy machine gun. The Type 69 was still in production up to the late 1990s, and about 6000 are estimated to have been built.*

Following the rift between China and the Soviet Union in 1960, the Russians withdrew their technical support from China's extensive armaments program, forcing the Chinese government to develop or improvise weapons of their own. The Type 69 was an early result of this program, and was a development of the Russian T-54A main battle tank, which had been produced in China as the T-59. Improvements included a dual-axis stabilized 3.94in (100mm) smoothbore gun, a new 580bhp (432kW) engine, and an infrared searchlight.

Chinese capture of T-62

The vehicle was not a success and did not enter series production, but in 1969, during a border clash with the Russians at the Ussuri river, the Chinese captured a T-62 and incorporated some of its components in the Type 69. The improvement was dramatic, but it was not until 1982 that the Type 69 was fully accepted for PLA service. Even then it was only used in limited quantities, as the Chinese Army was still not satisfied with its performance. When the tank was offered for export, however, it was an immediate success, with over 2000 vehicles being sold in the 1980s. A later upgrade of the Type 69, with western equipment, became the Type 79.

Specifications

Type 69

Armament: One 3.94in (100mm) gun; two 0.30in (7.62mm) MGs; one 0.50in (12.7mm) MG

Armor: 3.94in (100mm) steel

Crew: 4

Dimensions: Length 20ft 6in (6.24m); Width 10ft 9in (3.3m); Height 9ft 3in (2.81m)

Weight: 36.12 tons (36,700kg)

Powerplant: Type 12150L–7BW V-12 diesel, 580bhp (432kW)

Speed: 31mph (50km/h)

Range: 261 miles (420km)

The Armor Revolution
1980 Soviet Union

T-80 MAIN BATTLE TANK

Russia's T-80 main battle tank was used in Chechnya, where it proved vulnerable to rocket-propelled grenades. As a result, the latest model incorporates very sophisticated defenses.

Specifications

Armament: One 4.13in (105mm) gun; one 0.30in (7.62mm) MG; one 0.50in (12.7mm) MG
Armor: Steel; composite plates available
Crew: 4
Dimensions: Length 30ft 7in (9.33m); Width 11ft 1in (3.37m); Height 7ft 6in (2.29m)
Weight: 37.4 tons (38,000kg)
Powerplant: Model VR36 V-12 diesel, 730bhp (545kW)
Speed: 37mph (60km/h)
Range: 267 miles (430km)

Developed from the T-64, the Russian T-80 main battle tank first entered service in 1976 and was the first production tank in the world to be fitted with a gas turbine engine. The powerplant was developed by the Isotov design bureau and built by the Klimov factory, both of which had extensive experience in the design of gas turbines for helicopters. The engine provided more power than contemporary diesels, but it was fuel-hungry and the hull of the T-80 had to be redesigned to accommodate extra tankage.

Upgrades

Despite ongoing problems with the engine, and high manufacturing costs, the tank was ordered into production and subsequently underwent several upgrades, the first of which produced the T-80B in 1982. This was followed, in the mid-1980s, by the T-80U, which was equipped to fire the NK112 AT-8 Songster laser-beam-riding missile. The T-80U is fitted with new-generation Kontakt-5 armor and has an advanced fire control system incorporating an optical sight and laser rangefinder coupled with a stabilized image intensifier and active infrared sight. The latest version, the T-80UM-1 Bars (Snow Leopard) is fitted with very advanced antimissile equipment.

Below: *The T-80 pictured here is the T-80UK command tank version. It is fitted with laser detectors, aerosol mortars, and the Shtora-1 defensive system, of which its reactive armor forms an important part.*

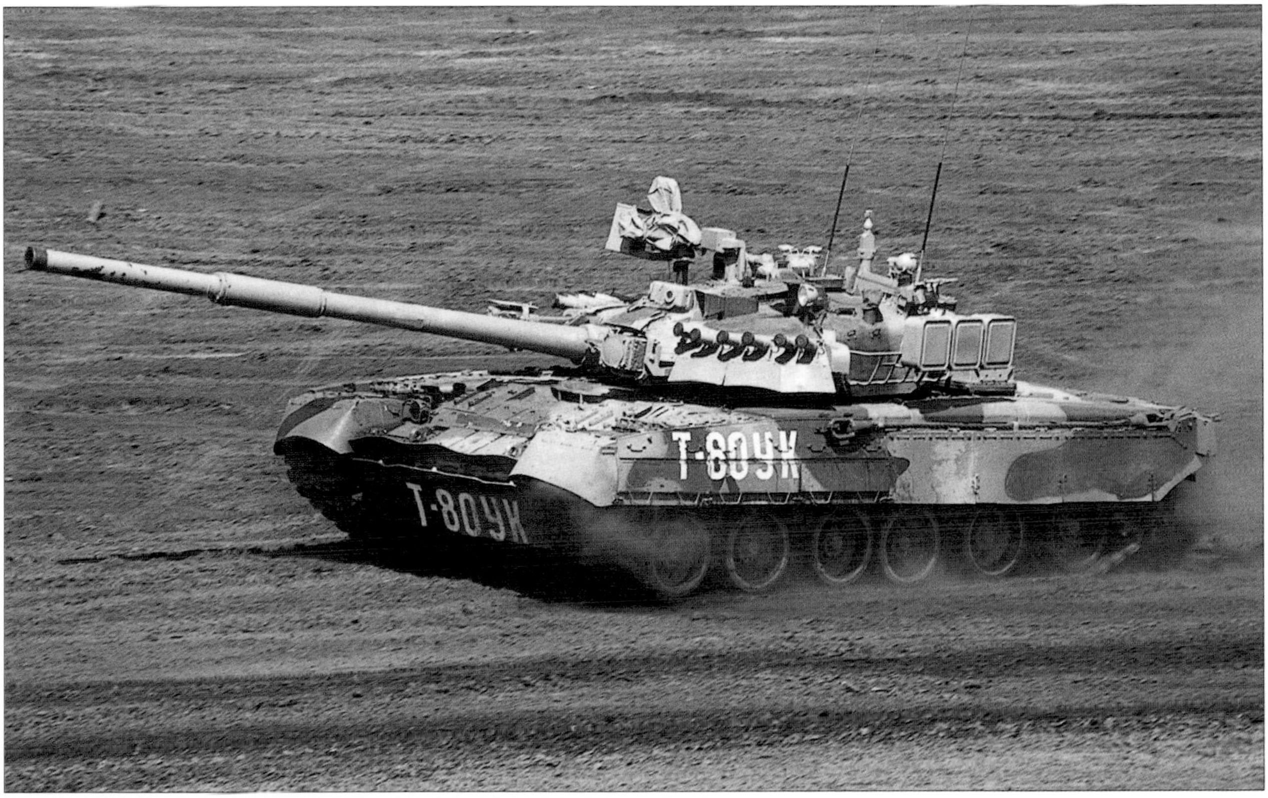

The Armor Revolution
1980 Spain

VEC ARMORED RECONNAISSANCE VEHICLE

Spain's VEC armored reconnaissance vehicle has good cross-country mobility, and can be made fully amphibious with a kit that includes water-jet propulsion as an optional extra.

Developed and produced by Santa Barbara Sistemas (now owned by General Dynamics) the VEC-M1 6x6 is the Spanish Army's principal cavalry reconnaissance fighting vehicle. It was first used by the Spanish Army in 1980, then as the BMR-625 VEC and subsequently underwent a major upgrade in the 1990s, emerging as the M1 version. The VEC (Vehiculo de Exploracion de Caballeria) shares many features with the BMR-600 6x6 infantry fighting vehicle. The first five propotypes were completed between 1977 and 1978, and the total Spanish Army order was for 235 vehicles.

Design features
The VEC mounts an automatic 0.98in (25mm) chain gun (M-242 Bushmaster) in a

Above: Seen here on duty with KFOR, the NATO Kosovo Force, the VEC cavalry reconnaissance vehicle has an option of three types of turret. This is fitted with a Boeing M242 0.98 in (25mm) chain gun cannon.

two-man turret and also a coaxial 0.30in (7.62mm) MG3S machine gun. Six electrically fired smoke-grenade launchers are located on the sides of the turret, three on the left side and three on the right. The vehicle has a five-man crew and is fully amphibious, propelled by its wheels; water jets are an optional extra. Steering is power-assisted on front and rear axles, and the suspension is adjustable. When produced for the export market, the VEC can be fitted with a wide range of turrets to meet different mission requirements.

Specifications

Armament: One 1.46in (37mm) gun; one 0.30in (7.62mm) MG

Armor: 0.354in (9mm)

Crew: 5 or 6

Dimensions: Length 15ft 9in (4.80m); Width 5ft 11in (1.79m); Height 9ft 1in (2.76m)

Weight: 5.90 tons (6000kg)

Powerplant: Scania D9 diesel, 310bhp (231kW) at 2200 rpm

Speed: 64mph (103km/h)

Range: 500 miles (800km)

The Armor Revolution
⚒ 1981 Sweden

BV 206S ARMORED PERSONNEL CARRIER

Sweden has produced an excellent range of tracked armored fighting vehicles since the end of World War II. One recent example is the Bv 206S.

Right: A Bv 206S at speed. The Bv 206 is unique among armored personnel carriers in that it consists of two units, connected by a steering unit. The vehicle is fully amphibious.

Specifications

Armament: None

Armor: Not revealed

Crew: 4 plus 8

Dimensions: Length 22ft 7in (6.88m); Width 6ft 7in (2m); Height 6ft 3in (1.90m)

Weight: 6.89 tons (7000kg)

Powerplant: Steyr M16 direct-injected 6-cylinder in-line diesel, 186bhp (138.8kW) at 4300rpm

Speed: 31mph (50km/h)

Range: 230 miles (370km)

The Bv 206S is the armored personnel carrier version of the Hägglunds Bv 206 all-terrain vehicle, fitted with two all-welded steel bodies to protect the occupants from small-arms fire and shell splinters. The vehicle is used by the British and Swedish armies, and also by Finland. The vehicle consists of two all-welded steel units joined together by a steering mechanism. Steering is accomplished by two hydraulic cylinders, controlled from a conventional steering wheel. The front unit has accommodation for a driver and three passengers, while the rear unit has seating capacity for eight soldiers. The Bv 206S is fully amphibious, propelled in the water by its tracks. Each track assembly contains four pairs of roadwheels on trailing arms sprung by rubber tension springs. The track assemblies are attached to a control bar by two transverse leaf springs. The armor provides protection from 0.30in (7.62mm) ammunition and the

windows provide protection equal to the body. The British Army's use of the vehicle stems from a dual requirement for a tracked APC capable of operating in conditions of snow or of sand. The first production vehicles were delivered to the Swedish Army in 1981.

Below: This convoy of Bv 206 APCs is seen in the environment for which the vehicle was intended, the snows of northern Sweden. The Bv 206 can be fitted with a roof-mounted Milan antitank missile unit.

The Armor Revolution

⚒ 1981 USA

M2 BRADLEY

The M2 Bradley had a protracted development history and not all US

Army chiefs were in favor of it, but it made a big impression in the Gulf

War of 1991, destroying more Iraqi armor than the M1 Abrams tank.

The M2 Bradley was the culmination of a program initiated by the US Army in the early 1960s to develop a new Mechanized Infantry Combat Vehicle (MICV). This was to act as a supplement to, rather than a replacement for, the M113 armored personnel carrier. The first two prototypes of the new vehicle, the XM2, were completed by the FMC Corporation (later to become United Defense Ground Systems) in 1978. These were named the M2 Bradley Infantry Fighting Vehicle (IFV) and

M3 Bradley Cavalry Fighting Vehicle (CFV). The former was designed to carry seven fully equipped troops, while the latter was intended for the reconnaissance and scout role.

Variants and upgrades

The M2 and M3 are similar in configuration. They are both equipped with an advanced two-person turret armed with an ATK Gun Systems Company stabilized 0.98in (25mm) M242 cannon and 0.30in (7.62mm)

Above: *A Bradley Infantry Fighting Vehicle plunging at speed though the Iraqi desert. The Bradley underwent a substantial modernization program following the 1991 Gulf War, being fitted with appliqué armor among other refinements.*

Right: *This photograph shows the commander and gunner of the Bradley in the central power-operated turret. This is the core of the vehicle's fighting capability, and is armed with a 0.98in (25mm) chain gun, a 0.3in (7.62mm) coaxial machine gun and a two-tube TOW missile launcher.*

Specifications

(M2A1)

Armament: One 0.98in (25mm) Bushmaster Chain Gun; one 0.3in (7.62mm) MG; two TOW missile launchers

Armor: Unknown thickness aluminum/steel

Crew: 3 plus 6

Dimensions: Length 21ft 6in (6.55m); Width 11ft 9in (3.61m); Height (turret roof) 8ft 5in (2.57m)

Weight: 22.58 tons (22,940kg)

Powerplant: Cummins VTA-903T turbocharged 8-cylinder diesel, 500hp (362.3kW)

Speed: 41mph (66km/h)

Range: 300 miles (483km)

Below: *Bradley IFVs traveling at speed through the desert. The Bradley confounded its critics by acquitting itself very well in the 1991 Gulf War.*

machine gun. The vehicles are also fitted with a twin launcher on the left side of the turret for a TOW antitank guided weapon. The first production Bradley AFVs were completed in 1981 and production continued up to 1995, with about 6800 units being built. Of these, 400 were supplied to Saudi Arabia, the only export customer. The latest models of the Bradley are fitted with explosive reactive armor, and automotive components of the vehicle are used as the basis for the Multiple Launch Rocket System (MLRS).

Improvements

Some of the improvements incorporated in the Bradley in recent years were a result of lessons learned in the Gulf War of 1991. The major improvements included an eye-safe laser rangefinder (ELRF), a tactical navigation system (TACNAV) incorporating the Precision Lightweight GPS Receiver (PLGR) and the Digital Compass System (DCS), a missile countermeasure device designed to defeat first-generation wire-guided missiles, and the Force XXI Battle Command Brigade and Below (FBCB2) Battlefield Command Information System. The internal stowage was further improved and a thermal-imaging system was added for the driver. During the Gulf War, M2 and M3 Bradleys destroyed more Iraqi armor than the M1 Abrams main battle tank. Twenty Bradleys were lost, three during combat and 17 due to friendly fire accidents. To remedy some problems that were identified as contributing factors in the friendly fire incidents, infrared identification panels and other marking measures were added to the Bradleys.

The Armor Revolution
✶ 1981 UK/Iran

KHALID 1981 MAIN BATTLE TANK

When the Islamic revolution swept through Iran in 1979, many arms orders placed with western governments were canceled. One of these was a tank called the Shir, which was then sold to Jordan as the Khalid.

Specifications

Armament: One 4.72in (120mm) L11A5 gun; two 0.30in (7.62mm) MGs

Armor: Not available

Crew: 4

Weight: 57.08 tons (58,000kg)

Dimensions: Length 21ft 10in (6.39m); Width 11ft 7in (3.42m); Height 9ft 11in (2.435m)

Powerplant: Perkins Engines (Shrewsbury) Condor V-12 1200 12-cylinder diesel, water-cooled, developing 1200bhp (894.8kW) at 2300rpm

Speed: 30mph (48km/h)

Range: Estimated, 248.5 miles (400km)

Left: *The Jordanian Army's Khalid was basically a mixture of the Chieftain and the Challenger, and a modified version was produced as the Challenger 1 for the British Army. The tank was originally intended for Iran.*

In 1974, the Royal Ordnance factory at Leeds, UK, received a contract from the Iranian Government for the production of 125 Shir 1 and 1225 Shir 2 main battle tanks. The Islamic revolution, accompanied by the overthrow of the Iranian royal dynasty and its government, upset this plan and the order was abruptly canceled. Production of the Shir 1 had already started, and some rapid negotiation by the British Government secured an order from Jordan for 274 slightly modified Shir 1s under the name of Khalid.

These were delivered from 1981. The tank was a late-production Chieftain with major changes to the fire control system and powerpack. It represented such an important advance over the Chieftain that the British Government ordered further developments, and it later emerged as the Challenger 1. The name Khalid means "sword" in Arabic, and has since been applied to a much later main battle tank developed jointly by China and Pakistan. The Royal Ordnance factory was taken over by Vickers Defence Systems in 1986.

The Armor Revolution
⚒ 1982 Finland

SISU XA-180 ARMORED PERSONNEL CARRIER

Below: Finland's SISU XA-180 is well suited to operations among the lakes and forests of Karelia. This is extremely difficult fighting terrain, as the Russians discovered to their cost in the "Winter War" of 1939–40.

Although it was produced for the Finnish Army, the XA-180 is a popular vehicle for United Nations police work. It has also been used by Austria, Ireland, Norway, and Sweden when their troops are required for UN duty.

Specifications

Armament: One 0.50in (12.7mm) MG

Armor: Not revealed

Crew: 2 plus 10

Dimensions: Length 24ft 2in (7.35m); Width 9ft 6in (2.9m); Height 7ft 6in (2.3m)

Weight: 15.25 tons (15,500kg)

Powerplant: Valmet 6-cylinder turbo-charged diesel

Speed: 62mph (100km/h)

Range: 500 miles (800km)

The XA-180 6x6 armored personnel carrier was developed as a replacement for Finland's ageing fleet of Russian BTR-60PB vehicles. Two prototypes were built, one by SISU and the other by Valmet. SISU was awarded the contract in 1983. The vehicle's hull is made of all-welded 0.39in (10mm) thick armor, with the commander and driver in front. The engine compartment is to the rear of the driver, on the left side, and the troop compartment at the rear. There is accommodation for 10 soldiers, seated five on each side on bench seats. The compartment also has two roof hatches, and

there are three firing ports on each side. The vehicle is fully amphibious, and is driven by two propellers at the rear of the hull.

Variants

Several variants of this tank have been produced, including the XA-181 air defense variant, armed with the Thomson-CSF Crotale Nouvelle Generation SAM system, a radar surveillance version, and a variant armed with a 4.72in (120mm) mortar. The XA-180 was followed into production by the improved XA-185, which has a more powerful engine.

Chapter 8

THE MODERN BLITZKRIEG

War produces classic remarks by military commanders; the 1991 Gulf War was no exception. On February 26, 1991 (day three of the 100-hour war against the Iraqi forces in Kuwait), tanks of the US 1st Armored Division encountered the allegedly elite Iraqi Republican Guard. The divisional commander, Major-General Ronald Griffiths, radioed his deputy, who was riding with the armored spearhead. "I understand we are engaging the Medina Division?" he said. "Negative, sir," came the reply. "We are destroying the Medina Division."

Above: *Yugoslavia's M-84 main battle tank in action in the desert. It has been exported to Kuwait and continues to be used widely.*

Left: *M1 Abrams tanks kick up clouds of dust during a desert exercise. In the 1991 Gulf War, the speed of the Abrams-equipped US armored divisions in their dash to eliminate the Iraqi Republican Guard surprised everyone.*

The destruction was carried out by a combination of close-support air power and the 1st Armored Division's M1A1 Abrams main battle tanks. Like the British Challenger, these tanks were being used for the first time, and their prowess against the Republican Guard's Russian-built T-72s exceeded all expectation. The deadly combination of the Panzer and the Stuka dive-bomber had been the key factor in the German Blitzkrieg in France in 1940, as well as in Russia in 1941. So it was again in 1991, although this time, the tanks and aircraft (especially the American Fairchild A-10A Thunderbolt II) were infinitely more deadly. The tanks had the benefit of technology that had been constantly developed and reviewed for nearly 20 years. This gave them the ability to fight at night, and to hit their targets while still on the move. Their armor protection was also something the German Panzer leaders could not have imagined 50 years earlier.

The Modern Blitzkrieg
⚒ **1982 Italy**

VCC-1 ARMORED PERSONNEL CARRIER

The VCC-1 armored personnel carrier is a modification of the well-used American M113, which was built under license in Italy. Its development was a cheap and effective way of extending the life of a proven design.

Left: Yet another variation on the excellent American M113, the VCC-1 armored personnel carrier offered the Italian Army a viable armored vehicle for service in the 1980s. It proved capable of further development.

The VCC-1 Camillino is a modified version of the M113 tracked armored personnel carrier, which was built under license for the Italian Army by Oto Melaro (later Otobreda) of La Spezia. The main modifications involved introducing firing ports (so the infantry could fire from inside the vehicle) and armor protection for the machine gunner on top of the hull. Both of these refinements were absent in the M113. In the modified vehicle, the commander is seated under a cupola to the rear of the driver. Over 1000 VCC-1s had been delivered to the Italian Army by 1983, and in

that year the Royal Saudi Army accepted 200 vehicles fitted with the improved TOW antitank missile launching system.

Design features

The VCC-1 is amphibious, propelled through the water by its tracks. This method is slower than the use of water jets and gives the vehicle a speed in the water of 3mph (5km/h). The VCC-2 version is basically the Italian-built M113 with appliqué armor on the front and sides, while the Mk 3 is fitted with a 0.79in (20mm) cannon in a mounting above the roof.

Specifications

Armament: Two MGs

Armor: Not revealed

Crew: 2 plus 7

Dimensions: Length 16ft 6in (5.04m); Width 8ft 10in (2.69m); Height 6ft 8in (2.03m)

Weight: 11.41 tons (11,600kg)

Powerplant: GMC V6 diesel, 210bhp (156kW) at 2800rpm

Speed: 40mph (65km/h)

Range: 340 miles (550km)

The Modern Blitzkrieg
⚔ 1982 UK

CHALLENGER 1 MAIN BATTLE TANK

The Challenger 1 main battle tank performed well enough in the Gulf War of 1991, but suffered from an inadequate fire control system. It was able to fire a wide range of ammunition.

Specifications

Armament: One 4.72in (120mm) L11A5 gun; three 0.30in (7.62mm) MGs

Armor: Not available

Crew: 4

Dimensions: Length 26ft 3in (8.327m); Width 11ft 7in (3.518m); Height 8ft 3in (2.5m)

Weight: 61.02 tons (62,000kg)

Powerplant: Perkins Engines (Shrewsbury) Condor V-12 1200 12-cylinder diesel, water-based cooled, developing 1200bhp (894.8kW) at 2300rpm. Auxiliary engine: Coventry Climax H30 diesel, 3-cylinder, developing 37bhp (27.6kW) at 3000rpm

Speed: 35mph (57km/h)

Range: 280 miles (450km)

The Challenger 1 main battle tank owed its existence to the Shir 2 tank, which had been ordered by Iran, but then canceled following the Islamic revolution. The UK Ministry of Defence authorized further development of the Shir 2 for service with the British Army, with modifications to suit a European rather than a Middle East environment. An order was placed with the Royal Ordnance factory (Leeds, UK) for the production of 237 vehicles. This order was later raised to 319. The first production Challengers were issued to the British Army in March 1983, and equipped five armored regiments in Germany. In 1990, 180 Challengers were deployed to Saudi Arabia from Germany, and these performed well during Operation Desert Storm early the following year.

Above: The Challenger 1 was similar to late-production versions of the Chieftain in most respects, and, with its powerful L11A5 rifled gun, it gave the British Army's armored formations a potent weapon that performed well in the 1991 Gulf War, although it was slower than the American M1 Abrams

They destroyed 300 enemy AFVs with no loss to themselves.

The Challenger's biggest asset, apart from its very accurate 4.72in (120mm) gun, was its Chobham armor, a new development that provided an unparalleled degree of protection against antitank warheads. Its main drawback was a poor fire control and sighting system, which resulted in a very slow rate of fire. This defect was remedied in a revised version, the Challenger 2.

The Modern Blitzkrieg

✖ **1983 USA**

M1 ABRAMS MAIN BATTLE TANK

This tank will forever be remembered for its epic dash through the Iraqi desert during the Gulf War of 1991. It was used by the US armored divisions to cut off and destroy Saddam Hussein's Republican Guard.

Named after General Creighton Abrams (a former US Army Chief of Staff and commander of the 37th Tank Battalion), the M1 was designed by Chrysler Defense (later purchased by General Dynamics Land Systems Division). It replaced the M60 as the principal US Army and US Marine Corps main battle tank. The tank entered production in 1980 at the Lima Army Tank Plant, Ohio, and at the Detroit Arsenal Tank Plant, Michigan, before production became centralized at Lima.

Right: *Cutaway showing the interior and crew stations of the M1 Abrams. This excellent fighting vehicle had never been in combat before the 1991 Gulf War, but during that conflict it acquitted itself superbly, earning the unqualified praise of its crews.*

Features and use

The primary aim of the Abrams tank is to close with and destroy enemy forces using mobility, firepower, and shock effect. Three variants are currently being used, the M1, M1A1, and M1A2. The 4.72in (120mm) main gun on the M1A1 and M1A2, combined with the powerful 1,500hp (1119.4kW) turbine engine and special

Specifications

Armament: One 4.72in (120mm) M256 gun; two 0.30in (7.62mm) MGs; one 0.50in (12.7mm) MG

Armor: Unknown thickness depleted uranium/steel

Crew: 4

Dimensions: Length (over gun) 32ft 3in (9.77m); Width 12ft (3.66m); Height 8ft (2.44m)

Weight: 56.3 tons (57,154kg)

Powerplant: Textron Lycoming AGT 1500 gas turbine, 1500hp (1119.4kW)

Speed: 42mph (67km/h)

Range: 289 miles (465km)

armor (the equivalent of the British-designed Chobham) make the Abrams tank able to attack or defend large numbers of heavy armored forces. The Abrams performed very well during the 1991 Gulf War, dispelling concerns that it might not do so against the latest Russian equipment used by the Iraqis. In all, 1848 Abrams were deployed to the Gulf for Desert Storm, and in 2003 it returned to Iraq to participate in Operation Iraqi Freedom.

Production

Production of M1A1 tanks for the US Army is complete. Over 8800 M1 and M1A1 tanks have been produced for the US Army and Marine Corps, as well as for the armies of Egypt, Saudi Arabia, and Kuwait. The M1A1 is currently undergoing a modernization program, features of which include increased armor protection, suspension improvements, and a nuclear, biological, and chemical (NBC) protection system. The M1A1D modification consists of an M1A1 with integrated appliqué computer and a far-target-designation capability.

Right: The Abrams' main asset is its Rheinmetall 4.72in (120mm) smoothbore gun, one of the most powerful tank weapons in the world.

Above: Thanks to its sophisticated fire control systems, the Abrams has an unprecedented first-shot kill power, as Iraq's Republican Guard—equipped with some of the latest Russian tanks—found to its cost.

Upgrades

The M1A2 modernization program includes a commander's independent thermal viewer, an improved commander's weapon station, position navigation equipment, a distributed data and power architecture, an embedded diagnostic system, and improved fire control systems. The M1A2 System Enhancement Program (SEP) adds second-generation thermal sensors and a thermal-management system. The SEP includes upgrades to the processors and memory that enable the M1A2 to use common command and control software, which enables the rapid transfer of digital situational data and overlays.

The Modern Blitzkrieg
⚔ 1984 Italy

IVECO TYPE 6614 ARMORED PERSONNEL CARRIER

The Type 6614 armored personnel carrier shares many features with the

Type 6616 armored car and with commercial vehicles. It transports 10

fully equipped troops.

The Type 6614 armored personnel carrier is a joint development by Fiat and Otobreda and has much in common with the Type 6616 armored car. Many of these components were taken from commercial vehicles in order to reduce production costs. The vehicle is used on a small scale by the Italian police and has been exported to Libya, Peru, and Tunisia. Over 1000 units have been produced, and the type is also produced under license by Asia Motors Inc. in the Republic of Korea, under the name of KM900.

Design features

There is accommodation in the troop compartment for 10 infantrymen, each of

Above: The Iveco Type 6614 has proved to be a cheap and effective little APC, and ideal for deployment on peacekeeping operations.

whom has an individual firing port. A range of optional equipment is available, including different weapon combinations, various types of night-vision equipment, a spare wheel and holder (often mounted on the roof of the troop compartment), smoke dischargers, an air-conditioning system, and a front-mounted winch for vehicle recovery. The vehicle is fully amphibious and is propelled by its wheels. Before it enters the water, four bilge pumps are switched on.

Specifications

Armament: One 0.50in (12.7mm) M2 MG

Armor: 0.315in (8mm)

Crew: 2 plus 8

Dimensions: Length 18ft 3in (5.56m); Width 7ft 8in (2.37m); Height 5ft 6in (1.68m)

Weight: 6.88 tons (7000kg)

Powerplant: Fiat Model 8062 6-cylinder, diesel, 128bhp (95.5kW) at 3200rpm

Speed: 60mph (96km/h)

Range: 435 miles (700km)

The Modern Blitzkrieg
⚒ 1984 Yugoslavia

M-84 MAIN BATTLE TANK

Yugoslavia's M-84 main battle tank was a license-built T-72 featuring a number of improvements, such as an automatic loading system. It has been exported to Kuwait and continues to be used widely.

Below: *Based on the Soviet T-72, the Yugoslav-built M-84 proved a surprising success, although many were lost during the fighting that tore Yugoslavia apart. One variant is used by Kuwait.*

Specifications
(M-84A)

Armament: One 4.92in (125mm) gun; two 0.30in (7.62mm) MGs; one 0.5in (12.7mm) AA MG

Armor: Unknown

Crew: 3

Weight: 41.3 tons (42,000kg)

Dimensions: Length 22ft 6in (6.86m); Width 11ft 7in (3.57m); Height 7ft 2in (2.19m)

Powerplant: V-46 TK V-12 turbocharged diesel, 1000bhp (746kW) at 2000rpm

Speed: 40mph (65km/h)

Range: 432 miles (700km)

The M-84 is a license-built T-72M1, with some local modifications. The Yugoslav Army received a small initial batch of T-72s for training purposes, so that by the time license production of the M-48 got going, the army already had crews who were experienced users of this tank. The first prototypes of the M-84 were completed between 1982 and 1983, and production deliveries began in 1984. It is estimated that over 600 units were built for the home and export markets. About 150 vehicles were exported to Kuwait, and these took part in the combat that followed the Iraqi invasion of 1990. Many M-84s were lost during the fighting that tore apart the former Yugoslavia. Production ceased for a time, but resumed at a later date with the M-84A. The version for Kuwait, the M-84AB, is also built in Slovenia.

M-2001 and M-95 Degman
The latest version of the M-84 is the M-2001, and this was unveiled in 2004. It features a new fire control system, Kontakt-5 ERA armor, AT-11 Sniper antitank missiles, Agava-2 thermal sight, and the Shtora defensive suite. It is very similar to the Russian T-90S. Croatia has developed an improved version of the M-84 under the name of M-95 Degman.

Below: *An M-84 seen in profile, with the antiaircraft machine gun in the deployed position.*

The Modern Blitzkrieg
1985 China

TYPE 85 ARMORED PERSONNEL CARRIER

There are numerous variants to the Type 85 chassis, including the YW 309 infantry combat vehicle, the Type 85 armored command post, the WZ 751 armored ambulance, and the Type 85 4.72in (120mm) self-propelled mortar.

The Type 85 armored personnel carrier is also known as the YW531H and the M-1967. It has replaced the 4x4 YW531 for the People's Liberation Army. The vehicle has five roadwheels, a hull of all-welded steel construction, and is fully amphibious. The driver sits at the front of the vehicle with the engine compartment to his right and the commander to his rear. The driver's one-piece hatch opens to the left and there are three forward-facing periscopes, one of which can be replaced by an infrared device for night driving. The troop compartment is at the rear, and the troops enter through a large hinged door. The door has a single firing port; there are two firing ports on the left side of the vehicle and three on the right. The Type 85 has a single circular roof hatch on each side in the forward part of the troop compartment, as well as two oblong roof hatches to the rear of the 0.50in (12.7mm) machine gun, and a trim vane that is erected before the vehicle enters the water.

Below: *The Type 85 APC has been produced in about a dozen different versions, including armored command post vehicle, armored ambulance, self-propelled mortar, recovery vehicle, and self-propelled howitzer.*

Specifications

Armament: One 0.50in (12.7mm) MG
Armor: Steel
Crew: 2 plus 13
Dimensions: Length 20ft (6.1m); Width 10ft (3.06m); Height 6ft 4in (1.91m)
Weight: 13.38 tons (13,600kg)
Powerplant: Type BF8L413F diesel, 320bhp (238kW)
Speed: 40.5mph (65km/h)
Range: 311 miles (500km)

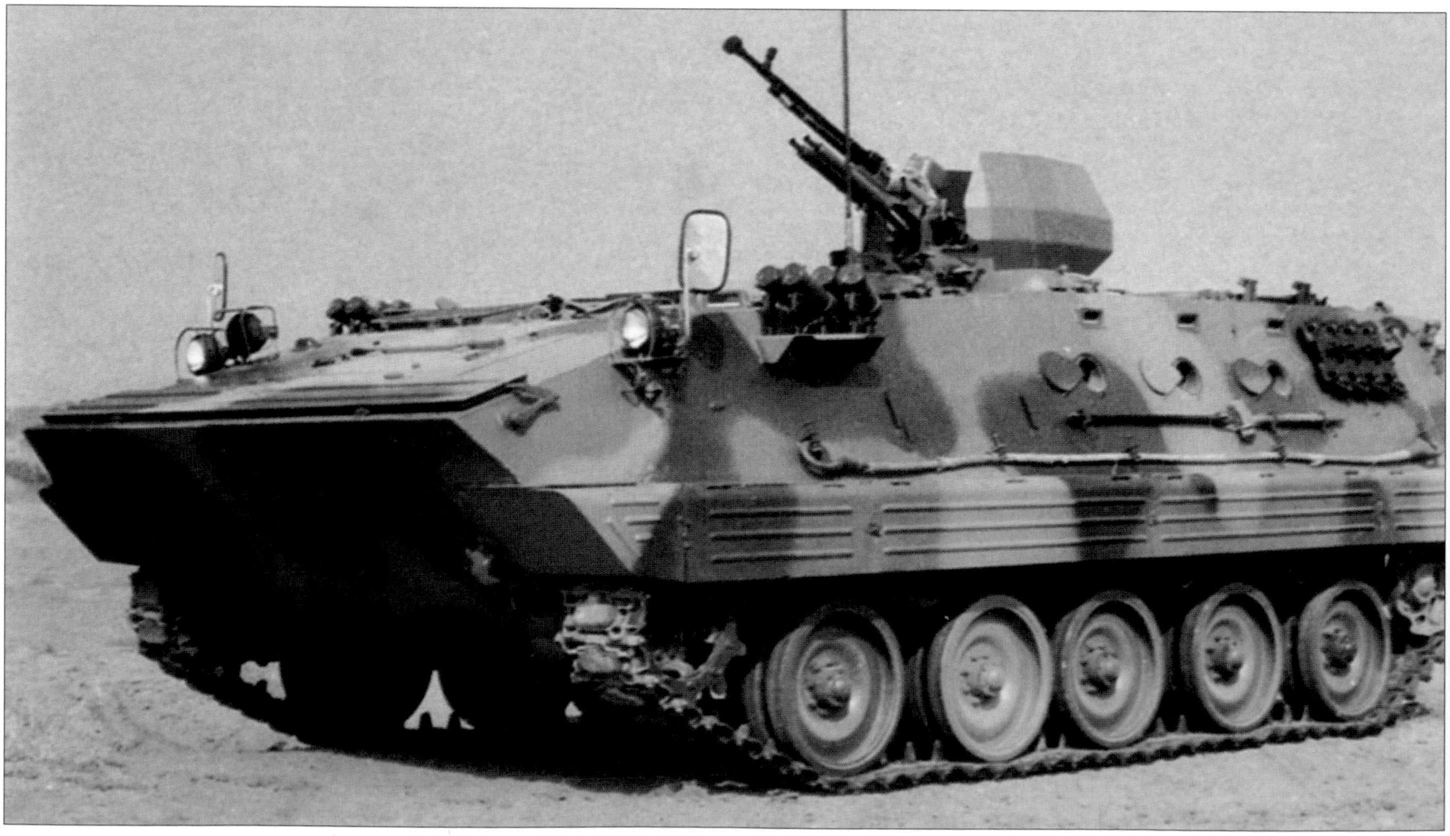

The Modern Blitzkrieg
⚒ **1985 China**

WZ 551 ARMORED PERSONNEL CARRIER

Below: *The six-wheeled WZ 551 has been built with a number of armament variations since it first appeared in the mid-1980s.*

The WZ 551 is one of many varieties of armored personnel carriers used by the Chinese People's Liberation Army today. The huge output of these vehicles is necessitated by the size of China's army.

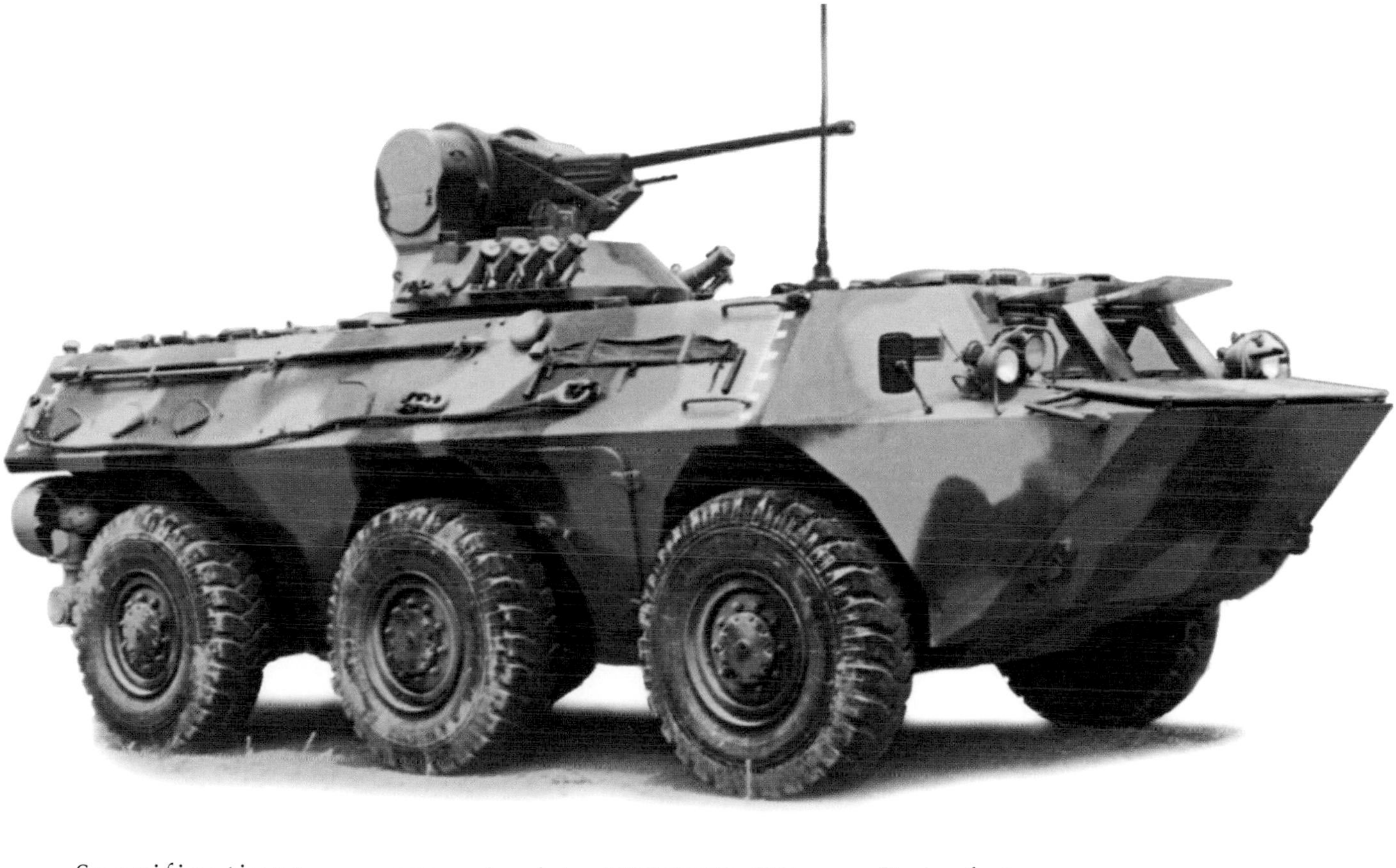

Specifications

(0.98in/25mm IFV version)

Armament: One 0.98in (25mm) Giat cannon; one 0.30in (7.62mm) MG

Armor: 0.315in (8mm) steel

Crew: 3 plus 9

Dimensions: Length 21ft 9in (6.65m); Width 9ft 3in (2.8m); Height 9ft 6in (2.89m)

Weight: 15.06 tons (15,300kg)

Powerplant: Deutz V-8 diesel, 256bhp (191kW)

Speed: 53mph (85km/h)

Range: 373 miles (600km)

Developed by NORINCO (Chinese North Industries Corporation), the WZ 551 armored personnel carrier is very similar to the French VAB series. The layout closely resembles that of the VAB, with the driver and commander at the front and the engine compartment to the rear of the driver. The troop compartment has a large door (which opens to the right), firing ports, and roof hatches. The Type WZ 551 can cross a 3.94ft (1.2m) trench, mount a 1.64ft (0.5m) vertical step, climb a 60 percent grade, climb a 30 percent side slope. It can also ford amphibiously.

Design features

The vehicle has air inlet and outlet louvres in the roof on the engine compartment, with the exhaust pipe running along the upper left side of the hull. The Type WZ 551 has an all-welded armored hull. The vehicle is fully amphibious, propelled through the water by two shrouded propellers mounted one on each side under the rear of the vehicle. These are swung backwards when in the water. More recent production vehicles have more powerful engines and slightly different specifications.

The Modern Blitzkrieg
⚒ **1985 Egypt**

FAHD ARMORED PERSONNEL CARRIER

The Egyptian Fahd APC is unsophisticated in comparison with other vehicles of its type, but it is cheap to produce and does an effective job in a variety of conditions.

Specifications

Armament: Optional	
Armor: Not revealed	
Crew: 2 plus 10	
Dimensions: Length 19ft 8in (6.0m); Width 8ft 10in (2.69m); Height 6ft 11in (2.1m)	
Weight: 11.07 tons (11,250kg)	
Powerplant: Mercedes-Benz 6-cylinder turbocharged diesel, 125kW (168bhp) at 2800rpm	
Speed: 52mph (84km/h)	
Range: 500 miles (800km)	

The Fahd four-wheeled armored personnel carrier was designed by the Henschel Wehrtechnik company in response to a request by the Egyptian Army. Its company name was TH390 and production began at the Kader works near Cairo in 1985. The first deliveries were made the following year. The Fahd comprises a modified Mercedes-Benz truck chassis with an armored body that provides complete protection from attack by small arms and shell splinters. The vehicle has a simple design and is optimized for desert conditions; standard equipment includes a central tire-pressure regulation system (allowing the driver to adjust the tire pressure to suit ground conditions), and power-assisted steering. The

Above: The Fahd 240/30 AFV , in service only with the Egyptian Army, is fitted with the BMP-2's two-man turret and armed with a 1.81in3 (0mm) cannon and 0.30in (7.62mm) caxial machine gun.

Fahd is a thoroughly unremarkable vehicle, cheap and unsophisticated, but it does its job remarkably well. The Fahd 240/30 is fitted with the complete turret of the Russian BMP-2 IFV with a 1.81in (30mm) cannon.

Export
The tank is not used in large numbers by the Egyptian Army, and some vehicles have reportedly been delivered to Kuwait, Oman, and the Sudan. Some have also been used by UN peacekeeping forces in Bosnia.

Below: A Fahd APC on duty with SFOR, the NATO-led stabilization force deployed to Bosnia and Herzogovina. It took over from IFOR in December 2004.

KOREAN INFANTRY FIGHTING VEHICLE (KIFV)

Produced by the Special Products Division of Daewoo, the Korean

Infantry Fighting Vehicle is used widely by the South Korean Army.

It has also been exported to Malaysia.

Specifications

Armament: One 12.7mm (0.5in)
MG; one 0.30in (7.62mm) MG

Armor: Unknown thickness
aluminum

Crew: 3 plus 9

Dimensions: Length 18ft 1in
(5.49m); Width 9ft 5in (2.85m);
Height 6ft 4in (1.93m)

Weight: 12.7 tons (12,900kg)

Powerplant: MAN D2848T V-8
diesel, 280bhp (209kW)

Speed: 46mph (74km/h)

Range: 298 miles (480km)

The Korean Infantry Fighting Vehicle (KIFV) is produced by Daewoo Heavy Industries. Its hull design is similar to that of the US Armored Infantry Fighting Vehicle. The powerplant is a MAN diesel, the self-changing gears are British, and the transmission is fully automatic. The vehicle carries a three-man crew, with space in the troop compartment for seven fully equipped infantry. The gunner has full front, side, and rear protection for the roof-mounted 0.50in (12.7mm) M2HB machine gun. Six electrically operated grenade dischargers are mounted on the glacis plate, firing forward. The vehicle is fully amphibious. Some 2000 KIFVs are in service with the Republic of Korea Army, and the vehicle has also been supplied to Malaysia.

Daewoo has produced an improved

Above: With a volatile communist regime just across the border, the Republic of Korea must have the ability to deploy thousands of troops at very short notice. The Korean Infantry Fighting Vehicle was introduced for just that purpose.

version of the basic KIFV, with a new powerpack consisting of a D2848T turbocharged diesel. This is coupled with an Allison X-200-5D series automatic transmission and attains 350 bhp (209kW). Another variant can be fitted with a 0.79in (20mm) Vulcan antiaircraft gun system license-produced in Korea, while a mortar carrier comes in two versions, one equipped to mount a 3.19in (81mm) mortar, the other a 4.21in (107mm). Other variants are equipped for recovery, antitank (fitted with the TOW missile system), NBC reconnaissance and command.

The Modern Blitzkrieg
⚒ 1985 UK

WARRIOR INFANTRY COMBAT VEHICLE

Developed by GKN (now a part of BAE Systems Land and Armaments) the Warrior has proved itself to be an excellent fighting vehicle in different kinds of environment, ranging from the desert of Iraq to the mountains of Bosnia.

Below: *An excellent fighting vehicle, the Warrior distinguished itself in the 1991 Gulf War and has supported the British Army in its deployments ever since, proving well suited to terrain that has ranged from the Balkans to Afghanistan.*

Specifications

Armament: One 1.18in (30mm) Rarden cannon; 0.30in (7.62mm) chain gun

Armor: Not available

Crew: 3 plus 7

Dimensions: Length 20ft 10in (6.34m); Width 9ft 11in (3.00m); Height 9ft 2in (2.791m)

Weight: 24.11 tons (25,500kg)

Powerplant: Perkins diesel developing 550bhp (410kW) at 2300rpm

Speed: 47mph (75km/h)

Range: 410 miles at 37.3mph (660km at 60km/h)

The Warrior family of infantry fighting vehicles, of which there are seven variants, was first used in 1988 and subsequently proved to be a resounding success in the 1991 Gulf War, Bosnia, Kosovo, and for a second time in Iraq in 2003. One of the most impressive features of the vehicle is its powerful diesel engine, which gives it a road speed of 46mph (75kph) and allows it to keep pace with the Challenger 2 main battle tank over the most difficult terrain. The vehicle is not amphibious, but can wade up to a depth of 4.2ft (1.3m).

Armor

The infantry combat versions of the warrior are armed with a turret-mounted 1.18in (30 mm) Rarden Cannon, which will defeat most light armored vehicles out to 4921.26ft (1500m). The OPV and BCV variants have the turret, but with a "dummy" cannon to make space for artillery fire control equipment. All variants are equipped with a 0.30in (7.62mm) chain gun. The chain gun and the Rarden Cannon have a low-level air defense capability against helicopters. The gun is not stabilized and therefore engagement of point targets must normally be conducted from static, hull-down positions. The vehicle is fitted with an image intensifying (II) magnification RAVEN sight eight times, and there is capacity to store eight LAW light antitank missiles in the back compartment.

Above: This photograph depicts the repair and recovery version of the Warrior, seen in operation during Operation Desert Storm in 1991.

Protection and facilities

The Warrior's armor is designed to withstand an explosion from a 6.10in (155mm) shell at 32.8ft (10m) and direct fire from machine guns up to a caliber of 0.57in (14.5mm). During the first Gulf War and operations in the Balkans and Iraq, additional armor was fitted for protection. Collective CBRN protection is provided when closed down and the section can remain fully closed down for 48 hours. A toilet is also located in the vehicle.

Design features

Warrior section vehicles are able to carry and support seven fully equipped soldiers together with supplies and weapons for a 48-hour battlefield period in nuclear/biological/chemical conditions. The protection provided against small arms, missiles, and antitank mines was proven during the UN operations in Bosnia. Additional (appliqué) armor can be fitted. Thales Optronics STAG thermal-imaging sights are being added to upgrade the night fighting capability as part of the BGTI (Battle Group Thermal Imaging) program. To date, 1043 Warriors (of all variants) have been produced, some for service with the Army of Kuwait.

The Modern Blitzkrieg
⚔ 1986 France

LECLERC MAIN BATTLE TANK

France has produced one of the finest main battle tanks in the world in the Leclerc. The famous general whose name it bears would have been justifiably proud.

Built by Giat Industries, the Leclerc main battle tank was named after the famous commander of the French 2nd Armored Division and liberator of Paris in World War II. It became operational with the French Army in 1992 and with the armed forces of Abu Dhabi in 1996. An improved version, the Leclerc Mk 2, went into production in 1998; this has updated software and engine-control system. The French Army has 400 Leclercs in use, while the United Arab Emirates use 390 tanks and 46 armored recovery vehicles. The Leclerc is fitted with the FINDERS (Fast Information, Navigation, Decision, and Reporting System) battlefield management system, developed by Giat. FINDERS includes a color map display, which shows the positions of the host tank, allied and hostile forces, and designated targets. This can be used for route and mission planning.

Below: *The Leclerc main battle tank a very effective fighting machine and incorporates all that is good in French tank design. Its 4.7in (120mm) main armament, coupled with a very advanced fire control system gives the French Army an armored capability that is second to none in the world today.*

Use by French Army

For many years the French Army had to rely on the ageing AMX-30 main battle tank as its principal armored spearhead. The introduction of the Leclerc, with its powerful 4.72in (120mm) gun and advanced fire control electronics, has given France's armored divisions new power.

Specifications

Armament: One 4.72in (120mm) gun; one 0.50in (12.7mm) MG; one 0.30in (7.62mm) MG

Armor: Not released

Crew: 3

Dimensions: Length overall, 32ft 4.5in (9.87m); Width 12ft 2in (3.71m); Height 8ft 3.6in (2.53m)

Weight: 55.61 tons (56,500kg)

Powerplant: SACM V8X-1500, 8-cylinder diesel, 1500hp (1118.5kW) or MTU 883, V-12 diesel, 1500hp (1119.4kW)

Speed: Road, 44.74mph (72km/h)

Range: Road, 279.5 miles (450km)

Left: *The Leclerc is well suited to desert warfare and has found an export customer in the United Arab Emirates, whose tanks have served on United Nations duty in Kosovo alongside their French counterparts.*

The Modern Blitzkrieg
✗ 1986   South Africa

LAND SYSTEMS OMC ROOIKAT ARMORED FIGHTING VEHICLE

The Land Systems OMC Rooikat has preformed exceptionally well for the South African defense forces for over a quarter of a century. It has a complex and very effective fire control system.

Below: *Diagram illustrating the interior of the Land Systems OMC Rooikat (the name is Afrikaans for caracal, a large, long-eared, reddish-fawn cat). The vehicle can be armed with either a 2.99in (76mm) or 4.13in (105mm) main gun, supported by two 0.3in (7.62mm) machine guns.*

Specifications

Armament: One 4.13in (105mm) gun; two 0.30in (7.62mm) MGs

Armor: Classified

Crew: 4

Dimensions: Length 23ft 3in (7.1m); Width 9ft 6in (2.9m); Height 8ft 2in (2.5m)

Weight: 27.5 tons (28,000kg)

Powerplant: ADE V-10 diesel, 563bhp (420kW)

Speed: 75mph (120km/h)

Range: 622 miles (1000km)

The Rooikat armored fighting vehicle was originally developed by Reemit, which later became Vickers OMC. (This in turn was renamed Alvis OMC in 2002, following the acquisition of Vickers Defence by Alvis, and Alvis is now part of BAE Systems Land Systems.) The Rooikat is designed for fast day and night combat operations and is equipped with thermal imaging for night driving, navigation, and weapons deployment. Armed with a 2.99in (76mm) gun, 240 vehicles have been delivered to the South African National Defense Force (SANDF) since 1980. In 1990, Reumech OMC further developed the Rooikat for the export market.

Armament and protection
The export version was armed with a 4.13in (105mm) gun. The vehicle is equipped with two banks of 3.19in (81mm) smoke-grenade launchers, mounted in a forward firing position on each side of the turret. The system is electrically operated. The Rooikat is protected against the explosion of a T46 antitank mine, giving full protection to the four-man crew, and is also proof against hits by rounds of up to 0.94in (24mm) over its frontal arc. The vehicle can remain mobile following the loss of one wheel, thanks to its eight-wheel configuration.

273

The Modern Blitzkrieg
⚒ 1987 India

ARJUN MAIN BATTLE TANK

The Arjun was an attempt by the Indian Army to produce its own main battle tank. Their program, however, has gone badly wrong.

Specifications

Armament: One 4.72in (120mm) gun; one 0.50in (12.7mm) MG; one 0.30in (7.62mm) MG

Armor: Not revealed

Crew: 4

Dimensions: Length 32ft 2in (9.8m); Width 10ft 5in (3.17m); Height 8ft (2.43m)

Weight: 57.08 tons (58,000kg)

Powerplant: MTU 636-Ka501 V12 diesel, 1045kW (1400bhp)

Speed: 45mph (72km/h)

Range: 250 miles (400km)

Left: *India's attempt to produce its own indigenous main battle tank was frustrated by continual delays and setbacks, and was seen by many senior army officers as a retrograde step. They argue that the funding could have been better spent on more foreign tank purchases.*

In the early 1970s, the Indian Defense Research and Development Organization (DRDO) gained experience in the license production of the Vijayanta main battle tank, and decided to produce their own MBT to meet the future requirements of the Indian Army. The new tank was designed by the Combat Vehicle Research and Development Establishment, with the assistance of other organizations throughout India, as well as some input from abroad. The first prototype of the tank, named Arjun after a hero in Indian mythology, was completed in 1984, and work proceeded on the construction of 12 more prototypes and a pre-series batch of 32 vehicles at the Heavy Vehicles Factory, Avadi (which had produced the Vijayanta). The Arjun program that followed was constantly hampered by delays and cost escalations, and it was not until 2004 that the first 15 tanks (out of an order for 124) were used by the Indian Army. Some senior Indian Army officers see the Arjun as a "white elephant," and suggest purchasing more T-90s from Russia as a more viable alternative.

Left: *In common with the tanks of Soviet design used by the Indian Army, the Arjun has provision for two long-range fuel drums at the rear of the hull. The missile in the background is a Prithvi short-range ballistic missile.*

The Modern Blitzkrieg

1987 Romania

TR-85 MAIN BATTLE TANK

Romania's TR-85 main battle tank is a much-modified version of the Russian T-55. It is still being upgraded with the help of new technology, as Romania seeks to become more compatible with NATO requirements.

Specifications

Armament: One 3.94in (100mm) gun; one 0.30in (7.62mm) MG; one 0.50in (12.7mm) AA MG

Armor: Unknown

Crew: 4

Dimensions: Length (including gun) 32ft 7in (9.96m); Width 11ft 3in (3.44m); Height 10ft 2in (3.10m)

Weight: 49.2 tons (50,000kg)

Powerplant: 8-cylinder diesel, 860bhp (641.8kW) at 2300rpm

Speed: 38mph (60km/h)

Range: 195 miles (310km)

Romania's TR-85 main battle tank is a drastically modified version of the T-55. It has a new turret, a new MAN German diesel engine (the same as that of the Leopard 1), as well as a completely redesigned suspension, stabilized main armament, muzzle reference system and thermal sleeve, and laser-and-thermal acquisition system. The tank is equipped with laser-warning receivers, which are able to pick up reflected laser radiation. There are 12 smoke grenades and a thermal trap. The newly designed 3.94in (100mm) APFSDS round BM-412Sg gives the main gun penetration of 17.71in (450mm) at over 0.62 miles (1km). The Romanian Armed Forces own 350 of these vehicles.

Upgrades

The TR-85 M1 is the modernized version of the TR 85, followed up by the TR-85-M2. The Romanian Army is currently upgrading about 150 old tanks (built on technology dating back to 1985). The upgraded TR-85 M1 medium tank is being produced in cooperation with the French firm Matra. At the end of 1999, the first batch of new tanks was delivered to operational units for testing.

Below: *Although nowhere near as effective as the main battle tanks produced by the leading nations of the world, the TR-85 and its various upgrades has been deemed sufficient to meet Romania's needs. The basic TR-85 has been given a substantial facelift with the help of French industry.*

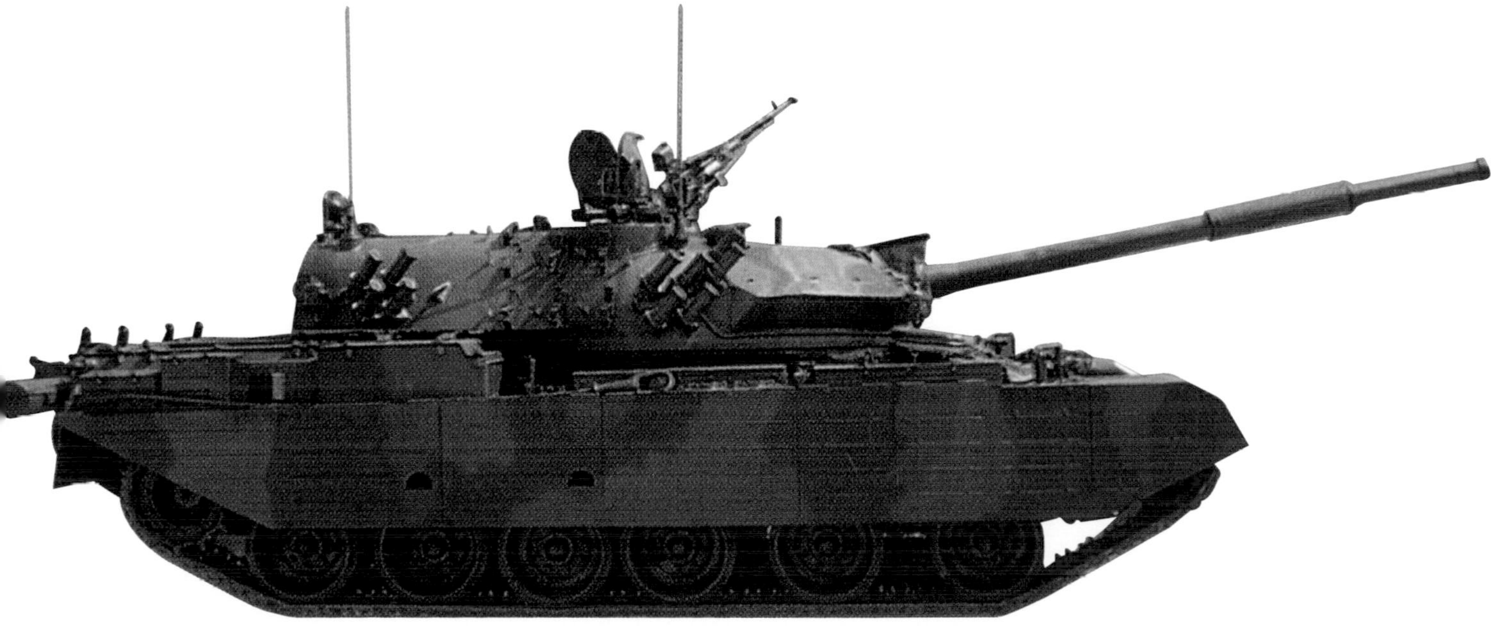

The Modern Blitzkrieg
⚒ **1987   South Korea**

TYPE 88 K1 MAIN BATTLE TANK

The Type 88 K1, a smaller version of the M1 Abrams main battle tank,

was developed to meet the threat posed by North Korea's Russian-built

T-62s. It has a fully computerized fire control system.

The Type 88 K1 was developed by what is now the General Dynamics Land Systems Division, the makers of the M1. It is not surprising, therefore, that this tank resembles a scaled–down version of the M1 Abrams. It was completed in prototype form in the United States in 1983. Series production was undertaken by the Hyundai Precision and Industrial Company at Changwon between 1985 and 1986. Possession of the K1 gave the Republic of Korean Army the means to outfight the North Koreans' T-62s, which had posed the main threat for some time.

Variants
An upgraded version of the K1, the K1A1, is similar to its predecessor, although a larger

Above: South Korea's K1 main battle tank was developed to counter the threat posed by North Korea's T-62s. The tank has been substantially upgraded since it was first deployed in 1987, and a variant has been supplied to Malaysia.

M-256 4.72in (120mm) main gun (the US licensed product of German Rheinmetall 4.72in [120mm] smoothbore gun) has vastly improved penetration power. The new version also includes an improved fire control system featuring thermal image KGPS (Korean Gunner's Primary Sight), KCPS (Korean Commander's Panoramic Sight), a new 32-bit ballistic computer, and improved survivablity for the engine. A further variant, the K1M, was developed to meet the requirements of the Malaysian armed forces.

Specifications

Armament: One 4.13in (105mm) gun; two 0.30in (7.62mm) MGs; one 0.50in (12.7mm) MG

Armor: Unknown thickness laminate/steel

Crew: 4

Dimensions: Length 31ft 8in (9.67m); Width 11ft 8in (3.59m); Height 7ft 5in (2.25m)

Weight: 50.29 tons (51,100kg)

Powerplant: MTU MB 871 Ka-501, diesel, 1200bhp (894kW)

Speed: 40km/h (65km/h)

Range: 272 miles (437km)

The Modern Blitzkrieg
⚒ **1988   China**

TYPE 80 MAIN BATTLE TANK

The Chinese Type 80 main battle tank is based on a design that began in 1978. It differs from its predecessor, the Type 69, in its redesigned hull and improvements to its armament and fire control.

Specifications

Armament: One 4.13in (105mm) gun, one 0.3in (7.62mm) MG, one 0.5in (12.7mm) MG

Armor: Steel; composite plates available

Crew: 4

Dimensions: Length 30ft 7in (9.33m); Width 11ft 1in (3.37m); Height 7ft 6in (2.29m)

Weight: 37.4 tons (38,000kg)

Powerplant: Model VR 36 V-12 diesel, 730bhp (545kW)

Speed: 37mph (60km/h)

Range: 267 miles (430km)

Unlike the earlier Type 69 main battle tank, which was a straightforward development of the Type 59, the Type 80 incorporated major new features, the most noticeable of which was a new hull. Design studies began in 1978 and production began a decade later. The main manufacturer was Norinco (China North Industries Corporation). Some 500 units were manufactured for the Chinese People's Liberation Army, and a few (no more than 20) were supplied to Myanmar (Burma). For deep fording, a snorkel can be fitted to the vehicle and a fire detection and suppression system is standard. If required, a layer of composite armor can be fitted to the glacis plate to improve battlefield survivability. An

Above: A Type 80 demonstrating its agility. The vehicle is fitted with a snorkel, enabling it to ford deep-water obstacles. The tank has not been produced in large numbers.

enhanced fire control system was introduced in the second model, the Type 80-II (Type 88B), and in this variant the transmission's former manually controlled gearbox was replaced by a semiautomatic system. The new fire control system has been retrofitted in some of the early model Type 80s. Another standard item of equipment is a ditching beam, and extra range can be achieved with the aid of two auxiliary fuel tanks at the rear of the vehicle, which can be jettisoned when empty.

The Modern Blitzkrieg
⚒ 1988 Italy

ARIETE MAIN BATTLE TANK

The Ariete main battle tank is one of a family of three armored vehicles, which also includes the Centauro tank destroyer and the Dardo infantry fighting vehicle. The Italian Army has 200 of these tanks in service.

The Ariete (Battering Ram) main battle tank was the product of a consortium formed in 1984 by Otobreda and Iveco specifically to develop a new family of armored fighting vehicles for the Italian Army. First deliveries of the Ariete were made in December 1995, the last examples of the 200 on order being issued in 2002.

Design features
The Ariete has an all-steel welded construction, with composite armor on the hull front and turret front and sides, and side-skirts protecting the top of the tracks. The tank also has a laser-warning sensor mounted

just ahead of the loader's hatch. The turret is in the center of the hull, with the commander and gunner on the right and the loader on the left. The commander has eight periscopes for all-round observation, while the loader has a single-piece hatch with two periscopes looking forward and to the left. The commander has a primary day and night (image intensification) stabilized panoramic sight (with magnification of x2.5 and x10). The gunner has a stabilized panoramic day and night (thermal) sight with laser rangefinder (of x5 magnification), which is linked to a ballistic computer, sensors, and muzzle reference system.

Left: *The Ariete has additional protection in the form of advanced armor over the frontal arc, offering protection against the latest high-explosive antitank (HEAT) warheads. The tank has a comprehensive suite of protective measures.*

Below: *The Ariete has four smoke grenade launchers on either side of the turret. The grenades can be automatically discharged when a laser warning system detects a threat. The system's sensor is mounted just in front of the loader's hatch.*

Specifications
Armament: One 4.72in (120mm) gun; two 0.30in (7.62mm) MGs

Armor: Not revealed

Crew: 4

Dimensions: Length (hull) 24ft 11in (7.59m); Width 11ft 10in (3.601m); Height 8ft 2in (2.5m)

Weight: 53 tons (54,000kg)

Powerplant: IVECO V12 MTCA turbocharged intercooled 12-cylinder diesel, 1300bhp (970kW) at 2300rpm

Speed: 40mph (65km/h)

Range: 342 miles (550km)

The Modern Blitzkrieg

1988 USA

STINGRAY LIGHT TANK

The Stingray light tank, despite being lightly armored, is a very capable fighting vehicle that combines good firepower with excellent mobility. It was developed for the export market.

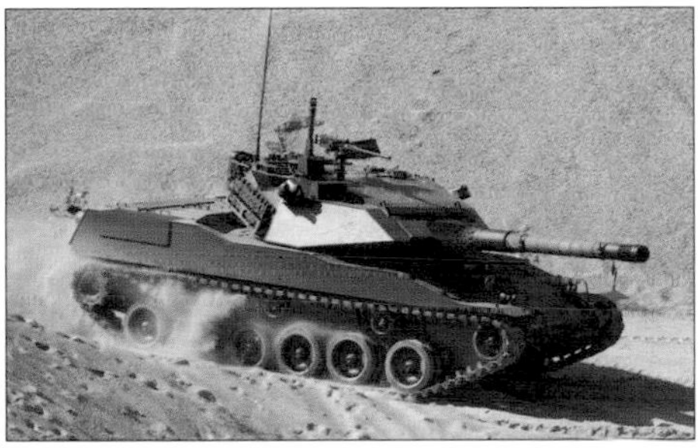

Left: *A lot of thought has gone into the Stingray design. The sides of its pointed turret slope inward for maximum protection, and smoke-grenade dischargers are mounted on either side.*

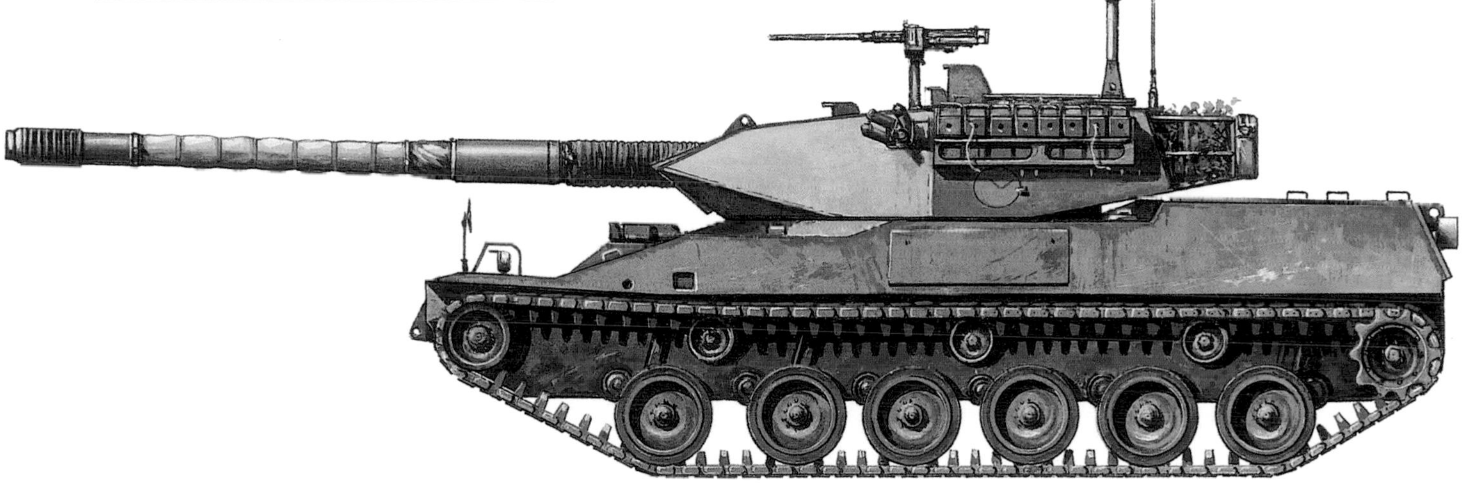

Specifications

Stingray I

Armament: One 4.13in (105mm) LRF gun; one 0.30in (7.62mm) MG; one 0.50in (12.7mm) MG

Armor: Unknown thickness Cadloy steel

Crew: 4

Dimensions: Length 30ft 6in (9.30m); Width 8ft 11in (2.71m); Height 8ft 4in (2.55m)

Weight: 19.9 tons (21,205kg)

Powerplant: Detroit Diesel 8V-92TA, 535hp (399kW)

Speed: 42mph (67km/h)

Range: 300 miles (483km)

The Stingray light tank started as a private venture, designed by Textron Marine and Land Systems (formerly Cadillac Gage Textron). Their aim was to produce a light and highly mobile AFV with the hitting power of a main battle tank. The first prototype was completed in 1985, and went to Thailand for operational trials and evaluation, after which the Thai Army placed an order for 106 examples. The Stingray II, appearing in 1996, is a more advanced version, with the same armament system as the Stingray, but with a more capable digital fire control system and NBC equipment. The primary armament of the Stingray is the LRF (Low Recoil Force) version of the British L7 series 4.13in (105mm) rifled gun.

Above: *The Stingray light tank is optimized for the reconnaissance role, and it possesses good firepower and mobility, but it is not designed to engage heavy armor on the battlefield. Stingray is the largest of the private-venture fighting vehicles developed by Cadillac Gage.*

Export

Up to 2006, the only export order for Stingray has come from Thailand. Despite claims that the vehicle combines the lethal power of a main battle tank with high mobility, it is too lightly armored for any real battlefield role, and is in effect a reconnaissance tank. The Thai order was completed in 1990 and the company is now concentrating on marketing the Stingray II.

The Modern Blitzkrieg
🔨 1989 China

TYPE 85-II, 85-III AND 96 MAIN BATTLE TANKS

The Type 85 series of main battle tanks all trace their ancestry back to the Russian T-54/55, but the design changes incorporated in them in recent years mean that it is hard to recognize any common features.

The Type 85-II, another product of Norinco, is a further development of the Type 80 main battle tank. It incorporates many improvements, including a redesigned hull and a turret with significantly improved armor protection, constructed of welded steel plates instead of cast metal. There are several models of the Type 85-II, including the Type 85-IIA and the Type 85-IIM. This variant features a Chinese indigenous 4.92in (125mm) smoothbore main gun, which is fitted with an autoloader copied from the Russian 2A46 design. The tank also has enhanced armor protection, a more sophisticated fire control system, and night-vision equipment. The vehicle is produced in Pakistan as the Type 85-IIAP. Further developments produced the Type 85-III, which has many improvements including a

Above: *The Type 85/96 is one of the Chinese People's Liberation Army's latest tanks, and shows many improvements over previous models. The tank is equipped with a Russian-type autoloader, enabling the crew to be reduced to three.*

1000bhp (745.70kW) diesel engine. The Type 85-III design received its design certificate in 1996, and was officially named by the PLA as the Type 96.

Service

The tank entered operational service with the PLA armored forces in 1997. The PLA had reportedly received over 1500 units of the Type 96 by 2005. Recent photos released by Chinese state media confirmed that all of the PLA's elite armored divisions are now equipped with the Type 96 MBT.

Specifications

(Type 85-IIM)
Armament: One 4.92in (125mm) gun; one 0.30in (7.62mm) MG; one 0.50in (12.7mm) MG

Armor: Unknown thickness steel/laminate

Crew: 3

Dimensions: Length 33ft 8in (10.28m); Width 11ft 4in (3.45m); Height 7ft 6in (2.30m)

Weight: 40.35 tons (41,000kg)

Powerplant: V-12 supercharged diesel, 730bhp (544kW)

Speed: 35mph (57km/h)

Range: 311 miles (500km)

The Modern Blitzkrieg
⚒ 1989 Germany

WIESEL SERIES

The Wiesel series of light armored fighting vehicles was designed to be air-portable. As well as the versions already in production, trials are ongoing with new variants.

Specifications

(Wiesel 1 TOW carrier)

Armament: One TOW antitank missile launcher plus seven missiles

Armor: Not released, estimated 0.39in (10mm)

Crew: 2

Dimensions: Length 10ft 10.3in (3.31m); Width 5ft 11.9in (1.827m); Height 6ft 2.7in (1.897m)

Weight: 2.75 tons (2800kg)

Powerplant: VW, 5-cylinder diesel, 86hp (64.1kW)

Speed: Road, 46.6mph (75km/h)

Range: Not recorded

The Wiesel AFV was developed by Porsche in response to a Bundeswehr request for a light, air-portable armored vehicle. Production was taken over by MaK (now part of Rheinmetall Landsysteme), which delivered the first of 345 vehicles to the German Army in 1989. Of these, 210 would be equipped with TOW antitank guided weapons and 135 with 0.79in (20mm) cannon. The Wiesel 1 can be adapted to a wide range of other roles, including command and control vehicles, battlefield surveillance vehicles with radar, recovery vehicles, air defense vehicles carrying the Bofors RBS-70 SAM system, and tank destroyers armed with HOT antitank missiles.

Wiesel 2

Further development by MaK, as a private venture, resulted in the Wiesel 2, the first prototype of which was completed in 1994. The Wiesel 2 is larger than the Wiesel 1 with an additional roadwheel station on either side, a higher hull, a more powerful engine, and more internal volume. It is therefore able to undertake a wider range of battlefield roles. At one time it thought that the Wiesel was light enough to be air-dropped, but trials (which destroyed four test vehicles) soon revealed that it was not.

Below: *This Wiesel is equipped with a TOW optically tracked, wire-guided missile system.*

The Modern Blitzkrieg
1990 China

TYPE 90 ARMORED PERSONNEL CARRIER

In recent years, the Chinese People's Republic has risen to the forefront of APC development, producing a range of successful vehicles that are adaptable to many roles.

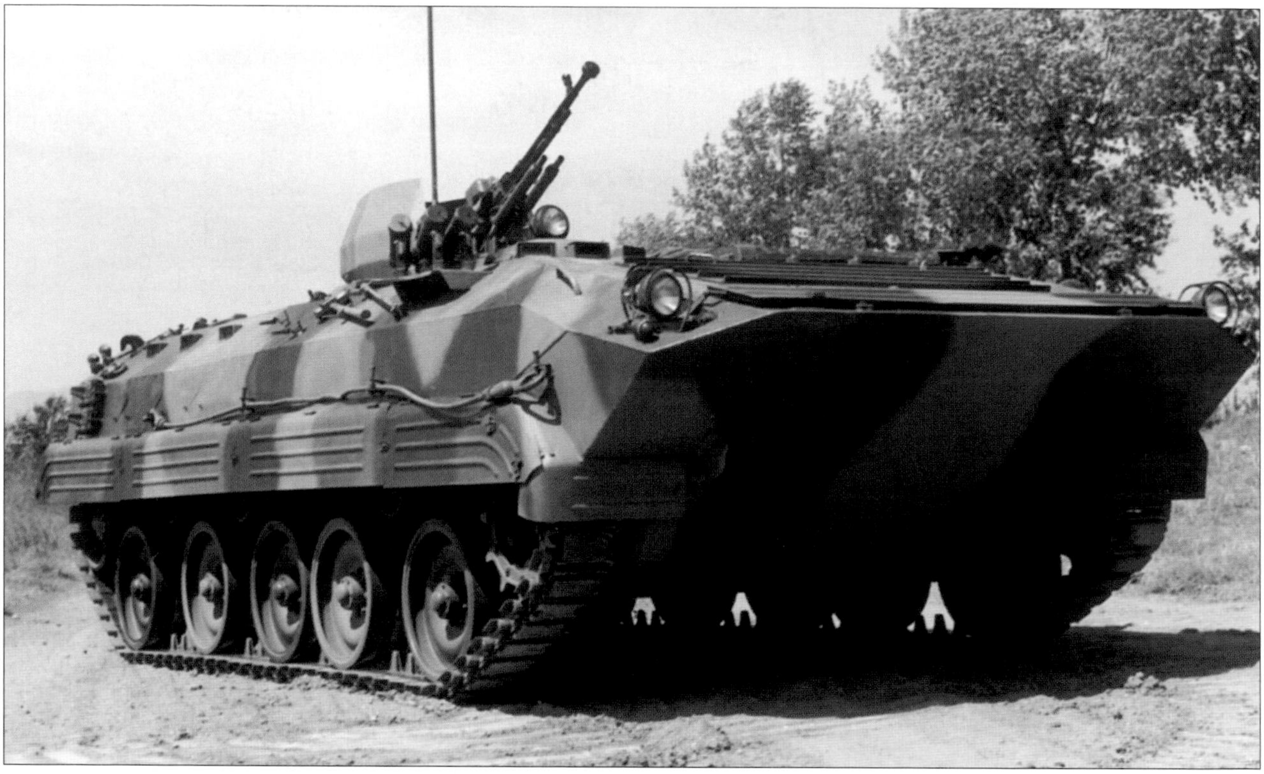

Above: *The Type 90 armored personnel carrier has provided the Chinese People's Liberation Army with a fine capability, and it is moreover produced in very large numbers.*

The Type 90 APC, derived from the WZ551, is one of a family of 10 6x6 wheeled armored fighting vehicles. Its members include a range of 4x4 and 8x8 configuration vehicles suited to a variety of roles. The Type 90 was introduced in 1986, and is based on the chassis of the Tiema XC2200 6X6 heavy-duty truck (which itself was derived from German Mercedes-Benz truck technology and designs). The Type 90 has been operational with the PLA ground force since 1992. The basic Type 90 has an overall combat weight of 15.3 tons (15,550kg). The vehicle has three crew (driver, commander, and gunner), and carries nine infantry soldiers in its troop compartment fitted with fire suppression and centralized NBC protection systems. The vehicle is fully amphibious. The first unit to be equipped with the Type 90 was the 127th Mechanized Infantry Division of the 54th Group Army in the Jinan Military Region. The earlier models are being progressively replaced by a later variant, the Type 92. Types 90 APC and 90 MICV of the People's Republic of China represent the most widely produced light-tracked vehicles in service anywhere.

Specifications

Armament: One 0.50in (12.7mm) MG

Armor: 0.7in (18mm) steel

Crew: 2 plus 13

Dimensions: Length 22ft 2in (6.74m); Width 10ft 4in (3.15m); Height 5ft 7in (1.72m)

Weight: 14.27 tons (14,500kg)

Powerplant: 8-cylinder turbocharged diesel, 360bhp (268kW)

Speed: 42mph (67km/h)

Range: 311 miles (500km)

The Modern Blitzkrieg
✴ **1990 Japan**

TYPE 89 INFANTRY COMBAT VEHICLE

The Type 89 infantry combat vehicle is in full use by the Japanese Ground Self-Defense Force. It has replaced the Type 75, which was lacking in protection and firepower, and became obsolete.

Specifications

Armament: One Oerlikion 1.38in (35mm) cannon; one 0.30in (7.62mm) MG; two Jyu-MAT wire-guided antitank missile launchers

Armor: Unknown thickness steel

Crew: 3 plus 7

Dimensions: Length 22ft (6.7m); Width 10ft 6in (3.2m); Height 8ft 3in (2.5m)

Weight: 26.57 tons (27,000kg)

Powerplant: Mitsubishi diesel, 600bhp (447kW)

Speed: 44mph (70km/h)

Range: 250 miles (400km)

Development of the Type 89 mechanized infantry combat vehicle for the Japanese Ground Self-Defense Force began in 1984. After successful evaluation, the vehicle was ordered into production. Mitsubishi Heavy Industries was the main contractor and Komatsu the main subcontractor. The layout of the vehicle is conventional, the driver seated at front right with the powerpack on his left. The two-man power-operated turret is in the center

Below: *The Type 89 represents a huge improvement over the earlier Type 75 Infantry Combat Vehicle, which lacked both armor and firepower. The vehicle is conventional, simple, and effective.*

and the troop compartment (which has entry doors, roof hatches and firing ports) at the rear. The commander sits on the right-hand side of the turret with the gunner on his left. Both crew members are provided with a single-piece roof hatch, periscopes for observation, and a main armament aiming sight. There are no variants of the Type 89, although there is provision for the vehicle to be fitted with mine-clearing equipment at the front of the hull. Main armament of the Type 89 is a 1.38in (35mm) cannon. The vehicle has almost entirely replaced the Type 75, which lacked both armor and firepower, and was declared obsolete.

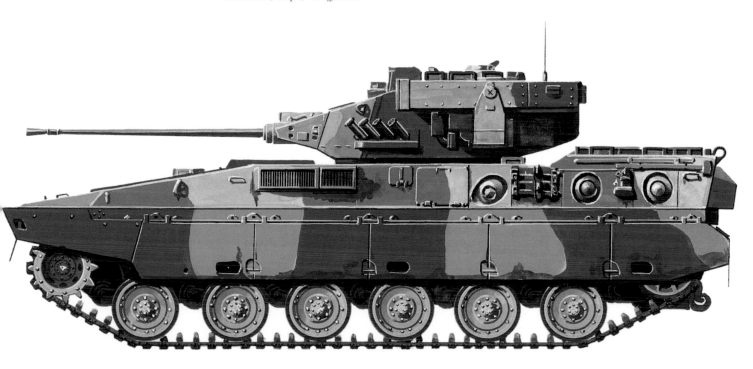

The Modern Blitzkrieg
1990 Soviet Union

BMP-3 INFANTRY COMBAT VEHICLE

The BMP-3 is very well armed. Its turret mounts a 3.94in (100mm) gun and 0.30in (7.62mm) machine gun. The main gun has a supply of 40 rounds, including 22 stacked in an automatic loader.

Developed by the Kurgan Machine Construction Plant, the BMP-3 infantry combat vehicle entered production in 1989. It is in service with the Russian Army, who had reportedly intended to replace the older BMP-2 with the new vehicle on a one-for-one basis. Lack of funds mean that the eventual total delivered was much less. Despite this, the vehicle has been a resounding success; over 600 have been exported to a number of countries, including the United Arab Emirates, Cyprus, Kuwait, and South Korea.

Variants

The BMP-3 is a tracked, armored, amphibious vehicle designed to engage armored ground and air targets while stationary, on the move and afloat. The BMP-3K is a command version (the same as the basic BMP-3) but it has additional communications and navigation equipment. The BMP-3F is designed for more sustained amphibious operations. It is able to remain at sea for seven hours and fire accurately in relatively high sea states. A reconnaissance version, the BRM-3K, is in use by the Russian Army.

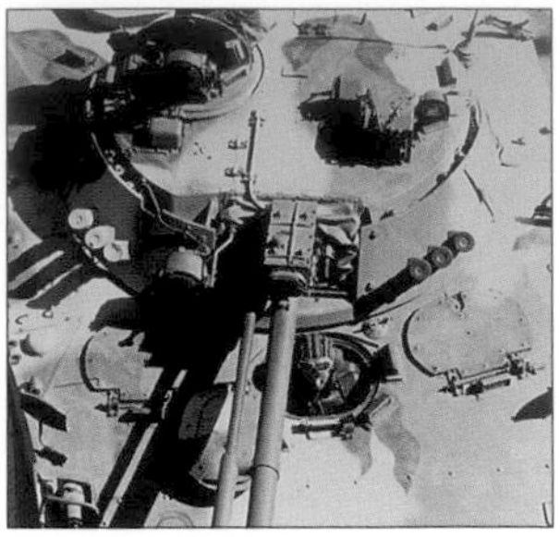

Above: *Bird's-eye view of the BMP-3's turret, showing the centrally positioned driver's station with hatches for additional crew to left and right. Note the grenade launchers mounted on the side of the turret.*

Specifications

Armament: One 3.94in (100mm) 2A70 rifled gun; one 1.18in (30mm) 2A72 automatic cannon; one 0.30in (7.62mm) PKT MG
Armor: Unknown
Crew: 3 plus 7
Dimensions: Length 23ft 7in (7.2m); Width 10ft 7in (3.23m); Height 7ft 7in (2.3m)
Weight: 18.4 tons (18,700kg)
Powerplant: One UTD-29 6-cylinder diesel, 500bhp (373kW)
Speed: 43mph (70km/h)
Range: 373 km (600km)

Below: *The BMP-3 is probably the best-armed infantry combat vehicle in the world, its main armament comprising a hefty 3.94in (100mm) rifled gun backed up by a 1.18in (30mm) automatic cannon and a 0.30in (7.62mm) machine gun.*

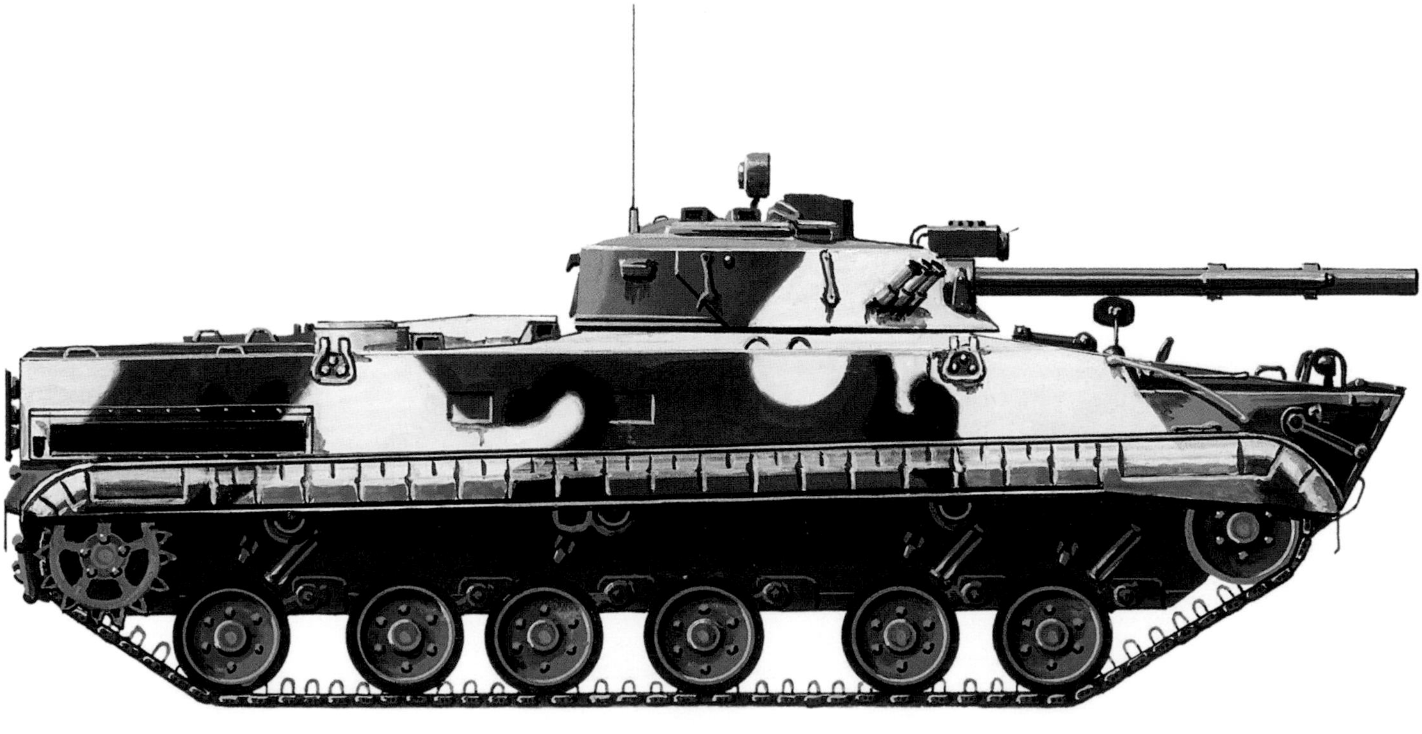

The Modern Blitzkrieg
✖ 1990 Taiwan

M48H (CM-11) MAIN BATTLE TANK

Taiwan's M48 tanks have undergone substantial upgrades over the years. Fitted with new guns and new armor, as well as advanced sighting systems, they are still a force to be reckoned with.

Right: Taiwan's CM-11 main battle tank would be hard put to fend off an assault by mainland China's latest main battle tanks. What it lacks in sophistication it makes up for in numbers, to some extent, and still forms an important component of Taiwan's armored forces.

Specifications

Armament: One 4.13in (105mm) gun; one 0.30in (7.62mm) MG

Armor: 5.63in (143mm)

Crew: 4

Dimensions: Length 30ft 6in (9.31m); Width 11ft 10in (3.63m); Height 10ft 2in (3.09m)

Weight: 49.2 tons (50,000kg)

Powerplant: General Dynamics AVDS-1790-2C, diesel, 750bhp (559kW)

Speed: 30mph (48km/h)

Range: 311 miles (500km)

The M48H is Taiwan's version of the well used Patton main battle tank. In 1990, Taiwan upgraded the design still further by producing a variant named the CM-11, which is a hybrid resulting from modified M48H turrets being added to new M60 hulls. It has an advanced fire control system which incorporates a ballistics computer and roof-mounted, stabilized sights with thermal-imaging channels similar to those installed on US M1 Abrams tanks. The imaging and targeting systems are joined to the 4.13in (105mm) gun, providing a high degree of accuracy. Dual-axis stabilization provides improved target tracking on the move. The firepower and mobility of the CM-11 is similar to that of the M60A3, but the turret armor is considered inferior and will not stand up to today's best antitank weapons. The Taiwanese version is named "Brave Tiger." The M48H/CM-11 forms a high proportion of Taiwan's armored defenses.

April 2006

The tank featured prominently in a large-scale military exercise held in April 2006 to demonstrate Taiwan's ability to fend off any potential invaders (which, in practice, means the Chinese People's Republic).

The Modern Blitzkrieg
⚒ 1991 Italy

CENTAURO TANK DESTROYER

The Centauro family of 8x8 vehicles consists of the reconnaissance antitank vehicle, the VBC infantry fighting vehicle, and the armored personnel carrier. All of these share a common chassis.

The Centauro family of wheeled armored fighting vehicles has been developed by Iveco Fiat Oto Melara Syndicated Company, based in Rome. Iveco Fiat is responsible for the vehicle and powerpack development, and Oto Melara developed the turrets and weapon systems. The Centauro entered production in 1991 and 400 of these tank destroyers are in service with the Italian Army. The Spanish Army has 22 Centauro vehicles in the armored reconnaissance configuration, with additional reactive armor package on the frontal arc, and ordered a further 62 vehicles in February 2002. Deliveries were scheduled to be completed in 2006.

Armament and protection

The Centauro has an all-welded steel armor

Above: The Centauro first appeared in prototype form in 1987. The low silhouette of this AFV is apparent in the photograph, which shows the 4.13in (105mm) gun locked in the transit position. The turret traverses through 360 degrees and has an elevation of minus 6 to plus 15 degrees.

hull, which provides protection against 0.50in (12.7mm) ammunition and shell fragments. Enhanced armor protection over the frontal arc provides protection against 0.79in (20mm) ammunition. A nuclear, chemical, and biological (NBC) warfare protection system is integrated into the vehicle's air-conditioning system. A laser-warning receiver can be installed on the vehicle. Centauro is capable of firing while stationary or on the move, against moving or stationary targets by day or night.

Specifications

Armament: One 4.13in (105mm) 52 caliber gun; two 0.30in (7.62mm) MGs

Armor: Not revealed

Crew: 4

Dimensions: Length 24ft 3in (7.40m); Width 9ft 8in (2.94m); Height 8ft (2.43m)

Weight: 23.62 tons (24,000kg)

Powerplant: IVECO V6 turbocharged diesel, 520bhp (388kW) at 2300rpm

Speed: 62mph (100km/h)

Range: 500 miles (800km)

The Modern Blitzkrieg
⚒ 1991 Japan

TYPE 90 MAIN BATTLE TANK

The Type 90 main battle tank is considered as one of the most advanced MTBs in the world. With over 200 in service with the Japanese Ground Self-Defense Force, it forms a large part of Japan's armored power.

Specifications

Armament: One 4.72in (120mm) gun, one 0.50in (12.7mm) MG; one 0.3in (7.62mm) MG

Armor: Unknown thickness steel/composite

Crew: 3

Dimensions: Length 32ft (9.76m); Width 11ft 4in (3.43m); Height 7ft 11in (2.34m)

Weight: 49.2 tons (50,000kg)

Powerplant: Mitsubishi 10ZG 10-cylinder diesel, 1500bhp (1118kW)

Speed: 43mph (70km/h)

Range: 250 miles (400km)

Development of the Type 90 main battle tank began in the mid-1970s, when the Japanese Self-Defense Agency and Mitsubishi Heavy Industries began work on a new MBT known as the TK-X. The first prototypes were completed in the mid-1980s and the vehicle was accepted for service in 1989 as the Type 90. The first production machines were completed in 1992. The Type 90's 4.72in (120mm) main armament was manufactured by Japan Steel works. This smoothbore weapon is essentially the same as the German Rheinmetall gun built under license in Japan, but it has its own recoil system and gun mount. The turret is similar to that of Germany's Leopard 2. The Type 90's crew is reduced to three as no loader is required.

Above: *The Type 90 main battle tank is reminiscent of Germany's Leopard 2, which is unsurprising, as it combines the same turret design with the Leopard's 4.72in (120mm) Rheinmetall smoothbore main gun. It has an effective recoil system. The type 90 is considered to be one of the most advanced MBTs in its class.*

Armament

An automatic loading system is provided for the 4.72in (120mm) gun, which fires HEAT-MP and APFSDS-T rounds with a semicombustible cartridge case. The computerized fire control system allows either the commander or gunner to aim and fire the main armament, whether the vehicle is on the move or stationary. It has a high probability of a first-round hit.

The Modern Blitzkrieg
⚔ 1991   Pakistan

AL KHALID MAIN BATTLE TANK

The Al Khalid is a joint venture between Pakistan, China, and the Ukraine, and is a very effective fighting machine. It compares favorably with the West's main battle tanks. Its reliable engine is one of the best of its kind.

Originally known as the MBT 2000, the Al Khalid (meaning "Sword") main battle tank is a joint venture between Pakistan, China, and the Ukraine (who supplied the diesel engine). Design work began in Pakistan in 1988, and in January 1990 an agreement was signed with China for the joint development and production of the vehicle. Several prototypes, produced in China, underwent field trials in 1992 to test the suitability of the tank for Pakistan's terrain and high temperatures. The choice of the Ukrainian 895kW (1200bhp) 6TD, optimized for "hot and high" conditions, was dictated by these factors. Series production of the Al Khalid began in 2000 at Taxila Heavy Industries, the first vehicles entering service

Above: *The Al Khalid represents a tri-nation attempt to produce an effective main battle tank cheaply, the costs being shared. The advantage is in the engine, which is produced in the Ukraine and is optimized for the type of conditions under which the tank will operate.*

with the Pakistan Army in 2001. Pakistan's armored forces reportedly has a requirement for 600 of these main battle tanks.

Design features

This tank has the capability of fighting at night as well as automatically tracking targets. It is a smaller tank than many of its contemporaries, with a crew of three. It has state-of-the-art automatic fire-extinguishing and explosion-suppression systems.

Specifications

Armament: One 4.92in (125mm) gun; one 0.30in (7.62mm) MG; one 0.5in (12.7mm) MG

Armor: Not revealed

Crew: 3

Dimensions: Length 22ft 8in (6.9m); Width 11ft 2in (3.4m); Height 7ft 7in (2.3m)

Weight: 45.3 tons (46,000kg)

Powerplant: 8-cylinder 4-stroke water-cooled diesel, 895kW (1200bhp)

Speed: 44mph (70km/h)

Range: 250 miles (400km)

The Modern Blitzkrieg
✗ 1992 Germany/Netherlands

FENNEK SCOUT CAR

The Fennek scout car was jointly developed by Germany and the Netherlands. It is a light and versatile vehicle that can be adapted to undertake a variety of roles. The name Fennek means "Desert Fox."

Right: *The Fennek is perhaps better described as a multipurpose carrier, as it is readily adaptable to a variety of roles. The interior can be configured to carry troops, supplies, or electronic equipment, and a small gun turret can be installed, as seen here.*

Specifications

Armament: One 1.57in (40mm) grenade-launcher or one 0.50in (12.7mm) MG, or one 0.30in (7.62mm) MG

Armor: Not revealed

Crew: 3 plus 5

Dimensions: Length 15ft 9in (4.8m); Width 8ft 3in (2.5m); Height 5ft 7in (1.7m)

Weight: 7.87 tons (8000kg)

Powerplant: DAF 6-cylinder turbocharged diesel, 210bhp (156.7kW)

Speed: 68mph (110km/h)

Range: 435–620 miles (700–1000km)

Originally known as the Multi-Purpose Carrier (MPC), the Fennek is a versatile light armored vehicle, in which modular design concepts have been fully exploited to make the vehicle adaptable. The vehicle is an international venture between Germany and the Netherlands. In 2006, 410 vehicles had been ordered by the German Army and 210 by the Dutch. Production is undertaken by the ARGE Fennek consortium, comprising SP of the Netherlands and Krauss Maffei Wegmann of Germany.

Design features

Fennek deliveries were scheduled to be completed in 2007. The tank has an all-welded aluminum armored hull, and the interior can be adapted considerably. Possible combat roles encompass those of battlefield reconnaissance and surveillance, command and communications, antitank missile carrier, supply vehicle, and combat engineer reconnaissance. For the antitank role, missiles can be launched from the roof of the vehicle, via remote weapon stations or manually from hatches, or alternatively from dismounted launchers at a distance from the carrier vehicle. The Fennek carries a sensor pod on a telescopic mast, enabling the crew to survey the surrounding area from an undercover position.

Chapter 9

TANKS FOR THE 21ST CENTURY

The practice of using armor to seize vital ground, and using it as a base from which to destroy the enemy, remains as valid today as it did in the 1930s, when Germany formed the concept of Blitzkrieg. A well-directed armored attack creates a confused and demoralized enemy; it did so in France in 1940 and in Iraq in 1991. The main battle tank remains the dominant weapon in any assault, and its future continues to be assured.

Above: *One of the most advanced AFVs of its kind, the Rheinmetall Landsysteme AGF has many self-protection devices, including a smokescreen system in the bumper and the ability to drive with punctured tyres.*

Left: *The Challenger II main battle tank is one of the finest main battle tanks in service today. It is used by the British army and the Royal army of Oman.*

Because modern armor provides such a high level of protection, the tank has achieved a new lease of life; a tank crew will feel most threatened if another tank similar to their own is armed with a high-velocity gun. The imperative move in today's combat is to get in the first killing shot. This depends on advanced stabilization and computerized fire control systems.

Research into tomorrow's tanks is ongoing. Prototypes of "stealth" tanks have already been built. These will be virtually invisible on the battlefield, where most engagements are now fought at night. Future tank designs look forward to manned turrets, with the crew in a single compartment in the hull of the tank, from which they can control the turret remotely. The turret's automatic loading system can then fire ammunition that is both too fast and too large for a human loader to handle. It can also store ammunition more efficiently, since there is no need for crew space in the turret.

Tanks for the 21st Century
⚒ 1992 UK

CHALLENGER 2 MAIN BATTLE TANK

The British Challenger 2 is arguably the finest main battle tank in service anywhere in the world today. Its design has the benefit of experience from the Challenger 1 in the Gulf War of 1991.

Challenger 2 is the new-generation main battle tank in service both with the British Army and the Royal Army of Oman. It is developed from Challenger 1, which proved very successful during the Gulf War despite a number of shortcomings, such as a poor fire control system that resulted in a slow rate of fire. The Challenger 2 is fitted with a completely new turret and is protected by advanced armor technology. The Challenger 2 entered service with the British Army in June 1998, and the first vehicles were issued to the Royal Scots Dragoon Guards. This tank has been used in operational service in Bosnia and Kosovo, and British Army Challenger 2 tanks were deployed on active service in Operation Iraqi Freedom in 2003.

Below: *Although the Challenger 2 closely resembles its predecessor, Challenger 1, it is essentially a new tank, 150 improvements having been made to the hull alone.*

Specifications

Armament: One 4.72in (120mm) L30A1 gun; three 0.30in (7.62mm) MGs

Armor: Not available

Crew: 4

Dimensions: Length 27ft 4in (8.327m); Width 11ft 6in (3.52m); Height 8ft 2in (2.49m)

Weight: 61.51 tons (62,500kg)

Powerplant: Perkins Engines (Shrewsbury) CV-12 TCA Condor V-12 12-cylinder 26.1 litre diesel developing 1200bhp (894.8kW) at 2300rpm

Speed: 37mph (60km/h)

Range: 280 miles (450km)

Export

The Challenger 2 is built by BAE Systems Land Systems (formerly Vickers Defence Systems, then Alvis Vickers Ltd). The UK placed orders for 127 Challenger 2 tanks in 1991 and an additional 259 in 1994, the last being delivered in April 2002. In 1993 Oman ordered 18 Challenger 2 tanks, and an order for a further 20 tanks was placed in November 1997. Deliveries for Oman were completed in 2001.

Design features

The totally integrated fire control system provides both the commander and gunner with an independently gyrostabilized, optical/thermal sights, equipped with a laser rangefinder. The gunner's sight has limited traverse, whilst the commander's is fully panoramic. The tank incorporates second-generation TOGS thermal imaging. Its fire control system enables it to consistently engage and destroy multiple targets using its new high pressure 4.72in (120mm) L30 gun. To make full use of its formidable and accurate firepower, the Challenger 2 is designed to optimize the crew's operational

Above: A Challenger 2 at speed. The Challenger 2 underwent an extremely demanding series of trials before being accepted for service—the most demanding ever set, according to the UK Ministry of Defence. The Challenger 2E is an export version.

environment. Levels of noise and vibration at crew stations are minimized, fresh filtered air maintains a workable environment, and the layout and operation of systems and controls maximizes the crew's ability to achieve first-round hits under all conditions.

Armament and protection

Stealth is designed into the tank's construction to reduce the probability of detection on the battlefield by visual, electronic, and thermal means. All explosive material is stowed below the turret ring in armored charge bins and a nuclear, biological, and chemical (NBC) filtration system provides collective protection against ingress and maintains a positive vehicle internal pressure. The advanced armor technology resisted penetration during prolonged trials with a wide range of modern antitank ordnance.

PT-91 MAIN BATTLE TANK

By upgrading the Russian T-72, the Polish Army has fielded a promising main battle tank that will remain at the core of its armored divisions for some time and eliminate the need to buy expensive new equipment.

Specifications

Armament: One 4.92in (125mm) gun; one 0.30in (7.62mm) MG; one 0.5in (12.7mm) AA MG

Armor: Unknown

Crew: 3

Dimensions: Length 22ft 10in (6.95m); Width 11ft 9in (3.59m); Height 7ft 2in (2.19m)

Weight: 44.6 tons (45,300kg)

Powerplant: S-12U V-12 supercharged diesel, 850bhp (634kW) at 2300rpm

Speed: 38mph (60km/h)

Range: 405 miles (650km)

Left: The turret of this PT-91 is fitted with explosive reactive armor plates, and is protected against HEAT projectiles by front and side skirts. Development of the PT-91 gained momentum after talks on purchasing new Russian tanks came to a halt in 1989.

The Polish PT-91 main battle tank is a much modified version of the Russian T-72M1, and is the outcome of a program, initiated by the Polish Ministry of Defense in the late 1980s, that aimed to modernize the later models of the Soviet tanks that were in Polish Army service. The Polish Army had already successfully upgraded its T-55 tanks to T-55AM standard, and it was decided to implement a similar project with the T-72M1. Work proceeded slowly at first, as the Polish General Staff was considering the purchase of a new T-72 variant, the T-72S. Nothing came of this, however: The Soviet Union fragmented and as a result, work on the upgraded T-72M1 accelerated.

PT-91 Twardy

The modernized tank, designated PT-91 Twardy (the name means "Hardy") was first used in 1995. Changes from the T-72 include a new dual-axis stabilized fire control system, reactive armor, a slightly more powerful 850bhp (634kW) S12-U engine, and hydraulic transmission with seven foward gears and one reverse. In 1995 the PT-91 Twardy underwent a second modernization, including a 1000bhp (745kW) engine, a more advanced fire control system, and an automatic loader. The newly upgraded vehicle was named the PT-91A.

Left: The explosive reactive armor plating is clearly visible in this shot of a PT-91. Note also the smoke-grenade launchers mounted on the turret.

Tanks for the 21st Century
✕ **1993 Soviet Union**

T-90 MAIN BATTLE TANK

Russia's T-90 main battle tank is the latest development of the T-72 line,
and is used in substantial numbers. It has also been purchased by India,
who have made further modifications.

Specifications

Armament: One 4.92in (125mm)
2A46M Rapira 3 smoothbore gun;
one coaxial 0.30in (7.62mm) PKT
MG; one 0.50in (12.7mm) NSVT
AA MG

Armor: Unknown

Crew: 3

Dimensions: Length (hull) 22ft 6in
(6.86m); Width 11ft 1in (3.37m);
Height 7ft 4in (2.23m)

Weight: 45.76 tons (46,500kg)

Powerplant: V-84MS 12-cylinder
multi-fuel diesel, 840bhp (627kW)
at 2000rpm

Speed: 40mph (65km/h)

Range: 400 miles (650km)

The T-90 main battle tank is the most modern tank owned by the Russian Army, and is a further development of the T-72. The tank entered production in 1993 and incorporates some subsystems of the T-80. It also features the latest development of the Kontakt-5 explosive reactive armor, which provides protection against chemical and kinetic energy warheads. By the mid-1990s, over 100 T-90s were in service with armored units in the Russian Far Eastern Military District. In 1996 an upgraded model made its appearance, featuring a fully welded turret in place of the original T-90's cast turret. In 2006 there were 241 T-90s serving with the Russian Army's 5th Tank Division in the Siberian Military District. In

2001, India was faced with a shortfall in modern armor following the debacle of it indigenous Arjun MBT design and purchased 310 T-90S tanks from Russia. Some of these vehicles were delivered in kit form for local assembly.

Indian variant

India has developed an improved version of the T-90S, known as the Bhishma. The name means "He of the Terrible Oath," and belonged to a hero in Indian mythology.

Below: *Although the T-90 is marketed by the Russians as a new tank, it is in fact an upgrade of the well-tried T-72. The T-90 is protected by both conventional and explosive reactive armor.*

COMBAT VEHICLE 90 (CV-90)

The CV-90 series, used by armies of northern Scandinavia, combines the firepower of a light tank with the ability to transport a section of infantry into battle. Its primary armament is larger than that of most other ICVs.

Specifications

(CV9040)

Armament: One 1.57in (40mm) gun; one 0.30in (7.62mm) MG

Armor: Not revealed

Crew: 3 plus 8

Dimensions: Length 21ft 3in (6.47m); Width 9ft 10in (3.01m); Height 8ft 3in (2.5m)

Weight: 22.04 tons (22,400kg)

Powerplant: Scania DS14 4-cylinder diesel, 550bhp (410kW)

Speed: 43mph (70km/h)

Range: Not revealed

Left: *The CV-90's hull has a well-sloped glacis plate, the turret being slightly offset to the left. The sides and rear of the hull are vertical, and there is a large door in the hull rear, as illustrated in this photograph.*

The Combat Vehicle 90 (CV-90) is one of a family of military vehicles developed by BAE Systems Land Systems Hagglunds. The development of the CV-90 began in 1984 in response to the needs of the Swedish Army for a family of armored combat vehicles with tactical and strategic mobility, air defense and antitank capability, good survivability and protection. Production began in 1993 and over 1125 vehicles were ordered by the armed forces of Sweden, Norway, Switzerland, and Finland. The CV-90's all-welded steel hull can be upgraded with add-on armor, which protects against 1.18in (30mm) APFSDS (armr-piercing fin-stabilized discarding sabot) rounds. The vehicle has a low radar, as well as acoustic and infrared signatures. A fire detection and extinguishing system is fitted and full nuclear, chemical, and biological (NBC) protection is provided.

Variants

Variants of the CV-90 IFV include the CV-9040 with a 1.57in (40mm) gun and the export variant, the CV-9030, with a 1.18in (30mm) gun. The CV-9040 has been used by the Swedish Army since 1993, with nearly 500 vehicles delivered. This is armed with a 1.57in (40mm) Bofors L/70 cannon. Final deliveries were completed in September 2002.

Left: *The turret of the 1.57in (40mm) version has a sloped front, as seen here, with vertical sides and rear. The 1.57in cannon has a distinctive muzzle with a large gunner's sight mounted on the right of the turret top.*

Tanks for the 21st Century
1993 USA

M1114 HUMVEE LIGHT UTILITY VEHICLE

Above: *The Humvee mounts a machine gun, as seen in these vehicles on night patrol. The vehicle was first used in Operation Just Cause—the 1989 invasion of Panama.*

The Humvee light utility vehicle has been used in massive numbers by the US armed forces in recent years. The provision of armor has been a necessity due to the losses suffered in action.

The M1114 Humvee owes its origin—and its name—to a US Army request in 1979, for a high mobility multipurpose wheeled vehicle (which became abbreviated to Humvee). The intention was to supplement and eventually replace the Jeep and other soft-skinned transport vehicles in US service. The US Government gave a development contract to AM General, an American heavy-vehicle manufacturer based at South Bend, Indiana and well known for its production of the civilian Hummer vehicle. The company began design work in July 1979, and just under a year later the first prototype, designated M998, was completed. After more prototypes were evaluated, the company received a US Army contract for the production of 55,000 units, to be delivered by 1985. The Humvee was first used in 1989 in Operation Just Cause, the US invasion of Panama. Over 10,000 vehicles were deployed in support of Operation Iraqi Freedom in 2003.

M1114

As the Humvee is unarmored, the losses created by small-arms fire and rocket-propelled grenades led to the development of an improved version, the M1114. This has a larger, more powerful engine with a turbocharger, air conditioning and a strengthened suspension. It also boasts a fully armored passenger area protected by hardened steel and bulletproof glass. This version now accounts for most of the Humvee production.

Below: *The M1114 Humvee features a vertical hull front with vertical louvers, flanked by headlamps.*

Specifications

Armament: One M60 0.30in (7.62mm) MG or one 0.50in (12.7mm) MG or one 1.57in (40mm) grenade launcher
Armor: Unknown thickness steel
Crew: 3–4
Dimensions: Length 16ft 3in (4.99m); Width 7ft 6in (2.3m); Height 6ft 2in (1.9m)
Weight: 5.4 tons (5489kg)
Powerplant: V-8 turbocharged fuel-injected diesel, 190hp (141.8kW)
Speed: 78mph (125km/h)
Range: 275 miles (443km)

PANDUR ARMORED PERSONNEL CARRIER

The Austrian Pandur can be fitted with a large number of sensory devices and weapons, and is fully amphibious, propelled by water jets. Its defensive features include engine and exhaust silencing .

Produced by Steyr-Daimler-Puch of Vienna, Austria, the Pandur 6x6 armored personnel carrier was developed as a private venture. The first prototypes appeared in 1985, and in 1994 the Austrian Army ordered 68 examples for use by Austrian forces on United Nations duty. The Pandur is also used by Kuwait, who accepted 70 vehicles, Belgium (54), and Slovenia (10). The vehicle is manufactured in small numbers in the United States by AV Technology International, a division of General Dynamics. The Pandur 8x8 is an improved version, combining many features of the 6x6 with new ones. It can be air-transported in a Lockheed Martin C-130 Hercules. The Pandur's driver sits at front left and the engine is to the right. The driver is provided with a single-piece hatch cover as well as three day periscopes, one of which can be replaced by a passive periscope for night missions. The vehicle is fitted with a two-stage synchronized distribution gear box for both road and cross-country use. Improved suspension will be fitted for optimum cross-country mobility.

Below: *The Pandur can be fitted with a variety of sensor equipment, as seen here with its sensor head elevated. This example is also carrying two Euromissile UTM 800 launchers for HOT antitank missiles.*

Above: *A 6x6 Pandur completing a river crossing. Note the waterjet under the starboard side of the hull. The armored front gives protection against 0.50in (12.7mm) projectiles.*

Tanks for the 21st Century
1994 Soviet Union

BTR-90 INFANTRY FIGHTING VEHICLE

The Russian Army has constantly upgraded its infantry fighting vehicles and some excellent designs have emerged. One of the latest is the BTR-90.

Specifications

Armament: One 1.18in (30mm) 2A42 automatic cannon; one coaxial 0.30in (7.62mm) PKT MG; one 1.18in (30mm) AG-17 grenade launcher; one AT-5 Spandrel ATGM system
Armor: Unknown
Crew: 3 plus 7
Dimensions: Length 25ft 1in (7.64m); Width 10ft 6in (3.2m); Height 9ft 9in (2.98m)
Weight: 20.57 tons (20,900kg)
Powerplant: Turbocharged multi-fuel engine
Speed: 62mph (100km/h)
Range: 500 miles (800km)

Development of the BTR-90 began in the early 1990s, with the first prototype completed in 1994. The vehicle is essentially a scaled-up version of the BTR-80, with improved armor protection and greater payload, which enables a wider range of weapon stations to be installed.

Design and layout

The BTR-90's overall layout is almost identical to the earlier BTR-80/BTR 80A vehicles, with the commander and driver seated at the front, the troop compartment and turret in the middle, and the power pack at the rear. The first example of the BTR-90 was fitted with the complete two-person turret of the BMP-2 infantry fighting vehicle (IFV), developed by the Kurgan Machine Construction Plant.

Above: *Russia has years of experience in building excellent infantry fighting vehicles, and has exported them widely across the world.*

This is armed with a 1.18in (30mm) 2A42 cannon, a 0.30in (7.62mm) PKT coaxial machine gun and a roof-mounted antitank guided weapon with a range of 13,123.36ft (4000m). More recent versions of the BTR-90 are equipped with a new turret developed from the one installed in the BMP-3 IFV. This turret mounts a 3.94in (100mm) gun; as well as firing conventional types of ammunition, it can also fire a laser-guided projectile fitted with a tandem high-explosive antitank (HEAT) warhead. The BTR-90 is fully amphibious and is propelled through the water by a single water jet.

LAV-25 COYOTE ARMORED RECONNAISSANCE VEHICLE

The Canadian Armed Forces' LAV-25 Coyote is an excellent armored reconnaissance vehicle, with sophisticated optical systems. It is linked to command centers by a comprehensive communications system.

Specifications

Armament: One 0.98in (25mm) cannon; two 0.30in (7.62mm) MGs

Armor: Classified

Crew: 4

Dimensions: Length 21ft (6.39m); Width 8ft 2in (2.5m); Height 8ft 10in (2.692m)

Weight: 13.19 tons (13,400kg)

Powerplant: Detroit Diesel Model 6V-53T, 275bhp (205kW) at 2800rpm

Speed: 62mph (100km/h)

Range: 410 miles (660km)

The Light Armored Vehicle 25 (LAV-25) was developed by the Diesel Division, General Motors of Canada, Alvis, and Cadillac Gage to meet a US Marine Corps requirement. The 8x8 wheeled vehicle was based on the Swiss MOHAG Piranha series, and following trials, 758 units were ordered for delivery over a five-year period. The first production LAV-25s were delivered in October 1983, with final deliveries taking place in 1987. In 1992, the LAV-25 was selected as the basis for a battlefield reconnaissance vehicle for the Canadian Armed Forces. A production order for 203 vehicles (which were known as LAV-25 Coyote) was placed in 1993.

Design features

The Coyote is armed with a M242 Bushmaster 0.98in (25mm) chain gun and a coaxial-mounted M240 0.30in (7.62mm) machine gun in a fully stabilized turret very similar to the M2 Bradley. The Coyote offers an extensive sensor suite, with remarkable target acquisition and identification capabilities. The first of these is a long-range television camera with high-performance

forward-looking infrared. This is capable of all-weather day or night target acquisition up to 9.32 miles (15km), and identification out to 6.21 miles (10km). A laser rangefinder linked to the vehicle's global positioning system can provide 10 digit grids to targets out to 6.21 miles (10km).

Right: *A LAV-25 armored reconnaissance vehicle with its sensor mast in the raised position. This gives the vehicle commander the ability to gain a panoramic view of the surrounding terrain while the vehicle remains under cover.*

Tanks for the 21st Century
✕ **1996 International**

ASCOD INFANTRY FIGHTING VEHICLE

Below: *The ASCOD infantry fighting vehicle is offered with a variety of armament fits. Pictured here is the LT 105 light tank variant, which is armed with a 4.13in (105mm) gun. Customers also have the choice of two engines.*

The ASCOD infantry fighting vehicle, also available as a light tank variant, is a joint effort by Austria and Spain to produce a mobile and effective fighting vehicle. It features the most up-to-date equipment.

Specifications

Armament: One 4.13in (105mm) gun; two 0.30in (7.62mm) MGs

Armor: Classified

Crew: 4

Dimensions: Length 21ft 8in (6.61m); Width 10ft 4in (3.15m); Height 9ft 1in (2.76m)

Weight: 28.05 tons (28,500kg)

Powerplant: MTU 8V 183 TE22 diesel, 600bhp (447kW) at 2300rpm

Speed: 43mph (70km/h)

Range: 310 miles (500km)

The ASCOD (Austrian Spanish Cooperation Development) infantry fighting vehicle is the result of a collaborative venture between Austrian Steyr-Daimler-Puch and Spanish Santa Barbara SA. The first production order was placed by the Spanish Government, who ordered 146 units in 1996. The vehicle is named Pizarro by the Spanish Army. They have placed a follow-on order for another 170 vehicles, with deliveries to be completed by 2010. The Austrian Army has acquired 112 units; the Austrian vehicles are named Ulan. The AIFV model is armed with a 1.18in (30mm) Mauser MK 30-2 automatic cannon and a 0.30in (7.62mm) coaxial gun. The turret is gyrostabilized to permit

accurate shooting when the vehicle is in motion. It has a computerized fire control system, night-vision equipment, and a laser-aiming device. The Austrian Ulan is powered by a 720bhp (536.90kW) MTU 8V 1999 diesel engine, while the Spanish Pizarro is fitted with a 600bhp (447.42kW) MTU 8V-183-TE22 diesel engine.

Variants

A light tank variant, the LT 105, is also on offer and is armed with a 4.13in (105mm) gun. Thailand is buying 15 units of this version. There are several other variants, including recovery vehicles and command vehicles.

Tanks for the 21st Century

1996 Iran

TYPE 72Z MAIN BATTLE TANK

In recent years, the Iranian Army has attempted to strengthen its armored forces by upgrading its existing tanks, or by building hybrids from spare parts.

Below: *The Iranian Army lost a huge amount of its armor in the war with Iraq in the 1980s. To fill the gap, it has resorted to upgrading the T-54/55 and the T-72Z.*

The Type 72Z is an Iranian Army upgrade of the T-54/55 main battle tank, achieved by replacing the existing 3.94in (100mm) gun with a 4.13in (105mm) rifled M68 tank gun. This was the type used in the American M60A1 main battle tanks acquired by Iran prior to 1979. To improve first-round hit probability, the Type 72Z has been fitted with a Fontana EFCS-3 computerized fire control system developed in Slovenia. This enables the upgraded tank to engage targets while stationary or on the move. The 0.30in (7.62mm) coaxial and roof-mounted 0.50mm (12.7mm) machine guns have been retained, as has the ability to lay a smoke screen by injecting diesel fuel into the exhaust outlet on the left of the hull. In addition, four electrically operated smoke-grenade dischargers have been mounted on each side of the turret. At least one example of the Type 72Z has been fitted with a roof-mounted laser warning device, probably coupled to a commander's display and the electrically operated smoke-grenade launchers either side of the turret. The Iranian Army has gone to great lengths to upgrade its armor in recent years, even building a hybrid main battle tank. This is called the Zulfiqar and is constructed from major components of T-72, M-48 and M-60 MBTs.

Specifications

Armament: One 4.13in (105mm) gun; one 0.50in (12.7mm) MG; one 0.30in (7.62mm) MG

Armor: 0.79–3.15in (20–80mm)

Crew: 4

Dimensions: Length 21ft 6in (6.54m); Width 11ft (3.35m); Height 7ft 9in (2.37m)

Weight: 35.4 tons (36,000kg)

Powerplant: V46-6 12-cylinder four-stroke water-cooled diesel, 582kW (780bhp) at 2000rpm

Speed: 40mph (65km/h)

Range: Not revealed

Tanks for the 21st Century
🛠 **1997 Singapore**

BIONIX INFANTRY FIGHTING VEHICLE

The Bionix infantry fighting vehicle was developed to meet the needs of the Singapore Armed Forces. It comes in two variants, the Bionix 25 and the Bionix 40/50.

Specifications

(Bionix infantry carrier vehicle [ICV])

Armament: One 0.50in (12.7mm) MG

Armor: Unknown, applique kit available

Crew: 2 plus 9

Dimensions: Length 21ft 7in (6.57m); Width 9ft 9in (2.98m); Height 8ft 4in (2.54m)

Weight: 23.6 tons (24,000kg) with armor kit

Powerplant: Detroit Diesel 6V-92TA, 475bhp (354kW)

Speed: 43mph (70km/h)

Range: 258 miles (415km)

The Bionix 25 infantry fighting vehicle was developed by Singapore Automotive Technologies to meet the requirements of the Singapore Armed Forces. Following trials with prototypes and preproduction vehicles, it was accepted for service and the first production vehicles were delivered in 1997. The infantry enter and leave via a power-operated ramp in the hull rear, and a 0.30in (7.62mm) machine gun can be mounted over the top of the troop compartment.

Variants

The 40/50 variant is fitted with a locally developed one-person cupola, armed with a 1.57in (40mm) grenade launcher and a 0.50in (12.7mm) machine gun. The Bionix family of vehicles offers a large range of variants for the full spectrum of battlefield operations. Built on a modular system with tremendous growth potential, this family of tanks can be adapted using various weapon stations, and used for command, recovery, and support roles.

Above: *The Bionix IFV features a well-sloped glacis plate, with the driver on the left-hand side. The hull top is horizontal. The large turret, with its pointed front and sloping sides, is positioned at the center of the hull.*

Tanks for the 21st Century
1998 Canada

LAV III ARMORED FIGHTING VEHICLE

The LAV III armored fighting vehicle is in service with the US military and the Canadian and New Zealand armed forces. It has proved its worth many times over on United Nations peacekeeping operations.

Below: *The LAV III is a robust fighting vehicle. It is widely used by the Canadian Armed Forces and has seen operational service on United Nations deployments overseas.*

The LAV III is the latest derivative of the LAV light armored vehicle family. It is based on the Swiss Piranha and was originally developed for service for the United States Marine Corps. The Canadian Army is the largest operator of the LAV III, and uses the vehicle in a variety of roles, including as an infantry carrier, a command post, for forward observation, engineer variants, and TOW missile carriers. The LAV III was first used by the Canadian Army in 1999, and 651 vehicles have been delivered. The New Zealand Army has also accepted 105. The infantry carrier version is able to accommodate up to seven infantrymen and a crew of three (gunner, driver, and commander). In addition to the 0.98in (25mm) cannon, the LAV III turret also features a coaxial 0.30in (7.62mm) machine gun, a top-mounted 0.218in (5.56mm) or 0.30in (7.62mm) machine gun, and one 0.30in (76mm) grenade launcher. Canadian LAV IIIs have been used overseas during United Nations deployments with the Canadian armed forces.

The Stryker

In US military service, the LAV III is known as the Stryker, in honor of two unrelated soldiers of that name, one killed in World War II and the other in Vietnam.

Specifications

Armament: One 0.98in (25mm) cannon; one 0.30in (7.62mm) MG; one 0.218in (5.56mm) MG
Armor: Classified
Crew: 3 plus 8
Dimensions: Length 22ft 9in (6.934m); Width 8ft 9in (2.667m); Height 9ft 3in (2.82m)
Weight: 16.24 tons (16,500kg)
Powerplant: Caterpillar 3126 series diesel, 350bhp (261kW)
Speed: 62mph (100km/h)
Range: 310 miles (500km)

Tanks for the 21st Century
⚒ 1998 China

TYPE 98 MAIN BATTLE TANK

Produced by Norinco, the Type 98 main battle tank has not performed well during its evaluation period with the Chinese Army. This has necessitated a series of modifications.

Specifications

Armament: One 4.92in (125mm) gun; one 0.30in (7.62mm) MG; one 0.50in (12.7mm) MG

Armor: Not available

Crew: 3

Dimensions: Not available

Weight: Not available

Powerplant: Not available

Speed: Not available

Range: Not available

Below: The Type 98 has a high power-to-weight ratio and as a consequence is likely to be an agile vehicle with a high speed.

This tank was first shown to the public in October 1999, when it took part in a parade to mark the 50th anniversary of the People's Republic of China. It was in effect the prototype of the Chinese Army's third-generation main battle tank. Four prototypes of the original Type 98 design were tested between 1995 and 1996. It is an updated and improved version of the Type 90, which is a derivative of the T-72 developed for export. The Type 98 comprises a T-72 chassis. This is surmounted by a new two-man turret armed with a 4.92in (125mm) smoothbore gun fed by an automatic loader.

Above: A Type 98 squats menacingly in the snow.

Type 98

The Type 98 was produced in limited numbers and gave way to the Type 98G, which has a modified turret and is now designated Type 99. The Type 99 possesses an advanced computer-based fire control system that enables it to engage targets on the move. Its 4.92in (125mm) main armament can fire a laser-guided projectile. The tank has a high power–weight ratio and possesses a high performance and considerable agility.

CV 90-120 ARMORED FIGHTING VEHICLE

This excellent Swedish armored fighting vehicle combines the lightness of a scout or reconnaissance tank with the powerful main armament of a main battle tank.

This light tank was developed by BAE Systems Hägglunds from the CV 90 infantry combat vehicle, and features an all-new turret. The CV 90-120 is an impressive light tank with a powerful armament. It retains features of the CV 90 infantry combat vehicle upon which it is based, including a rear door and the capacity to carry four infantry. The tank has an all-welded steel hull and the driver is seated at the front left with the engine to his right. The gunner and commander are positioned on the right and the loader on the left of the all-welded steel turret. The commander and gunner have individual roof hatches, and both are equipped with a periscope. A coaxial machine gun is installed to the left of the main armament, alongside electrically operated smoke-grenade dischargers. The tank features an antiaircraft-sighting system and a semiautomatic loading system.

Armament and protection

The main armament consists of a 4.72in (120mm) 50 caliber compact tank gun developed by Swiss Ordnance Enterprise Corporation. The gun is fitted with a vertical sliding breech magazine, a pepperpot muzzle brake, thermal sleeve, and fume extractor. The CV90120 tank is equipped with an active protection system. It weighs only 32 tons with added protection, but retains the high level of protection and firepower of a conventional tank.

Specifications

Armament:	One 4.72in (120mm) gun; one MG
Armor:	Not revealed
Crew:	4
Dimensions:	Length 21ft 3in (6.47m); Width 10ft 2in (3.10m); Height 9ft 6in (2.90m)
Weight:	24.60 tons (25,000kg)
Powerplant:	Scania 4-cylinder diesel, 600bhp (448kW) at 2200rpm
Speed:	43mph (70km/h)
Range:	415 miles (670km)

Below: *The disparity in size between the CV 90-120 and its main armament is evident in this photograph. The L/50 high-pressure smoothbore gun is fully stabilized and has a maximum rate of fire of 12 rounds per minute.*

Tanks for the 21st Century
⚒ **1999   Australia**

BUSHMASTER INFANTRY MOBILITY VEHICLE

The Bushmaster infantry mobility vehicle embodies a high degree of safety factors to protect its crew in an environment where the vehicle may be subjected to roadside bombs or rocket-propelled grenades.

Specifications

Armament: One 0.50in (12.7mm) MG if required

Armor: Unknown thickness steel

Crew: 2 plus 7

Dimensions: Length 23ft 1in (7.02m); Width 8ft 3in (2.5m); Height 8ft 8in (2.65m)

Weight: 13.78 tons (14,000kg)

Powerplant: Caterpillar 3126 ATAAC, 6-cylinder, diesel, 300bhp (224kW)

Speed: 75mph (120km/h)

Range: 621 miles (1000km)

Below: The Bushmaster is a very workmanlike design that was subjected to very extensive testing before being accepted for service with the Australian Army. Among other things, it underwent 155,250 miles (250,000km) of controlled trials.

The Bushmaster was specifically developed by Australian Defence Industries to meet the Australian Army's demands for a highly maneuverable and safe infantry mobility vehicle. Bushmaster carries up to 10 troops, including the driver, in a spacious air-conditioned environment designed to minimize fatigue. The crew compartment can be configured to carry eight troops sitting face-to-face while the driver and one passenger are seated in the cab. The vehicle's large-capacity fuel tanks give it a range of over 500 miles (800km) at sustained road speeds of up to 62mph (100km/h).

Use in dangerous environments

The V-shaped armored hull protects the occupants by deflecting landmine blasts anywhere under the vehicle. Protection is provided against side blasts from improvised explosive roadside devices and fragment-shaped projectiles. These may be encountered in the dangerous environment of Iraq, where the Bushmaster is deployed. Its fuel and hydraulic tanks are positioned outside the crew compartment to ensure that the crew is protected from fires that may result from blasts. A protected emergency fuel tank ensures it can keep moving in dangerous situations.

M-95 DEGMAN MAIN BATTLE TANK

Croatia's M-95 Degman main battle tank is an M-84 upgraded with new systems, some acquired from Sweden. It is intended to counter any potential threat from Serbia's T-84s.

Below: *The Degman main battle tank is a Croatian improvement of the Yugoslav M-84A.*

Developed in Croatia, the M-95 Degman main battle tank is a modified version of the Yugoslav M-84. This is in service with the Serbian Army, and is the very vehicle that the M-95 is intended to counter. The four-stroke, 12-cylinder, water-cooled, turbocharged, multi-fuel diesel engine is identical to the M-84A and M-84AB variants; the main improvement on the M-84 is the application of explosive reactive armor on the turret, hull front, and side skirts, offering more protection against HEAT shaped-charge munitions. The manufacturer (Đuro Đaković) offers optional thermal imaging, allowing enhanced night activity, and an optional

1,200bhp (894.84kW) engine, which would raise the power-to-weight ratio to approximately 27 hp/t. There are also numerous smaller changes, for example in fire control, communications equipment, and track. Much of the new equipment has been obtained from Sweden.

Production delays

The M-95 was not yet in series production in 2006 because of funding problems, but compared to other MBTs the vehicle is relatively inexpensive, and this will probably find it an outlet in the export market. Two prototypes, ordered by the Croatian Government, are currently being evaluated.

Specifications

Armament: One 4.92in (125mm) gun; one 0.30in (7.62mm) MG; one 0.50in (12.7mm) AA MG

Armor: Unknown

Crew: 3

Dimensions: Unknown

Weight: Unknown

Powerplant: 1000bhp (746kW)

Speed: Unknown

Range: Unknown

Tanks for the 21st Century
⚒ 1999 Iran

BORAGH ARMORED PERSONNEL CARRIER

Iran's Boragh armored personnel carrier, now available in several versions, is an attempt by the Iranian Government to avoid reliance on military imports.

Specifications

Armament: One 0.50in (12.7mm) MG

Armor: Not revealed

Crew: 2 plus 8 or 12

Dimensions: Length 22ft (6.72m); Width 10ft (2in3.1m); Height 5ft 3in (1.6m)

Weight: 12.8 tons (13,000kg)

Powerplant: V8 air-cooled turbocharged diesel, 246kW (330bhp) at 2300rpm

Speed: 40mph (65km/h)

Range: 370 miles (600km)

The Iranian Army's Boragh armored personnel carrier clearly draws its inspiration from the Russian BMP-1 and its Chinese equivalent, the Norinco Wz 501 series. The Boragh originated during the Iran–Iraq war that raged throughout the 1980s. During this time, the Iranian Army suffered huge losses in obsolete Russian-built equipment supplied following the halting of arms supplies from the West in the wake of the Islamic revolution. Determined to sever its reliance on foreign arms imports, the Iranian Government initiated a program of its own arms production, one offshoot of which was the Boragh. The 6x6 vehicle features a similar low pressure 2.87in (73mm) gun and the Sagger ATG. It is fully

Above: The Boragh is one of Iran's better efforts at producing a family of indigenous fighting vehicles. Iran has come to realize that it has the technological capability to produce armaments as good as any in the world.

amphibious and is fitted with an NBC system and infrared night-vision equipment for the commander, driver, and gunner.

Variants

In May 2002, the Iranian Defense Industries Organization (DIO) revealed that three new variants of the Boragh had been developed, comprising a 4.72in (120mm) self-propelled mortar variant, an ammunition resupply vehicle, and an APC fitted with improved armament.

Tanks for the 21st Century
✗ 1999 Israel

SABRA MAIN BATTLE TANK

Israel is in the process of updating its earlier main battle tanks by fitting them with the latest technology, thereby enabling them to remain effective for the foreseeable future.

The Sabra main battle tank is a modernized upgraded M60A3 developed by Israel Military Industries Slavin heavy weapons plant at Ramat Hasharon. It is an upgraded version of the M60A3, fitted with a 4.72in (120mm) smoothbore main armament similar to that developed for the Merkava. The gun is fitted with a fume extractor and a thermal sleeve for reduction of wear and to maximize the first-round hit probability by reducing thermally induced distortion of the barrel. There is stowage capacity for 42 rounds of ammunition. The gun can fire NATO standard 4.72in (120mm) smoothbore ammunition. The Sabra is equipped with an automatic fire and explosion suppression system, a threat warning system and smoke-grenade launchers. It is fitted with modular passive armor protection, which is upgraded to explosive reactive armor in the Sabra Mk II. The tank is equipped with a computerized fire control system supplied by El-Op (Electro-Optics) Industries Ltd of Rehovot and Elbit Systems of Haifa. The Turkish Army is currently upgrading 170 of its M60 main battle tanks with the Sabra Mk II upgrade package.

Below: *The Sabra is a very agile fighting vehicle, with a good power-to-weight ratio. From a standing start, it can accelerate to 20mph (32km/h) in 9.6 seconds.*

Specifications

Armament: One 4.72in (120mm) gun; three 0.30in (7.62mm) MGs

Armor: Not revealed

Crew: 4

Dimensions: Length 27ft 1in (8.26m); Width 11ft 11in (3.63m); Height 10ft (3.05m)

Weight: 54.13 tons (55,000kg)

Powerplant: General Dynamics V12 turbocharged diesel, 678kW (908bhp) at 2400rpm

Speed: 30mph (48km/h)

Range: 280 miles (450km)

Tanks for the 21st Century

1999 Japan

TYPE 96 ARMORED PERSONNEL CARRIER

With a long coastline indented with many places where an aggressor might make an amphibious landing, the Japanese Self-Defense Force relies on the rapid deployment of troops in vehicles like the Type 96.

Above: *The Type 96 armored personnel carrier is tailor-made to suit the requirements of the Japanese Self-Defense Forces.*

Specifications

Armament: One 0.50in (12.7mm) MG or one 1.57in (40mm) grenade launcher
Armor: Unknown
Crew: 3 plus 7
Dimensions: Unknown
Weight: Unknown
Powerplant: Unknown
Speed: 63mph (100km/h)
Range: 313 miles (500km)

The Type 96 8x8 armored personnel carrier is in full-scale production for the Japanese Self-Defense Force, which, in 2006, is the sole operator of the type. With a height of only 6ft (1.83m), the vehicle has a very low profile. It can carry up to eight fully armed infantrymen in addition to the driver and gunner, and the weapons comprising a roof-mounted 1.57in (40mm) grenade launcher and a 0.50in (12.7mm) machine gun. Armored personnel carriers are in service with all three arms of the Japanese Self-Defense Force, being used by the Navy's marine units and the airfield defense components of the Japanese Air Self-Defense force. Like other modern APCs, the Type 96 is designed to give as much protection as possible against landmines, small-arms fire, and rocket-propelled grenades. The rapid deployment of forces is a key element in Japan's defense strategy; the Home Islands have many places where an aggressor might land an amphibious force by surprise and establish a foothold. The number of Type 96 on order for the Japanese forces has not been revealed.

Tanks for the 21st Century

2002 **Italy**

DARDO INFANTRY FIGHTING VEHICLE

This tank was developed by the Consorzio Iveco Oto to meet a need of the Italian Army for a modern vehicle to carry out UN peacekeeping and security operations. The Dardo was previously called the VCC-80 IV.

Specifications

Armament: 0.98in (25mm) cannon; 0.3in (7.62mm) coaxial machine gun

Armor: All-welded aluminum with ballistic steel on hull and turret

Crew: 2 plus 7

Dimensions: Length 22 ft (6.71m); Width 9ft 10in (3m); Height 8ft 8in (2.64 m)

Weight: 22.64 tons (23,000kg)

Powerplant: IVECO 8260 liquid-cooled V-6 diesel, 520hp (388 kW)

Speed: 43.5 mph (70 km/h)

Range: 311 miles (500 km)

The Dardo is an infantry fighting vehicle designed to operate together with MBTs and provide a soldier squad with adequate protection, fast deployment, and fire support. In 1999, the Italian Army ordered 200 Dardo vehicles in basic configuration, armed with an Oto Melara 0.98in (25mm) HITFIST turret, plus four vehicles in special versions (command and control, ambulance, mortar carrier, and antitank). The first Dardo was delivered in May 2002. By adopting this vehicle, the Italian Army is now equipped with a modern system. It is also effective in peacekeeping missions thanks to its high protection (the hull and turret are made of all-welded aluminum with outer plates of high hardness steel), mobility (the Iveco engine and the automatic transmission allow the Dardo to achieve a speed exceeding 19.44mph [70 km/h] on the road) and the capacity to perform surgical firing actions with its TOW missiles. The Italian Army is considering the acquisition of another batch of several hundred vehicles, including special versions.

Above: *The Dardo Infantry Fighting Vehicle can carry its own antitank capability in the form of two single-tube TOW missile launchers mounted on the turret. The TOW missile is effective up to 3750 yards (3430m).*

Below: *This shows the large rear ramp through which the infantry enter and leave the vehicle. The ramp is power-operated, although it incorporates a manually operated door for emergency use.*

Above: *Front view of the AGF.*
The vehicle can carry a variety of
armaments, including 1.57in
(40mm) grenade launchers.

Specifications

Armament: 0.50in (12.7mm)
machine gun or 1.57in (40mm)
grenade launcher

Armor: Unknown

Crew: Unknown

Dimensions: Length 18ft 6in
(5.64m); Width 8ft 2 in (2.50m);
Height 7ft 6in (2.30m)

Weight: 3.3-5.2 tons (3,300-
5,200kg)

Powerplant: DC 270 CDI EURO
III, 154hp (115 kW)

Speed: Unknown

Range: Unknown

Tanks for the 21st Century

✗ 2003 Germany

AGF ARMORED FIGHTING VEHICLE

One of the most advanced AFVs of its kind, the AGF is optimized for special operations by elite forces. It can be carried into conflict under a helicopter or dropped from a transport aircraft.

Following the award of a contract in March 2002, Rheinmetall Landsysteme GmbH developed a reconnaissance and combat vehicle (AGF) for special operations forces in the space of just 10 months. The first 21 of these vehicles were delivered in January 2003. This small-scale production series was completed by the middle of the year. The vehicle is based on the new Wolf G 270 CDI from DaimlerChrysler.

Design features

The permissible total weight (with a useful load of 1.18 tons [1200kg]) comes to 4.43 tons (4500kg); the engine output is 156bph

(115kW). A single reconnaissance and combat vehicle can be airlifted using a medium lift-capacity CH-53 transport helicopter, and can carry four troops. The tank is capable of driving with punctured tires and is also equipped with a smokescreen system in the bumper. The vehicle's RLS 609 K weapon station, which can be swiftly disassembled for transport by air, can be equipped with 0.50in (12.7mm) machine gun or a 1.57in (40mm) grenade launcher. A 0.30in (7.62mm) machine gun can be mounted either at the front or the rear of the vehicle. The AGF is known as the Light Infantry Vehicle for Special Operations LIV (SO).

Below: *One of the most attractive aspects of the AGF*
is that it combines very good off-road capability with
low running costs.

Above: *The Nyala is a popular choice for service with the United Nations peacekeeping forces.*

Tanks for the 21st Century
✖ **2006 South Africa**

RG31 NYALA ARMORED PERSONNEL CARRIER

South Africa's RG31 Nyala state-of-the art armored personnel carrier continues to operate under combat conditions with NATO and UN forces in trouble spots around the world.

Specifications

Armament: 0.3in (7.62) x 1.5in (39mm) AK, 0.2 in (5.56) x 1.7in (45mm) NATO

Armor: Mine-protected, 31lb (14kg) under wheel; 15lb (7 kg) under belly.

Crew: 1 plus 10

Dimensions: Length 17ft 11in (5.46m); Width 7ft 3in (2.21m); Height 8ft 2in (2.5m)

Weight: 6.69 tons (6,800kg)

Powerplant: 123hp (92kW); 1.25 gallon (5.7 litre) 6-cylinder Daimler OM352A

Speed: 62mph (100 km/h)

Range: 559m (900 km)

The BAE Land Systems/OEG RG31 4x4 APC is well protected against road mines and roadside bombs, which makes it extremely attractive to military forces operating in a terrorist-dominated environment. The RG31 has an all-steel welded monocoque hull and accommodates a crew of 10 (including the driver).

Geographical use

The RG31 is currently in service with US Army Task Force Pathfinder attached to the 82nd Airborne Division in Iraq. It is also used by Explosive Ordinance Disposal units of the US Marine Corps, whose task is to locate and neutralize explosive devices. The vehicle is also in service with the Canadian Armed

Above: *The Nyala's V-shaped monocoque welded steel hull and high suspension are designed to resist a blast equivalent to two TM-57 antitank mines detonating simultaneously underneath it.*

Forces, whose version incorporates a Kongsberg Protector M151 Remote Weapon Station, and is equipped with a day-and-night sighting system. This allows the operator to fire the weapon while remaining protected within the vehicle. The Canadian RG31s have been tested under combat conditions in Afghanistan; others have been extensively used with NATO forces in the former Yugoslavia and by United Nations (UN) forces in Lebanon, Georgia, Syria, Bosnia and Herzegovina, and Kosovo.

Tanks for the 21st Century
2007 Germany

BOXER

The Boxer multi-role armored vehicle began as a joint venture between the UK, Germany, and the Netherlands, but the UK pulled out of the program in 2003.

Specifications

Armament: Reconfigurable to suit operations and national requirements
Armor: Unknown
Crew: Up to 11
Dimensions: Length 25ft 7in (7.88m); Width 11ft 10in (3.61m); Height 9ft 9in (2.99m)
Weight: 25.2 tons (25,604kg)
Powerplant: 711hp (530kW)
Speed: 64 mph (103 km/h)
Range: 652m (1050 km)

Left: *The Boxer design makes provision for an 8x8 armored personnel carrier (pictured here) and command vehicle versions, and also allows for the development of other variants using the same base vehicle.*

In November 1999, the governments of the UK and Germany signed a contract for the collaborative development and initial production of the family of next-generation armored utility vehicles. The program was known as the Multi-Role Armoured Vehicle (MRAV) in the UK, and the Gepanzertes Transport-Kraftfahrzeug (GTK) in Germany. In February 2001, the Netherlands signed a Memorandum of Understanding to join the program. The Dutch program is called the Pantser Wiel Voertuig (PWV). In December 2002, it was announced that the vehicle would be called the Boxer. An industrial group, ARTEC GmbH (consisting of Krauss-Maffei Wegmann [KMW] and Rheinmetall Landsysteme from Germany, and Stork of the Netherlands) is the prime contractor for the program. The UK withdrew from the program in 2003 but the other two nations went ahead.

Prototypes and production

The first prototype, in German APC configuration, was completed in December 2002 and the first Dutch prototype, a Command Post version, was completed in October 2003. Germany has ordered 1000 vehicles and the Netherlands have ordered 384. The Boxer will replace M113 and Fuchs Tpz 1 vehicles in the Germany Army, and YPR and M577 vehicles in the Royal Netherlands Army.

Left: *In July 2003, the UK Ministry of Defence announced that it would withdraw from the program to pursue a new national program, the Future Rapid Effect System (FRES). The MoD requires a lighter more easily deployable vehicle.*

INDEX